Making Sense of the
CHURCH

Works by Wayne Grudem

Bible Doctrine: Essential Teachings of the Christian Faith

Christian Beliefs: Twenty Basics Every Christian Should Know

Counterpoints: Are Miraculous Gifts for Today? (General Editor)

Politics According to the Bible

Systematic Theology

Systematic Theology Laminated Sheet

Making Sense of Series

Making Sense of the Bible

Making Sense of Who God Is

Making Sense of Man and Sin

Making Sense of Christ and the Spirit

Making Sense of Salvation

Making Sense of the Church

Making Sense of the Future

MAKING SENSE OF THE
CHURCH

ONE OF SEVEN PARTS FROM GRUDEM'S
SYSTEMATIC THEOLOGY

WAYNE GRUDEM

ZONDERVAN®

ZONDERVAN.com/
AUTHORTRACKER
follow your favorite authors

ZONDERVAN

Making Sense of the Church
Copyright © 1994, 2011 by Wayne Grudem

Previously published in *Systematic Theology*

This title is also available as a Zondervan ebook. Visit www.zondervan.com/ebooks.

Requests for information should be addressed to:

Zondervan, *Grand Rapids, Michigan 49530*

This edition: ISBN 978-0-310-49316-7 (softcover)

The Library of Congress has cataloged the complete volume as:

Grudem, Wayne Arden.
    Systematic theology: an introduction to biblical doctrine / Wayne Grudem.
        p.   cm.
    Includes index.
    ISBN 978-0-310-28670-7
    1. Theology, Doctrinal. I. Title.
  BT75.2.G78 — 1994
  230'.046—dc20   94-8300

Cover design: Rob Monacelli
Interior design: Mark Sheeres

Printed in the United States of America

11 12 13 14 15 16 /DCI/ 33 32 31 30 29 28 27 26 25 24 23 22 21 20 19 18 17 16 15 14 13 12 11 10 9 8 7 6 5 4 3 2 1

CONTENTS

PREFACE

I have not written this book for other teachers of theology (though I hope many of them will read it). I have written it for students—and not only for students, but also for every Christian who has a hunger to know the central doctrines of the Bible in greater depth.

I have tried to make it understandable even for Christians who have never studied theology before. I have avoided using technical terms without first explaining them. And most of the chapters can be read on their own, so that someone can begin at any chapter and grasp it without having read the earlier material.

Introductory studies do not have to be shallow or simplistic. I am convinced that most Christians are able to understand the doctrinal teachings of the Bible in considerable depth, provided that they are presented clearly and without the use of highly technical language. Therefore I have not hesitated to treat theological disputes in some detail where it seemed necessary.

Yet this book is still an *introduction* to systematic theology. Entire books have been written about the topics covered in each chapter of this book, and entire articles have been written about many of the verses quoted in this book. Therefore each chapter is capable of opening out into additional study in more breadth or more depth for those who are interested. The bibliographies at the end of each chapter give some help in that direction.

The following six distinctive features of this book grow out of my convictions about what systematic theology is and how it should be taught:

1. A Clear Biblical Basis for Doctrines. Because I believe that theology should be explicitly based on the teachings of Scripture, in each chapter I have attempted to show where the Bible gives support for the doctrines under consideration. In fact, because I believe that the words of Scripture themselves have power and authority greater than any human words, I have not just given Bible references; I have frequently quoted Bible passages at length so that readers can easily examine for themselves the scriptural evidence and in that way be like the noble Bereans, who were "examining the scriptures daily to see if these things were so" (Acts 17:11). This conviction about the unique nature of the Bible as God's words has also led to the inclusion of a Scripture memory passage at the end of each chapter.

2. Clarity in the Explanation of Doctrines. I do not believe that God intended the study of theology to result in confusion and frustration. A student who comes out of a course in theology filled only with doctrinal uncertainty and a thousand unanswered questions is hardly "able to give instruction in sound doctrine and also to confute those who contradict it" (Titus 1:9). Therefore I have tried to state the doctrinal positions of this book clearly and to show where in Scripture I find convincing evidence for those positions. I do not expect that everyone reading this book will agree with me at every point of doctrine; I do think that every reader will understand the positions I am arguing for and where Scripture can be found to support those positions.

This does not mean that I ignore other views. Where there are doctrinal differences within evangelical Christianity I have tried to represent other positions fairly, to explain why I disagree with them, and to give references to the best available defenses of the opposing positions. In fact, I have made it easy for students to find a conservative evangelical statement on each topic from within their own theological traditions, because each chapter contains an index to treatments of that chapter's subject in thirty-four other theology texts classified by denominational background.

3. Application to Life. I do not believe that God intended the study of theology to be dry and boring. Theology is the study of God and all his works! Theology is meant to be lived and prayed and sung! All of the great doctrinal writings of the Bible (such as Paul's epistle to the Romans) are full of praise to God and personal application to life. For this reason I have incorporated notes on application from time to time in the text, and have added "Questions for Personal Application" at the end of each chapter, as well as a hymn related to the topic of the chapter. True theology is "teaching which accords with godliness" (1 Tim. 6:3), and theology when studied rightly will lead to growth in our Christian lives, and to worship.

4. Focus on the Evangelical World. I do not think that a true system of theology can be constructed from within what we may call the "liberal" theological tradition—that is, by people who deny the absolute truthfulness of the Bible, or who do not think the words of the Bible to be God's very words. For this reason, the other writers I interact with in this book are mostly within what is today called the larger "conservative evangelical" tradition—from the great Reformers John Calvin and Martin Luther, down to the writings of evangelical scholars today. I write as an evangelical and for evangelicals. This does not mean that those in the liberal tradition have nothing valuable to say; it simply means that differences with them almost always boil down to differences over the nature of the Bible and its authority. The amount of doctrinal agreement that can be reached by people with widely divergent bases of authority is quite limited. I am thankful for my evangelical friends who write extensive critiques of liberal theology, but I do not think that everyone is called to do that, or that an extensive analysis of liberal views is the most helpful way to build a positive system of theology based on the total truthfulness of the whole Bible. In fact, somewhat like the boy in Hans Christian Andersen's tale who shouted, "The Emperor has no clothes!" I think someone needs to say that it is doubtful that liberal theologians have given us any significant insights into the doctrinal teachings of Scripture that are not already to be found in evangelical writers.

It is not always appreciated that the world of conservative evangelical scholarship is so rich and diverse that it affords ample opportunity for exploration of different viewpoints and insights into Scripture. I think that ultimately we will attain much more depth of understanding of Scripture when we are able to study it in the company of a great number of scholars who all begin with the conviction that the Bible is completely true and absolutely authoritative. The cross-references to thirty-four other evangelical systematic theologies that I have put at the end of each chapter reflect this conviction: though they are broken down into seven broad theological traditions (Anglican/Episcopalian, Arminian/Wesleyan/Methodist, Baptist, Dispensational, Lutheran, Reformed/Presbyterian, and Renewal/Charismatic/ Pentecostal), they all would hold to the inerrancy of the Bible and would belong to what would be called a conservative evangelical position today. (In addition to these thirty-four conservative evangelical works, I have also added to each chapter a section of cross-references to two representative Roman Catholic theologies, because Roman Catholicism continues to exercise such a significant influence worldwide.)

5. Hope for Progress in Doctrinal Unity in the Church. I believe that there is still much hope for the church to attain deeper and purer doctrinal understanding, and to overcome old barriers, even those that have persisted for centuries. Jesus is at work perfecting his church "that he might present the church to himself in splendor, without spot or wrinkle or any such thing, that she might be holy and without blemish" (Eph. 5:27), and he has given gifts to equip the church "until we all attain to the unity of the faith and of the knowledge of the Son of God" (Eph. 4:13). Though the past history of the church may discourage us, these Scriptures remain true, and we should not abandon hope of greater agreement. In fact, in this century we have already seen much greater understanding and some greater doctrinal agreement between Covenant and Dispensational theologians, and between charismatics and noncharismatics; moreover, I think the church's understanding of biblical inerrancy and of spiritual gifts has also increased significantly in the last few decades. I believe that the current debate over appropriate roles for men and women in marriage and the church will eventually result in much greater understanding of the teaching of Scripture as well, painful though the controversy may be at the present time. Therefore, in this book I have not hesitated to raise again some of the old differences (over baptism, the Lord's Supper, church government, the millennium and the tribulation, and predestination, for example) in the hope that, in some cases at least, a fresh look at Scripture may provoke a new examination of these doctrines and may perhaps prompt some movement not just toward greater understanding and tolerance of other viewpoints, but even toward greater doctrinal consensus in the church.

6. A Sense of the Urgent Need for Greater Doctrinal Understanding in the Whole Church. I am convinced that there is an urgent need in the church today for much greater understanding of Christian doctrine, or systematic theology. Not only pastors and teachers need to understand theology in greater depth—the whole church does as well. One day by God's grace we may have churches full of Christians who can discuss, apply, and live the doctrinal teachings of the Bible as readily as they can discuss the details of their own jobs or hobbies—or the fortunes of their favorite sports team or television program. It is not that Christians lack the ability to understand doctrine; it is just that they must have access to it in an understandable form. Once that happens, I think that many Christians will find that understanding (and living) the doctrines of Scripture is one of their greatest joys.

> *"O give thanks to the LORD, for he is good; for his steadfast love endures for ever!" (Ps. 118:29).*

> *"Not to us, O LORD, not to us, but to your name give glory" (Ps. 115:1).*

WAYNE GRUDEM
Phoenix Seminary
4222 E. Thomas Road/Suite 400
Phoenix, Arizona 85018
USA

ABBREVIATIONS

BAGD	*A Greek-English Lexicon of the New Testament and Other Early Christian Literature.* Ed. Walter Bauer. Rev. and trans. Wm. Arndt, F. W. Gingrich, and F. Danker. Chicago: University of Chicago Press, 1979.
BDB	*A Hebrew and English Lexicon of the Old Testament.* F. Brown, S. R. Driver, and C. Briggs. Oxford: Clarendon Press, 1907; reprinted, with corrections, 1968.
BETS	*Bulletin of the Evangelical Theological Society*
BibSac	*Bibliotheca Sacra*
cf.	compare
CRSQ	*Creation Research Society Quarterly*
CT	*Christianity Today*
CThRev	*Criswell Theological Review*
DPCM	*Dictionary of Pentecostal and Charismatic Movements.* Stanley M. Burgess and Gary B. McGee, eds. Grand Rapids: Zondervan, 1988.
EBC	*Expositor's Bible Commentary.* Frank E. Gaebelein, ed. Grand Rapids: Zondervan, 1976.
ed.	edited by, edition
EDT	*Evangelical Dictionary of Theology.* Walter Elwell, ed. Grand Rapids: Baker, 1984.
et al.	and others
IBD	*The Illustrated Bible Dictionary.* Ed. J. D. Douglas, et al. 3 vols. Leicester: Inter-Varsity Press, and Wheaton: Tyndale House, 1980.
ISBE	*International Standard Bible Encyclopedia.* Revised edition. G. W. Bromiley, ed. Grand Rapids: Eerdmans, 1982.
JAMA	*Journal of the American Medical Association*
JBL	*Journal of Biblical Literature*
JETS	*Journal of the Evangelical Theological Society*
JSOT	*Journal for the Study of the Old Testament*
KJV	King James Version (Authorized Version)
LSJ	*A Greek-English Lexicon,* ninth edition. Henry Liddell, Robert Scott, H. S. Jones, R. McKenzie. Oxford: Clarendon Press, 1940.
LXX	Septuagint
mg.	margin or marginal notes
n.	note
n.d.	no date of publication given
n.p.	no place of publication given

NASB	New American Standard Bible
NDT	*New Dictionary of Theology.* S. B. Ferguson, D. F. Wright, J. I. Packer, eds. Leicester and Downers Grove, Ill.: InterVarsity Press, 1988.
NIDCC	*New International Dictionary of the Christian Church.* Ed. J. D. Douglas et al. Grand Rapids: Zondervan, 1974.
NIDNTT	*The New International Dictionary of New Testament Theology.* 3 vols. Colin Brown, gen. ed. Grand Rapids: Zondervan, 1975–78.
NIGTC	New International Greek Testament Commentaries
NIV	New International Version
NKJV	New King James Version
NTS	*New Testament Studies*
ODCC	*Oxford Dictionary of the Christian Church.* Ed. F. L. Cross. London and New York: Oxford University Press, 1977.
rev.	revised
RSV	Revised Standard Version
TB	*Tyndale Bulletin*
TDNT	*Theological Dictionary of the New Testament.* 10 vols. G. Kittel and G. Friedrich, eds.; trans. G. W. Bromiley. Grand Rapids: Eerdmans, 1964–76.
TNTC	Tyndale New Testament Commentaries
TOTC	Tyndale Old Testament Commentaries
trans.	translated by
TrinJ	*Trinity Journal*
vol.	volume
WBC	Word Biblical Commentary
WTJ	*Westminster Theological Journal*

Chapter 1

INTRODUCTION TO SYSTEMATIC THEOLOGY

What is systematic theology?
Why should Christians study it?
How should we study it?

EXPLANATION AND SCRIPTURAL BASIS

A. Definition of Systematic Theology

What is systematic theology? Many different definitions have been given, but for the purposes of this book the following definition will be used: *Systematic theology is any study that answers the question, "What does the whole Bible teach us today?" about any given topic.*[1]

This definition indicates that systematic theology involves collecting and understanding all the relevant passages in the Bible on various topics and then summarizing their teachings clearly so that we know what to believe about each topic.

1. Relationship to Other Disciplines. The emphasis of this book will not therefore be on *historical theology* (a historical study of how Christians in different periods have understood various theological topics) or *philosophical theology* (studying theological topics largely without use of the Bible, but using the tools and methods of philosophical reasoning and what can be known about God from observing the universe) or *apologetics*

---

[1]This definition of systematic theology is taken from Professor John Frame, now of Westminster Seminary in Escondido, California, under whom I was privileged to study in 1971–73 (at Westminster Seminary, Philadelphia). Though it is impossible to acknowledge my indebtedness to him at every point, it is appropriate to express gratitude to him at this point, and to say that he has probably influenced my theological thinking more than anyone else, especially in the crucial areas of the nature of systematic theology and the doctrine of the Word of God. Many of his former students will recognize echoes of his teaching in the following pages, especially in those two areas.

(providing a defense of the truthfulness of the Christian faith for the purpose of convincing unbelievers). These three subjects, which are worthwhile subjects for Christians to pursue, are sometimes also included in a broader definition of the term *systematic theology*. In fact, some consideration of historical, philosophical, and apologetic matters will be found at points throughout this book. This is because historical study informs us of the insights gained and the mistakes made by others previously in understanding Scripture; philosophical study helps us understand right and wrong thought forms common in our culture and others; and apologetic study helps us bring the teachings of Scripture to bear on the objections raised by unbelievers. But these areas of study are not the focus of this volume, which rather interacts directly with the biblical text in order to understand what the Bible itself says to us about various theological subjects.

If someone prefers to use the term *systematic theology* in the broader sense just mentioned instead of the narrow sense which has been defined above, it will not make much difference.[2] Those who use the narrower definition will agree that these other areas of study definitely contribute in a positive way to our understanding of systematic theology, and those who use the broader definition will certainly agree that historical theology, philosophical theology, and apologetics can be distinguished from the process of collecting and synthesizing all the relevant Scripture passages for various topics. Moreover, even though historical and philosophical studies do contribute to our understanding of theological questions, only Scripture has the final authority to define what we are to believe,[3] and it is therefore appropriate to spend some time focusing on the process of analyzing the teaching of Scripture itself.

Systematic theology, as we have defined it, also differs from *Old Testament theology, New Testament theology,* and *biblical theology.* These three disciplines organize their topics historically and in the order the topics are presented in the Bible. Therefore, in Old Testament theology, one might ask, "What does Deuteronomy teach about prayer?" or "What do the Psalms teach about prayer?" or "What does Isaiah teach about prayer?" or even, "What does the whole Old Testament teach about prayer and how is that teaching developed over the history of the Old Testament?" In New Testament theology one might ask, "What does John's gospel teach about prayer?" or "What does Paul teach about prayer?" or even "What does the New Testament teach about prayer and what is the historical development of that teaching as it progresses through the New Testament?"

"Biblical theology" has a technical meaning in theological studies. It is the larger category that contains both Old Testament theology and New Testament theology as we have defined them above. Biblical theology gives special attention to the teachings of *individual authors and sections* of Scripture, and to the place of each teaching in the *historical development* of Scripture.[4] So one might ask, "What is the historical development

---

[2]Gordon Lewis and Bruce Demarest have coined a new phrase, "integrative theology," to refer to systematic theology in this broader sense: see their excellent work, *Integrative Theology* (Grand Rapids: Zondervan, 1996). For each doctrine, they analyze historical alternatives and relevant biblical passages, give a coherent summary of the doctrine, answer philosophical objections, and give practical application.

[3]Charles Hodge says, "The Scriptures contain all the Facts of Theology" (section heading in *Systematic Theology,* 1:15). He argues that ideas gained from intuition or observation or experience are valid in theology only if they are supported by the teaching of Scripture.

[4]The term "biblical theology" might seem to be a natural and appropriate one for the process I have called

of the teaching about prayer as it is seen throughout the history of the Old Testament and then of the New Testament?" Of course, this question comes very close to the question, "What does the whole Bible teach us today about prayer?" (which would be *systematic theology* by our definition). It then becomes evident that the boundary lines between these various disciplines often overlap at the edges, and parts of one study blend into the next. Yet there is still a difference, for biblical theology traces the historical development of a doctrine and the way in which one's place at some point in that historical development affects one's understanding and application of that particular doctrine. Biblical theology also focuses on the understanding of each doctrine that the biblical authors and their original hearers or readers possessed.

Systematic theology, on the other hand, makes use of the material of biblical theology and often builds on the results of biblical theology. At some points, especially where great detail and care is needed in the development of a doctrine, systematic theology will even use a biblical-theological method, analyzing the development of each doctrine through the historical development of Scripture. But the focus of systematic theology remains different: its focus is on the collection and then the summary of the teaching of all the biblical passages on a particular subject. Thus systematic theology asks, for example, "What does the whole Bible teach us today about prayer?" It attempts to summarize the teaching of Scripture in a brief, understandable, and very carefully formulated statement.

2. Application to Life. Furthermore, systematic theology focuses on summarizing each doctrine as it should be understood by present-day Christians. This will sometimes involve the use of terms and even concepts that were not themselves used by any individual biblical author, but that are the proper result of combining the teachings of two or more biblical authors on a particular subject. The terms *Trinity, incarnation,* and *deity of Christ,* for example, are not found in the Bible, but they usefully summarize biblical concepts.

Defining systematic theology to include "what the whole Bible *teaches us* today" implies that application to life is a necessary part of the proper pursuit of systematic theology. Thus a doctrine under consideration is seen in terms of its practical value for living the Christian life. Nowhere in Scripture do we find doctrine studied for its own sake or in isolation from life. The biblical writers consistently apply their teaching to life. Therefore, any Christian reading this book should find his or her Christian life enriched and deepened during this study; indeed, if personal spiritual growth does not occur, then the book has not been written properly by the author or the material has not been rightly studied by the reader.

3. Systematic Theology and Disorganized Theology. If we use this definition of systematic theology, it will be seen that most Christians actually do systematic theology (or at least make systematic-theological statements) many times a week. For example: "The Bible says that everyone who believes in Jesus Christ will be saved." "The Bible says

---

"systematic theology." However, its usage in theological studies to refer to tracing the historical development of doctrines throughout the Bible is too well established, so that starting now

to use the term biblical theology to refer to what I have called systematic theology would only result in confusion.

that Jesus Christ is the only way to God." "The Bible says that Jesus is coming again." These are all summaries of what Scripture says and, as such, they are systematic-theological statements. In fact, every time a Christian says something about what the whole Bible says, he or she is in a sense doing "systematic theology"—according to our definition—by thinking about various topics and answering the question, "What does the whole Bible teach us today?"[5]

How then does this book differ from the "systematic theology" that most Christians do? First, it treats biblical topics in a *carefully organized way* to guarantee that all important topics will receive thorough consideration. This organization also provides one sort of check against inaccurate analysis of individual topics, for it means that all other doctrines that are treated can be compared with each topic for consistency in methodology and absence of contradictions in the relationships between the doctrines. This also helps to ensure balanced consideration of complementary doctrines: Christ's deity and humanity are studied together, for example, as are God's sovereignty and man's responsibility, so that wrong conclusions will not be drawn from an imbalanced emphasis on only one aspect of the full biblical presentation.

In fact, the adjective *systematic* in systematic theology should be understood to mean something like "carefully organized by topics," with the understanding that the topics studied will be seen to fit together in a consistent way, and will include all the major doctrinal topics of the Bible. Thus "systematic" should be thought of as the opposite of "randomly arranged" or "disorganized." In systematic theology topics are treated in an orderly or "systematic" way.

A second difference between this book and the way most Christians do systematic theology is that it treats topics in *much more detail* than most Christians do. For example, an ordinary Christian as a result of regular reading of the Bible may make the theological statement, "The Bible says that everyone who believes in Jesus Christ will be saved." That is a perfectly true summary of a major biblical teaching. However, it can take several pages to elaborate more precisely what it means to "believe in Jesus Christ," and it could take several chapters to explain what it means to "be saved" in all of the many implications of that term.

Third, a formal study of systematic theology will make it possible to formulate summaries of biblical teachings with *much more accuracy* than Christians would normally arrive at without such a study. In systematic theology, summaries of biblical teachings must be worded precisely to guard against misunderstandings and to exclude false teachings.

Fourth, a good theological analysis must find and treat fairly *all the relevant Bible passages* for each particular topic, not just some or a few of the relevant passages. This

---

[5]Robert L. Reymond, "The Justification of Theology with a Special Application to Contemporary Christology," in Nigel M. Cameron, ed., *The Challenge of Evangelical Theology: Essays in Approach and Method* (Edinburgh: Rutherford House, 1987), pp. 82–104, cites several examples from the New Testament of this kind of searching through all of Scripture to demonstrate doctrinal conclusions: Jesus in Luke 24:25–27 (and elsewhere); Apollos in Acts 18:28; the Jerusalem Council in Acts 15; and Paul in Acts 17:2–3; 20:27; and all of Romans. To this list could be added Heb. 1 (on Christ's divine Sonship), Heb. 11 (on the nature of true faith), and many other passages from the Epistles.

often means that it must depend on the results of careful exegesis (or interpretation) of Scripture generally agreed upon by evangelical interpreters or, where there are significant differences of interpretation, systematic theology will include detailed exegesis at certain points.

Because of the large number of topics covered in a study of systematic theology and because of the great detail with which these topics are analyzed, it is inevitable that someone studying a systematic theology text or taking a course in systematic theology for the first time will have many of his or her own personal beliefs challenged or modified, refined or enriched. It is of utmost importance therefore that each person beginning such a course firmly resolve in his or her own mind to abandon as false any idea which is found to be clearly contradicted by the teaching of Scripture. But it is also very important for each person to resolve not to believe any individual doctrine simply because this textbook or some other textbook or teacher says that it is true, unless this book or the instructor in a course can convince the student from the text of Scripture itself. It is Scripture alone, not "conservative evangelical tradition" or any other human authority, that must function as the normative authority for the definition of what we should believe.

4. What Are Doctrines? In this book, the word *doctrine* will be understood in the following way: *A doctrine is what the whole Bible teaches us today about some particular topic.* This definition is directly related to our earlier definition of systematic theology, since it shows that a "doctrine" is simply the result of the process of doing systematic theology with regard to one particular topic. Understood in this way, doctrines can be very broad or very narrow. We can speak of "the doctrine of God" as a major doctrinal category, including a summary of all that the Bible teaches us today about God. Such a doctrine would be exceptionally large. On the other hand, we may also speak more narrowly of the doctrine of God's eternity, or the doctrine of the Trinity, or the doctrine of God's justice.[6]

Within the major doctrinal category of this book, many more specific teachings have been selected as appropriate for inclusion. Generally these meet at least one of the following three criteria: (1) they are doctrines that are most emphasized in Scripture; (2) they are doctrines that have been most significant throughout the history of the church and have been important for all Christians at all times; (3) they are doctrines that have become important for Christians in the present situation in the history of the church (even though some of these doctrines may not have been of such great interest earlier in church history). Some examples of doctrines in the third category would be the doctrine of the inerrancy of Scripture, the doctrine of baptism in the Holy Spirit, the doctrine of Satan and demons with particular reference to spiritual warfare, the doctrine of spiritual gifts in the New Testament age, and the doctrine of the creation of man as male and female in relation to the understanding of roles appropriate to men and women today.

---

[6]The word *dogma* is an approximate synonym for *doctrine*, but I have not used it in this book. *Dogma* is a term more often used by Roman Catholic and Lutheran theologians, and the term frequently refers to doctrines that have official church endorsement. *Dogmatic theology* is another term for *systematic theology*.

Finally, what is the difference between systematic theology and *Christian ethics?* Although there is inevitably some overlap between the study of theology and the study of ethics, I have tried to maintain a distinction in emphasis. The emphasis of systematic theology is on what God wants us to *believe* and to *know,* while the emphasis in Christian ethics is on what God wants us to *do* and what *attitudes* he wants us to have. Such a distinction is reflected in the following definition: *Christian ethics is any study that answers the question, "What does God require us to do and what attitudes does he require us to have today?" with regard to any given situation.* Thus theology focuses on ideas while ethics focuses on situations in life. Theology tells us how we should think while ethics tells us how we should live. A textbook on ethics, for example, would discuss topics such as marriage and divorce, lying and telling the truth, stealing and ownership of property, abortion, birth control, homosexuality, the role of civil government, discipline of children, capital punishment, war, care for the poor, racial discrimination, and so forth. Of course there is some overlap: theology must be applied to life (therefore it is often ethical to some degree). And ethics must be based on proper ideas of God and his world (therefore it is theological to some degree).

This book will emphasize systematic theology, though it will not hesitate to apply theology to life where such application comes readily. Still, for a thorough treatment of Christian ethics, another textbook similar to this in scope would be necessary.

B. Initial Assumptions of This Book

We begin with two assumptions or presuppositions: (1) that the Bible is true and that it is, in fact, our only absolute standard of truth; (2) that the God who is spoken of in the Bible exists, and that he is who the Bible says he is: the Creator of heaven and earth and all things in them. These two presuppositions, of course, are always open to later adjustment or modification or deeper confirmation, but at this point, these two assumptions form the point at which we begin.

C. Why Should Christians Study Theology?

Why should Christians study systematic theology? That is, why should we engage in the process of collecting and summarizing the teachings of many individual Bible passages on particular topics? Why is it not sufficient simply to continue reading the Bible regularly every day of our lives?

1. The Basic Reason. Many answers have been given to this question, but too often they leave the impression that systematic theology somehow can "improve" on the Bible by doing a better job of organizing its teachings or explaining them more clearly than the Bible itself has done. Thus we may begin implicitly to deny the clarity of Scripture or the sufficiency of Scripture.

However, Jesus commanded his disciples and now commands us also to *teach* believers to observe all that he commanded:

> Go therefore and make disciples of all nations, baptizing them in the name of the Father and of the Son and of the Holy Spirit, *teaching them* to observe all

that I have commanded you; and lo, I am with you always, to the close of the age. (Matt. 28:19–20)

Now to teach all that Jesus commanded, in a narrow sense, is simply to teach the content of the oral teaching of Jesus as it is recorded in the gospel narratives. However, in a broader sense, "all that Jesus commanded" includes the interpretation and application of his life and teachings, because in the book of Acts it is implied that it contains a narrative of what Jesus *continued* to do and teach through the apostles after his resurrection (note that 1:1 speaks of "all that Jesus *began* to do and teach"). "All that Jesus commanded" can also include the Epistles, since they were written under the supervision of the Holy Spirit and were also considered to be a "command of the Lord" (1 Cor. 14:37; see also John 14:26; 16:13; 1 Thess. 4:15; 2 Peter 3:2; and Rev. 1:1–3). Thus in a larger sense, "all that Jesus commanded" includes all of the New Testament.

Furthermore, when we consider that the New Testament writings endorse the absolute confidence Jesus had in the authority and reliability of the Old Testament Scriptures as God's words, and when we realize that the New Testament epistles also endorse this view of the Old Testament as absolutely authoritative words of God, then it becomes evident that we cannot teach "all that Jesus commanded" without including all of the Old Testament (rightly understood in the various ways in which it applies to the new covenant age in the history of redemption) as well.

The task of fulfilling the Great Commission includes therefore not only evangelism but also *teaching.* And the task of teaching all that Jesus commanded us is, in a broad sense, the task of teaching what the whole Bible says to us today. To effectively teach ourselves and to teach others what the whole Bible says, it is necessary to *collect* and *summarize* all the Scripture passages on a particular subject.

For example, if someone asks me, "What does the Bible teach about Christ's return?" I could say, "Just keep reading your Bible and you'll find out." But if the questioner begins reading at Genesis 1:1 it will be a long time before he or she finds the answer to his question. By that time many other questions will have needed answers, and his list of unanswered questions will begin to grow very long indeed. What does the Bible teach about the work of the Holy Spirit? What does the Bible teach about prayer? What does the Bible teach about sin? There simply is not time in our lifetimes to read through the entire Bible looking for an answer for ourselves every time a doctrinal question arises. Therefore, for us to learn what the Bible says, it is very helpful to have the benefit of the work of others who have searched through Scripture and found answers to these various topics.

We can teach others most effectively if we can direct them to the most relevant passages and suggest an appropriate summary of the teachings of those passages. Then the person who questions us can inspect those passages quickly for himself or herself and learn much more rapidly what the teaching of the Bible is on a particular subject. Thus the necessity of systematic theology for teaching what the Bible says comes about primarily because we are finite in our memory and in the amount of time at our disposal.

The basic reason for studying systematic theology, then, is that it enables us to teach ourselves and others what the whole Bible says, thus fulfilling the second part of the Great Commission.

2. The Benefits to Our Lives. Although the basic reason for studying systematic theology is that it is a means of obedience to our Lord's command, there are some additional specific benefits that come from such study.

First, studying theology helps us *overcome our wrong ideas.* If there were no sin in our hearts, we could read the Bible from cover to cover and, although we would not immediately learn everything in the Bible, we would most likely learn only true things about God and his creation. Every time we read it we would learn more true things and we would not rebel or refuse to accept anything we found written there. But with sin in our hearts we retain some rebelliousness against God. At various points there are—for all of us—biblical teachings which for one reason or another we do not want to accept. The study of systematic theology is of help in overcoming those rebellious ideas.

For example, suppose there is someone who does not want to believe that Jesus is personally coming back to earth again. We could show this person one verse or perhaps two that speak of Jesus' return to earth, but the person might still find a way to evade the force of those verses or read a different meaning into them. But if we collect twenty-five or thirty verses that say that Jesus is coming back to earth personally and write them all out on paper, our friend who hesitated to believe in Christ's return is much more likely to be persuaded by the breadth and diversity of biblical evidence for this doctrine. Of course, we all have areas like that, areas where our understanding of the Bible's teaching is inadequate. In these areas, it is helpful for us to be confronted with the *total weight of the teaching of Scripture* on that subject, so that we will more readily be persuaded even against our initial wrongful inclinations.

Second, studying systematic theology helps us to be *able to make better decisions later* on new questions of doctrine that may arise. We cannot know what new doctrinal controversies will arise in the churches in which we will live and minister ten, twenty, or thirty years from now, if the Lord does not return before then. These new doctrinal controversies will sometimes include questions that no one has faced very carefully before. Christians will be asking, "What does the whole Bible say about this subject?" (The precise nature of biblical inerrancy and the appropriate understanding of biblical teaching on gifts of the Holy Spirit are two examples of questions that have arisen in our century with much more forcefulness than ever before in the history of the church.)

Whatever the new doctrinal controversies are in future years, those who have learned systematic theology well will be much better able to answer the new questions that arise. The reason for this is that everything that the Bible says is somehow related to everything else the Bible says (for it all fits together in a consistent way, at least within God's own understanding of reality, and in the nature of God and creation as they really are). Thus the new question will be related to much that has already been learned from Scripture. The more thoroughly that earlier material has been learned, the better able we will be to deal with those new questions.

This benefit extends even more broadly. We face problems of applying Scripture to life in many more contexts than formal doctrinal discussions. What does the Bible teach about husband-wife relationships? About raising children? About witnessing to a friend at work? What principles does Scripture give us for studying psychology, or economics, or the natural sciences? How does it guide us in spending money, or in saving, or in tithing? In every area of inquiry certain theological principles will come to bear, and those who have learned well the theological teachings of the Bible will be much better able to make decisions that are pleasing to God.

A helpful analogy at this point is that of a jigsaw puzzle. If the puzzle represents "what the whole Bible teaches us today about everything" then a course in systematic theology would be like filling in the border and some of the major items pictured in the puzzle. But we will never know everything that the Bible teaches about everything, so our jigsaw puzzle will have many gaps, many pieces that remain to be put in. Solving a new real-life problem is analogous to filling in another section of the jigsaw puzzle: the more pieces one has in place correctly to begin with, the easier it is to fit new pieces in, and the less apt one is to make mistakes. In this book the goal is to enable Christians to put into their "theological jigsaw puzzle" as many pieces with as much accuracy as possible, and to encourage Christians to go on putting in more and more correct pieces for the rest of their lives. The Christian doctrines studied here will act as guidelines to help in the filling in of all other areas, areas that pertain to all aspects of truth in all aspects of life.

Third, studying systematic theology will *help us grow as Christians.* The more we know about God, about his Word, about his relationships to the world and mankind, the better we will trust him, the more fully we will praise him, and the more readily we will obey him. Studying systematic theology rightly will make us more mature Christians. If it does not do this, we are not studying it in the way God intends.

In fact, the Bible often connects sound doctrine with maturity in Christian living: Paul speaks of "*the teaching which accords with godliness*" (1 Tim. 6:3) and says that his work as an apostle is "to further the faith of God's elect and their knowledge of *the truth which accords with godliness*" (Titus 1:1). By contrast, he indicates that all kinds of disobedience and immorality are "contrary to sound doctrine" (1 Tim. 1:10).

In connection with this idea it is appropriate to ask what the difference is between a "major doctrine" and a "minor doctrine." Christians often say they want to seek agreement in the church on major doctrines but also to allow for differences on minor doctrines. I have found the following guideline useful:

> A major doctrine is one that has a significant impact on our thinking about other doctrines, or that has a significant impact on how we live the Christian life. A minor doctrine is one that has very little impact on how we think about other doctrines, and very little impact on how we live the Christian life.

By this standard doctrines such as the authority of the Bible, the Trinity, the deity of Christ, justification by faith, and many others would rightly be considered major doctrines. People who disagree with the historic evangelical understanding of any of these doctrines will have wide areas of difference with evangelical Christians who affirm these doctrines. By contrast, it seems to me that differences over forms of church government or some details about the Lord's Supper or the timing of the great tribulation concern minor doctrines. Christians who differ over these things can agree on perhaps every other area of doctrine, can live Christian lives that differ in no important way, and can have genuine fellowship with one another.

Of course, we may find doctrines that fall somewhere between "major" and "minor" according to this standard. For example, Christians may differ over the degree of significance that should attach to the doctrine of baptism or the millennium or the extent of the atonement. That is only natural, because many doctrines have *some* influence on other doctrines or on life, but we may differ over whether we think it to be a "significant" influence. We could even recognize that there will be a range of significance here and just say that the more influence a doctrine has on other doctrines and on life, the more "major" it becomes. This amount of influence may even vary according to the historical circumstances and needs of the church at any given time. In such cases, Christians will need to ask God to give them mature wisdom and sound judgment as they try to determine to what extent a doctrine should be considered "major" in their particular circumstances.

D. A Note on Two Objections to the Study of Systematic Theology

1. "The Conclusions Are 'Too Neat' to be True." Some scholars look with suspicion at systematic theology when—or even because—its teachings fit together in a noncontradictory way. They object that the results are "too neat" and that systematic theologians must therefore be squeezing the Bible's teachings into an artificial mold, distorting the true meaning of Scripture to get an orderly set of beliefs.

To this objection two responses can be made: (1) We must first ask the people making the objection to tell us at what specific points Scripture has been misinterpreted, and then we must deal with the understanding of those passages. Perhaps mistakes have been made, and in that case there should be corrections.

Yet it is also possible that the objector will have no specific passages in mind, or no clearly erroneous interpretations to point to in the works of the most responsible evangelical theologians. Of course, incompetent exegesis can be found in the writings of the less competent scholars in *any* field of biblical studies, not just in systematic theology, but those "bad examples" constitute an objection not against the scholar's field but against the incompetent scholar himself.

It is very important that the objector be specific at this point because this objection is sometimes made by those who—perhaps unconsciously—have adopted from our culture a skeptical view of the possibility of finding universally true conclusions about anything, even about God from his Word. This kind of skepticism regarding theological truth is especially common in the modern university world where "systematic theology"—if it is studied at all—is studied only from the perspectives of philosophical theology and historical theology (including perhaps a historical study of the various ideas that were believed by the early Christians who wrote the New Testament, and by other Christians at that time and throughout church history). In this kind of intellectual climate the study of "systematic theology" as defined in this chapter would be considered impossible, because the Bible would be assumed to be merely the work of many human authors who wrote out of diverse cultures and experiences over the course of more than one thousand years: trying to find "what the whole Bible teaches" about any subject would be thought nearly as hopeless as trying to find "what all philosophers teach" about some question, for the answer in both cases would be thought to be not one view but many diverse and often conflicting views. This skeptical viewpoint must be rejected by evangelicals who see Scripture as the product of human *and* divine authorship, and therefore as a collection of writings that teach noncontradictory truths about God and about the universe he created.

(2) Second, it must be answered that in God's own mind, and in the nature of reality itself, *true* facts and ideas are all consistent with one another. Therefore if we have accurately understood the teachings of God in Scripture we should expect our conclusions to "fit together" and be mutually consistent. Internal consistency, then, is an argument for, not against, any individual results of systematic theology.

2. "The Choice of Topics Dictates the Conclusions." Another general objection to systematic theology concerns the choice and arrangement of topics, and even the fact that such topically arranged study of Scripture, using categories sometimes different from those found in Scripture itself, is done at all. Why are *these* theological topics treated rather than just the topics emphasized by the biblical authors, and why are the topics *arranged in this way* rather than in some other way? Perhaps—this objection would say—our traditions and our cultures have determined the topics we treat and the arrangement of topics, so that the results of this systematic-theological study of Scripture, though acceptable in our own theological tradition, will in fact be untrue to Scripture itself.

A variant of this objection is the statement that our starting point often determines our conclusions on controversial topics: if we decide to start with an emphasis on the divine authorship of Scripture, for example, we will end up believing in biblical inerrancy, but if we start with an emphasis on the human authorship of Scripture, we will end up believing there are some errors in the Bible. Similarly, if we start with an emphasis on God's sovereignty, we will end up as Calvinists, but if we start with an emphasis on man's ability to make free choices, we will end up as Arminians, and so forth. This objection makes it sound as if the most important theological questions could probably be decided by flipping a coin to decide where to start, since *different* and *equally valid* conclusions will inevitably be reached from the different starting points.

Those who make such an objection often suggest that the best way to avoid this problem is not to study or teach systematic theology at all, but to limit our topical studies to the field of biblical theology, treating only the topics and themes the biblical authors themselves emphasize and describing the historical development of these biblical themes through the Bible.

In response to this objection, much of the discussion in this chapter about the necessity to teach Scripture will be relevant. Our choice of topics need not be restricted to the main concerns of the biblical authors, for our goal is to find out what God requires of us in all areas of concern to us today.

For example, it was not the *main* concern of any New Testament author to explain such topics as "baptism in the Holy Spirit," or women's roles in the church, or the doctrine of the Trinity, but these are valid areas of concern for us today, and we must look at all the places in Scripture that have relevance for those topics (whether those specific terms are mentioned or not, and whether those themes are of primary concern to each passage we examine or not) if we are going to be able to understand and explain to others "what the whole Bible teaches" about them.

The only alternative—for we *will* think *something* about those subjects—is to form our opinions haphazardly from a general impression of what we feel to be a "biblical" position on each subject, or perhaps to buttress our positions with careful analysis of one or two relevant texts, yet with no guarantee that those texts present a balanced view of "the whole counsel of God" (Acts 20:27) on the subject being considered. In fact this approach—one all too common in evangelical circles today—could, I suppose, be called "unsystematic theology" or even "disorderly and random theology"! Such an alternative is too subjective and too subject to cultural pressures. It tends toward doctrinal fragmentation and widespread doctrinal uncertainty, leaving the church theologically immature, like "children, tossed to and fro and carried about with every wind of doctrine" (Eph. 4:14).

Concerning the objection about the choice and sequence of topics, there is nothing to prevent us from going to Scripture to look for answers to *any* doctrinal questions, considered in *any sequence*. The sequence of topics in this book is a very common one and has been adopted because it is orderly and lends itself well to learning and teaching. But the chapters could be read in any sequence one wanted and the conclusions should not be different, nor should the persuasiveness of the arguments—if they are rightly derived from Scripture—be significantly diminished. I have tried to write the chapters so that they can be read as independent units.

E. How Should Christians Study Systematic Theology?

How then should we study systematic theology? The Bible provides some guidelines for answering this question.

1. We Should Study Systematic Theology With Prayer. If studying systematic theology is simply a certain way of studying the Bible, then the passages in Scripture that talk about the way in which we should study God's Word give guidance to us in this task. Just as the psalmist prays in Psalm 119:18, "Open my eyes, that I may behold wondrous things out of your law," so we should pray and seek God's help in understanding his Word. Paul tells us in 1 Corinthians 2:14 that "the unspiritual man does not receive the gifts of the Spirit of God, for they are folly to him, and he is not able to understand them because they are spiritually discerned." Studying theology is therefore a spiritual activity in which we need the help of the Holy Spirit.

No matter how intelligent, if the student does not continue to pray for God to give him or her an understanding mind and a believing and humble heart, and the student does not maintain a personal walk with the Lord, then the teachings of Scripture will be misunderstood and disbelieved, doctrinal error will result, and the mind and heart of the student will not be changed for the better but for the worse. Students of systematic theology should resolve at the beginning to keep their lives free from any disobedience to God or any known sin that would disrupt their relationship with him. They should resolve to maintain with great regularity their own personal devotional lives. They should continually pray for wisdom and understanding of Scripture.

Since it is the Holy Spirit who gives us the ability rightly to understand Scripture, we need to realize that the proper thing to do, particularly when we are unable to understand some passage or some doctrine of Scripture, is to pray for God's help. Often what we need is not more data but more insight into the data we already have available. This insight is given only by the Holy Spirit (cf. 1 Cor. 2:14; Eph. 1:17–19).

2. We Should Study Systematic Theology With Humility. Peter tells us, "Clothe yourselves, all of you, with humility toward one another, for 'God opposes the proud, but gives grace to the humble'" (1 Peter 5:5). Those who study systematic theology will learn many things about the teachings of Scripture that are perhaps not known or not known well by other Christians in their churches or by relatives who are older in the Lord than they are. They may also find that they understand things about Scripture that some of their church officers do not understand, and that even their pastor has perhaps forgotten or never learned well.

In all of these situations it would be very easy to adopt an attitude of pride or superiority toward others who have not made such a study. But how ugly it would be if anyone were to use this knowledge of God's Word simply to win arguments or to put down a fellow Christian in conversation, or to make another believer feel insignificant in the Lord's work. James' counsel is good for us at this point: "Let every man be quick to hear, slow to speak, slow to anger, for the anger of man does not work the righteousness of God" (James 1:19–20). He tells us that one's understanding of Scripture is to be imparted in humility and love:

> Who is wise and understanding among you? By his good life let him show his works in the meekness of wisdom. . . . But the wisdom from above is first pure, then peaceable, gentle, open to reason, full of mercy and good fruits, without uncertainty or insincerity. And the harvest of righteousness is sown in peace by those who make peace. (James 3:13, 17–18)

Systematic theology rightly studied will not lead to the knowledge that "puffs up" (1 Cor. 8:1) but to humility and love for others.

3. We Should Study Systematic Theology With Reason. We find in the New Testament that Jesus and the New Testament authors will often quote a verse of Scripture and then draw logical conclusions from it. They *reason* from Scripture. It is therefore not wrong to use human understanding, human logic, and human reason to draw conclusions from the statements of Scripture. Nevertheless, when we reason and draw what we think to be correct logical deductions from Scripture, we sometimes make mistakes. The deductions we draw from the statements of Scripture are not equal to the statements of Scripture themselves in certainty or authority, for our ability to reason and draw conclusions is not the ultimate standard of truth—only Scripture is.

What then are the limits on our use of our reasoning abilities to draw deductions from the statements of Scripture? The fact that reasoning to conclusions that go beyond the mere statements of Scripture is appropriate and even necessary for studying Scripture, and the fact that Scripture itself is the ultimate standard of truth, combine to indicate to us that *we are free to use our reasoning abilities to draw deductions from any passage of Scripture so long as these deductions do not contradict the clear teaching of some other passage of Scripture.*[7]

This principle puts a safeguard on our use of what we think to be logical deductions from Scripture. Our supposedly logical deductions may be erroneous, but Scripture itself cannot be erroneous. Thus, for example, we may read Scripture and find that God the Father is called God (1 Cor. 1:3), that God the Son is called God (John 20:28; Titus 2:13), and that God the Holy Spirit is called God (Acts 5:3–4). We might deduce from this that there are three Gods. But then we find the Bible explicitly teaching us that God is one (Deut. 6:4; James 2:19). Thus we conclude that what we *thought* to be a valid logical deduction about three Gods was wrong and that Scripture teaches both (a) that there are three separate persons (the Father, the Son, and the Holy Spirit), each of whom is fully God, and (b) that there is one God.

We cannot understand exactly how these two statements can both be true, so together they constitute a *paradox* ("a seemingly contradictory statement that may nonetheless be true").[8] We can tolerate a paradox (such as "God is three persons and one God") because we have confidence that ultimately God knows fully the truth about himself and about the nature of reality, and that in his understanding the different elements of a paradox are fully reconciled, even though at this point God's thoughts are higher than our thoughts (Isa. 55:8–9). But a true contradiction (such as, "God is three persons and God is not three persons") would imply ultimate contradiction in God's own understanding of himself or of reality, and this cannot be.

---

[7]This guideline is also adopted from Professor John Frame at Westminster Seminary.

[8]The *American Heritage Dictionary of the English Language*, ed. William Morris (Boston: Houghton-Mifflin, 1980), p. 950 (first definition). Essentially the same meaning is adopted by the *Oxford English Dictionary* (1913 ed., 7:450), the *Concise Oxford Dictionary* (1981 ed., p. 742), the *Random House College Dictionary* (1979 ed., p. 964), and the *Chambers Twentieth Century Dictionary* (p. 780), though all note that *paradox* can also mean "contradiction" (though less commonly); compare the *Encyclopedia of Philosophy*, ed. Paul Edwards (New York: Macmillan and The Free Press, 1967), 5:45, and the entire article "Logical Paradoxes" by John van Heijenoort on pp. 45–51 of the same volume, which proposes solutions to many of the classical paradoxes in the history of philosophy. (If *paradox* meant "contradiction," such solutions would be impossible.)

When I use the word *paradox* in the primary sense defined by these dictionaries today I realize that I am differing somewhat with the article "Paradox" by K. S. Kantzer in the *EDT*, ed. Walter Elwell, pp. 826–27 (which takes *paradox* to mean essentially "contradiction"). However, I am using *paradox* in an ordinary English sense and one also familiar in philosophy. There seems to me to be available no better word than *paradox* to refer to an apparent but not real contradiction.

There is, however, some lack of uniformity in the use of the term *paradox* and a related term, *antinomy,* in con-

temporary evangelical discussion. The word *antinomy* has sometimes been used to apply to what I here call *paradox,* that is, "seemingly contradictory statements that may nonetheless both be true" (see, for example, John Jefferson Davis, *Theology Primer* [Grand Rapids: Baker, 1981], p. 18). Such a sense for *antinomy* gained support in a widely read book, *Evangelism and the Sovereignty of God,* by J. I. Packer (London: Inter-Varsity Press, 1961). On pp. 18–22 Packer defines *antinomy* as "an appearance of contradiction" (but admits on p. 18 that his definition differs with the *Shorter Oxford Dictionary*). My problem with using *antinomy* in this sense is that the word is so unfamiliar in ordinary English that it just increases the stock of technical terms Christians have to learn in order to understand theologians, and moreover such a sense is unsupported by any of the dictionaries cited above, all of which define *antinomy* to mean "contradiction" (e.g., *Oxford English Dictionary,* 1:371). The problem is not serious, but it would help communication if evangelicals could agree on uniform senses for these terms.

A paradox is certainly acceptable in systematic theology, and paradoxes are in fact inevitable so long as we have finite understanding of any theological topic. However, it is important to recognize that Christian theology should never affirm a *contradiction* (a set of two statements, one of which denies the other). A contradiction would be, "God is three persons and God is not three persons" (where the term *persons* has the same sense in both halves of the sentence).

When the psalmist says, "The sum of your word is truth; and every one of your righteous ordinances endures for ever" (Ps. 119:160), he implies that God's words are not only true individually but also viewed together as a whole. Viewed collectively, their "sum" is also "truth." Ultimately, there is no internal contradiction either in Scripture or in God's own thoughts.

4. We Should Study Systematic Theology With Help From Others. We need to be thankful that God has put teachers in the church ("And God has appointed in the church first apostles, second prophets, third *teachers . . .*" [1 Cor. 12:28]. We should allow those with gifts of teaching to help us understand Scripture. This means that we should make use of systematic theologies and other books that have been written by some of the teachers that God has given to the church over the course of its history. It also means that our study of theology should include *talking with other Christians* about the things we study. Among those with whom we talk will often be some with gifts of teaching who can explain biblical teachings clearly and help us to understand more easily. In fact, some of the most effective learning in systematic theology courses in colleges and seminaries often occurs outside the classroom in informal conversations among students who are attempting to understand Bible doctrines for themselves.

5. We Should Study Systematic Theology by Collecting and Understanding All the Relevant Passages of Scripture on Any Topic. This point was mentioned in our definition of systematic theology at the beginning of the chapter, but the actual process needs to be described here. How does one go about making a doctrinal summary of what all the passages of Scripture teach on a certain topic? For topics covered in this book, many people will think that studying the chapters in this book and reading the Bible verses noted in the chapters is enough. But some people will want to do further study of Scripture on a particular topic or study some new topic not covered here. How could a student go about using the Bible to research its teachings on some new subject, perhaps one not discussed explicitly in any of his or her systematic theology textbooks?

The process would look like this: (1) Find all the relevant verses. The best help in this step is a good concordance, which enables one to look up key words and find the verses in which the subject is treated. For example, in studying what it means that man is created in the image and likeness of God, one needs to find all the verses in which "image" and "likeness" and "create" occur. (The words "man" and "God" occur too often to be useful for a concordance search.) In studying the doctrine of prayer, many words could be looked up (*pray, prayer, intercede, petition, supplication, confess, confession, praise, thanks, thanksgiving,* et al.)—and perhaps the list of verses would grow too long to be manageable, so that the student would have to skim the concordance entries without looking up the verses, or the search would probably have to be divided into sections or limited in some other way. Verses can also be found by thinking through the overall history of the Bible and then turning to sections where there would be information on the topic at hand—for example, a student studying prayer would want to read passages like the one about Hannah's prayer for a son (in 1 Sam. 1), Solomon's prayer at the dedication of the temple (in 1 Kings 8), Jesus' prayer in the Garden of Gethsemane (in Matt. 26 and parallels), and so forth. Then in addition to concordance work and reading other passages that one can find on the subject, checking the relevant sections in some systematic theology books will often bring to light other verses that had been missed, sometimes because none of the key words used for the concordance were in those verses.[9]

(2) The second step is to read, make notes on, and try to summarize the points made in the relevant verses. Sometimes a theme will be repeated often and the summary of the various verses will be relatively easy. At other times, there will be verses difficult to understand, and the student will need to take some time to study a verse in depth (just by reading the verse in context over and over, or by using specialized tools such as commentaries and dictionaries) until a satisfactory understanding is reached.

(3) Finally, the teachings of the various verses should be summarized into one or more points that the Bible affirms about that subject. The summary does not have to take the exact form of anyone else's conclusions on the subject, because we each may see things in Scripture that others have missed, or we may organize the subject differently or emphasize different things.

On the other hand, at this point it is also helpful to read related sections, if any can be found, in several systematic theology books. This provides a useful check against error and oversight, and often makes one aware of alternative perspectives and arguments that may cause us to modify or strengthen our position. If a student finds that others have argued for strongly differing conclusions, then these other views need to be stated fairly and then answered. Sometimes other theology books will alert us to historical or philosophical considerations that have been raised before in the history of the church, and these will provide additional insight or warnings against error.

The process outlined above is possible for any Christian who can read his or her Bible and can look up words in a concordance. Of course people will become faster and more accurate in this process with time and experience and Christian maturity, but it would be a tremendous help to the church if Christians generally would give much more time to searching out topics in Scripture for themselves and drawing conclusions in the way outlined above. The joy of discovery of biblical themes would be richly rewarding. Especially pastors and those who lead Bible studies would find added freshness in their understanding of Scripture and in their teaching.

6. We Should Study Systematic Theology With Rejoicing and Praise. The study of theology is not merely a theoretical exercise of the intellect. It is a study of the living God, and of the wonders of all his works in creation and redemption. We cannot study this subject dispassionately! We must love all that God is, all that he says and all that he does. "You shall love the LORD your God with all your heart" (Deut. 6:5). Our response to the study of the theology of Scripture should be that of the psalmist who said, "How precious to me are your thoughts, O God!" (Ps. 139:17). In the study of the teachings of

---

[9]I have read a number of student papers telling me that John's gospel says nothing about how Christians should pray, for example, because they looked at a concordance and found that the word *prayer* was not in John, and the word *pray* only occurs four times in reference to Jesus praying in John 14, 16, and 17. They overlooked the fact that John contains several important verses where the word *ask* rather than the word *pray* is used (John 14:13–14; 15:7, 16, et al.).

God's Word, it should not surprise us if we often find our hearts spontaneously breaking forth in expressions of praise and delight like those of the psalmist:

> The precepts of the LORD are right,
> rejoicing the heart. (Ps. 19:8)

> In the way of your testimonies I delight
> as much as in all riches. (Ps. 119:14)

> How sweet are your words to my taste,
> sweeter than honey to my mouth! (Ps. 119:103)

> Your testimonies are my heritage for ever;
> yea, they are the joy of my heart. (Ps. 119:111)

> I rejoice at your word
> like one who finds great spoil. (Ps. 119:162)

Often in the study of theology the response of the Christian should be similar to that of Paul in reflecting on the long theological argument that he has just completed at the end of Romans 11:32. He breaks forth into joyful praise at the richness of the doctrine which God has enabled him to express:

> O the depth of the riches and wisdom and knowledge of God! How unsearchable are his judgments and how inscrutable his ways!

> "For who has known the mind of the Lord,
> or who has been his counselor?"
> "Or who has given a gift to him
> that he might be repaid?"

> For from him and through him and to him are all things. To him be glory for ever. Amen. (Rom. 11:33–36)

QUESTIONS FOR PERSONAL APPLICATION

These questions at the end of each chapter focus on application to life. Because I think doctrine is to be felt at the emotional level as well as understood at the intellectual level, in many chapters I have included some questions about how a reader *feels* regarding a point of doctrine. I think these questions will prove quite valuable for those who take the time to reflect on them.

1. In what ways (if any) has this chapter changed your understanding of what systematic theology is? What was your attitude toward the study of systematic theology before reading this chapter? What is your attitude now?

2. What is likely to happen to a church or denomination that gives up learning systematic theology for a generation or longer? Has that been true of your church?

3. Are there any doctrines listed in the Contents for which a fuller understanding would help to solve a personal difficulty in your life at the present time? What

are the spiritual and emotional dangers that you personally need to be aware of in studying systematic theology?

4. Pray for God to make this study of basic Christian doctrines a time of spiritual growth and deeper fellowship with him, and a time in which you understand and apply the teachings of Scripture rightly.

SPECIAL TERMS

apologetics

minor doctrine

biblical theology

New Testament theology

Christian ethics

Old Testament theology

contradiction

paradox

doctrine

philosophical theology

dogmatic theology

presupposition

historical theology

systematic theology

major doctrine

BIBLIOGRAPHY

Baker, D. L. "Biblical Theology." In *NDT,* p. 671.

Berkhof, Louis. *Introduction to Systematic Theology.* Grand Rapids: Eerdmans, 1982, pp. 15–75 (first published 1932).

Bray, Gerald L., ed. *Contours of Christian Theology.* Downers Grove, Ill.: InterVarsity Press, 1993.

_____. "Systematic Theology, History of." In *NDT,* pp. 671–72.

Cameron, Nigel M., ed. *The Challenge of Evangelical Theology: Essays in Approach and Method.* Edinburgh: Rutherford House, 1987.

Carson, D. A. "Unity and Diversity in the New Testament: The Possibility of Systematic Theology." In *Scripture and Truth.* Ed. by D. A. Carson and John Woodbridge. Grand Rapids: Zondervan, 1983, pp. 65–95.

Davis, John Jefferson. *Foundations of Evangelical Theology.* Grand Rapids: Baker, 1984.

_____. *The Necessity of Systematic Theology.* Grand Rapids: Baker, 1980.

_____. *Theology Primer: Resources for the Theological Student.* Grand Rapids: Baker, 1981.

Demarest, Bruce. "Systematic Theology." In *EDT,* pp. 1064–66.

Erickson, Millard. *Concise Dictionary of Christian Theology.* Grand Rapids: Baker, 1986.

Frame, John. *Van Til the Theologian.* Phillipsburg, N.J.: Pilgrim, 1976.

Geehan, E. R., ed. *Jerusalem and Athens.* Nutley, N.J.: Craig Press, 1971.

Grenz, Stanley J. *Revisioning Evangelical Theology: A Fresh Agenda for the 21st Century.* Downers Grove, Ill.: InterVarsity Press, 1993.

House, H. Wayne. *Charts of Christian Theology and Doctrine.* Grand Rapids: Zondervan, 1992.

Kuyper, Abraham. *Principles of Sacred Theology.* Trans. by J. H. DeVries. Grand Rapids: Eerdmans, 1968 (reprint; first published as *Encyclopedia of Sacred Theology* in 1898).

Machen, J. Gresham. *Christianity and Liberalism.* Grand Rapids: Eerdmans, 1923. (This 180-page book is, in my opinion, one of the most significant theological studies ever written. It gives a clear overview of major biblical doctrines and shows the vital differences with Protestant liberal theology at every point, differences that still confront us today. It is required reading in all my introductory theology classes.)

Morrow, T. W. "Systematic Theology." In *NDT,* p. 671.

Poythress, Vern. *Symphonic Theology: The Validity of Multiple Perspectives in Theology.* Grand Rapids: Zondervan, 1987.

Preus, Robert D. *The Theology of Post-Reformation Lutheranism: A Study of Theological Prolegomena.* 2 vols. St. Louis: Concordia, 1970.

Van Til, Cornelius. *In Defense of the Faith,* vol. 5: *An Introduction to Systematic Theology.* N.p.: Presbyterian and Reformed, 1976, pp. 1–61, 253–62.

_____. *The Defense of the Faith.* Philadelphia: Presbyterian and Reformed, 1955.

Vos, Geerhardus. "The Idea of Biblical Theology as a Science and as a Theological Discipline." In *Redemptive History and Biblical Interpretation,* pp. 3–24. Ed. by Richard Gaffin. Phillipsburg, N.J.: Presbyterian and Reformed, 1980 (article first published 1894).

Warfield, B. B. "The Indispensableness of Systematic Theology to the Preacher." In *Selected Shorter Writings of Benjamin B. Warfield,* 2:280–88. Ed. by John E. Meeter. Nutley, N.J.: Presbyterian and Reformed, 1973 (article first published 1897).

_____. "The Right of Systematic Theology." In *Selected Shorter Writings of Benjamin B. Warfield,* 2:21–279. Ed. by John E. Meeter. Nutley, N.J.: Presbyterian and Reformed, 1973 (article first published 1896).

Wells, David. *No Place for Truth, or, Whatever Happened to Evangelical Theology?* Grand Rapids: Eerdmans, 1993.

Woodbridge, John D., and Thomas E. McComiskey, eds. *Doing Theology in Today's World: Essays in Honor of Kenneth S. Kantzer.* Grand Rapids: Zondervan, 1991.

SCRIPTURE MEMORY PASSAGE

Students have repeatedly mentioned that one of the most valuable parts of any of their courses in college or seminary has been the Scripture passages they were required to memorize. "I have hidden your word in my heart that I might not sin against you" (Ps. 119:11 NIV). In each chapter, therefore, I have included an appropriate memory passage so that instructors may incorporate Scripture memory into the course requirements wherever possible. (Scripture memory passages at the end of each chapter are taken from the RSV. These same passages in the NIV and NASB may be found in appendix 2.)

Matthew 28:18–20: *And Jesus came and said to them, "All authority in heaven and on earth has been given to me. Go therefore and make disciples of all nations, baptizing them in the name of the Father and of the Son and of the Holy Spirit, teaching them to observe all that I have commanded you; and lo, I am with you always, to the close of the age."*

HYMN

Systematic theology at its best will result in praise. It is appropriate therefore at the end of each chapter to include a hymn related to the subject of that chapter. In a classroom setting, the hymn can be sung together at the beginning or end of class. Alternatively, an individual reader can sing it privately or simply meditate quietly on the words.

For almost every chapter the words of the hymns were found in *Trinity Hymnal* (Philadelphia: Great Commission Publications, 1990),[10] the hymnal of the Presbyterian Church in America and the Orthodox Presbyterian Church, but most of them are found in many other common hymnals. Unless otherwise noted, the words of these hymns are now in public domain and no longer subject to copyright restrictions: therefore they may be freely copied for overhead projector use or photocopied.

Why have I used so many old hymns? Although I personally like many of the more recent worship songs that have come into wide use, when I began to select hymns that would correspond to the great doctrines of the Christian faith, I realized that the great hymns of the church throughout history have a doctrinal richness and breadth that is still unequaled. For several of the chapters in this book, I know of no modern worship song that covers the same subject in an extended way — perhaps this can be a challenge to modern songwriters to study these chapters and then write songs reflecting the teaching of Scripture on the respective subjects.

For this chapter, however, I found no hymn ancient or modern that thanked God for the privilege of studying systematic theology from the pages of Scripture. Therefore I have selected a hymn of general praise, which is always appropriate.

"O for a Thousand Tongues to Sing"

This hymn by Charles Wesley (1707–88) begins by wishing for "a thousand tongues" to sing God's praise. Verse 2 is a prayer that God would "assist me" in singing his praise throughout the earth. The remaining verses give praise to Jesus (vv. 3–6) and to God the Father (v. 7).

> O for a thousand tongues to sing
> My great Redeemer's praise,
> The glories of my God and King,
> The triumphs of His grace.
>
> My gracious Master and my God,
> Assist me to proclaim,
> To spread through all the earth abroad,
> The honors of Thy name.
>
> Jesus! the name that charms our fears,
> That bids our sorrows cease;

---

[10]This hymn book is completely revised from a similar hymnal of the same title published by the Orthodox Presbyterian Church in WW 1961.

'Tis music in the sinner's ears,
'Tis life and health and peace.

He breaks the pow'r of reigning sin,
He sets the prisoner free;
His blood can make the foulest clean;
His blood availed for me.

He speaks and, list'ning to His voice,
New life the dead receive;
The mournful, broken hearts rejoice;
The humble poor believe.

Hear him, ye deaf; his praise, ye dumb,
Your loosened tongues employ,
Ye blind, behold your Savior come;
And leap, ye lame, for joy.

Glory to God and praise and love
Be ever, ever giv'n
By saints below and saints above—
The church in earth and heav'n.

AUTHOR: CHARLES WESLEY, 1739, ALT.

Chapter 2

THE CHURCH: ITS NATURE, ITS MARKS, AND ITS PURPOSES

What is necessary to make a church?
How can we recognize a true church?
The purposes of the church.

EXPLANATION AND SCRIPTURAL BASIS

A. The Nature of the Church

1. Definition: The Church Is the Community of All True Believers for All Time. This definition understands the church to be made of all those who are truly saved. Paul says, "Christ loved *the church* and gave himself up for her" (Eph. 5:25). Here the term "the church" is used to apply to all those whom Christ died to redeem, all those who are saved by the death of Christ. But that must include all true believers for all time, both believers in the New Testament age and believers in the Old Testament age as well.[1] So great is God's plan for the church that he has exalted Christ to a position of highest authority for the sake of the church: "He has put all things under his feet and has made him the head over all things *for the church,* which is his body, the fulness of him who fills all in all" (Eph. 1:22–23).

Jesus Christ himself builds the church by calling his people to himself. He promised, "I will build my church" (Matt. 16:18). And Luke is careful to tell us that the growth of the church came not by human effort alone, but that "*the Lord* added to their number day by day those who were being saved" (Acts 2:47). But this process whereby Christ builds the church is just a continuation of the pattern established by God in the Old Testament

---

[1]See section 5 below for a discussion of the dispensational view that the church and Israel must be thought of as distinct groups. In this book I have taken a non-dispensational position on that question, though it should be pointed out that many evangelicals who agree with much of the rest of this book will differ with me on this particular question.

whereby he called people to himself to be a worshiping assembly before him. There are several indications *in the Old Testament* that God thought of his people as a "church," a people assembled for the purpose of worshiping God. When Moses tells the people that the Lord said to him, *"Gather the people to me,* that I may let them hear my words, so that they may learn to fear me all the days that they live upon the earth . . ."* (Deut. 4:10), the Septuagint translates the word for "gather" (Heb. *qāhal*) with the Greek term *ekklēsiazō,* "to summon an assembly," the verb that is cognate to the New Testament noun *ekklēsia,* "church."[2]

It is not surprising, then, that the New Testament authors can speak of the Old Testament people of Israel as a "church" (*ekklēsia*). For example, Stephen speaks of the people of Israel in the wilderness as "the *church* (*ekklēsia*) in the wilderness" (Acts 7:38, author's translation). And the author of Hebrews quotes Christ as saying that he would sing praise to God in the midst of the great assembly of God's people in heaven: "In the midst of the church (*ekklēsia*) I will sing praise to you" (Heb. 2:12, author's translation, quoting Ps. 22:22).

Therefore the author of Hebrews understands the present-day Christians who constitute the church on earth to be surrounded by a great "cloud of witnesses" (Heb. 12:1) that reaches back into the earliest eras of the Old Testament and includes Abel, Enoch, Noah, Abraham, Sarah, Gideon, Barak, Samson, Jephthah, David, Samuel, and the prophets (Heb. 11:4–32). All these "witnesses" surround the present-day people of God, and it seems only appropriate that they, together with the New Testament people of God, should be thought of as God's great spiritual "assembly" or "church."[3] Moreover, later in chapter 12 the author of Hebrews says that when New Testament Christians worship we come into the presence of "the *assembly* (lit. "church," Gk. *ekklēsia*) of the first-born who are enrolled in heaven." This emphasis is not surprising in light of the fact that the New Testament authors see Jewish believers and Gentile believers alike to be now united in the church. Together they have been made "one" (Eph. 2:14), they are "one new man" (v. 15) and "fellow citizens" (v. 19), and "members of the household of God" (v. 19).

Therefore, even though there are certainly new privileges and new blessings that are given to the people of God in the New Testament, both the usage of the term "church"

---

[2]In fact, the Greek word *ekklēsia,* the term translated "church" in the New Testament, is the word that the Septuagint most frequently uses to translate the Old Testament term *qāhal,* the word used to speak of the "congregation" or the "assembly" of God's people. *Ekklēsia* translates *qāhal,* "assembly," 69 times in the Septuagint. The next most frequent translation is *synagōgē,* "synagogue" or "meeting, place of meeting" (37 times). Chafer objects to this analysis, for he says that the Septuagint use of the word *ekklēsia* does not reflect the New Testament meaning of the word "church" but is a common term for an "assembly." Therefore we should not call the "assembly" in the theater at Ephesus a church (Acts 19:32) even though the word *ekklēsia* is used there to refer to that group of people. Similarly, when Stephen refers to Israel in the wilderness (Acts 7:38) as an *ekklēsia,* it does not imply that he thinks of it as a "church" but only an assembly of people. Chafer sees this usage of the term as different from its distinctive New Testament meaning to refer to the church (*Systematic*

Theology, 4:39). However, the extensive use of the word *ekklēsia* in the Septuagint to refer to assemblies not of pagan mobs but specifically of God's people certainly must be taken into account in understanding the meaning of the word when used by New Testament authors. The Septuagint was the Bible that they most commonly used, and they are certainly using the word *ekklēsia* with awareness of its Old Testament content. This would explain why Luke can so easily record Stephen as referring to the "church" in the wilderness with Moses and yet many times in the surrounding chapters in Acts speak of the growth of the "church" after Pentecost with no indication that there is any difference in meaning intended. The New Testament church is an assembly of God's people that simply continues in the pattern of assemblies of God's people found throughout the Old Testament.

[3]The Greek word *ekklēsia,* translated "church" in the New Testament, simply means "assembly."

in Scripture and the fact that throughout Scripture God has always called his people to assemble to worship himself, indicate that it is appropriate to think of the church as constituting all the people of God for all time, both Old Testament believers and New Testament believers.[4]

2. The Church Is Invisible, Yet Visible. In its true spiritual reality as the fellowship of all genuine believers, the church is invisible. This is because we cannot see the spiritual condition of people's hearts. We can see those who outwardly attend the church, and we can see outward evidences of inward spiritual change, but we cannot actually see into people's hearts and view their spiritual state—only God can do that. This is why Paul says, *"The Lord knows those who are his"* (2 Tim. 2:19). Even in our own churches and our own neighborhoods, only God knows who are true believers with certainty and without error. In speaking of the church as invisible the author of Hebrews speaks of the "assembly (literally, "church") of the first-born who are enrolled in heaven" (Heb. 12:23), and says that present-day Christians join with that assembly in worship.

We can give the following definition: *The invisible church is the church as God sees it.*

Both Martin Luther and John Calvin were eager to affirm this invisible aspect of the church over against the Roman Catholic teaching that the church was the one visible organization that had descended from the apostles in an unbroken line of succession (through the bishops of the church). The Roman Catholic Church had argued that only in the visible organization of the Roman Church could we find the one true church, the only true church. Even today such a view is held by the Roman Catholic Church. In their "Pastoral Statement for Catholics on Biblical Fundamentalism" issued March 25, 1987, the (United States) National Conference of Catholic Bishops Ad Hoc Committee on Biblical Fundamentalism criticized evangelical Christianity

---

[4]For a discussion of the question of whether there remains a distinction between "the church" and "Israel" as two separate peoples of God, see section 5 below.

Millard Erickson, *Christian Theology* (Grand Rapids: Baker, 1983–85), p. 1048, argues that the church does not start until Pentecost because Luke does not use the word "church" (*ekklēsia*) in his gospel, but uses it twenty-four times in Acts. If the church existed before Pentecost, he reasons, why did Luke not speak of it before that time? Yet the reason Luke did not use the word "church" to speak of the people of God during Jesus' earthly ministry is probably because there was no clearly defined or visible group to which it could refer during Jesus' earthly ministry. The true church *did* exist in the sense that it consisted of all true believers in Israel during that time, but this was such a small remnant of faithful Jews (such as Joseph and Mary, Zechariah and Elizabeth, Simeon, Anna, and others like them), that it was not an outwardly evident or well-defined group at all. Large segments of the Jewish population had strayed from God and had substituted other kinds of religious activities, such as legalism (the Pharisees), unbelieving "liberalism" (the Sadducees), speculative mysticism (those who wrote or believed apocalyptic literature and fol-

lowers of sects such as those in the Qumran community), crass materialism (the tax collectors and others for whom wealth was a false god), or political or military activism (the Zealots and others who sought salvation through political or military means). Though there were no doubt genuine believers among many or all of these groups, the nation as a whole did not constitute an assembly of people who worshiped God rightly.

Moreover, the idea of a people of God newly "called out" as an assembly to follow Christ first came to fruition on the day of Pentecost. Therefore, although the "church" in the sense of the group of all who truly believed in God did exist before the day of Pentecost, it came to much clearer visible expression on the day of Pentecost, and it is natural that Luke should begin to use the name "the church" at that point. Before that point the name "church" could not have referred to any clearly established entity apart from the nation of Israel as a whole; after Pentecost, however, it readily could be used to refer to those who willingly and visibly identified themselves with this new people of God.

We should also note that Jesus did use the word "church" (*ekklēsia*) twice in Matthew's gospel (16:18 and 18:17).

(which it called "biblical fundamentalism") primarily because it took people away from the one true church:

> The basic characteristic of biblical fundamentalism is that it eliminates from Christianity the church as the Lord Jesus founded it. . . . There is no mention of the historic, authoritative church in continuity with Peter and the other apostles. . . . A study of the New Testament . . . demonstrates the importance of belonging to the church started by Jesus Christ. Christ chose Peter and the other apostles as foundations of his church. . . . Peter and the other apostles have been succeeded by the bishop of Rome and the other bishops, and . . . the flock of Christ still has, under Christ, a universal shepherd.[5]

In response to that kind of teaching both Luther and Calvin disagreed. They said that the Roman Catholic Church had the outward form, the organization, but it was just a shell. Calvin argued that just as Caiaphas (the high priest at the time of Christ) was descended from Aaron but was no true priest, so the Roman Catholic bishops had "descended" from the apostles in a line of succession but they were not true bishops in Christ's church. Because they had departed from the true preaching of the gospel, their visible organization was not the true church. Calvin said, "This pretense of succession is vain unless their descendants conserve safe and uncorrupted the truth of Christ which they have received at their fathers' hands, and abide in it. . . . See what value this succession has, unless it also include a true and uninterrupted emulation on the part of the successors!"[6]

On the other hand, the true church of Christ certainly has a visible aspect as well. We may use the following definition: *The visible church is the church as Christians on earth see it.* In this sense the visible church includes all who profess faith in Christ and give evidence of that faith in their lives.[7]

In this definition we do not say that the visible church is the church as any person in the world (such as an unbeliever or someone who held heretical teachings) might see it, but we mean to speak of the church as it is perceived by those who are genuine believers and have an understanding of the difference between believers and unbelievers.

When Paul writes his epistles he writes to the visible church in each community: "To the *church* of God which is at Corinth" (1 Cor. 1:2); "To the *church* of the Thessalonians" (1 Thess. 1:1); "To Philemon . . . and Apphia . . . and Archippus . . . and the *church* in your house" (Philem. 1–2). Paul certainly realized that there were unbelievers in some of those churches, some who had made a profession of faith that was not genuine, who appeared to be Christians but would eventually fall away. Yet neither Paul nor anyone else could tell with certainty who those people were. Paul simply wrote to the entire church that met together in any one place. In this sense, we could say today that the visible

---

[5]The full text of the Bishops' statement can be obtained from the National Catholic News Service, 1312 Massachusetts Avenue NW, Washington, D.C. 20005. The text was published in "Pastoral Statement for Catholics on Biblical Fundamentalism," in Origins vol. 17:21 (Nov. 5, 1987), pp. 376–77.

[6]John Calvin, *Institutes* 4.2.2–3 (pp. 1043, 1045).

[7]Both Calvin and Luther would add the third qualification that those who are considered part of the visible church must partake of the sacraments of baptism and the Lord's Supper. Others might consider this as a subcategory of the requirement that people give evidence of faith in their life.

church is the group of people who come together each week to worship as a church and profess faith in Christ.

The visible church throughout the world will always include some unbelievers, and individual congregations will usually include some unbelievers, because we cannot see hearts as God sees them. Paul speaks of "Hymenaeus and Philetus, who have swerved from the truth" and who "are upsetting the faith of some" (2 Tim. 2:17–18). But he is confident that "The Lord knows those who are his" (2 Tim. 2:19). Paul says with sorrow, "Demas, in love with this present world, has deserted me and gone to Thessalonica" (2 Tim. 4:10).

Similarly, Paul warns the Ephesian elders that after his departure "fierce wolves will come in among you, not sparing the flock; and *from among your own selves* will arise men speaking perverse things, to draw away the disciples after them" (Acts 20:29–30). Jesus himself warned, "Beware of false prophets, *who come to you in sheep's clothing* but inwardly are ravenous wolves. You will know them by their fruits" (Matt. 7:15–16). Realizing this distinction between the church invisible and the church visible, Augustine said of the visible church, "Many sheep are without and many wolves are within."[8]

When we recognize that there are unbelievers in the visible church, there is a danger that we may become overly suspicious. We may begin to doubt the salvation of many true believers and thereby bring great confusion into the church. Calvin warned against this danger by saying that we must make a "charitable judgment" whereby we recognize as members of the church all who "by confession of faith, by example of life, and by partaking of the sacraments, profess the same God and Christ with us."[9] We should not try to exclude people from the fellowship of the church until they by public sin bring discipline upon themselves. On the other hand, of course, the church should not tolerate in its membership "public unbelievers" who by profession or life clearly proclaim themselves to be outside the true church.

3. The Church Is Local and Universal. In the New Testament the word "church" may be applied to a group of believers at any level, ranging from a very small group meeting in a private home all the way to the group of all true believers in the universal church. A "house church" is called a "church" in Romans 16:5 ("greet also *the church in their house*"), 1 Corinthians 16:19 ("Aquila and Prisca, together with *the church in their house,* send you hearty greetings in the Lord"). The church in an entire city is also called "a church" (1 Cor. 1:2; 2 Cor. 1:1; and 1 Thess. 1:1). The church in a region is referred to as a "church" in Acts 9:31: "So *the church throughout all Judea and Galilee and Samaria* had peace and was built up."[10] Finally, the church throughout the entire world can be referred to as "the church." Paul says, "Christ loved *the church* and gave himself up for her" (Eph.

[8]Quoted in John Calvin, *Institutes* 4.1.8 (p. 1022).
[9]John Calvin, *Institutes,* 4.1.8 (pp. 1022–23).
[10]There is a textual variant among the Greek manuscripts of Acts 9:31, with some manuscripts having "the church" and some having "the churches." The singular reading "the church" is far preferable to the variant that has the plural. The singular reading is given a "B" probability (next to highest degree of probability) in the United Bible Societies' text. The singular is represented by many early and diverse texts while the plural reading is found in the Byzantine text tradition but in no texts before the fifth century A.D. (In order for the grammar to be consistent, six words have to be changed in the Greek text; therefore the variant is an intentional alteration in one direction or the other.)

5:25) and says, "God has appointed *in the church* first apostles, second prophets, third teachers . . ." (1 Cor. 12:28). In this latter verse the mention of "apostles," who were not given to any individual church, guarantees that the reference is to the church universal.

We may conclude that the group of God's people considered at any level from local to universal may rightly be called "a church." We should not make the mistake of saying that only a church meeting in houses expresses the true nature of the church, or only a church considered at a city-wide level can rightly be called a church, or only the church universal can rightly be called by the name "church." Rather, the community of God's people considered at any level can be rightly called a church.

4. Metaphors for the Church.[11] To help us understand the nature of the church, Scripture uses a wide range of metaphors and images to describe to us what the church is like.[12] There are several family images—for example, Paul views the church as a *family* when he tells Timothy to act as if all the church members were members of a larger family: "Do not rebuke an older man but exhort him as you would a father; treat younger men like brothers, older women like mothers, younger women like sisters, in all purity" (1 Tim. 5:1–2). God is our heavenly Father (Eph. 3:14), and we are his sons and daughters, for God says to us, "I will be a father to you, and you shall be my sons and daughters, says the Lord Almighty" (2 Cor. 6:18). We are therefore brothers and sisters with each other in God's family (Matt. 12:49–50; 1 John 3:14–18). A somewhat different family metaphor is seen when Paul refers to the church as the *bride of Christ.* He says that the relationship between a husband and wife "refers to Christ and the church" (Eph. 5:32), and he says that he brought about the engagement between Christ and the church at Corinth and that it resembles an engagement between a bride and her husband-to-be: "I betrothed you to one husband, that to Christ I might present you as a pure virgin" (2 Cor. 11:2 NASB)—here Paul is looking forward to the time of Christ's return as the time when the church will be presented to him as his bride.

In other metaphors Scripture compares the church to *branches on a vine* (John 15:5), *an olive tree* (Rom. 11:17–24), *a field of crops* (1 Cor. 3:6–9), *a building* (1 Cor. 3:9), and *a harvest* (Matt. 13:1–30; John 4:35). The church is also viewed as *a new temple* not built with literal stones but built with Christian people who are "living stones" (1 Peter 2:5) built up on the "cornerstone" who is Christ Jesus (1 Peter 2:4–8). Yet the church is not only a new temple for worship of God; it is also *a new group of priests,* a "holy priesthood" that can offer "spiritual sacrifices acceptable to God" (1 Peter 2:5). We are also viewed as *God's house:* "And we are his house" (Heb. 3:6), with Jesus Christ himself viewed as the "builder" of the house (Heb. 3:3). The church is also viewed as *"the pillar* and *bulwark of the truth"* (1 Tim. 3:15).

Finally, another familiar metaphor views the church as *the body of Christ* (1 Cor. 12:12–27). We should recognize that Paul in fact uses two different metaphors of the human body when he speaks of the church. In 1 Corinthians 12 *the whole body* is taken as

---

[11]For more discussion of this topic see Edmund P. Clowney, "Interpreting the Biblical Models of the Church," in *Biblical Interpretation and the Church,* ed. by D. A. Carson (Nashville: Thomas Nelson, 1985), pp. 64–109.

[12]The list of metaphors given in this section is not intended to be exhaustive.

a metaphor for the church, because Paul speaks of the "ear" and the "eye" and the "sense of smell" (1 Cor. 12:16–17). In this metaphor, Christ is not viewed as the head joined to the body, because the individual members are themselves the individual parts of the head. Christ is in this metaphor the Lord who is "outside" of that body that represents the church and is the one whom the church serves and worships.

But in Ephesians 1:22–23; 4:15–16, and in Colossians 2:19, Paul uses a different body metaphor to refer to the church. In these passages Paul says that Christ is the head and the church is like *the rest of the body, as distinguished from the head:* "We are to grow up in every way into him who is the head, into Christ, from whom the whole body, joined and knit together by every joint with which it is supplied, when each part is working properly, makes bodily growth and upbuilds itself in love" (Eph. 4:15–16).[13] We should not confuse these two metaphors in 1 Corinthians 12 and Ephesians 4, but keep them distinct.

The wide range of metaphors used for the church in the New Testament should remind us not to focus exclusively on any one. For example, while it is true that the church is the body of Christ, we must remember that this is only one metaphor among many. If we focus exclusively on that metaphor we will be likely to forget that Christ is our Lord reigning in heaven as well as the one who dwells among us. Certainly we should not agree to the Roman Catholic view that the church is the "continuing incarnation" of the Son of God on earth today. The church is not the Son of God in the flesh, for Christ rose in his human body, he ascended in his human body into heaven, and he now reigns as the incarnate Christ in heaven, one who is clearly distinct from the church here on earth.

Each of the metaphors used for the church can help us to appreciate more of the richness of privilege that God has given us by incorporating us into the church. The fact that the church is like a family should increase our love and fellowship with one another. The thought that the church is like the bride of Christ should stimulate us to strive for greater purity and holiness, and also greater love for Christ and submission to him. The image of the church as branches in a vine should cause us to rest in him more fully. The idea of an agricultural crop should encourage us to continue growing in the Christian life and obtaining for ourselves and others the proper spiritual nutrients to grow. The picture of the church as God's new temple should increase our awareness of God's very presence dwelling in our midst as we meet. The concept of the church as a priesthood should help us to see more clearly the delight God has in the sacrifices of praise and good deeds that we offer to him (see Heb. 13:15–16). The metaphor of the church as the body of Christ should increase our interdependence on one another and our appreciation of the diversity of gifts within the body. Many other applications could be drawn from these and other metaphors for the church listed in Scripture.

5. The Church and Israel. Among evangelical Protestants there has been a difference of viewpoint on the question of the relationship between Israel and the church. This question was brought into prominence by those who hold to a "dispensational" system of theology. The most extensive systematic theology written by a dispensationalist, Lewis

---

[13]This second metaphor is not even a complete or "proper" metaphor, for bodily parts do not grow up into the head, but Paul is mixing the idea of Christ's headship (or authority), the idea of the church as a body, and the idea that we grow to maturity in Christ, and he combines them into one complex statement.

Sperry Chafer's *Systematic Theology,*[14] points out many distinctions between Israel and the church, and even between believing Israel in the Old Testament and the church in the New Testament.[15] Chafer argues that God has two distinct plans for the two different groups of people that he has redeemed: God's purposes and promises for *Israel* are for *earthly blessings,* and they will yet be fulfilled on this earth at some time in the future. On the other hand, God's purposes and promises for *the church* are for *heavenly blessings,* and those promises will be fulfilled in heaven. This distinction between the two different groups that God saves will especially be seen in the millennium, according to Chafer, for at that time Israel will reign on earth as God's people and enjoy the fulfillment of Old Testament promises, but the church will already have been taken up into heaven at the time of Christ's secret return for his saints ("the rapture"). On this view, the church did not begin until Pentecost (Acts 2). And it is not right to think of Old Testament believers together with New Testament believers as constituting one church.

While Chafer's position continues to have influence in some dispensational circles, and certainly in more popular preaching, a number of leaders among more recent dispensationalists have not followed Chafer in many of these points. Several current dispensational theologians, such as Robert Saucy, Craig Blaising, and Darrell Bock, refer to themselves as "progressive dispensationalists,"[16] and they have gained a wide following. They *would not see the church as a parenthesis* in God's plan but as the first step toward the establishment of the kingdom of God. On a progressive dispensational view, *God does not have two separate purposes for Israel and the church,* but a single purpose — the establishment of the kingdom of God — in which Israel and the church will both share. Progressive dispensationalists would see *no distinction between Israel and the church in the future eternal state,* for all will be part of the one people of God. Moreover, they would hold that the church will reign with Christ in *glorified bodies on earth during the millennium.*

However, there is still a difference between progressive dispensationalists and the rest of evangelicalism on one point: they would say that *the Old Testament prophecies concerning Israel will still be fulfilled in the millennium by ethnic Jewish people* who will believe in Christ and live in the land of Israel as a "model nation" for all nations to see and learn from. Therefore they would not say that the church is the "new Israel" or that all the Old Testament prophecies about Israel will be fulfilled in the church, for these prophecies will yet be fulfilled in ethnic Israel.

---

[14]Lewis Sperry Chafer, *Systematic Theology.* Although there are several other distinctive doctrines that usually characterize dispensationalists, the distinction between Israel and the church as two groups in God's overall plan is probably the most important. Other doctrines held by dispensationalists usually include a pretribulational rapture of the church into heaven, a future literal fulfillment of Old Testament prophecies concerning Israel, the dividing of biblical history into seven periods or "dispensations" of God's ways of relating to his people, and an understanding of the church age as a parenthesis in God's plan for the ages, a parenthesis instituted when the Jews largely rejected Jesus as their Messiah. How-ever, many present-day dispensationalists would qualify or reject several of these other distinctives. Dispensationalism as a system began with the writings of J. N. Darby (1800 – 1882) in Great Britain, but was popularized in the USA through the Scofield Reference Bible.

[15]Chafer, *Systematic Theology,* 4:45 – 53.

[16]See Robert L. Saucy, *The Case for Progressive Dispensationalism* (Grand Rapids: Zondervan, 1993), and Darrell L. Bock and Craig A. Blaising, eds., *Progressive Dispensationalism* (Wheaton: Victor, 1993). See also John S. Feinberg, ed., *Continuity and Discontinuity: Perspectives on the Relationship Between the Old and New Testaments* (Wheaton: Crossway, 1988).

The position taken in this book differs quite a bit from Chafer's views on this issue and also differs somewhat with progressive dispensationalists. However, it must be said here that questions about the exact way in which biblical prophecies about the future will be fulfilled are, in the nature of the case, difficult to decide with certainty, and it is wise to have some tentativeness in our conclusions on these matters. With this in mind, the following may be said.

Both Protestant and Catholic theologians outside of the dispensational position have said that the church includes both Old Testament believers and New Testament believers in one church or one body of Christ. Even on the nondispensational view, a person may hold that there will be a future large-scale conversion of the Jewish people (Rom. 11:12, 15, 23–24, 25–26, 28–31),[17] yet that this conversion will only result in Jewish believers becoming part of the one true church of God—they will be "grafted back into their own olive tree" (Rom. 11:24).

With regard to this question, we should notice the many New Testament verses that understand the church as the "new Israel" or new "people of God." The fact that "Christ loved *the church* and gave himself up for her" (Eph. 5:25) would suggest this. Moreover, this present church age, which has brought the salvation of many millions of Christians in the church, is not an interruption or a parenthesis in God's plan,[18] but a continuation of his plan expressed throughout the Old Testament to call a people to himself. Paul says, "For he is not a real Jew who is one outwardly, nor is true circumcision something external and physical. *He is a Jew who is one inwardly*, and real circumcision is a matter of the heart, spiritual and not literal" (Rom. 2:28–29). Paul recognizes that though there is a literal or natural sense in which people who physically descended from Abraham are to be called Jews, there is also a deeper or spiritual sense in which a "true Jew" is one who is inwardly a believer and whose heart has been cleansed by God.

Paul says that Abraham is not only to be considered the father of the Jewish people in a physical sense. He is also in a deeper and more true sense *the father of all who believe without being circumcised . . . and likewise the father of the circumcised who are not merely circumcised but also follow the example of the faith which our father Abraham had* (Rom. 4:11–12; cf. vv. 16, 18). Therefore Paul can say, "not all who are descended from Israel belong to Israel, and not all are children of Abraham because they are his descendants . . . it is not the children of the flesh who are the children of God, but the children of the promise are reckoned as descendants" (Rom. 9:6–8). Paul here implies that the true children of Abraham, those who are in the most true sense "Israel," are not the nation of Israel by physical descent from Abraham but those who have believed in Christ. Those who truly believe in Christ are now the ones who have the privilege of being called "my people" by the Lord (Rom. 9:25, quoting Hos. 2:23); therefore, the church is now God's chosen people. This means that when Jewish people according to the flesh are saved in large numbers at some time in the future, they will not constitute

---

[17]I affirm the conviction that Rom. 9–11 teaches a future large-scale conversion of the Jewish people, even though I am not a dispensationalist in the commonly understood sense of that term.

[18]Chafer's term is "an intercalation," meaning an inser-

tion of a period of time into a previously planned schedule or calendar of events (p. 41). Here Chafer says, "The present age of the church is an intercalation into the revealed calendar or program of God as that program was foreseen by the prophets of old."

a separate people of God or be like a separate olive tree, but they will be "grafted back *into their own olive tree*" (Rom. 11:24). Another passage indicating this is Galatians 3:29: "And if you are Christ's, then you are Abraham's offspring, heirs according to promise." Similarly, Paul says that Christians are the "true circumcision" (Phil. 3:3).

Far from thinking of the church as a separate group from the Jewish people, Paul writes to Gentile believers at Ephesus telling them that they were formerly "alienated from the commonwealth of Israel, and strangers to the covenants of promise" (Eph. 2:12), but that now they have been "brought near in the blood of Christ" (Eph. 2:13). And when the Gentiles were brought into the church, Jews and Gentiles were united into one new body. Paul says that God "*has made us both one,* and has broken down the dividing wall of hostility . . . that he might create in himself one new man in place of the two, so making peace, and might *reconcile us both to God in one body* through the cross" (Eph. 2:14–16). Therefore Paul can say that Gentiles are "*fellow citizens with the saints* and members of the household of God, built upon the foundation of the apostles and prophets, Christ Jesus himself being the cornerstone" (Eph. 2:19–20). With his extensive awareness of the Old Testament background to the New Testament church, Paul can still say that "the Gentiles are fellow heirs, members of the same body" (Eph. 3:6). The entire passage speaks strongly of the unity of Jewish and Gentile believers in one body in Christ and gives no indication of any distinctive plan for Jewish people ever to be saved apart from inclusion in the one body of Christ, the church. The church incorporates into itself all the true people of God, and almost all of the titles used of God's people in the Old Testament are in one place or another applied to the church in the New Testament.

Hebrews 8 provides another strong argument for seeing the church as the recipient, and the fulfillment, of the Old Testament promises concerning Israel. In the context of speaking about the new covenant to which Christians belong, the author of Hebrews gives an extensive quotation from Jeremiah 31:31–34, in which he says, "The days will come, says the Lord, when I will establish a new *covenant with the house of Israel and with the house of Judah.* . . . This is the covenant that I will make with the house of Israel after those days, says the Lord: I will put my laws into their minds, and write them on their hearts, and I will be their God, and they shall be my people" (Heb. 8:8–10). Here the author quotes the Lord's promise that he will make a new covenant with the house of Israel and *with the house of Judah,* and says that that is the new covenant that has now been made *with the church.* That new covenant is the covenant of which believers in the church are now members. It seems hard to avoid the conclusion that the author views the church as the true Israel of God in which the Old Testament promises to Israel find their fulfillment.

Similarly, James can write a general letter to many early Christian churches and say that he is writing "To the twelve tribes in the Dispersion" (James 1:1). This indicates that he is evidently viewing New Testament Christians as the successors to and fulfillment of the twelve tribes of Israel.

Peter also speaks in the same way. From the first verse in which he calls his readers "exiles of the Dispersion" (1 Peter 1:1)[19] to the next-to-last verse in which he calls the city

---

[19]The "Dispersion" was a term used to refer to the Jewish people scattered abroad from the land of Israel and living throughout the ancient Mediterranean world.

of Rome "Babylon" (1 Peter 5:13), Peter frequently speaks of New Testament Christians in terms of Old Testament imagery and promises given to the Jews. This theme comes to prominence in 1 Peter 2:4–10, where[20] Peter says that God has bestowed on the church almost all the blessings promised to Israel in the Old Testament. The dwelling-place of God is no longer the Jerusalem temple, for Christians are the new "temple" of God (v. 5). The priesthood able to offer acceptable sacrifices to God is no longer descended from Aaron, for Christians are now the true "royal priesthood" with access before God's throne (vv. 4–5, 9). God's chosen people are no longer said to be those physically descended from Abraham, for Christians are now the true "chosen race" (v. 9). The nation blessed by God is no longer said to be the nation of Israel, for Christians are now God's true "holy nation" (v. 9). The people of Israel are no longer said to be the people of God, for Christians—both Jewish Christians and Gentile Christians—are now "God's people" and those who have "received mercy" (v. 10). Moreover, Peter takes these quotations from contexts in the Old Testament that repeatedly warn that God will reject his people who persist in rebellion against him and who reject the precious "cornerstone" (v. 6) that he has established. What further statement could be needed in order for us to say with assurance that the church has now become the true Israel of God and will receive all the blessings promised to Israel in the Old Testament?[21]

6. The Church and the Kingdom of God. What is the relationship between the church and the kingdom of God? The differences have been summarized well by George Ladd:

> The Kingdom is primarily the dynamic reign or kingly rule of God, and, derivatively, the sphere in which the rule is experienced. In biblical idiom, the Kingdom is not identified with its subjects. They are the people of God's rule who enter it, live under it, and are governed by it. The church is the community of the Kingdom but never the Kingdom itself. Jesus' disciples belong to the Kingdom as the Kingdom belongs to them; but they are not the Kingdom. The Kingdom is the rule of God; the church is a society of men.[22]

Ladd goes on to summarize five specific aspects of the relationship between the kingdom and the church: (1) The church is not the kingdom (for Jesus and the early Christians preached that the kingdom of God was near, not that the church was near, and preached the good news of the kingdom, not the good news of the church: Acts 8:12; 19:8; 20:25; 28:23, 31). (2) The kingdom creates the church (for as people enter into God's kingdom they become joined to the human fellowship of the church). (3) The church witnesses to the kingdom (for Jesus said, "this gospel of the kingdom will be preached throughout the whole world," Matt. 24:14). (4) The church is the instrument of the kingdom (for the Holy Spirit, manifesting the power of the kingdom, works through the disciples to heal

---

[20]The remainder of this paragraph is largely taken from Wayne Grudem, *1 Peter,* TNTC (Grand Rapids: Eerdmans, 1988), p. 113.

[21]A dispensationalist may grant at this point that the church has been the recipient of many *applications* of Old Testament prophecies concerning Israel, but that the true *fulfillment* of these promises will yet come in the future for ethnic Israel. But with all these evident New Testament examples of clear application of these promises to the church, there does not seem to be any strong reason to deny that this really is the only fulfillment that God is going to give for these promises.

[22]George Eldon Ladd, *A Theology of the New Testament,* (Grand Rapids: Eerdmans, 1974), p. 111.

the sick and cast out demons, as he did in the ministry of Jesus: Matt. 10:8; Luke 10:17). (5) The church is the custodian of the kingdom (for the church has been given the keys of the kingdom of heaven: Matt. 16:19).[23]

Therefore we should not identify the kingdom of God and the church (as in Roman Catholic theology), nor should we see the kingdom of God as entirely future, something distinct from the church age (as in older dispensational theology). Rather, we should recognize that there is a close connection between the kingdom of God and the church. As the church proclaims the good news of the kingdom, people will come into the church and begin to experience the blessings of God's rule in their lives. The kingdom manifests itself through the church, and thereby the future reign of God breaks into the present (it is "already" here: Matt. 12:28; Rom. 14:17; and "not yet" here fully: Matt. 25:34; 1 Cor. 6:9–10). Therefore those who believe in Christ will begin to experience something of what God's final kingdom reign will be like: they will know some measure of victory over sin (Rom. 6:14; 14:17), over demonic opposition (Luke 10:17), and over disease (Luke 10:9). They will live in the power of the Holy Spirit (Matt. 12:28; Rom. 8:4–17; 14:17), who is the dynamic power of the coming kingdom. Eventually Jesus will return and his kingdom reign will extend over all creation (1 Cor. 15:24–28).

B. The "Marks" of the Church (Distinguishing Characteristics)

1. There Are True Churches and False Churches. What makes a church a church? What is necessary to have a church? Might a group of people who claim to be Christians become so unlike what a church should be that they should no longer be called a church?

In the early centuries of the Christian church, there was little controversy about what was a true church. There was only one world-wide church, the "visible" church throughout the world, and that was, of course, the true church. This church had bishops and local clergymen and church buildings which everyone could see. Any heretics who were found to be in serious doctrinal error were simply excluded from the church.

But at the Reformation a crucial question came up: how can we recognize a true church? Is the Roman Catholic Church a true church or not? In order to answer that question people had to decide what were the "marks" of a true church, the distinguishing characteristics that lead us to recognize it as a true church. Scripture certainly speaks of false churches. Paul says of the pagan temples in Corinth, "What pagans sacrifice they offer to demons and not to God" (1 Cor. 10:20). He tells the Corinthians that "when you were heathen, you were led astray to dumb idols" (1 Cor. 12:2). These pagan temples were certainly false churches or false religious assemblies. Moreover, Scripture speaks of a religious assembly that is really a "synagogue of Satan" (Rev. 2:9; 3:9). Here the risen Lord Jesus seems to be referring to Jewish assemblies that claim to be Jews but were not true Jews who had saving faith. Their religious assembly was not an assembly of Christ's people but of those who still belonged to the kingdom of darkness, the kingdom of Satan. This also would certainly be a false church.

In large measure there was agreement between Luther and Calvin on the question of what constituted a true church. The Lutheran statement of faith, which is called the

Augsburg Confession (1530), defined the church as "the congregation of saints in which the gospel is rightly taught and the Sacraments rightly administered" (Article 7).[24] Similarly, John Calvin said, "Wherever we see the Word of God purely preached and heard, and the sacraments administered according to Christ's institution, there, it is not to be doubted, a church of God exists."[25] Although Calvin spoke of the pure preaching of the Word (whereas the Lutheran Confession spoke of the right preaching of the gospel) and although Calvin said that the Word must not only be preached but heard (whereas the Augsburg Confession merely mentioned that it had to be rightly taught), their understanding of the distinguishing marks of a true church is quite similar.[26] In contrast to the view of Luther and Calvin regarding the marks of a church, the Roman Catholic position has been that *the visible church* that descended from Peter and the apostles *is the true church*.

It seems appropriate that we take Luther and Calvin's view on the marks of a true church as correct still today. Certainly if the Word of God is not being preached, but simply false doctrines or doctrines of men, then there is no true church. In some cases we might have difficulty determining just how much wrong doctrine can be tolerated before a church can no longer be considered a true church, but there are many clear cases where we can say that a true church does not exist. For example, the Church of Jesus Christ of Latter Day Saints (the Mormon Church) does not hold to any major Christian doctrines concerning salvation or the person of God or the person and work of Christ. It is clearly a false church. Similarly, the Jehovah's Witnesses teach salvation by works, not by trusting in Jesus Christ alone. This is a fundamental doctrinal deviation because if people believe the teachings of the Jehovah's Witnesses, they simply will not be saved. So the Jehovah's Witnesses also must be considered a false church. When the preaching of a church conceals the gospel message of salvation by faith alone from its members, so that the gospel message is not clearly proclaimed, and has not been proclaimed for some time, the group meeting there is not a church.

The second mark of the church, the right administration of the sacraments (baptism and the Lord's Supper) was probably stated in opposition to the Roman Catholic view that saving grace came through the sacraments and thereby the sacraments were made "works" by which we earned merit for salvation. In this way, the Roman Catholic Church was insisting on payment rather than teaching faith as the means of obtaining salvation.

But another reason exists for including the sacraments as a mark of the church. Once an organization begins to practice baptism and the Lord's Supper, it is a continuing organization and is *attempting to function as a church*. (In modern American society, an organization that begins to meet for worship and prayer and Bible teachings on Sunday mornings also would clearly be attempting to function as a church.)

Baptism and the Lord's Supper also serve as "membership controls" for the church. Baptism is the means for admitting people into the church, and the Lord's Supper is the means for allowing people to give a sign of continuing in the membership of the

---

[24]Quoted from Philip Schaff, *The Creeds of Christendom*, 3 vols. (Grand Rapids: Baker, 1983 reprint of 1931 edition), 1:11–12.

[25]Calvin, *Institutes* 4.1.9 (p. 1023).

[26]Later confessions sometimes added a third mark of the church (the right exercise of church discipline), but neither Luther nor Calvin themselves listed this mark.

church—the church signifies that it considers those who receive baptism and the Lord's Supper to be saved. Therefore these activities indicate what a church thinks about salvation, and they are appropriately listed as a mark of the church today as well. By contrast, groups who do not administer baptism and the Lord's Supper signify that they are not intending to function as a church. Someone may stand on a street corner with a small crowd and have true preaching and hearing of the Word, but the people there would not be a church. Even a neighborhood Bible study meeting in a home can have the true teaching and hearing of the Word without becoming a church. But if a local Bible study began baptizing its own new converts and regularly participating in the Lord's Supper, these things would signify *an intention to function as a church,* and it would be difficult to say why it should not be considered a church in itself.[27]

2. True and False Churches Today. In view of the question posed during the Reformation, what about the Roman Catholic Church today? Is it a true church? Here it seems that we cannot simply make a decision regarding the Roman Catholic Church as a whole, because it is far too diverse. To ask whether the Roman Catholic Church is a true church or a false church today is somewhat similar to asking whether Protestant churches are true or false today—there is great variety among them. Some Roman Catholic parishes certainly lack both marks: there is no pure preaching of the Word and the gospel message of salvation by faith in Christ alone is not known or received by people in the parish. Participation in the sacraments is seen as a "work" that can earn merit with God. Such a group of people is not a true Christian church. On the other hand, there are many Roman Catholic parishes in various parts of the world today where the local priest has a genuine saving knowledge of Christ and a vital personal relationship with Christ in prayer and Bible study. His own homilies and private teaching of the Bible place much emphasis on personal faith and the need for individual Bible reading and prayer. His teaching on the sacraments emphasizes their symbolic and commemorative aspects much more than it speaks of them as acts that merit some infusion of saving grace from God. In such a case, although we would have to say that we still have profound differences with Roman Catholic teaching on some doctrines,[28] nonetheless, it would seem that such a church would have a close enough approximation to the two marks of the church that it would be hard to deny that it is in fact a true church. It would seem to be a genuine congregation of believers in which the gospel is taught (though not purely) and the sacraments are administered more rightly than wrongly.

Are there false churches within Protestantism? If we again look at the two distinguishing marks of the church, in the judgment of this present writer it seems appropriate to say that many liberal Protestant churches are in fact false churches today.[29] Is the gospel of

---

[27]The Salvation Army is an unusual case because it does not observe baptism or the Lord's Supper, yet it seems in every other way to be a true church. In this case the organization has substituted other means of signifying membership and continuing participation in the church, and these other means of signifying membership provide a substitute for baptism and the Lord's Supper in terms of "membership controls."

[28]Significant doctrinal differences would still include matters such as the continuing sacrifice of the mass, the authority of the pope and the church councils, the veneration of the Virgin Mary and her role in redemption, the doctrine of purgatory, and the extent of the biblical canon.

[29]A similar conclusion was expressed by J. Gresham Machen as long ago as 1923: "The Church of Rome may

works-righteousness and unbelief in Scripture that these churches teach any more likely to save people than did Roman Catholic teaching at the time of the Reformation? And is not their administration of the sacraments without sound teaching to anyone who walks in the door likely to give as much false assurance to unregenerate sinners as did the Roman Catholic use of the sacraments at the time of the Reformation? When there is an assembly of people who take the name "Christian" but consistently teach that people cannot believe their Bibles—indeed a church whose pastor and congregation seldom read their Bibles or pray in any meaningful way, and do not believe or perhaps even understand the gospel of salvation by faith in Christ alone, then how can we say that this is a true church?[30]

C. The Purposes of the Church

We can understand the purposes of the church in terms of ministry to God, ministry to believers, and ministry to the world.

1. Ministry to God: Worship. In relationship to God the church's purpose is to worship him. Paul directs the church at Colossae to "sing psalms and hymns and spiritual songs with thankfulness in your hearts to God" (Col. 3:16). God has destined us and appointed us in Christ "to live for the praise of his glory" (Eph. 1:12). Worship in the church is not merely a preparation for something else: it is in itself fulfilling the major purpose of the church with reference to its Lord. That is why Paul can follow an exhortation that we are to be "making the most of the time" with a command to be filled with the Spirit and then to be "singing and making melody to the Lord with all your heart" (Eph. 5:16–19).

2. Ministry to Believers: Nurture. According to Scripture, the church has an obligation to nurture those who are already believers and build them up to maturity in the faith. Paul said that his own goal was not simply to bring people to initial saving faith but to "present every man *mature in Christ*" (Col. 1:28). And he told the church at Ephesus that God gave the church gifted persons "to equip the saints for the work of ministry, *for building up the body of Christ,* until we all attain to the unity of the faith and of the knowledge of the Son of God, to mature manhood, to the measure of the stature of the fullness of Christ" (Eph. 4:12–13). It is clearly contrary to the New Testament pattern to think that our only goal with people is to bring them to initial saving faith. Our goal as a church must be to present to God every Christian "mature in Christ" (Col. 1:28).

3. Ministry to the World: Evangelism and Mercy. Jesus told his disciples that they should "make disciples of all nations" (Matt. 28:19). This evangelistic work of declaring the gos-

---

represent a perversion of the Christian religion; but naturalistic liberalism is not Christianity at all" (*Christianity and Liberalism* [Grand Rapids: Eerdmans, 1923], p. 52).

[30]In the next chapter we shall discuss the question of the purity of the church. Although Christians should not voluntarily associate with a false church, we must recognize that among true churches there are more-pure and less-pure

churches (see discussion in chapter 3, below). It is also important to note here that some liberal Protestant denominations today can have many false churches within the denomination (churches where the gospel is not preached or heard) and still have some local congregations that preach the gospel clearly and faithfully and are true churches.

pel is the primary ministry that the church has toward the world.[31] Yet accompanying the work of evangelism is also a ministry of mercy, a ministry that includes caring for the poor and needy in the name of the Lord. Although the emphasis of the New Testament is on giving material help to those who are part of the church (Acts 11:29; 2 Cor. 8:4; 1 John 3:17), there is still an affirmation that it is right to help unbelievers even if they do not respond with gratitude or acceptance of the gospel message. Jesus tells us,

> Love your enemies, and do good, and lend, expecting nothing in return; and your reward will be great, and you will be sons of the Most High; for *he is kind to the ungrateful and the selfish.* Be merciful, even as your Father is merciful. (Luke 6:35–36)

The point of Jesus' explanation is that we are to imitate God in being kind to those who are being ungrateful and selfish as well. Moreover, we have the example of Jesus who did not attempt to heal only those who accepted him as Messiah. Rather, when great crowds came to him, "he laid his hands *on every one of them* and healed them" (Luke 4:40). This should give us encouragement to carry out deeds of kindness, and to pray for healing and other needs, in the lives of unbelievers as well as believers. Such ministries of mercy to the world may also include participation in civic activities or attempting to influence governmental policies to make them more consistent with biblical moral principles. In areas where there is systematic injustice manifested in the treatment of the poor and/or ethnic or religious minorities, the church should also pray and—as it has opportunity—speak against such injustice. All of these are ways in which the church can supplement its evangelistic ministry to the world and indeed adorn the gospel that it professes. But such ministries of mercy to the world should never become a substitute for genuine evangelism or for the other areas of ministry to God and to believers mentioned above.

4. Keeping These Purposes in Balance. Once we have listed these three purposes for the church someone might ask, Which is most important? Or someone else might ask, Might we neglect one of these three as less important than the others?

To that we must respond that all three purposes of the church are commanded by the Lord in Scripture; therefore all three are important and none can be neglected. In fact, a strong church will have effective ministries in all three of these areas. We should beware of any attempts to reduce the purpose of the church to only one of these three and to say that it should be our primary focus. In fact, such attempts to make one of these purposes primary will always result in some neglect of the other two. A church that emphasizes only worship will end up with inadequate Bible teaching of believers and its members will remain shallow in their understanding of Scripture and immature in their Christian lives. If it also begins to neglect evangelism the church will cease to grow and influence others; it will become ingrown and eventually begin to wither.

---

[31]I do not mean to say that evangelism is more important than worship or nurture, but only that it is our primary ministry towards the world.

A church that places the edification of believers as a purpose that takes precedence over the other two will tend to produce Christians who know much Bible doctrine but have spiritual dryness in their lives because they know little of the joy of worshiping God or telling others about Christ.

But a church that makes evangelism such a priority that it causes the other two purposes to be neglected will also end up with immature Christians who emphasize growth in numbers but have less and less genuine love for God expressed in their worship and less and less doctrinal maturity and personal holiness in their lives. All three purposes must be emphasized continually in a healthy church.

However, *individuals* are different from churches in placing a relative priority on one or another of these purposes of the church. Because we are like a body with diverse spiritual gifts and abilities, it is right for us to place most of our emphasis on the fulfillment of that purpose of the church that is most closely related to the gifts and interests God has given to us. There is certainly no obligation for every believer to attempt to give exactly one third of his or her time in the church to worship, one-third to nurturing other believers, and one-third to evangelism or deeds of mercy. Someone with the gift of evangelism should of course spend some time in worship and caring for other believers, but may end up spending the vast majority of his or her time in evangelistic work. Someone who is a gifted worship leader may end up devoting 90 percent of his time in the church toward preparation for and leading of worship. This is only an appropriate response to the diversity of gifts that God has given us.

QUESTIONS FOR PERSONAL APPLICATION

1. When you think of the church as the invisible fellowship of all true believers throughout all time, how does it affect the way you think of yourself as an individual Christian? In the community in which you live, is there much visible unity among genuine believers (that is, is there much visible evidence of the true nature of the invisible church)? Does the New Testament say anything about the ideal size for an individual church?

2. Would you consider the church that you are now in to be a true church? Have you ever been a member of a church that you would think to be a false church? Do you think there is any harm done when evangelical Christians continue to give the impression that they think liberal Protestant churches are true Christian churches? Viewed from the perspective of the final judgment, what good and what harm might come from our failure to state that we think unbelieving churches are false churches?

3. Did any of the metaphors for the church give you a new appreciation for the church that you currently attend?

4. To which purpose of the church do you think you can most effectively contribute? Which purpose has God placed in your heart a strong desire to fulfill?

SPECIAL TERMS

body of Christ
church
ekklēsia

invisible church
marks of the church
visible church

BIBLIOGRAPHY

Banks, Robert J. *Paul's Idea of Community: The Early House Churches in Their Historical Setting.* Grand Rapids: Eerdmans, 1980.

Bannerman, James. *The Church of Christ.* Cherry Hill, N.J.: Mack Publishing, 1972. (First published in 1869.)

Berkouwer, G. C. *The Church.* Trans. by James E. Davidson. Grand Rapids: Eerdmans, 1976.

Bock, Darrell L., and Craig A. Blaising, eds. *Progressive Dispensationalism.* Wheaton: Victor, 1993.

Carson, D. A., ed. *Biblical Interpretation and the Church: Text and Context.* Exeter: Paternoster, 1984.

_____. *The Church in the Bible and the World.* Grand Rapids: Baker, and Exeter: Paternoster, 1987.

Clowney, Edmund. "Church." In *NDT,* pp. 140–43.

_____. *The Doctrine of the Church.* Philadelphia: Presbyterian and Reformed, 1969.

Feinberg, John S., ed. *Continuity and Discontinuity: Perspectives on the Relationship Between the Old and New Testaments.* Wheaton: Crossway, 1988.

Gaffin, Richard B. "Kingdom of God." In *NDT,* pp. 367–69.

Ladd, George Eldon. "The Kingdom and the Church." In *A Theology of the New Testament.* Grand Rapids: Eerdmans, 1974, pp. 105–19.

Martin, Ralph P. *The Family and the Fellowship: New Testament Images of the Church.* Grand Rapids: Eerdmans, 1979.

Omanson, R. L. "Church, The." In *EDT,* pp. 231–33.

Poythress, Vern. *Understanding Dispensationalists.* Grand Rapids: Zondervan, 1987.

Saucy, Robert. *The Case for Progressive Dispensationalism.* Grand Rapids: Zondervan, 1993.

_____. *The Church in God's Program.* Chicago: Moody, 1972.

Snyder, Howard A. *The Community of the King.* Downers Grove, Ill.: InterVarsity Press, 1977.

VanGemeren, Willem. *The Progress of Redemption.* Grand Rapids: Zondervan, 1988.

Watson, David C. *I Believe in the Church.* Grand Rapids: Eerdmans, 1979.

SCRIPTURE MEMORY PASSAGE

Ephesians 4:11–13: *And his gifts were that some should be apostles, some prophets, some evangelists, some pastors and teachers, to equip the saints for the work of ministry, for building up the body of Christ, until we all attain to the unity of the faith and of the knowledge of the Son of God, to mature manhood, to the measure of the stature of the fulness of Christ.*

HYMN

"The Church's One Foundation"

The church's one foundation is Jesus Christ her Lord;
    She is his new creation by water and the Word:
From heav'n he came and sought her to be his holy bride;
    With his own blood he bought her, and for her life he died.

Elect from ev'ry nation, yet one o'er all the earth,
    Her charter of salvation one Lord, one faith, one birth;
One holy name she blesses, partakes one holy food,
    And to one hope she presses, with ev'ry grace endued.

Though with a scornful wonder men see her sore oppressed,
    By schisms rent asunder, by heresies distressed,
Yet saints their watch are keeping, their cry goes up, "How long?"
    And soon the night of weeping shall be the morn of song.

The church shall never perish! Her dear Lord to defend,
    To guide, sustain and cherish, is with her to the end;
Though there be those that hate her, and false sons in her pale,
    Against or foe or traitor she ever shall prevail.

'Mid toil and tribulation, and tumult of her war,
    She waits the consummation of peace forevermore;
Til with the vision glorious her longing eyes are blest,
    And the great church victorious shall be the church at rest.

Yet she on earth hath union with God the Three in One,
    And mystic sweet communion with those whose rest is won:
O happy ones and holy! Lord, give us grace that we,
    Like them, the meek and lowly, on high may dwell with thee.

AUTHOR: SAMUEL J. STONE, 1866

Chapter 3

THE PURITY AND UNITY OF THE CHURCH

What makes a church more or less pleasing to God? What kinds of churches should we cooperate with or join?

EXPLANATION AND SCRIPTURAL BASIS

A. More Pure and Less Pure Churches

In the previous chapter we saw that there are "true churches" and "false churches." In this chapter a further distinction must be made: there are *more pure* and *less pure* churches.

This fact is evident from a brief comparison of Paul's epistles. When we look at Philippians or 1 Thessalonians we find evidence of Paul's great joy in these churches and the relative absence of major doctrinal or moral problems (see Phil. 1:3–11; 4:10–16; 1 Thess. 1:2–10; 3:6–10; 2 Thess. 1:3–4; 2:13; cf. 2 Cor. 8:1–5). On the other hand, there were all sorts of serious doctrinal and moral problems in the churches of Galatia (Gal. 1:6–9; 3:1–5) and Corinth (1 Cor. 3:1–4; 4:18–21; 5:1–2, 6; 6:1–8; 11:17–22; 14:20–23; 15:12; 2 Cor. 1:23–2:11; 11:3–5, 12–15; 12:20–13:10). Other examples could be given, but it should be clear that among true churches there are *less pure* and *more pure* churches. This may be represented as in figure 3.1.

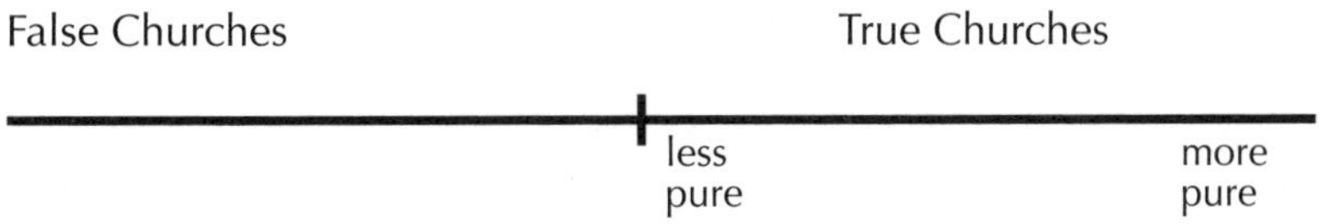

False Churches   True Churches

less   more
pure   pure

AMONG TRUE CHURCHES, THERE ARE LESS PURE
AND MORE PURE CHURCHES
Figure 3.1

B. Definitions of Purity and Unity

We may define the purity of the church as follows: *The purity of the church is its degree of freedom from wrong doctrine and conduct, and its degree of conformity to God's revealed will for the church.*

As we shall see in the following discussion, it is right to pray and work for the greater purity of the church. But purity cannot be our only concern, or Christians would have a tendency to separate into tiny groups of very "pure" Christians and tend to exclude anyone who showed the slightest deviation in doctrine or conduct of life. Therefore the New Testament also speaks frequently about the need to strive for the *unity* of the visible church. This may be defined in the following way: *The unity of the church is its degree of freedom from divisions among true Christians.*

The definition specifies "true Christians" because, as we saw in the previous chapter, there are those who are Christian in name only, but have had no genuine experience of regeneration by the Holy Spirit. Nonetheless, many of these people take the name "Christian" and many churches that are filled with such unbelievers still call themselves Christian churches. We should not expect or work for organizational or functional unity that includes all of those people, and therefore there will never be unity with all churches that call themselves "Christian." But, as we shall also see in the following discussion, the New Testament certainly encourages us to work for the unity of all true believers.

C. Signs of a More Pure Church

Factors that make a church "more pure" include:

1. Biblical doctrine (or right preaching of the Word)
2. Proper use of the sacraments (or ordinances)
3. Right use of church discipline
4. Genuine worship
5. Effective prayer
6. Effective witness
7. Effective fellowship
8. Biblical church government
9. Spiritual power in ministry
10. Personal holiness of life among members
11. Care for the poor
12. Love for Christ

There may be other signs than these, but at least these can be mentioned as factors that increase a church's conformity to God's purposes. Of course, churches can be more pure in some areas and less pure in others—a church may have excellent doctrine and sound preaching, for example, yet be a dismal failure in witness to others or in meaningful worship. Or a church may have a dynamic witness and very God-honoring times of worship but be weak in doctrinal understanding and Bible teaching.

Most churches will tend to think that the areas in which they are strong are the most important areas, and the areas where they are weak are less important. But the New Testament encourages us to work for the purity of the church in all of these areas. Christ's goal for the church is *"that he might sanctify her,* having cleansed her by the washing of water with the word, *that he might present the church to himself* in splendor, *without spot or wrinkle or any such thing,* that she might be holy and without blemish" (Eph. 5:26–27). Paul's ministry was one of "warning every man and teaching every man in all wisdom, that we may present every man mature in Christ" (Col. 1:28). Moreover, Paul told Titus that elders must "be able to give instruction in sound doctrine and also to confute those who contradict it" (Titus 1:9), and he said that false teachers "must be silenced" (Titus 1:11). Jude urged Christians to "contend for the faith which was once for all delivered to the saints" (Jude 3). Proper use of the sacraments is commanded in 1 Corinthians 11:17–34, and right use of church discipline to protect the purity of the church is required in 1 Corinthians 5:6–7, 12–13.

The New Testament also mentions a number of other factors: we are to strive for spiritual worship (Eph. 5:18–20; Col. 3:16–17), effective witness (Matt. 28:19–20; John 13:34–35; Acts 2:44–47; 1 John 4:7), proper government of the church (1 Tim. 3:1–13), spiritual power in ministry (Acts 1:8; Rom. 1:16; 1 Cor. 4:20; 2 Cor. 10:3–4; Gal. 3:3–5; 2 Tim. 3:5; James 5:16), personal holiness (1 Thess. 4:3; Heb. 12:14), care for the poor (Acts 4:32–35; Rom. 15:26; Gal. 2:10), and love for Christ (1 Peter 1:8; Rev. 2:4). In fact, all Christians are to "strive to excel in *building up the church*" (1 Cor. 14:12), an exhortation that applies not only to an increase in the number of church members, but also (and in fact primarily) to the "edification" or growth of the church toward Christian maturity. The force of all of these passages is to remind us that *we are to work for the purity of the visible church.*

Of course, if we are to work for the purity of the church, especially of the local church of which we are a part, we must recognize that this is a process, and that any church of which we are a part will be somewhat impure in various areas. There were no perfect churches at the time of the New Testament and there will be no perfect churches until Christ returns.[1] This means that Christians have no obligation to seek the *purest church* they can find and stay there, and then leave it if an even purer church comes to their attention. Rather, they should find a *true church* in which they can have effective ministry and in which they will experience Christian growth as well, and then should stay there and minister, continually working for the purity of that church. God will often bless their prayers and faithful witness and the church will gradually grow in many areas of purity.

But we must realize that not all churches will respond well to influences that would bring them to greater purity. Sometimes, in spite of a few faithful Christians within a church, its dominant direction will be set by others who are determined to lead it on another course. Unless God graciously intervenes to bring reformation, some of these churches will become cults, and others will just die and close their doors. But more commonly these churches will simply drift into liberal Protestantism.

---

[1]This is recognized by the Westminster Confession of Faith: "The purest Churches under heaven are subject both to mixture and error" (25.5).

It is helpful at this point to remember that classical liberal Protestantism is humanistic, and its approaches are *primarily man-centered* rather than God-centered.[2] When a church begins to stray from faithfulness to Christ, this will be evident not only in the shift to impure doctrine (which can sometimes be concealed from church members by the use of evasive language) but also in the daily life of the church: its activities, its preaching, its counseling, and even the casual conversations among members will tend to become more and more man-centered and less and less God-centered. There will tend to be a repeated emphasis on the typical kinds of self-help advice given in popular journals and by secular psychologists. There will be a horizontal orientation as opposed to a vertical or God-centered orientation, there will be fewer and fewer extended times of prayer and less and less emphasis on the direct application of Scripture to daily situations, but more emphasis on simply being a caring and sensitive person, and on affirming others and acting in love toward them. The conversation and activities of the church will have very little genuine spiritual content—little emphasis on the need for daily prayer for individual concerns and for forgiveness of sins, little emphasis on daily personal reading of Scripture, and little emphasis on moment-by-moment trust in Christ and knowing the reality of his presence in our lives. Where there are admonitions to moral reformation, these will often be viewed as human deficiencies that people can correct by their own discipline and effort, and perhaps encouragement from others, but these moral aspects of life will not primarily be viewed as sin against a holy God, sin which can only effectively be overcome by the power of the Holy Spirit working within. When such humanistic emphases become dominant in a church, it has moved far toward the "less-pure" end of the scale in many of the areas listed above, and it is moving in the direction of becoming a false church.

D. New Testament Teaching on the Unity of the Church

There is a strong emphasis in the New Testament on the unity of the church. Jesus' goal is that "there shall be *one flock, one shepherd*" (John 10:16), and he prays for all future believers "that they may all be one" (John 17:21). This unity will be a witness to unbelievers, for Jesus prays "that they may become *perfectly one, so that the world may know that you have sent me* and have loved them even as you have loved me" (John 17:23).

Paul reminds the Corinthians that they are "called to be saints *together with all those who in every place call on the name of our Lord Jesus Christ,* both their Lord and ours" (1 Cor. 1:2). Then Paul writes to Corinth, "I appeal to you, brethren, by the name of our Lord Jesus Christ, that *all of you agree* and that there be no dissensions among you, but *that you be united* in the same mind and the same judgment" (1 Cor. 1:10; cf. v. 13).

He encourages the Philippians, "complete my joy by being of the same mind, having the same love, *being in full accord and of one mind*" (Phil. 2:2). He tells the Ephesians that Christians are to be "eager to maintain the *unity* of the Spirit in the bond of peace" (Eph. 4:3), and that the Lord gives gifts to the church "for building up the body of Christ, *until*

---

[2]See the remarkably accurate analysis by J. Gresham Machen, *Christianity and Liberalism* (repr. ed., Grand Rapids: Eerdmans, 1968; first published in 1923), esp. pp. 64–68.

we all attain to the unity of the faith and of the knowledge of the Son of God, to mature manhood, to the measure of the stature of the fulness of Christ" (Eph. 4:12–13).

Paul can *command* the church to live in unity because there already is an *actual* spiritual unity in Christ which exists among genuine believers. He says, "There is one body and one Spirit, just as you were called to the one hope that belongs to your call, one Lord, one faith, one baptism, one God and Father of us all, who is above all and through all and in all" (Eph. 4:4–6). And though the body of Christ consists of many members, those members are all *"one body"* (1 Cor. 10:17; 12:12–26).

Because they are jealous to protect this unity of the church, the New Testament writers give strong warnings against those who cause divisions:

> I appeal to you, brethren, to take note of those who create dissensions and difficulties, in opposition to the doctrine which you have been taught; avoid them. For such persons do not serve our Lord Christ, but their own appetites. (Rom. 16:17–18)

Paul opposed Peter to his face because he separated from Gentile Christians and began eating only with Jewish Christians (Gal. 2:11–14). Those who promote "strife . . . dissension, party spirit . . . shall not inherit the kingdom of God" (Gal. 5:20–21). And Jude warns that those who "set up divisions" are "worldly people, devoid of the Spirit" (Jude 19).

Consistent with this New Testament emphasis on the unity of believers is the fact that the direct commands to *separate* from other people are always commands to separate *from unbelievers,* not from Christians with whom one disagrees. When Paul says, "Therefore come out from them, and *be separate from them"* (2 Cor. 6:17), it is in support of his opening command of that section, "Do not be mismated *with unbelievers"* (2 Cor. 6:14). And Paul tells Timothy that he is to "avoid such people" (2 Tim. 3:5), referring not to believers but to unbelievers, those who are "lovers of pleasure rather than lovers of God, holding the form of religion but denying the power of it" (2 Tim. 3:4–5). He says that these people are "men of corrupt mind and counterfeit faith" (2 Tim. 3:8). Of course, there is a kind of church discipline that requires separation from an individual who is causing trouble within the church (Matt. 18:17; 1 Cor. 5:11–13), and there may be other reasons for which Christians conclude that separation is required,[3] but it is important to note here, in discussing the unity of the church, that there are no direct New Testament commands to separate from Christians with whom one has doctrinal differences (unless those differences involve such serious heresy that the Christian faith itself is denied).[4]

These passages on church unity tell us that, in addition to working for the purity of the visible church, *we are also to work for the unity of the visible church.* Yet we must realize that such unity does not actually require one worldwide church government over all Christians. In fact, the unity of believers is often demonstrated quite effectively through voluntary cooperation and affiliation among Christian groups. Moreover, different types of ministries and different emphases in ministry may result in different organizations, all

---

[3]See the discussion on reasons for separation in section F below.

[4]2 John 10 forbids Christians to give a greeting to itinerant heretical teachers who were not proclaiming the true gospel at all; see discussion below.

under the universal headship of Christ as Lord of the church. Therefore the existence of different denominations, mission boards, Christian educational institutions, college ministries, and so forth is not necessarily a mark of disunity of the church (though in some cases it may be), for there may be a great deal of cooperation and frequent demonstrations of unity among such diverse bodies as these. (I think the modern term *parachurch organization* is unfortunate, because it implies that these organizations are somehow "beside" and therefore "outside of" the church, whereas in reality they are simply different parts of the one universal church.) Moreover, many Christians argue that there *should not* be a worldwide government of the church, because the New Testament pattern of church government never shows elders having authority over any more than their own local congregations (see chapter 5 below). In fact, even in the New Testament the apostles agreed that Paul should emphasize missionary work to the Gentiles while Peter would emphasize missionary work to the Jews (Gal. 2:7), and Paul and Barnabas went their separate ways for a time because of a disagreement over whether they should take Mark with them (Acts 15:39–40), though certainly they had unity in every other way.[5]

E. Brief History of Organizational Separation in the Church

There are sometimes reasons why the outward or visible unity of the church cannot be maintained. A brief survey of the history of organizational separation in the church may highlight some of these reasons,[6] and help explain where present-day denominational divisions came from.

During the first thousand years of the church there was for the most part outward unity. There had been some minor divisions during controversies with groups like the Montanists (second century) and the Donatists (fourth century), and there was a minor separation by some Monophysite churches (fifth and sixth centuries), but the prevailing sentiment was one of strong opposition to division in the body of Christ. For example, Irenaeus, a second century bishop, said about those who cause divisions in the church, "No reformation able to be effected by them will be of great enough importance to compensate for the damage arising from their schism" (*Against Heresies* 4.33.7).

The first major division in the church came in A.D. 1054 when the Eastern (now Orthodox) church separated from the Western (Roman Catholic) church. The reason was that the pope had changed a church creed simply on his own authority, and the Eastern church protested that he had no right to do that.

The Reformation in the sixteenth century then separated the Western church into Roman Catholic and Protestant branches, yet there was often a strong reluctance to cause formal division. Martin Luther wanted to reform the church without dividing it, but he

---

[5]Scripture hints that Paul was right and Barnabas wrong in this controversy, since it tells us that Paul and Silas left Antioch "being commended by the brethren to the grace of the Lord" (Acts 15:40), whereas nothing similar is said about Barnabas. This incident is simply reported in Acts but is not strong evidence for the appropriateness of diversification of ministry, since the report of a "sharp contention" (v.

39) between Paul and Barnabas indicates that we should not think of them as entirely free from fault.

[6]From this point to the end of the chapter much of the material has been taken from the article, "Separation, Ecclesiastical" by Wayne Grudem, prepared for *The Tyndale Encyclopedia of Christian Knowledge* (Wheaton, Ill.: Tyndale House, copyright 1971, but never published). Used by permission.

was excommunicated in 1521. The Anglican (Episcopalian) church did not separate from Rome, but was excommunicated in 1570; thus it can say, "We suffer schism, we did not cause it." On the other hand, there were many Protestants, especially among the Anabaptists, who wanted to form churches of believers only, and began as early as 1525 to form separate churches in Switzerland and then other parts of Europe.

In the centuries following the Reformation, Protestantism splintered into hundreds of smaller groups. Sometimes leaders of the new groups regretted such divisions: John Wesley, although he was the founder of Methodism, claimed that he lived and died a member of the Anglican church. It was often the case that matters of conscience or religious freedom forced the division, as with the Puritans and many Pietist groups. On the other hand, sometimes language differences among immigrant groups in America led to the founding of separate churches.

Have the reasons for separation into different organizations and denominations always been proper ones? Although there have almost always been strong theological differences in major church divisions, one fears that too often, especially in more recent history, the real motives for beginning or maintaining separation have been selfish ones, and that John Calvin may have been correct in saying, "Pride or self-glorification is the cause and starting point of all controversies, when each person, claiming for himself more than he is entitled to have, is eager to have others in his power."[7] Moreover, he says, "Ambition has been, and still is, the mother of all errors, of all disturbances and sects."[8]

In the mid-twentieth century the ecumenical movement sought greater organizational unity among denominations, but without noteworthy success. It by no means received wholehearted approval or support from evangelicals. On the other hand, since the 1960s, the growth of the charismatic movement across almost all denominational lines, the rise of neighborhood Bible study and prayer groups, and a greatly diminished doctrinal awareness among laypeople, have brought about a remarkable increase in actual unity of fellowship — even between Protestants and Catholics — at the local level.

Although the previous paragraphs spoke of separation in the sense of (1) the formation of *separate organizations*, there are two other, more severe kinds of separation that should be mentioned: (2) *"No cooperation"*: in this case a church or Christian organization refuses to cooperate in joint activities with other churches (activities such as evangelistic campaigns or joint worship services or mutual recognition of ordination). (3) *"No personal fellowship"*: this involves the extremely strict avoidance of all personal fellowship with members of another church, and prohibits any joint prayer or Bible study, and sometimes even ordinary social contact, with members of another church group. We will discuss the possible reasons for these kinds of separation in the following section.

F. Reasons for Separation

As we examine the motives people have had for church separation throughout history, and as we compare those motives with the New Testament requirements that we seek

---

[7]Commentary on 1 Cor. 4:6. [8]Commentary on Num. 12:1.

both the unity and the purity of the visible church, we can find *both right and wrong reasons for separation*. Wrong reasons would include such things as personal ambition and pride, or differences on minor doctrines or practices (doctrinal or behavioral patterns that would not affect any other doctrine and that would not have a significant effect on the way one lives the Christian life).

On the other hand, there are some reasons for separation that we may consider to be right (or possibly right, depending on the specific circumstances). In most cases these reasons will flow from the need to work for the purity of the church as well as its unity. These reasons for separation can be considered in three categories: (1) doctrinal reasons; (2) reasons of conscience; (3) practical considerations. In the following section, I have listed some situations where it seems to me that Christians would be *required* to leave a church. Then I have listed some other situations that seem to me less clear, in which some Christians may think it *wise* to leave a church, and others will think it *unwise*. In these less-clear cases, I have generally not drawn any conclusions, but simply listed the kinds of factors that Christians will want to consider.

1. Doctrinal Reasons. A need for separation may arise when the doctrinal position of a church deviates from biblical standards in a serious way. This deviation may be in official statements or in actual belief and practice, insofar as that can be determined. But when does doctrinal deviation become so serious that it requires withdrawing from a church or forming a separate church? As we noted above, there are no commands in the New Testament to separate from any true church, so long as it is still a part of the body of Christ. Paul's response even to people in erring churches (even in churches like the one at Corinth, which tolerated serious doctrinal and moral error, and for a time tolerated some who rejected Paul's apostolic authority) is not to tell faithful Christians to separate from those churches, but to admonish the churches, work for their repentance, and pray for them. Of course there are commands to discipline those who cause trouble within the church, sometimes by excluding them from church fellowship (1 Cor. 5:11–13; 2 Thess. 3:14–15; Titus 3:10–11), but there are no instructions to leave the church and cause division if this cannot be done immediately (see Rev. 2:14–16, 20–25; cf. Luke 9:50; 11:23).

Second John 10–11, which forbids the receiving of false teachers, makes perhaps the strongest statement in the entire New Testament: "Do not take him into your house or welcome him. Anyone who welcomes him shares in his wicked work" (NIV). But it should be noted that such a visitor is teaching a serious heresy about the person of Christ, one that prevents people from having saving faith. (John is talking about anyone who "does not abide in the doctrine of Christ" and "does not have God" [v. 9].) Moreover, this verse refers to false teachers, not to all individuals who hold false beliefs, because it speaks of someone who comes to you and "does not bring this doctrine" (v. 10; cf. v. 7, "Many deceivers have gone out into the world, men who will not acknowledge the coming of Jesus Christ in the flesh"). John even uses the word *antichrist* for such teachers. Finally, the greeting John has in mind refers either to an official church greeting or one that would give an appearance of endorsement of this doctrine, because the prohibition talks about someone who "*comes to you* and does not *bring this doctrine*" (v. 10), which suggests that the person in view is a traveling teacher who comes not to an individual home but to address the church as a whole.[9]

On the principle of separation from unbelievers or from fundamental error that would involve the denial of the Christian faith, Christians would seem to be *required* on doctrinal grounds to withdraw from a church and join or form a new organization only when the doctrinal error is so serious and so pervasive that the parent church *has become a false church,* no longer part of the body of Christ. This would be a church which is no longer a fellowship of true believers, no longer a true part of the body of Christ, or no longer a place where those who believe its teachings will find salvation.[10] In the case of leaving a false church, those who separate will claim that in fact they have not *left* the true church, but that they *are* the true church, and that the parent organization has left by means of its error. In fact, both Luther and Calvin eventually said that the Roman Catholic Church was not a true church.

However, even when withdrawal or separation is not absolutely required, many Christians may find that it is *wise* or *expedient* to withdraw before the church has become a false church, but when serious doctrinal deviation occurs. For instance, some would argue that doctrinal deviation has become intolerable whenever heretical views on major doctrines (such as the Trinity, the person of Christ, the atonement, the resurrection, etc.) can be advocated by a church leader without causing him to be subject to church discipline or to exclusion from the fellowship of the church. In other cases many would say that separation should occur when the church as a body publicly approves of some serious doctrinal or moral error (such as endorsing a doctrinal error in a church creed or statement of faith). However, other Christians would not think separation to be wise or expedient in such cases, but would advocate praying and working for revival and reformation within the church, and giving clear public statements of disagreement with any doctrinal error that has been tolerated. In such cases, those who decide to stay and those who decide they must leave should both recognize that God may call different Christians to different roles and ministries, and therefore to different decisions, and we would do well to give considerable freedom to others to seek God's wisdom in such a case and to obey it as they best understand it for their own lives.

2. Matters of Conscience. In the area of conscience, if a Christian had no freedom to preach or teach as his or her conscience, informed by Scripture, would dictate, it might be thought that separation was necessary or at least wise. But caution and great humility are in order here: individual judgment may be distorted, especially if it is not informed by the consensus of faithful believers throughout history, and by the counsel of believers in the present.

Moreover, the command in 2 Corinthians 6:14 not to be yoked together with unbelievers could also require a person to separate if the parent church became so dominated by those who gave no evidence of saving faith that such "yoking together" could not be

---

[9]See the discussion in John Stott, *The Epistles of John,* TNTC (London: Tyndale Press, 1964), pp. 212–15.

[10]After saying that "The purist Churches under heaven are subject both to mixture and error," the Westminster Confession of Faith adds, "and some have so degenerated, as to become no Churches of Christ, but synagogues of Satan" (25.5).

avoided. In this passage the prohibition against being "yoked together" with unbelievers forbids not mere association or even acceptance of help (cf. Luke 9:50, but also 3 John 7), but rather *the giving up of control over one's activities and the loss of freedom to act in obedience to God,* for these restraints are what is implied in the metaphor of being "yoked" together. Some people might also find it necessary or at least wise to leave a church on the basis of conscience if staying implied approval of some unbiblical doctrine or practice within the church, and thereby encouraged others to follow that wrong doctrine or practice. But others may think it right to stay in the church and voice clear disapproval of the faulty doctrine.

In other cases, some have argued that it is required to leave a denomination when a higher governing authority in that denomination, which one has promised to obey, commands an action which is clearly sinful (that is, an action which is clearly contrary to Scripture). In such a case some would say that leaving the denomination is the only way to avoid doing either the sinful act which is commanded or the sinful act of disobedience to those in authority. But this does not seem to be a necessary requirement, for many Scripture passages could be cited showing that disobedience to a higher authority is not wrong when one is commanded to sin (see Acts 5:29; Dan. 3:18; 6:10), and that one may disobey but remain in the parent church until forced out.

3. Practical Considerations. Christians may decide to separate from a parent church if, after prayerful consideration, it seems that staying in the parent church will very likely result in more harm than good. This could be because their work for the Lord would become frustrated and ineffectual due to opposition to it from within the parent church, or because they would find little or no fellowship with others in that church. Moreover, some may decide that staying in the church would harm the faith of other believers or would hinder unbelievers from coming to true faith because their continued affiliation with the parent church would seem to imply approval of false teachings within that church. Again, Christians might find themselves in situations where they have prayed and worked for change for some time but there seems to be no reasonable hope for change in the parent church, perhaps because the present leadership group is resistant to correction from Scripture, is firmly entrenched, and is self-perpetuating. In all of these situations much prayer and mature judgment will be required, because withdrawing from a church, especially by people who have been there a long time or have established leadership functions in the church, is a serious action.

4. Are There Times When Cooperation and Personal Fellowship Are Prohibited? Finally, when should Christians take stronger steps than those mentioned above and engage in the kind of separation that we earlier called "no cooperation" or "no personal fellowship"? The biblical passages we have looked at seem to require that Christians practice "no cooperation" in certain activities with another group only when the other group is an unbelieving one, and then, it seems, only when the unbelieving group shares control of the activity (this is implied in the metaphor of being "yoked together" in 2 Cor. 6:14). Of course, it may be found wise or expedient on other grounds to decide not to cooperate in a particular function, but non-cooperation would not seem to be required except when the other group is an unbelieving one. Certainly *opposition* to activities such as evangelistic campaigns by other true believers would be seen by the New Testament authors as divisiveness and a failure to demonstrate the unity of the body of Christ.[11]

The third and most extreme kind of separation, the avoidance of all personal fellowship with members of another entire church group, is never commanded in the New Testament. Such an extreme measure of "no fellowship" is only implied in serious cases of church discipline of individuals, not in cases of differences with entire churches.

QUESTIONS FOR PERSONAL APPLICATION

1. In what areas is your own church "more pure"? In what areas do you think it is "less pure"?

2. On a scale of 1 to 10 (1 equals less pure; 10 equals more pure), where would you rank your church in each of the categories that mark a more-pure church?

3. What do you think that you should be doing in order to work for greater purity in your own church? Does the fact that you recognize a specific need in the church mean that God is calling you (rather than someone else) to meet that need?

4. Do you know of other churches in your area that you would consider more pure than your own? What are the reasons that you might think it right to stay in your own church even though it may not be the most pure church you know of?

5. Are there marks of a more-pure church that evangelicals generally in this century have been negligent in emphasizing?

6. Since the first century, do you think that by and large the church has continued to increase in purity over time? Can you give specific reasons to support your answer?

7. In your lifetime, what encouraging signs do you see that the church is increasing in purity? What signs do you see that the church is increasing in unity?

8. In what ways do you think your own local church could grow in unity among its members?

9. In what ways could your church demonstrate greater unity with other true churches in the same geographical area? What do you think are the barriers to that unity (if any)? In what ways could that unity be expressed? What might be the benefits of such expressions of unity?

10. Are you in a church where you have wondered if God would have you leave and join another church? After reading this chapter, do you now think that you should stay in your present church or leave it? Has there been significant change for the better

---

[11]The New Testament authors would probably also think it tragic that most divisions among Protestants have come about or been maintained today because of differences over some of the least emphasized and least clearly taught doctrines in the New Testament, such as the form of church government, the exact nature of Christ's presence in the Lord's Supper, and the details of the end times. (Many people would want to add to that list: differences over the proper subjects for baptism.)

in your church in the last ten years? If you knew that the church were to remain substantially the same for the next ten years, would you decide to stay now or to leave it?

11. What are some ways in which the worldwide unity of true believers is already being expressed and demonstrated? What would the church around the world look like if there were much greater demonstration of the unity of the church? What would be the result in the world as a whole?

12. If a community already has several active and effective evangelical churches, is there any justification for another evangelical denomination to attempt to plant its own church in that community?

13. Do you think it hinders evangelism and witness to society generally when the popular culture thinks of unbelieving or false churches and believing churches both as "Christians"? Can anything be done to change that impression?

14. What kinds of unity and cooperation can appropriately be demonstrated with believers within the Roman Catholic Church today? What are the limits to such cooperation?

SPECIAL TERMS

Eastern church
purity of the church
separation

unity of the church
Western church

BIBLIOGRAPHY

Bromiley, G. W. "Unity." In *EDT*, pp. 1127–28.
Carson, Donald A. "Evangelicals, Ecumenism and the Church." In *Evangelical Affirmations*. Ed. by Kenneth S. Kantzer and Carl F. H. Henry. Grand Rapids: Zondervan, 1990, pp. 347–85.
Puritan and Reformed Studies Conference. *Approaches to Reformation of the Church.* London: *The Evangelical* magazine, 1965. Contains papers by D. W. Marshall, D. P. Kingdon, J. I. Packer, G. S. R. Cox, S. M. Houghton, and D. M. Lloyd-Jones.

SCRIPTURE MEMORY PASSAGE

Ephesians 4:14–16: *So that we may no longer be children, tossed to and fro and carried about with every wind of doctrine, by the cunning of men, by their craftiness in deceitful wiles. Rather, speaking the truth in love, we are to grow up in every way into him who is the head, into Christ, from whom the whole body, joined and knit together by every joint with which it is supplied, when each part is working properly, makes bodily growth and upbuilds itself in love.*

HYMN

"Blest Be the Tie That Binds"

This hymn speaks of the unity or the "tie" that binds the hearts of Christians together in love. It continues to speak of fellowship as like the fellowship of heaven: it is "like to that above." It also speaks of sharing in prayer and concern for each other and bearing of one another's burdens. The hymn goes on to speak of our hope that we will one day be united in "perfect love and friendship" for eternity in heaven.

> Blest be the tie that binds
>   Our hearts in Christian love:
> The fellowship of kindred minds
>   Is like to that above.
>
> Before our Father's throne
>   We pour our ardent prayers;
> Our fears, our hopes, our aims, are one,
>   Our comforts and our cares.
>
> We share our mutual woes,
>   Our mutual burdens bear,
> And often for each other flows
>   The sympathizing tear.
>
> When we asunder part,
>   It gives us inward pain;
> But we shall still be joined in heart,
>   And hope to meet again.
>
> This glorious hope revives
>   Our courage by the way,
> While each in expectation lives,
>   And longs to see the day.
>
> From sorrow, toil and pain,
>   And sin, we shall be free;
> And perfect love and friendship reign
>   Through all eternity.

AUTHOR: JOHN FAWCETT, 1782

Chapter 4

THE POWER OF THE CHURCH

What kind of authority does the church have?
How should church discipline function?

EXPLANATION AND SCRIPTURAL BASIS

When we look at the powerful governments of the world and at other business and educational organizations that have great influence, and then consider our local churches, or even our denominational headquarters, the church may seem to us to be weak and ineffective. Moreover, when we recognize the rapid growth of evil that is seen daily in our society, we may wonder if the church has power to make any changes at all.

On the other hand, in some countries the officially recognized church has great influence on the conduct of national affairs. This was certainly true of the influence of the Roman Catholic Church in former times in some southern European and Latin American countries (and is still true today to some extent). It was true of the Church of England in previous centuries, and of John Calvin's church in Geneva, Switzerland, while he was alive, and of the church founded by the pilgrims in the Massachusetts Bay Colony in 1620. Situations like these where the church appears to have great influence cause us to ask whether Scripture places any limitations on the church's power.

We may define the power of the church as follows: *The power of the church is its God-given authority to carry on spiritual warfare, proclaim the gospel, and exercise church discipline.*

Although these three areas overlap and could be treated in any order, since the category of "spiritual warfare" is the broader category it will be treated first. This perspective on the church's power also reminds us that the power of the church, unlike the worldly influence exercised by human armies and governments, directly affects the spiritual realm.

A. Spiritual Warfare

Paul reminds the Corinthians, "For though we live in the world we are not carrying on a worldly war, for *the weapons of our warfare are not worldly but have divine power to destroy strongholds*" (2 Cor. 10:3–4). These weapons, used against demonic forces that hinder the spread of the gospel and the progress of the church, include such things as prayer, worship, the authority to rebuke demonic forces, the words of Scripture, faith, and righteous conduct on the part of the members of the church. (Paul gives further details about our spiritual conflict and the armor we wear for it in Eph. 6:10–18.)

When we consider this spiritual power in a broad sense, it certainly includes the power of the gospel to break through sin and hardened opposition and awaken faith in the hearts of unbelievers (see Rom. 10:17; James 1:18; 1 Peter 1:23). But this power also includes spiritual power that will render demonic opposition to the gospel ineffective. We see examples of this in Acts 13:8–11, where Paul pronounced judgment on Elymas the magician, who was opposing the preaching of the gospel, and in Acts 16:16–18, where Paul rebuked an evil spirit in the soothsaying girl who was annoying Paul while he proclaimed the gospel.[1] Such spiritual power to defeat evil opposition was seen frequently in the early church, such as in the freeing of Peter from prison (Acts 12:1–17), and perhaps also in the subsequent judgment on King Herod Agrippa I (Acts 12:20–24).[2]

Yet Paul realizes that he can use this spiritual power not only against those outside the church who oppose the gospel, but also against those within the church who are active opponents of his apostolic ministry. He says about some arrogant troublemakers in the church, "I will come to you soon, if the Lord wills, and I will find out not the talk of these arrogant people but their power. For the kingdom of God does not consist in talk but in power" (1 Cor. 4:19–20). Such power was not to be trifled with, for it was the same power of the Holy Spirit that had brought death to Ananias and Sapphira (Acts 5:1–11) and blindness to Elymas (Acts 13:8–11). Paul did not wish to use this power in a judgmental capacity, but he was prepared to do so if necessary. Later he wrote again to the Corinthians that his actions when present would be as powerful as his letters when absent (2 Cor. 10:8–11), and he warned those who opposed his authority and had sinned publicly and not repented, "If I come again I will not spare them—since you desire proof that Christ is speaking in me. . . . For we are weak in him, but in dealing with you we shall live with him by the power of God" (2 Cor. 13:2–4). He then adds a final reminder of his reluctance to use this authority, telling them that he is writing before he comes "in order that when I come I may not have to be severe in my use of the authority which the Lord has given me for building up and not for tearing down" (2 Cor. 13:10).

---

[1] Jesus often rebuked demonic spirits that created disturbances when he was ministering to people: see Mark 1:23–26; 5:1–13, et al.

[2] The text does not specify that Herod's death was in any way connected to the "earnest prayer" (Acts 12:5) that was made for Peter by the church, but the fact that the narrative about Herod's death follows immediately upon the story of his killing James the brother of John with the sword and his putting Peter in prison certainly hints at the fact that God intended this as a judgment upon one of the primary enemies of the church, showing that no opposition could stand against the progress of the gospel. This understanding is also supported by the fact that the sentence immediately following the narrative of Herod's death is, "But the word of God grew and multiplied" (Acts 12:24).

Now we may question whether the church today has the same degree of spiritual power that the apostles Peter or Paul did. Certainly there is a distinction between the apostles and the other early Christians even in the book of Acts (note that immediately after the death of Ananias and Sapphira "many signs and wonders" were done "by the hands of the apostles," but "None of the rest dared join them, but the people held them in high honor," Acts 5:12–13). Moreover, Paul did not instruct any leaders of the church at Corinth, or even Timothy or Titus, to exercise that spiritual power at Corinth against his opponents. He spoke about the power which the Lord "has given *me*" (2 Cor. 13:10), not about the power which the Lord had given to the church or to Christians generally.

On the other hand, Paul did direct the Corinthian church to exercise church discipline in a case of incest in the church at Corinth, and to do it "when you are assembled, and my spirit is present, with the power of our Lord Jesus" (1 Cor. 5:4). Moreover, the descriptions of spiritual warfare in Ephesians 6:10–18 and 2 Corinthians 10:3–4 seem applicable to Christians generally, and few today would deny that the church has authority to pray against and to speak with authority against demonic opposition to the work of the gospel. So there would seem to be at least some significant degree of spiritual power against evil opposition that God is willing to grant to the church in every age (including the present one). Perhaps it is impossible to define more specifically the degree of spiritual power God will grant to the church in times of conflict against evil, but we do not need to know the details in advance: our calling is simply to be faithful to Scripture in praying and in exercising church discipline, and then to leave the rest in God's hands, knowing that he will grant sufficient power to accomplish his purposes through the church.

B. The Keys of the Kingdom

The phrase "the keys of the kingdom" occurs only once in the Bible, in Matthew 16:19, where Jesus is speaking to Peter: "I will give you the keys of the kingdom of heaven; and whatever you shall bind on earth shall have been bound in heaven and whatever you shall loose on earth shall have been loosed in heaven" (NASB). What is the meaning of these "keys of the kingdom of heaven"?[3]

Elsewhere in the New Testament a key always implies *authority to open a door and give entrance to a place or realm.* Jesus says, "Woe to you lawyers! for you have taken away the key of knowledge; you did not enter yourselves, and you hindered those who were entering" (Luke 11:52). Moreover, Jesus says in Revelation 1:18, "I have the keys of Death and Hades," implying that he has the authority to grant entrance and exit from those realms. (Cf. also Rev. 3:7; 9:1; 20:1; also the messianic prediction in Isa. 22:22.)

The "keys of the kingdom of heaven" therefore represent at least the authority to preach the gospel of Christ (cf. Matt. 16:16) and thus to open the door of the kingdom of heaven and allow people to enter.

Peter first used this authority by preaching the gospel at Pentecost (Acts 2:14–42). But the other apostles also were given this authority in a primary sense (they wrote the gospel

---

[3]The rest of this section discussing the keys of the kingdom of heaven is adapted from the article, "Keys of the Kingdom" by Wayne Grudem, in *EDT,* pp. 604–5, and is used here by permission.

in permanent form in the New Testament). And all believers have this "key" in a secondary sense, for they can all share the gospel with others, and thereby open the kingdom of heaven to those who will enter it.

But is there any other authority, in addition to this, that Jesus implies by the phrase "the keys of the kingdom of heaven"? There are two factors suggesting that the authority of the keys here also includes *the authority to exercise discipline within the church:* (1) The plural "keys" suggests authority over more than one door. Thus, more than simply entrance into the kingdom is implied; some authority *within* the kingdom is also suggested. (2) Jesus completes the promise about the keys with a statement about "binding" and "loosing," which closely parallels another saying of his in Matthew 18, in which "binding" and "loosing" mean placing under church discipline and releasing from church discipline:

> If he refuses to listen even to the church, let him be to you as a Gentile and a tax-gatherer. Truly I say to you, whatever you shall *bind* on earth shall have been bound in heaven; and whatever you *loose* on earth shall have been loosed in heaven. (Matt. 18:17–18 NASB)

But if "binding" and "loosing" clearly refer to church discipline in Matthew 18, then it seems likely that they would also refer to church discipline in Matthew 16, where Jesus' words are very similar.[4]

This understanding of binding and loosing in terms of church discipline also fits the context of Matthew 16:19, for, on this understanding, after promising to build his church (v. 18), Jesus promises to give not only the authority to open the door of entrance into the kingdom, but also some administrative authority to regulate the conduct of people once they are inside.[5] Therefore it seems that "the keys of the kingdom of heaven" which Jesus promised to Peter in Matthew 16:19 included both (1) ability to admit people to the kingdom through preaching the gospel, and (2) authority to exercise church discipline for those who do enter.

In Matthew 16:16–19, Jesus does not indicate whether the authority of the keys will later be given to others besides Peter. But certainly the authority to preach the gospel is given to others at a later time, and in Matthew 18:18 Jesus does state explicitly that the authority to exercise church discipline is given to the church generally whenever it meets and corporately carries out such discipline ("Tell it to the church," Matt. 18:17). Thus both aspects of the authority of the keys, though first given to Peter, were soon expanded

---

[4]The statement in Matt. 16:19 uses singular pronouns for "whatever" and "you" (referring to Peter), while Matt. 18:18 uses plurals (referring to Christians generally), but the same Greek words are used for "bind" (*deō*) and "loose" (*luō*), and the grammatical construction (periphrastic future perfect) is the same.

[5]Some have argued that binding and loosing do not refer to actions of church discipline, but to an authority to make various rules for conduct, because in the rabbinic literature that comes from Jewish teachers around the time of Jesus the words *bind* and *loose* are sometimes used for forbidding and

permitting various kinds of conduct. This interpretation does not seem persuasive, however, because these rabbinic statements are a much more distant parallel than the statement of Jesus himself in Matt. 18:18, where church discipline is clearly in view. Moreover, it is difficult to know whether any of the rabbinic parallels pre-date the time of the New Testament, or to show that such words would have functioned as technical terms in the ordinary vocabulary of Jesus and his hearers—in fact, Matt. 18:18 shows that they did not function as technical terms in that way, because they were used rather to refer to church discipline in that verse.

to include the authority given to the church as a whole. In preaching the gospel and in exercising discipline the church now exercises the authority of the keys of the kingdom.

What persons or actions are subject to the kind of church discipline implied by the authority of the keys? In both Matthew 16:19 and 18:18, the term "whatever" is neuter in Greek, and seems to indicate that Jesus is speaking not specifically to *persons* ("whoever," for which a masculine plural would be ordinarily expected), but rather more generally to *situations* and *relationships* that come up within the church. This would not exclude the authority to exercise discipline over individuals, but the phrase is broader than that, and includes specific actions that are subject to discipline as well.

Yet the authority of the keys with respect to church discipline is not completely unlimited. It will only be effective against true sin (cf. Matt. 18:15), sin as defined by God's Word. The church does not have authority on its own to legislate what is morally right and wrong in an absolute sense, for the authority to define right and wrong belongs to God alone (see Rom. 1:32; 2:16; 3:4–8; 9:20; Ps. 119:89, 142, 160; Matt. 5:18). The church can only declare and teach what God has already commanded in his Word. Nor can the authority of the keys involve authority to forgive sins in any absolute sense, because in Scripture it is clear that that can only be done by God himself (Isa. 43:25; 55:7; Mark 2:7, 10; Ps. 103:3; 1 John 1:9).[6] Therefore the authority to carry out discipline in the church is an authority that must be carried out in accordance with the standards of Scripture.

Is it possible to be any more specific about the kind of spiritual authority that is involved in this use of the keys of the kingdom of heaven? Both Matthew 16:19 and 18:18 use an unusual Greek verbal construction (a periphrastic future perfect). It is best translated by the NASB, "Whatever you shall bind on earth *shall have been bound* in heaven, and whatever you shall loose on earth *shall have been loosed* in heaven."[7] Several other examples of this construction show that it indicates not just a future action ("shall be bound"), for which a common Greek tense was available (future passive), but rather *an action that would be completed before some future point,* with effects that would continue to be felt.[8] Thus, Jesus is teaching that church discipline will have heavenly sanction. But it is not as if the church must wait for God to endorse its actions after the actions have occurred. Rather, whenever the church *enacts discipline* it can be confident that God has already begun the process spiritually. Whenever it *releases from discipline,* forgives the sinner, and restores personal relationships, the church can be confident that God has already begun the restoration spiritually (cf. John 20:23). In this way Jesus promises that the spiritual relationship between God and the person subject to discipline will be immediately affected in ways consistent with the direction of the church's disciplinary action. Legitimate church discipline, therefore, involves the awesome certainty that corresponding heavenly discipline has already begun.

Moreover, this teaching on the power of the keys has a significant application to individual Christians who begin to be subject to the discipline of a true church: Christians

---

[6]In John 20:23, the forgiveness of sins by the disciples is best understood as freeing from church discipline and restoring personal relationships in a sense similar to the "loosing" of Matt. 16:19 and 18:18.

[7]See the grammatical discussion in D. A. Carson, "Matthew," *EBC*, 8:370–72.

[8]See examples in Luke 12:52; Gen. 43:9; 44:32; Ex. 12:6; Sirach 7:25; Hermas, *Similitudes* 5.4.2; *Letter of Aristeas* 40.

should submit to this discipline and not run from it, because God himself has also put them under discipline for that sin.

C. The Power of the Church and the Power of the State

The previous sections have discussed spiritual power and spiritual warfare to be exercised by the church. But should the church ever use physical force (weapons and armies, for example) to carry out its mission? The phrase commonly used to refer to the idea of physical, worldly warfare is "to take up the sword."

There are several indications in Scripture that the church must never take up the sword to carry out its purposes in the new covenant age. This was a dreadful mistake made in the Crusades, when church-sponsored armies marched across Europe and Asia to attempt to reclaim the land of Israel. In these cases the church was trying to use physical force to bring about its triumph over earthly territories. But Jesus said, *"My kingdom is not of this world. If it were, my servants would fight"* (John 18:36 NIV). The church has the power of the keys, which is spiritual power. It is to carry out spiritual battles using spiritual weapons, but is not to use the power of the sword to accomplish its purposes. "The weapons of our warfare are not worldly" (2 Cor. 10:4).

Certainly God does give *to civil government* the right to bear the sword, that is, to use force to punish evil in the world (Rom. 13:1–7). But there is no indication that the power of government is to be used to enforce adherence to Christianity upon any people.[9] Moreover, there are several indications that Jesus refused to use the power of physical force to compel people to accept the gospel. For example, when a Samaritan village would not receive Jesus, James and John asked, "Lord, do you want us to bid fire come down from heaven and consume them?" (Luke 9:54). But Jesus "rebuked them" (v. 55) for even making that suggestion. Jesus came the first time to offer the gospel to all who would receive it, not to execute punishment on those who rejected it. This is why he could say, "For God sent the Son into the world, not to condemn the world, but that the world might be saved through him" (John 3:17). He will one day come again in judgment, at the end of the church age, but during this age it is not the prerogative of the church to use physical force to carry out judgment.

Jesus clearly made a distinction between the authority granted to the government and the authority that God exercises in our personal allegiance to him when he said, "Render therefore to Caesar the things that are Caesar's, and to God the things that are God's" (Matt. 22:21). And though Jesus recognized the authority of civil government, he refused to usurp that authority himself, telling someone, "Man, who made me a judge or divider over you?" with respect to a matter of family inheritance (Luke 12:13–14).

A further reason why the government should not use force to require allegiance to Christianity is that in the new covenant, membership in the church and allegiance to Christ must be voluntary. They cannot be compelled by family or by the state. In fact, faith in Christ, to be truly held and practiced, cannot be compelled by force. If it is

---

[9]Edmund Clowney rightly observes, "We may not suppose that Christ denied to his apostles the right to bring in his kingdom with the sword, but conceded that right to Pilate" ("The Biblical Theology of the Church," in *The Church in the Bible and the World,* ed. by D. A. Carson [Exeter: Paternoster, and Grand Rapids: Baker, 1987], p. 33).

compelled, it changes its essential quality and is no longer a voluntary act of the individual, and cannot be true faith.

From this it also follows that *the civil government should not enforce laws requiring or prohibiting kinds of church doctrine, or abridging the people's freedom to worship as they choose.* On the other hand, the church does not and should not rule over the state, as if it were some kind of higher authority over the state; it is not. Rather, the authority of the church and that of the state belong to distinct spheres (Matt. 22:21; John 18:36; 2 Cor. 10:3–4), and each should respect the authority God has given the other in its own sphere of operation.

These limitations on the activities of the church and the state are different from the practice of the Catholic Church through much of the Middle Ages, where it often had more power than the civil government. These principles also differ from the practice of the Church of England, which is subject to the authority of the Queen and Parliament in the appointment of bishops and any change in doctrinal standards. The failure to respect the distinct roles of church and state is seen in many Roman Catholic countries today, where the church still has strong influence on the government, and in the compulsory membership in state-sponsored Protestant churches of Northern Europe after the Reformation, a situation that caused many emigrants to flee to America for religious freedom.

However, it should be said that the degree of state-enforced religion in Protestant or Catholic countries is mild indeed compared to state-sponsored and state-enforced religion in most Muslim countries today, and in many Hindu and Buddhist countries as well. In fact, it is difficult to find genuine freedom of religion apart from the strong influence of healthy evangelical Christianity in any country around the world (except where various religions are so weak or so evenly balanced that no one religion has dominant political power). Whenever Christians are involved in the political realm, they ought clearly to affirm freedom of religion as a political policy that is nonnegotiable, and they should be willing to defend that freedom for religions other than their own as well. The Christian faith can stand on its own two feet and compete very well in the marketplace of ideas in any society and in any culture, provided it has the freedom to do so.

Finally, what has been said above should not be misunderstood as a prohibition against Christians attempting to bring positive moral influence on government and attempting to persuade governments to make laws consistent with biblical standards of morality. It is right for Christians to attempt to persuade governments to make laws that protect families and private property and the lives of human beings—laws that both outlaw and punish murder, theft, and the breaking of contracts (things that violate the Ten Commandments), as well as prohibit homosexual "marriage," incest, slander, drug abuse, abortion, and other things that are inconsistent with biblical standards of morality. These things are far different from requiring belief in certain types of church doctrine or theological conviction, and from requiring that people attend certain kinds of church or worship services. The latter are clearly "religious" activities in the narrow sense in that they pertain to our relationship to God and our beliefs about him.[10] Governments should refrain from making laws about these things.

---

[10]The fact that Christians should try to influence government to make laws consistent with biblical standards is indicated by passages such as Matt. 6:10; 14:4; Acts 24:25; and 1 Tim. 2:1–4. We may hope that the moral standards of Scripture

D. Church Discipline

Since church discipline is one aspect of the use of the power of the church, it is appropriate here to give some discussion of the biblical principles relevant to the practice of church discipline.

1. The Purpose of Church Discipline.

a. Restoration and Reconciliation of the Believer Who Is Going Astray: Sin hinders fellowship among believers and with God. In order for reconciliation to occur, the sin must be dealt with. Therefore, the primary purpose of church discipline is to pursue the twofold goal of *restoration* (of the offender to right behavior) and *reconciliation* (between believers, and with God).[11] Just as wise parents discipline their children (Prov. 13:24: "He who loves [his son] is diligent to discipline him"), and just as God our Father disciplines those whom he loves (Heb. 12:6; Rev. 3:19), so the church in its discipline is acting in love to bring back a brother or sister who has gone astray, reestablishing that person in right fellowship and rescuing him or her from destructive patterns of life. In Matthew 18:15, the hope is that discipline will stop at the first step, when someone goes alone: "If he listens to you, you have gained your brother." The phrase "you have gained your brother" implies that those carrying out discipline should keep the goal of personal reconciliation among Christians always in mind. Paul reminds us that we are to "restore" the sinning brother or sister "in a spirit of gentleness" (Gal. 6:1), and James encourages us to "bring back a sinner from the error of his way" (James 5:20).

In fact, if church members were actively involved in giving private words of gentle admonition and in praying for one another when the first clear evidence of sinful conduct is seen, very little formal church discipline would have to be carried out, because the process would begin and end with a conversation between two people that never becomes known to anyone else.

Even when the final step of "excommunication" (that is, putting someone out of the fellowship or "communion" of the church) is taken, it is still with the hope that repentance will result. Paul delivered Hymenaeus and Alexander to Satan *that they may learn not to blaspheme* (1 Tim. 1:20), and the man living in incest at Corinth was to be

---

will also eventually gain general consent from most of the people of a given society, since those moral standards have also been inscribed on their hearts and therefore they have a witness in their consciences that these standards are correct (see Rom. 2:14–15). It is also the case that God holds all societies and cultures responsible for obeying his moral standards, and often in the Old Testament God's prophets pronounced judgments upon not only the people of Israel but also upon immoral pagan societies, even though they did not have his written laws (see Deut. 9:5; Isa. 13–23; Ezek. 25–32; Dan. 4:27; Amos 1–2; Obadiah [written to Edom]; Jonah [prophesied to Nineveh]; Nahum [prophesied to Nineveh]; Hab. 2; Zeph. 2). In fact, civil

governments are sent by God "to punish those who do wrong and to praise those who do right" (1 Peter 2:14).

[11]In their excellent book on church discipline, *Church Discipline That Heals* (Downers Grove, Ill.: InterVarsity Press, 1985; originally published as *Healing the Wounded*), John White and Ken Blue note that a failure to keep reconciliation as the primary goal of church discipline has led to many abuses of the process in the history of the church (see esp. pp. 45–56). But they themselves say that "true reconciliation never takes place without change in the parties involved" (p. 46). Therefore I have combined reconciliation and restoration in this first section.

delivered to Satan "that his spirit may be saved in the day of the Lord Jesus" (1 Cor. 5:5).[12]

If Christians who must take steps of church discipline will continue to remember this first purpose—the reconciliation of believers who are going astray with each other and with God, and their restoration to right patterns of life—then it will be much easier to continue to act in genuine love for the parties involved, and feelings of anger or desires for revenge on the part of those who have been hurt, which often lie near the surface, will much more easily be avoided.

b. To Keep the Sin From Spreading to Others: Although the primary goal of church discipline is restoration and reconciliation for the erring believer, in this present age reconciliation and restoration will not always come about. But whether restoration comes about or not, the church is told to carry out discipline because two other purposes are served as well.

One other purpose is that the sin will be kept from spreading to others. The author of Hebrews tells Christians to see to it that "no 'root of bitterness' spring up and cause trouble, and by it *the many become defiled*" (Heb. 12:15). This means that if conflict between persons is not resolved quickly, the effects may spread to many others—something that sadly seems to be true in many cases of church division. Paul also says, "*A little leaven leavens the whole lump,*" and tells the Corinthians to put out of the church a man living in incest (1 Cor. 5:2, 6–7), lest his sin affect the whole church. If that man were not disciplined, the effects of the sin would spread to many others who were aware of it and saw that the church paid little attention to it. This would cause many to think that perhaps that sin was not as bad as they had thought, and others might be tempted to commit similar or related kinds of sin. Moreover, if discipline against one specific offense is not carried out, then it will be much more difficult for the church to carry out discipline if a similar kind of sin is committed by someone else in the future.

Paul also told Timothy that elders who persist in sin are to be rebuked in the presence of all, "*so that the rest may stand in fear*" (1 Tim. 5:20)—that is, so that many others would realize that the sin will not be tolerated but will receive discipline both from the church and from God himself. In fact, Paul rebuked Peter publicly, in order that others would not follow Peter's bad example of separating himself and eating only with Jewish believers (Gal. 2:11).

c. To Protect the Purity of the Church and the Honor of Christ: A third purpose of church discipline is that the purity of the church is to be protected, so that Christ will not be dishonored. Of course, no believer in this age has a completely pure heart, and we all have remaining sin in our lives. But when a church member continues to sin in a way that is outwardly evident to others, especially to unbelievers,[13] this clearly brings dishonor to Christ. It is similar to the situation of Jews who disobeyed God's law and led unbelievers to scoff and blaspheme God's name (Rom. 2:24: "The name of God is blasphemed among the Gentiles because of you").

---

[12]The unusual phrase "deliver to Satan" in these verses seems to mean "put out of the church" since that is clearly what Paul tells the Corinthians to do in 1 Cor. 5:2, 7, 13.

Putting someone out of the church puts that person back into the kingdom of this sinful age, which is ruled by Satan.

[13]But also to angels (see Eph. 3:10; 1 Tim. 5:21).

This is why Paul is shocked that the Corinthians have not disciplined the man who continued in willful sin that was publicly known in the church (1 Cor. 5:1–2: "And you are arrogant! Ought you not rather to mourn?"). He is also greatly distressed to know that "brother goes to law against brother, and that before unbelievers" (1 Cor. 6:6). Rather than allowing such moral blemishes on the character of the church, Peter encourages believers to "be zealous to be found by [Christ] without spot or blemish, and at peace" (2 Peter 3:14). And our Lord Jesus wants to present to himself a church "without spot or wrinkle . . . holy and without blemish" (Eph. 5:27), for he is the head of the church, and its character reflects on his reputation. Even angels and demons look at the church and behold the wisdom of God expressed in it (Eph. 3:10); therefore (Eph. 4:1) Paul encourages Christians to be "eager to maintain the unity of the Spirit in the bond of peace" (Eph. 4:3).

This is a very serious matter. Since the Lord Jesus is jealous for his own honor, if the church does not exercise proper discipline, he will do it himself, as he did at Corinth, where the Lord's discipline resulted in sickness and death (1 Cor. 11:27–34), and as he warned he would do both at Pergamum (Rev. 2:14–15) and at Thyatira (Rev. 2:20). In these last two cases the Lord was displeased with the whole church for tolerating outward disobedience and not exercising discipline: "But I have this against you, that *you tolerate the woman Jezebel,* who calls herself a prophetess and is teaching and beguiling my servants to practice immorality and to eat food sacrificed to idols" (Rev. 2:20; cf. vv. 14–16).[14]

2. For What Sins Should Church Discipline Be Exercised? On the one hand, Jesus' teaching in Matthew 18:15–20 tells us that if a situation involving personal sin against someone else cannot be resolved in a private or small group meeting, then the matter must be brought to the church:

> If your brother sins against you, go and tell him his fault, between you and him alone. If he listens to you, you have gained your brother. But if he does not listen, take one or two others along with you, that every word may be confirmed by the evidence of two or three witnesses. If he refuses to listen to them, tell it to the church; and if he refuses to listen even to the church, let him be to you as a Gentile and a tax collector. (Matt. 18:15–17)

In this case the matter has progressed from a private and informal situation to a public and much more formal process of discipline by the whole church.

On the other hand, there does not seem to be any explicit limitation specified for the kinds of sin that should be subject to church discipline. The examples of sins subject to church discipline in the New Testament are extremely diverse: divisiveness (Rom. 16:17; Titus 3:10), incest (1 Cor. 5:1), laziness and refusing to work (2 Thess. 3:6–10), disobeying what Paul writes (2 Thess. 3:14–15), blasphemy (1 Tim. 1:20), and teaching heretical doctrine (2 John 10–11).

---

[14]The purposes of church discipline discussed above are well summarized in the Westminster Confession of Faith, chapter 30, paragraph 3: "Church censures are necessary, for the reclaiming and gaining of offending brethren, for deterring of others from the like offenses, for purging out of that leaven which might infect the whole lump, for vindicating the honor of Christ, and the holy profession of the gospel, and for preventing the wrath of God, which might justly fall upon the church, if they should suffer his covenant, and the seals thereof, to be profaned by notorious and obstinate offenders."

Nonetheless, a definite principle appears to be at work: all sins that were explicitly disciplined in the New Testament were publicly known or outwardly evident sins,[15] and many of them had continued over a period of time. The fact that the sins were publicly known meant that reproach was being brought on the church, Christ was being dishonored, and there was a real possibility that others would be encouraged to follow the wrongful patterns of life that were being publicly tolerated.

There is always the need, however, for mature judgment in the exercise of church discipline, because there is lack of complete sanctification in all our lives. Furthermore, when we realize that someone is already aware of a sin and struggling to overcome it, a word of admonition may in fact do more harm than good. We should also remember that where there are issues of conduct on which Christians legitimately disagree, Paul encourages a wide degree of tolerance (Rom. 14:1–23).

3. How Should Church Discipline Be Carried Out?

a. Knowledge of the Sin Should Be Kept to the Smallest Group Possible: This seems to be the purpose in Matthew 18:15–17 behind the gradual progression from a private meeting, to a meeting with two or three others, to telling the entire church. The fewer people who know about some sin, the better, because repentance is easier, fewer people are led astray, and less harm is done to the reputation of the person, the reputation of the church, and the reputation of Christ.[16]

b. Disciplinary Measures Should Increase in Strength Until There Is a Solution: Once again in Matthew 18 Jesus teaches us that we cannot stop simply with a private conversation if that has not brought satisfactory results. He requires that the wronged person first go alone, and then take one or two others (Matt. 18:15–16). Moreover, if a Christian thinks that he or she has wronged someone else (or even if that other person *thinks* that he or she has been wronged), Jesus requires that the person who has done the wrong (or is thought to have done the wrong) go to the person who considers himself the victim of wrongdoing (Matt. 5:23). This means that whether we have been wronged or others think they have been wronged, *it is always our responsibility* to take the initiative and go to the other person. Jesus does not allow us to wait for the other person to come to us.

After a private meeting and a small group meeting, Jesus does not specify that the elders or officers of the church are next to be consulted as a group, but certainly this intermediate step seems to be appropriate, because Jesus may simply be summarizing the process without necessarily mentioning every possible step in it. In fact, there are several examples of small group admonition in the New Testament which are carried out by elders or other church officers (see 1 Thess. 5:12; 2 Tim. 4:2; Titus 1:13; 2:15; 3:10; James 5:19–20). Moreover, the principle of keeping the knowledge of sin to the smallest group possible would certainly encourage this intermediate step as well.

---

[15]One exception was the secret sin of Ananias and Sapphira in Acts 5:1–11. In this situation the Holy Spirit (vv. 3, 8) was so powerfully present that he brought an intrusion of final judgment, when the secrets of all hearts will be disclosed, into the church age, "and great fear came upon the whole church" (v. 11).

[16]However, see section c below on the requirement for public disclosure of the serious sins of a church leader.

Finally, if the situation cannot be resolved Jesus says to "tell it to the church" (Matt. 18:17). In this case the church would be assembled to hear the facts of the case and to come to a decision. Since Jesus allows for the possibility that the person "refuses to listen even to the church" (v. 17), the church may have to meet once to decide what to say to the offender, and then meet again to exclude that person from the fellowship of the church.[17]

When Jesus gives these directions about church discipline, he reminds the church that his own presence and his own power are behind the decisions made by the church: "Again I say to you, if two of you agree on earth about anything they ask, it will be done for them by my Father in heaven. For where two or three are gathered in my name, *there am I in the midst of them*" (Matt. 18:19–20). Jesus promises to be present in church gatherings generally, but specifically here with respect to the church being gathered for discipline of an offending member. And Paul similarly tells the Corinthians to discipline the erring member when they are assembled *"with the power of our Lord Jesus"* (1 Cor. 5:4). This is not an activity to be taken lightly, but is carried out in the presence of the Lord, the spiritual component of it actually being carried out by the Lord himself.

If this ever must be done, the whole church will then know that the erring person is no longer considered a member of the church, and that person would not be allowed to take Communion, since partaking in the Lord's Supper is a sign of partaking in the unity of the church (1 Cor. 10:17: "Because there is one bread, we who are many are one body, *for we all partake of the one bread"*).

There are other passages in the New Testament that speak of avoiding fellowship with the excommunicated person. Paul tells the Corinthians, "I wrote to you *not to associate* with any one who bears the name of brother if he is guilty of immorality or greed, or is an idolater, reviler, drunkard, or robber—not even to eat with such a one" (1 Cor. 5:11). He tells the Thessalonians, "Now we command you, brethren, in the name of our Lord Jesus Christ, that you keep away from any brother who is living in idleness and not in accord with the tradition that you received from us" (2 Thess. 3:6). Moreover, he says, "If any one refuses to obey what we say in this letter, note that man, and have nothing to do with him, that he may be ashamed. Do not look on him as an enemy, but warn him as a brother" (2 Thess. 3:14–15). Second John 10–11 also prohibits greeting or welcoming into the house anyone who is promoting false teaching. These instructions are apparently given to prevent the church from giving to others the impression that it approves of the disobedience of the erring person.

c. Discipline of Church Leaders: In one passage Paul gives special directives concerning the discipline of church elders:

> Never admit any charge *against an elder* except on the evidence of two or three witnesses. As for those who persist in sin, *rebuke them in the presence of all, so that the rest may stand in fear.* In the presence of God and of Christ Jesus and of the elect angels I charge you to keep these rules without favor, doing nothing from partiality. (1 Tim. 5:19–21)

---

[17]1 Cor. 5:4 also requires that the church be assembled for this final step in church discipline.

Paul here gives a special caution to protect elders from individual attacks: action regarding wrongdoing in this case should require the evidence of two or three witnesses. "Those who persist in sin"[18] are to be rebuked *"in the presence of all."* This is because the bad example of wrongful conduct by elders will very likely have a widespread negative effect on others who see their lives. Then Paul reminds Timothy to do "nothing from partiality" in this situation, a very helpful warning, since Timothy was probably a close friend to many of the elders in the church at Ephesus.

Paul's command to rebuke a sinning elder publicly means that some statement of the nature of the offense must be made to the church (*"rebuke them* in the presence of all," v. 20).[19] On the other hand, not every detail of the sin has to be disclosed to the church. A helpful guideline is that the church should be told enough that (1) they will understand how serious the offense was, (2) they will be able to understand and support the discipline process, and (3) they will not subsequently feel the sin was minimized or covered up if more details somehow leak out later.

Such a public disclosure of the sin of a leader will signal to the congregation that the leaders of the church will not hide such matters from them in the future. This will increase the confidence of the church in the integrity of the leadership board. It will also allow the sinning leader to begin the gradual process of rebuilding relationships and trust with the congregation, because he will not have to deal with people who have a hundred different speculations about what his sin was, but with people who know the specific sin, and can see the genuine repentance and change regarding that area of sin in his life.

What about the serious sins of people who are not church leaders? Scripture gives no command to disclose publicly the sins of people who are ordinary members but not recognized leaders in the church. Leaders, however, are treated differently because their lives are to be "above reproach" (1 Tim. 3:2), and their lives should be examples for other Christians to imitate (see 1 Tim. 4:12).[20]

d. Other Aspects of Church Discipline: Once discipline has occurred, as soon as there is repentance at any stage of the process, the Christians who have known about the discipline should welcome the repentant person back quickly into the fellowship of the church. Paul says, "You should rather turn to *forgive and comfort him,* or he may be overwhelmed by excessive sorrow. . . . I beg you to reaffirm your love for him" (2 Cor. 2:7–8; cf. 7:8–11). Once again, our purpose in church discipline should never be to punish out of a desire for vengeance, but always to restore and heal.

The attitude with which discipline is carried out at any stage is also very important. It must be done with gentleness and humility, and with a genuine appreciation for our

---

[18]This is apparently the sense of *tous harmartanontas* in 1 Tim. 5:20, since the present participle gives the sense of continuing in an action over a period of time.

[19]When churches have to discipline a church leader, an easy mistake to make is failing to take Paul's command seriously, and thereby failing to give adequate disclosure to the church of the nature of the sin involved. If that happens, the congregation only hears that a leader was removed from office because of some sin (or maybe a general category of sin is mentioned).

But this is not really an effective public rebuke. Because it is so vague, it will only result in confusion, speculation, and gossip. Moreover, serious divisions can arise in the church because in the absence of information some people will think the discipline process too harsh and others will think it too lenient, and the church will not be united in supporting the process.

[20]I understand "above reproach" to mean that their lives are such that no charge of serious wrongdoing can be rightfully brought against them.

own weakness and with a fear that we might fall into similar sins. "If a man is overtaken in any trespass, you who are spiritual should restore him *in a spirit of gentleness. Look to yourself, lest you too be tempted*" (Gal. 6:1).

It is unwise to set any timetable in advance, telling people how long the discipline process is expected to last. This is because it is impossible for us to predict how long it will be until the Holy Spirit brings about deep, genuine repentance and a change in the condition of the person's heart that led to the sin in the first place.

Finally, we should notice that immediately following the passage on church discipline in Matthew 18:15–20, Jesus strongly teaches the need for personal forgiveness of those who sin against us (Matt. 18:21–35). We are to forgive those who harm us "seventy times seven" (v. 22), and Jesus tells us that our heavenly Father will punish us severely if we do not *forgive our brother from the heart* (v. 35). We should see the passage on church discipline and this passage as complementary, not contradictory. As individuals we must always forgive in our hearts and not bear grudges. Yet we can certainly forgive someone in our hearts and still seek church discipline for the good of the person who is committing a sin, for the good of the church, for the honor of Christ, and because God's Word commands it.

QUESTIONS FOR PERSONAL APPLICATION

1. Have you previously thought of the church as rather weak or rather strong in its influence on the affairs of the world? How has your thinking changed as a result of this chapter? Do you now think there is any hope for transforming society apart from the strong redemptive influence of the church?

2. Have you previously thought of yourself as holding any of the "keys of the kingdom of heaven"? Do you in fact have some of those keys now? What are you doing with them?

3. In what ways could your church exercise its spiritual power against the forces of the enemy more effectively? In what ways could you use this power more effectively yourself?

4. What is the strongest enemy to the effective proclamation of the gospel in your community now? How might the power of the church be used against that enemy?

5. If you accept the principles that the church should not rule the state and the state should not rule over or restrict the freedom of the church, are these principles being played out effectively in your own country or local situation? What could be done to increase conformity to these principles? (Do you agree with these principles?)

6. Are you aware of situations where a gentle word of admonition has resulted in a positive change in your own behavior or the behavior of another Christian? Are you aware of situations where church discipline has gone a step or two further than

this and has resulted in restoration of the erring person? If you are aware of situations where the practice of church discipline has not brought a good result, what could have been done differently to bring about a better result?

7. If a church refuses to carry out church discipline at all for a number of years, even though there is an evident need for it, what will be the harmful results in the church? Are you aware of situations where those harmful results have occurred?

8. Have there been times when you wished that someone would have come to you earlier with a word of admonition or counsel concerning an area of sin that you were unaware of or that you were uncertain about? If so, why didn't that happen?

9. Are there now any relationships in your life where Matthew 5:23 and Matthew 18:15 combine to tell you that you have an obligation to go to another person and seek to make the situation right?

SPECIAL TERMS

binding and loosing
excommunication
keys of the kingdom

power of the church
to take up the sword

BIBLIOGRAPHY

Adams, Jay E. *Handbook of Church Discipline.* Grand Rapids: Ministry Resources Library, 1986.

Bauckham, Richard. *The Bible in Politics: How to Read the Bible Politically.* Louisville: Westminster/John Knox, 1989.

DeKoster, L. "Church Discipline." In *EDT,* p. 238.

Eidsmoe, John. *God and Caesar: Christian Faith and Political Action.* Westchester, Ill.: Crossway, 1984.

Grudem, W. A. "Keys of the Kingdom." In *EDT,* pp. 604–6.

Laney, J. Carl. *A Guide to Church Discipline.* Minneapolis: Bethany, 1985.

Linder, R. D. "Church and State." In *EDT,* pp. 233–38.

Robertson, O. Palmer. "Reflections on New Testament Testimony Concerning Civil Disobedience." *JETS.* Vol. 33, No. 3 (Sept., 1990), pp. 331–51.

Schaeffer, Francis. *A Christian Manifesto.* Westchester, Ill.: Crossway, 1981.

Stott, John R. W. *The Preacher's Portrait: Some New Testament Word Studies.* Grand Rapids: Eerdmans, 1961.

White, John, and Ken Blue. *Church Discipline That Heals: Putting Costly Love into Action.* (First published as *Healing the Wounded.*) Downers Grove, Ill.: InterVarsity Press, 1985.

SCRIPTURE MEMORY PASSAGE

2 Corinthians 10:3 – 4: *For though we live in the world we are not carrying on a worldly war, for the weapons of our warfare are not worldly but have divine power to destroy strongholds.*

HYMN

"Onward Christian Soldiers"

This hymn does not talk about earthly warfare with swords and shields, but with the spiritual warfare of prayer and praise, and the enemies are not earthly unbelievers but Satan and his demonic hosts: "Hell's foundations quiver at the shout of praise;/Brothers, lift your voices, loud your anthems raise."

The hymn pictures the church moving as a worldwide army of God against the forces of Satan, and it proclaims the unity of the church as well: "We are not divided, all one body we, /One in hope and doctrine, one in charity." It is a triumphant, joyful song of spiritual warfare by a church that will not be divided and will not be defeated.

> Onward, Christian soldiers, marching as to war,
>   With the cross of Jesus going on before:
> Christ the royal Master leads against the foe;
>   Forward into battle, see his banners go.
>
> *Refrain:*
> Onward, Christian soldiers, marching as to war,
>   With the cross of Jesus going on before.
>
> At the sign of triumph Satan's host doth flee;
>   On then, Christian soldiers, on to victory:
> Hell's foundations quiver at the shout of praise;
>   Brothers, lift your voices, loud your anthems raise.
>
> Like a mighty army moves the church of God;
>   Brothers, we are treading where the saints have trod;
> We are not divided, all one body we,
>   One in hope and doctrine, one in charity.
>
> Crowns and thrones may perish, kingdoms rise and wane,
>   But the church of Jesus constant will remain;
> Gates of hell can never 'gainst that church prevail;
>   We have Christ's own promise, and that cannot fail.
>
> Onward, then ye people, join our happy throng,
>   Blend with ours your voices in the triumph song;
> Glory, laud, and honor unto Christ the King;
>   This through countless ages men and angels sing.

AUTHOR: SABINE BARING-GOULD, 1865

Chapter 5

CHURCH GOVERNMENT

How should a church be governed?
How should church officers be chosen?
Should women serve as pastors of churches?

EXPLANATION AND SCRIPTURAL BASIS

Churches today have many different forms of government. The Roman Catholic Church has a worldwide government under the authority of the Pope. Episcopalian churches have bishops with regional authority, and archbishops over them. Presbyterian churches grant regional authority to presbyteries and national authority to general assemblies. On the other hand, Baptist churches and many other independent churches have no formal governing authority beyond the local congregation, and affiliation with denominations is on a voluntary basis.

Within local churches, Baptists often have a single pastor with a board of deacons, but some have a board of elders as well. Presbyterians have a board of elders and Episcopalians have a vestry. Other churches simply have a church board.

Is there a New Testament pattern for church government? Is any one form of church government to be preferred over another? These are the questions addressed in this chapter.

However, at the outset it must be said that the form of church government is not a major doctrine like the Trinity, the deity of Christ, substitutionary atonement, or the authority of Scripture. Although I believe, after examining the New Testament evidence, that one particular form of church government is preferable to the others, nevertheless, each form has some weaknesses as well as strengths. And church history attests that several different forms of government have worked fairly well for several centuries. Moreover, while some aspects of church government seem to be reasonably clear from the New Testament, other matters (such as the way in which church officers should be chosen) are less clear, mainly because the New Testament evidence on them is not extensive, and thus our inferences from this evidence are less certain. It seems to me, then, that there ought to be room for evangelical Christians to differ amicably over this question, in the hope that further understanding may be gained. And it also seems that individual Christians—while they may have a preference for one system or another, and while they may wish at appropriate times to argue forcefully for one system over another—should nevertheless be willing to live and minister within any of several different Protestant systems of church government in which they may find themselves from time to time.

But I do not mean to say that this is an entirely unimportant matter. In this area as well as others, a church may be more or less pure. If there are clear New Testament patterns regarding some aspects of church government, then there will be negative consequences in our churches if we disregard them, even if we cannot foresee all of those consequences at the present time. Therefore Christians are certainly free to speak and write on this subject in order to work for increased purity in the church.

In this chapter we shall first survey the New Testament data concerning church officers, especially *apostle, elder,* and *deacon.* Then we shall ask how church officers should be chosen. After that we shall look at two controversial questions: Which form of church government—if any—is closest to the New Testament pattern? And, may women serve as officers in the church?

A. Church Officers

For purposes of this chapter, we will use the following definition: *A church officer is someone who has been publicly recognized as having the right and responsibility to perform certain functions for the benefit of the whole church.*

According to this definition, elders and deacons would be considered officers in a church, as would the pastor (if that is a distinct office). The church treasurer and church moderator would also be officers (these titles may vary from church to church). All of these people have had public recognition, usually at a service in which they are "installed" or "ordained" in an office. In fact, they *need* public recognition in order to fulfill their responsibilities: for example, it would not be appropriate for people to wonder from week to week who was to receive the offering and deposit it in the bank, or for various people to argue that they had been gifted to take that responsibility in any particular week! The orderly functioning of the church requires that one person be recognized as having that responsibility. Similarly, the pastor who is responsible to do Bible teaching each Sunday morning must be recognized as having the right and responsibility to do that (at least, in most forms of church government). If this were not the case, then many people might prepare sermons and all claim the right to preach, or on some Sundays no one might prepare. Similarly, in order for people to follow the elders of the church and look to them for guidance, they must know who the elders are.

By contrast, many other people exercise gifts in the church, but we do not say they have an "office" because they do not need formal public recognition for their gifts to function. Those who have a gift of "helps" (see 1 Cor. 12:28), or who have a gift of especially strong faith, or a gift of "distinguishing between spirits" (1 Cor. 12:10), or a gift of exhorting or contributing (Rom. 12:8) do not need public recognition in order to function effectively in the church.

In the material that follows, we shall see that the New Testament discusses one church office which was limited to the time when the early church was founded (the office of apostle), and two other church offices which continue throughout the church age (the offices of elder and deacon).

1. Apostle. The New Testament *apostles* had a unique kind of authority in the early church: authority to speak and write words which were "words of God" in an absolute sense. To disbelieve or disobey them was to disbelieve or disobey God. The apostles, therefore, had the authority to write words which became words of Scripture. This fact in itself should suggest to us that there was something unique about the office of apostle, and that we would not expect it to continue today, for no one today can add words to the Bible and have them be counted as God's very words or as part of Scripture.

In addition, the New Testament information on the qualifications of an apostle and the identity of the apostles also leads us to conclude that the office was unique and limited to the first century, and that we are to expect no more apostles today.[1] We shall see this as we ask the following questions: What were the requirements for being an apostle? Who were the apostles? How many apostles were there? And are there apostles today?

At the outset it must be made clear that the answers to these questions depend on what one means by the word *apostle*. Today some people use the word *apostle* in a very broad sense, to refer to an effective church planter, or to a significant missionary pioneer ("William Carey was an apostle to India," for example). If we use the word *apostle* in this broad sense, everyone would agree that there are still apostles today—for there are certainly effective missionaries and church planters today.

The New Testament itself has three verses in which the word *apostle* (Gk. *apostolos*) is used in a broad sense, not to refer to any specific church office, but simply to mean "messenger." In Philippians 2:25, Paul calls Epaphroditus "your *messenger* (*apostolos*) and minister to my need"; in 2 Corinthians 8:23, Paul refers to those who accompanied the offering that he was taking to Jerusalem as "*messengers [apostoloi] of the churches*"; and in John 13:16, Jesus says, "Nor is *he who is sent [apostolos]* greater than he who sent him."

But there is another sense for the word *apostle*. Much more frequently in the New Testament the word refers to a special office, "*apostle of Jesus Christ*." In this narrow sense of the term, there are no more apostles today, and we are to expect no more. This is because of what the New Testament says about the qualifications for being an apostle and about who the apostles were.

a. Qualifications of an Apostle: The two qualifications for being an apostle were (1) having seen Jesus after his resurrection with one's own eyes (thus, being an "eyewitness of the resurrection"), and (2) having been specifically commissioned by Christ as his apostle.[2]

---

[1]The material from this point through through the end of section 1 has been taken from Wayne Grudem, *The Gift of Prophecy in the New Testament and Today* (Eastbourne, U.K.: Kingsway, and Westchester, Ill.: Crossway, 1988), pp. 269–76, and is used by permission.

[2]These two qualifications are discussed in detail in the classic essay by J. B. Lightfoot, "The Name and Office of an Apostle," in his commentary, *The Epistle of St. Paul to the Galatians* (first published 1865; repr. Grand Rapids: Zondervan, 1957), pp. 92–101; see also K. H. Rengstorf, "*apostolos*," *TDNT*, 1:398–447.

The fact that an apostle had to have seen the risen Lord with his own eyes is indicated by Acts 1:22, where Peter said that person to replace Judas "must become with us *a witness to his resurrection*." Moreover, it was "to the apostles whom he had chosen" that "he presented himself alive after his passion by many proofs, appearing to them during forty days" (Acts 1:2–3; cf. 4:33).

Paul makes much of the fact that he did meet this qualification even though it was in an unusual way (Christ appeared to him in a vision on the road to Damascus and appointed him as an apostle: Acts 9:5–6; 26:15–18). When he is defending his apostleship he says, "Am I not an apostle? *Have I not seen Jesus our Lord?*" (1 Cor. 9:1). And when recounting the people to whom Christ appeared after his resurrection, Paul says, "Then *he appeared to James,* then *to all the apostles.* Last of all, as to one untimely born, *he appeared also to me.* For I am the least of the apostles, unfit to be called an apostle" (1 Cor. 15:7–9).

These verses combine to indicate that unless someone had seen Jesus after the resurrection with his own eyes, he could not be an apostle.

The second qualification, specific appointment by Christ as an apostle, is also evident from several verses. First, though the term *apostle* is not common in the gospels, the twelve disciples are called "apostles" specifically in a context where Jesus is commissioning them, "sending them out" to preach in his name:

> And he called to him his twelve disciples and gave them authority over unclean spirits, to cast them out, and to heal every disease and every infirmity. The names of the twelve *apostles* are these. . . . *These twelve Jesus sent out,* charging them, ". . . preach as you go, saying, 'The kingdom of heaven is at hand.'" (Matt. 10:1–7)

Similarly, Jesus commissions his apostles in a special sense to be his "witnesses . . . to the end of the earth" (Acts 1:8). And in choosing another apostle to replace Judas, the eleven apostles did not take the responsibility on themselves, but prayed and asked the ascended Christ to make the appointment:

> "Lord, who knows the hearts of all men, *show which one of these two you have chosen* to take the place in this ministry and apostleship from which Judas turned aside. . . ." And they cast lots for them, and the lot fell on Matthias; and he was enrolled with the eleven apostles. (Acts 1:24–26)

Paul himself insists that Christ personally appointed him as an apostle. He tells how, on the Damascus Road, Jesus told him that he was appointing him as an apostle to the Gentiles: "I have appeared to you for this purpose, to appoint you to serve and to bear witness . . . delivering you from the people and from the Gentiles—to whom I send you" (Acts 26:16–17). He later affirms that he was specifically appointed by Christ as an apostle (see Rom. 1:1; Gal. 1:1; 1 Tim. 1:12; 2:7; 2 Tim. 1:11).

b. Who Were Apostles? The initial group of apostles numbered twelve—the eleven original disciples who remained after Judas died, plus Matthias, who replaced Judas: "And they cast lots for them, and the lot fell on Matthias; and *he was enrolled with the* *eleven apostles"* (Acts 1:26). So important was this original group of twelve apostles, the "charter members" of the office of apostle, that we read that their names are inscribed on the foundations of the heavenly city, the New Jerusalem: "And the wall of the city had twelve foundations, and on them *the twelve names of the twelve apostles of the Lamb"* (Rev. 21:14).

We might at first think that such a group could never be expanded, that no one could be added to it. But then Paul clearly claims that he, also, is an apostle. And Acts 14:14 calls both Barnabas and Paul apostles: "when *the apostles Barnabas and Paul* heard of it. . . ." So with Paul and Barnabas there are fourteen "apostles of Jesus Christ."[3]

Then James the brother of Jesus (who was not one of the twelve original disciples) seems to be called an apostle in Galatians 1:19: Paul tells how, when he went to Jerusalem, "I saw none of *the other apostles* except James the Lord's brother."[4] Then in Galatians 2:9 James is classified with Peter and John as "pillars" of the Jerusalem church. And in Acts 15:13–21, James, along with Peter, exercises a significant leadership function in the Jerusalem Council, a function which would be appropriate to the office of apostle. Furthermore, when Paul is listing the resurrection appearances of Jesus he once again readily classifies James with the apostles:

> Then he appeared *to James,* then *to all the apostles.* Last of all, as to one untimely born, he appeared also to me. For I am the least of the apostles, unfit to be called an apostle, because I persecuted the church of God. (1 Cor. 15:7–9)

Finally, the fact that James could write the New Testament epistle which bears his name would also be entirely consistent with his having the authority which belonged to the office of apostle, the authority to write words which were the words of God. All these considerations combine to indicate that James the Lord's brother was also commissioned by Christ as an apostle. That would bring the number to fifteen "apostles of Jesus Christ" (the twelve plus Paul, Barnabas, and James).

Were there more than these fifteen? There may possibly have been a few more, though we know little if anything about them, and it is not certain that there were any more. Others, of course, had seen Jesus after his resurrection ("Then he appeared to more than five hundred brethren at one time," 1 Cor. 15:6). From this large group it is possible that

---

[3]If the apostles' writings were accepted as Scripture, someone may wonder why the extrabiblical document called *The Epistle of Barnabas* is not included in Scripture. The answer is that nearly unanimous scholarly opinion has concluded that it was not written by Barnabas, but by some unknown Christian who probably lived in Alexandria between A.D. 70 and 100. The epistle claims that much of the Old Testament, including animal sacrifices, much of the Mosaic law, and the construction of a physical temple, were mistakes that were contrary to God's will (see ODCC, p. 134). (Text and translation are found in Kirsopp Lake, translator, *The Apostolic Fathers* [Cambridge, Mass.: Harvard University Press, and London: Heinemann, 1970], 1:335–409).

[4]It is not absolutely necessary to translate the verse this way, including James among the apostles. (The NIV reads, "I saw none of the other apostles—only James, the Lord's brother.") Yet the translation "except James the Lord's brother" seems clearly preferable, because (1) the Greek phrase is *ei mē,* which ordinarily means "except" (BAGD, p. 22, 8a), and in the great majority of New Testament uses designates something that is part of the previous group but is "excepted" from it; and (2) in the context of Gal. 1:18, it would not make much sense for Paul to say that when he went to Jerusalem he saw Peter, and no other people except James—or Peter, and no other church leaders except James—for he stayed there "fifteen days" (Gal. 1:18). So he must mean he saw Peter, and *no other apostles* except James. But this classifies James with the apostles. See discussion in E. D. Burton, *The Epistle to the Galatians,* ICC (Edinburgh: T. & T. Clark, 1920), p. 60. (Burton says, "*ei mē* means here, as always before a noun, 'except'" [ibid.].)

Christ appointed some others as apostles—but it is also very possible that he did not. The evidence is not sufficient to decide the issue.

Romans 16:7 says, "Greet *Andronicus and Junias,* my kinsmen and my fellow prisoners; they are *men of note among the apostles,* and they were in Christ before me." Because there are several translation problems in the verse, no clear conclusions can be reached. "Men of note" may be also translated "men noted by" (the apostles). "Junias" (a man's name) may also be translated "Junia" (a woman's name).[5] "Apostles" here may not mean the office "apostles of Jesus Christ," but may simply mean "messengers" (the broader sense which the word takes in Phil. 2:25; 2 Cor. 8:23; John 13:16). The verse has too little clear information to allow us to draw a conclusion.

Others have been suggested as apostles. Silas (Silvanus) and sometimes Timothy are mentioned because of 1 Thessalonians 2:6: "though *we* might have made demands *as apostles of Christ.*" Does Paul include Silas and Timothy here, since the letter begins, "Paul, Silvanus, and Timothy" (1 Thess. 1:1)?

It is not likely that Paul is including Timothy in this statement, for two reasons. (1) He says just four verses earlier, "we had already suffered and been shamefully treated at Philippi, as you know" (1 Thess. 2:2), but this refers to the beating and imprisonment which happened just to Paul and Silas, not to Timothy (Acts 16:19). So the "we" in verse 6 does not seem to include all of the people (Paul, Silvanus, Timothy) mentioned in the first verse. The letter in general is from Paul, Silas and Timothy, but Paul knows that the readers will naturally understand the appropriate members of the "we" statements when he does not mean to include all three of them in certain sections of the letter. He does not specify "we—that is, Silas and I—had already suffered and been shamefully treated at Philippi, as you know," because the Thessalonians will know who the "we" are that he is talking about.

(2) This is also seen in 1 Thessalonians 3:1–2, where the "we" certainly cannot include Timothy:

> Therefore when we could bear it no longer, we were willing to be left behind at Athens alone, and *we sent Timothy,* our brother and God's servant in the gospel of Christ, to establish you in your faith and to exhort you. (1 Thess. 3:1–2)

In this case, the "we" refers either to Paul and Silas, or else just to Paul alone (see Acts 17:14–15; 18:5). Apparently Silas and Timothy had come to Paul in Athens "as soon as possible" (Acts 17:15)—though Luke does not mention their arrival in Athens—and

---

[5]For an extensive discussion of whether to translate "Junias" or "Junia" here, see John Piper and Wayne Grudem, eds., *Recovering Biblical Manhood and Womanhood* (Wheaton: Crossway, 1991), pp. 79–81, 214, 221–22. Some have claimed that Junia was a common woman's name in ancient Greece, but this is incorrect, at least in written Greek literature: A computer search of 2,889 ancient Greek authors over thirteen centuries (ninth century B.C.–fifth century A.D.) turned up only two examples of Junia as a woman's name, one in Plutarch (c. A.D. 50–c. 120) and one in the church father Chrysostom (A.D. 347–407), who referred to Junia as a woman in a sermon on Rom. 16:7. It is not common as a man's name either, since this search found only one example of Junias as a man's name, in Epiphanius (A.D. 315–403), bishop of Salimis in Cyprus, who refers to Junias in Rom. 16:7 and says he became bishop of Apameia in Syria (*Index of Disciples* 125.19–20; this quotation is the most significant, since Epiphanius knows more information about Junias). The Latin text of the church father Origen (d. A.D. 252) also refers to Junias in Rom. 16:7 as a man (J. P. Migne, *Patrologia Graeca,* vol. 14, col. 1289). Therefore the available data give some support to the view that Junias was a man, but the information is too sparse to be conclusive.

Paul had sent them back to Thessalonica again to help the church there. Then he himself went to Corinth, and they later joined him there (Acts 18:5).

It is most likely that "*We* were willing to be left behind at Athens alone" (1 Thess. 3:1), refers to Paul alone, both because he picks up the argument again in verse 5 with the singular "I" ("When I could bear it no longer, I sent that I might know your faith," 1 Thess. 3:5), and because the point concerning extreme loneliness in Athens would not be made if Silas had stayed with him.[6] In fact, in the previous paragraph, Paul means "I," for he says, "We wanted to come to you — I, Paul, again and again — but Satan hindered us" (1 Thess. 2:18). Apparently he is using "we" more frequently in this epistle as a courteous way of including Silas and Timothy, who had spent so much time in the Thessalonian church, in the letter to that church. But the Thessalonians would have had little doubt who was really in charge of this great mission to the Gentiles, and on whose apostolic authority the letter primarily (or exclusively) depended.

So it is just possible that Silas was himself an apostle, and that 1 Thessalonians 2:6 hints at that. He was a leading member of the Jerusalem church (Acts 15:22), and could well have seen Jesus after his resurrection, and then been appointed as an apostle. But we cannot be very certain.

The situation with Timothy is different, however. Just as he is excluded from the "we" of 1 Thessalonians 2:2 (and 3:1–2), so he seems to be excluded from the "we" of 1 Thessalonians 2:6. Moreover, as a native of Lystra (Acts 16:1–3) who had learned of Christ from his grandmother and mother (2 Tim. 1:5), it seems impossible that he would have been in Jerusalem before Pentecost and would there have seen the risen Lord and come to believe in him, and then suddenly have been appointed as an apostle. In addition, *Paul's pattern of address in his letters always jealously guards the title "apostle" for himself,* never allowing it to be applied to Timothy or others of his traveling companions (note 2 Cor. 1:1; Col. 1:1: "*Paul, an apostle* of Christ Jesus . . . *and Timothy our brother*"; and then Phil. 1:1: "*Paul and Timothy, servants* of Christ Jesus"). So Timothy, as important a role as he had, should not rightly be considered one of the apostles.

This gives us a limited but somewhat imprecisely numbered group who had the office "apostles of Jesus Christ." There seem to have been at least fifteen, and perhaps sixteen or even a few more who are not recorded in the New Testament.

Yet it seems quite certain that there were none appointed after Paul. When Paul lists the resurrection appearances of Christ, he emphasizes the unusual way in which Christ appeared to him, and connects that with the statement that this was the "last" appearance of all, and that he himself is indeed "the least of the apostles, unfit to be called an apostle."

> He appeared to Cephas (Peter), then to the twelve. Then he appeared to more than five hundred brethren at one time, most of whom are still alive, though some have fallen asleep. Then he appeared to James, then to all the apostles. *Last*

---

[6]See the discussion in Leon Morris, *The First and Second Epistles to the Thessalonians,* NIC (Grand Rapids: Eerdmans, 1959), pp. 98–99. Morris says, "The practice in this epistle differs somewhat from that in the Pauline epistles generally. The plural is used almost throughout, whereas in most of his letters Paul prefers the singular" (p. 98; cf. pp. 46–47). Morris takes the plurals here to refer only to Paul himself.

of all, as to one untimely born, *he appeared also to me.* For I am the least of the apostles, unfit to be called an apostle. (1 Cor. 15:5–9)

c. Summary: The word *apostle* can be used in a broad or narrow sense. In a broad sense, it just means "messenger" or "pioneer missionary." But in a narrow sense, the most common sense in the New Testament, it refers to a specific office, "apostle of Jesus Christ." These apostles had unique authority to found and govern the early church, and they could speak and write words of God. Many of their written words became the New Testament Scriptures.

In order to qualify as an apostle, someone (1) had to have seen Christ with his own eyes after he rose from the dead, and (2) had to have been specifically appointed by Christ as an apostle. There was a limited number of apostles, perhaps fifteen or sixteen or a few more—the New Testament is not explicit on the number. The twelve original apostles (the eleven plus Matthias) were joined by Barnabas and Paul, very probably James, perhaps Silas, and maybe even Andronicus and Junias or a few unnamed others. It seems that no apostles were appointed after Paul, and certainly, since no one today can meet the qualification of having seen the risen Christ with his own eyes, there are no apostles today.[7] In place of living apostles present in the church to teach and govern it, we have instead the writings of the apostles in the books of the New Testament. Those New Testament Scriptures fulfill for the church today the absolutely authoritative teaching and governing functions which were fulfilled by the apostles themselves during the early years of the church.

Though some may use the word *apostle* in English today to refer to very effective church planters or evangelists, it seems inappropriate and unhelpful to do so, for it simply confuses people who read the New Testament and see the high authority that is attributed to the office of "apostle" there. It is noteworthy that no major leader in the history of the church—not Athanasius or Augustine, not Luther or Calvin, not Wesley or Whitefield—has taken to himself the title of "apostle" or let himself be called an apostle. If any in modern times want to take the title "apostle" to themselves, they immediately raise the suspicion that they may be motivated by inappropriate pride and desires for

---

[7]Someone may object that Christ could appear to someone today and appoint that person as an apostle. But the foundational nature of the office of apostle (Eph. 2:20; Rev. 21:14) and the fact that Paul views himself as the last one whom Christ appeared to and appointed as an apostle ("last of all, as to one untimely born," 1 Cor. 15:8), indicate that this will not happen. Moreover, God's purpose in the history of redemption seems to have been to give apostles only at the beginning of the church age (see Eph. 2:20).

Another objection to the idea that there are no apostles today, one that comes especially from people in the charismatic movement, is the argument that the "fivefold ministry" of Eph. 4:11 should continue today, and we should have (1) apostles, (2) prophets, (3) evangelists, (4) pastors, and (5) teachers, since Paul says that Christ "gave some as apostles, and some as prophets, and some as evangelists, and some as pastors and teachers" (Eph. 4:11 NASB).

However, Eph. 4:11 talks about a one-time event in the past (note the aorist *kai edōken,* "and he *gave*"), when Christ ascended into heaven (vv. 8–10) and then at Pentecost poured out initial giftings on the church, giving the church apostles, prophets, evangelists, and pastor-teachers (or pastors and teachers). Whether or not Christ would later give more people for each of these offices *cannot be decided from this verse alone,* but must be decided based on other New Testament teachings on the nature of these offices and whether they were expected to continue. In fact, we see that there were many prophets, evangelists, and pastor-teachers established by Christ throughout all of the early churches, but there was only one more apostle given after this initial time (Paul, "last of all," in unusual circumstances on the Damascus Road).

self-exaltation, along with excessive ambition and a desire for much more authority in the church than any one person should rightfully have.

2. Elder (Pastor/Overseer/Bishop).

a. Plural Elders: The Pattern in All New Testament Churches: The next church office to be considered is that of "elder." Although some have argued that different forms of church government are evident in the New Testament,[8] a survey of the relevant texts shows the opposite to be true: there is quite a consistent pattern of *plural elders* as the main governing group in New Testament churches. For instance, in Acts 14:23 we read, "And when they had appointed *elders*[9] for them in every church, with prayer and fasting, they committed them to the Lord in whom they believed." This is on Paul's first missionary journey, when he is returning through the cities of Lystra, Iconium, and Antioch. It indicates that Paul's normal procedure from the time of his first missionary journey was to establish a group of elders in each church shortly after the church began. We know that Paul also established elders in the church at Ephesus, for we read, "From Miletus he sent to Ephesus and called to him the *elders* of the church" (Acts 20:17). Moreover, Paul's apostolic assistants apparently were instructed to carry out a similar process, for Paul wrote to Titus, "This is why I left you in Crete, that you might amend what was defective, and *appoint elders in every town* as I directed you" (Titus 1:5). Shortly after a church has been established, once again we see elders being established in office, in "every town" in which there was a church. And Paul reminded Timothy of the time "when the *elders* laid their hands upon you" (1 Tim. 4:14).

James writes, "Is any among you sick? Let him call for the *elders* of the church, and let them pray over him, anointing him with oil in the name of the Lord" (James 5:14). This is a significant statement because the epistle of James is a general letter written to many churches, all the believers scattered abroad, whom James characterizes as "the twelve tribes in the Dispersion" (James 1:1). It indicates that James expected that there would be elders *in every New Testament church to which his general epistle went*—that is, in *all the churches in existence at that time.*

A similar conclusion can be drawn from 1 Peter. Peter writes, "So I exhort the *elders* among you. . . . Tend the flock of God that is your charge . . ." (1 Peter 5:1–2). First Peter is also a general epistle, written to dozens of churches scattered throughout four Roman provinces in Asia Minor (see 1 Peter 1:1; Bithynia and Pontus constituted one Roman province). Far from expecting different kinds of church government when he was writing (around A.D. 62, more than thirty years after Pentecost), Peter assumes that *all* these churches, whether founded by Paul or by others, whether predominantly Gentile or predominantly Jewish or evenly divided in their make-up, would have elders leading them. Moreover, there were elders in the Jerusalem church (Acts 11:30; 15:2), and, though the word *elders* is not used, there is a plurality of leaders in the congregation to which the epistle to the Hebrews is directed, for the author says, "Obey your leaders and submit to

---

[8]See, for example, Millard Erickson, *Christian Theology,* (Grand Rapids: Baker, 1983–85), p. 1084.

[9]The word translated "elder" in the New Testament is the Greek word *presbyteros,* which also was used in other contexts to mean simply an older person.

them; for they are keeping watch over your souls, as men who will have to give account" (Heb. 13:17).

Two significant conclusions may be drawn from this survey of the New Testament evidence. First, no passage suggests that any church, no matter how small, had only one elder. The consistent New Testament pattern is a plurality of elders "in every church" (Acts 14:23) and "in every town" (Titus 1:5).[10] Second, we do not see a diversity of forms of government in the New Testament church, but a unified and consistent pattern in which every church had elders governing it and keeping watch over it (Acts 20:28; Heb. 13:17; 1 Peter 5:2–3).

b. Other Names for Elders: Pastors, Overseers, Bishops: Elders are also called "pastors" or "bishops" or "overseers" in the New Testament. The least commonly used word (at least in the noun form) is *pastor* (Gk. *poimēn*). It may be surprising to us to find that this word, which has become so common in English, only occurs once in the New Testament when speaking about a church officer. In Ephesians 4:11, Paul writes, "And his gifts were that some should be apostles, some prophets, some evangelists, some *pastors* and teachers." The verse is probably better translated "pastor-teachers" (one group) rather than "pastors and teachers" (suggesting two groups) because of the Greek construction (though not every New Testament scholar agrees with that translation).[11] The connection with teaching suggests that these pastors were some (or perhaps all) of the elders who carried on the work of teaching, for one qualification for an elder is that he be "able to teach" (1 Tim. 3:2).

Although the noun *pastor* (*poimēn*) is not used of church officers elsewhere in the New Testament,[12] the related verb which means "to act as a shepherd" or "to act as a pastor" (Gk. *poimainō*) is applied to elders in Paul's address to the Ephesian elders. He tells them "to *shepherd* the church of God" (Acts 20:28, literally translating the verb *poimainō*), and in the same sentence he referred to God's people as "all the *flock*," using another related noun (Gk. *poimnion*) which means "a flock of sheep." So Paul directly charges these Ephesian elders to act as shepherds or "pastors."[13]

The same verb is used in 1 Peter 5:2 where Peter tells the elders to "*shepherd* (*poimainō*) the flock of God that is your charge" (author's translation). Then two verses later Jesus is

---

[10]Some have suggested that perhaps there was one elder in every "house church" in a town, and that all of those elders from the different house churches together constituted the elders that Titus was to appoint in each town. If this was true, perhaps some support could be given for the idea of one pastor ("elder") over every church.

In response to this suggestion, we must note that this is a theory without any evidence to support it, for no verse in the New Testament hints at the idea that there was one elder in each "house church." In terms of supporting evidence, this suggestion stands in the same category as the statement, "Perhaps all the elders in Crete were blind in the left eye." Of course, scholars can say "perhaps" to any event for which there is no evidence, but such statements should carry no weight in our attempts to determine what pattern of church government actually existed in the first century.

[11]The phrase "some pastors and teachers" has one definite article in front of two nouns joined by *kai* ("and"), a construction that always in Greek indicates that the two nouns are viewed by the writer as unified in some way. This construction often is used where two nouns refer to the same person or thing, but it is sometimes used of two different persons or groups viewed as a unity. In either case, the phrase ties together "pastors" and "teachers" more closely than any other titles.

[12]It is used several times to speak of a "shepherd" who cares for his sheep, however.

[13]The English word *pastor* is derived from a Latin term that means "one who cares for sheep," and the English word *pastor* earlier meant "shepherd" in the literal sense of one who took care of sheep (see *Oxford English Dictionary*, Vol. P, p. 542).

called the chief pastor or "chief shepherd" (Gk. *archipoimēn*, 1 Peter 5:4), implying quite clearly that Peter also viewed the elders as shepherds or "pastors" in the church. Therefore, although the noun *pastor* is only used once to refer to elders, the related verb is used twice in passages that explicitly identify the task of shepherding with the office of elder.

Another term used for elders in the New Testament is a Greek word *episkopos*, which is variously translated as "overseer" or "bishop," depending on the individual passage and the English translation.[14] But this word also seems quite clearly to be another term for elders in New Testament usage. For example, when Paul has called to him the *elders* of the church at Ephesus (Acts 20:17), he says to them, "Take heed to yourselves and to all the flock, in which the Holy Spirit has made you *overseers* (Gk. *episkopos*)" (Acts 20:28). Paul quite readily refers to these Ephesian elders as "overseers" (or "bishops").

In 1 Timothy 3:1–2, Paul writes, "If any one aspires to the office of *bishop,* he desires a noble task. Now a bishop must be above reproach. . . ." We must remember that Paul is writing to Timothy when Timothy is at Ephesus (see 1 Tim. 1:3, "remain at Ephesus") and we already know from Acts 20 that there are *elders* at Ephesus (Acts 20:17–38). Furthermore, in 1 Timothy 5:17, we see that elders were ruling the church at Ephesus when Timothy was there, because it says, "Let the *elders who rule well* be considered worthy of double honor." Now the "bishops" in 1 Timothy 3:1–2 *also* are to rule over the church at Ephesus because one qualification is that "He must manage his own household well . . . for if a man does not know how to manage his own household, how can he care for God's church?" (1 Tim. 3:4–5). So here it also seems that "bishop" or "overseer" is simply another term for "elder," since these "bishops" fulfill the same function as elders quite clearly do elsewhere in this epistle and in Acts 20.

In Titus 1:5, Paul tells Titus to "appoint *elders* in every town" and gives some qualifications (v. 6). Then in the very next sentence (v. 7), he gives reasons for those qualifications, and he begins by saying, "For a *bishop,* as God's steward, must be blameless." Here again he uses the word "bishop" to refer to the elders whom Titus was to appoint, giving another indication that the terms *elder* and *bishop* were interchangeable.

Finally, in Philippians 1:1, Paul writes "To all the saints in Christ Jesus who are at Philippi, with the *bishops* and deacons." Here it also seems appropriate to think that "bishops" is another name for "elders," because there certainly were elders at Philippi, since it was Paul's practice to establish elders in every church (see Acts 14:23). And if there were elders ruling in the church at Philippi, it is unthinkable that Paul would write to the church and single out bishops and deacons—but not elders—if their offices were both different from that of the elders. Therefore, by "bishops and deacons" Paul must have meant the same thing as "elders and deacons."[15] Although in some parts of the church from the second century A.D. onward, the word *bishop* has been used to refer to a single individual with authority over several churches, this was a later development of the term and is not found in the New Testament itself.

---

[14]The NIV regularly uses "overseer" instead of "bishop" to translate *episkopos*.

[15]Even the Anglican scholar J. B. Lightfoot, says, "It is a fact now generally recognised by theologians of all shades of opinion, that in the language of the New Testament the same officer in the Church is called indifferently 'bishop' (*episkopos*) and 'elder' or 'presbyter' (*presbyteros*)" (*St. Paul's Epistle to the Philippians* [Grand Rapids: Zondervan, 1953; first published 1868], p. 95; on pp. 95–99 Lightfoot discusses the data to support this conclusion).

c. The Functions of Elders: One of the major roles of elders in the New Testament is to govern the New Testament churches. In 1 Timothy 5:17 we read, "Let the elders who *rule* well be considered worthy of double honor." Earlier in the same epistle Paul says that an overseer (or elder) "must manage his own household well, keeping his children submissive and respectful in every way; for if a man does not know how to manage his own household, how can he care for God's church?" (1 Tim. 3:4–5).

Peter also indicates a ruling function for elders when he exhorts them:

> Tend the flock of God that is your charge, not by constraint but willingly, not for shameful gain but eagerly, not as domineering over those in your charge but being examples to the flock. And when the chief Shepherd is manifested you will obtain the unfading crown of glory. Likewise you that are younger be subject to the elders. (1 Peter 5:2–5)

The fact that they are to act as shepherds of the flock of God, and the fact that they are not to domineer (that is, not to rule harshly or oppressively) strongly suggest that elders have ruling or governing functions in the churches to which Peter is writing. This is consistent with his charge that especially those who are younger should "be subject to the elders" (v. 5).[16]

Although Hebrews 13:17 does not name elders, certainly there are some church officers with governing authority over the church, for the author says, "*Obey your leaders and submit to them;* for they are keeping watch over your souls, as men who will have to give account." Since the New Testament gives no indication of any other officers in the church with this kind of authority, it is reasonable to conclude that the congregation is to submit to and obey its elders. (This conclusion is also consistent with the description of responsibilities Paul gives to the Ephesian elders in Acts 20:28.)

In addition to governing responsibility, elders also seem to have had some *teaching responsibilities* in the New Testament churches. In Ephesians 4:11, elders are referred to as "pastor-teachers" (or, on an alternative translation, pastors who are viewed as quite closely united to teachers). And in 1 Timothy 3:2, an overseer (elder) must be "an *apt teacher.*" Then in 1 Timothy 5:17, Paul says, "Let the elders who rule well be considered worthy of double honor, especially those who labor in *preaching and teaching.*" Here Paul seems to imply that there is a special group of elders who "labor in preaching and teaching." This means at least that there are some among the elders who give more time to the activities of preaching and teaching, and may even mean that there are some who "labor" in the sense of earning their living from that preaching and teaching. The same conclusions can be drawn from Titus, where Paul says that an elder "must hold firm to the sure word as taught, so that he may be *able to give instruction* in sound doctrine and also to confute those who contradict it" (Titus 1:9).[17]

---

[16]For a defense of the view that church officers and not just older people are referred to in 1 Peter 5:5, see Wayne Grudem, *1 Peter,* TNTC (Grand Rapids: Eerdmans, 1988), pp. 192–93.

[17]Paul never says that all the elders are to be able to teach publicly or to preach sermons to the congregation, and it would be reasonable to think that an "apt teacher" could be someone who is able to explain God's Word privately. So perhaps not all elders are called to do public teaching—perhaps not all have gifts for teaching in that specific way. What is clear here is that Paul wants to guarantee that elders have a mature and sound understanding of Scripture and can explain it to others.

Elders, then, had responsibility to rule and to teach in New Testament churches.

d. Qualifications for Elders: When Paul lists the qualifications for elders, it is significant that he combines requirements concerning character traits and heart attitudes with requirements that cannot be fulfilled in a short time but will only become evident over a period of several years of faithful Christian living:

> Now a bishop must be above reproach, the husband of one wife, temperate, sensible, dignified, hospitable, an apt teacher, no drunkard, not violent but gentle, not quarrelsome, and no lover of money. He must manage his own household well, keeping his children submissive and respectful in every way; for if a man does not know how to manage his own household, how can he care for God's church? He must not be a recent convert, or he may be puffed up with conceit and fall into the condemnation of the devil; moreover he must be well thought of by outsiders, or he may fall into reproach and the snare of the devil. (1 Tim. 3:2–7)

Similar but differently worded qualifications are found in Titus 1:6–9, where Paul says that Titus is to appoint elders in every town:

> If any man is blameless, the husband of one wife, and his children are believers and not open to the charge of being profligate or insubordinate. For a bishop, as God's steward, must be blameless; he must not be arrogant or quick-tempered or a drunkard or violent or greedy for gain, but hospitable, a lover of goodness, master of himself, upright, holy, and self-controlled; he must hold firm to the sure word as taught, so that he may be able to give instruction in sound doctrine and also to confute those who contradict it. (Titus 1:6–9)

Those who are choosing elders in churches today would do well to look carefully at candidates in the light of these qualifications, and to look for these character traits and patterns of godly living rather than worldly achievement, fame, or success. Especially in churches in western industrial societies, there seems to be a tendency to think that success in the world of business (or law, or medicine, or government) is an indication of suitability for the office of elder, but this is not the teaching of the New Testament. It reminds us that elders are to be "examples to the flock" in their daily lives, and that would certainly include their own personal relationships with God in Bible reading, prayer, and worship. Just as Paul could say, "*Be imitators of me,* as I am of Christ" (1 Cor. 11:1; cf. 2 Tim. 3:10–11), and just as he could command Timothy to "*set the believers an example* in speech and conduct, in love, in faith, in purity" (1 Tim. 4:12), and just as he could tell Titus, "Show yourself in all respects a *model of good deeds,* and in your teaching show integrity, gravity, and sound speech that cannot be censured" (Titus 2:7), so the pattern is to be continued in the lives of all church leaders today. It is not optional that their lives be examples for others to follow; it is a requirement.

e. What Is the Meaning of "Husband of One Wife"? The qualification *"the husband of one wife"* (1 Tim. 3:2; Titus 1:6) has been understood in different ways. Some people have thought that it excludes from the office of elder men who have been divorced and have then married someone else, since they have then been the husband of two wives. But this does not seem to be a correct understanding of these verses. A better interpretation is that Paul was prohibiting a polygamist (a man who *presently* has more than one wife) from being an elder. Several reasons support this view: (1) All the other qualifications listed by Paul refer to a man's *present status,* not his entire past life. For example, 1 Timothy 3:1–7 does not mean "one who has *never been* violent," but "one who is *not now* violent, but gentle." It does not mean "one who has *never been* a lover of money," but "one who is *not now* a lover of money." It does not mean "one who has been above reproach for his whole life," but "one who is now above reproach." If we made these qualifications apply to one's entire past life, then we would exclude from office almost everyone who became a Christian as an adult, for it is doubtful that any non-Christian could meet these qualifications.

(2) Paul could have said "having been married only once" if he had wanted to, but he did not.[18] (3) We should not prevent remarried widowers from being elders, but that would be necessary if we take the phrase to mean "having been married only once." The qualifications for elders are all based on a man's moral and spiritual character, and there is nothing in Scripture to suggest that a man who remarried after his wife had died has lower moral or spiritual qualifications.[19] (4) Polygamy was possible in the first century. Although it was not common, polygamy was practiced, especially among the Jews. The Jewish historian Josephus says, "For it is an ancestral custom of ours to have several wives at the same time."[20] Rabbinic legislation also regulated inheritance customs and other aspects of polygamy.[21]

Therefore it is best to understand "the husband of one wife" to prohibit a polygamist from holding the office of elder. The verses say nothing about divorce and remarriage with respect to qualifications for church office.

f. The Public Installation of Elders: In connection with the discussion of elders Paul says, "Do not be hasty in the laying on of hands" (1 Tim. 5:22). Although the context

[18]The Greek expression for "having been married only once" would be *hapax gegamēmenos,* using the word "once" (*hapax*) plus a perfect participle, giving the sense, "having been married once and continuing in the state resulting from that marriage." (Such a construction is found, for example, in Heb. 10:2, and a similar construction is found in Heb. 9:26. Related expressions with aorist verbs are found in Heb. 6:4; 9:28; and Jude 3.)

Another way Paul could have expressed the idea of having been married only once is using a perfect participle of *ginomai* to say "having been a husband of one wife" (*gegonōs mias gunaikos anēr*). This is, in fact, the force of the requirement for widows in 1 Tim. 5:9, "having been the wife of one husband" (the force of the perfect participle *gegonuia* carries over from the previous phrase, and all the qualifications for enrolling widows in 1 Tim. 5:9–10 speak of past history in their lives). But in 1 Tim. 3:2 and Titus 1:6 the sense is different, because present tense forms of *eimi* ("to be") are used: (literally) "It is necessary for a bishop *to be* blameless, the husband of one wife. . . ."

[19]Some interpreters in the early church did try to exclude remarried widowers from church office (see, for example, *Apostolic Constitutions* 2.2; 6.17 [third or fourth century A.D.], and *Apostolic Canons* 17 [fourth or fifth century A.D.]), but these statements reflect not a biblical perspective but a false asceticism which held that celibacy in general was superior to marriage. (These texts can be found in the *Ante-Nicene Fathers* series, 7:396, 457, and 501.)

However, Chrysostom (d. A.D. 407) understood 1 Tim. 3:2 to prohibit polygamy, not second marriages after death or divorce (see his *Homilies* on 1 Tim. 3:2).

[20]Josephus, *Antiquities* 17.14; in 17.19 he lists the nine women who were married to King Herod at the same time.

[21]See Mishnah, *Yebamoth* 4:11; *Ketuboth* 10:1, 4, 5; *Sanhedrin* 2:4; *Kerithoth* 3:7; *Kiddushin* 2:7; *Bechoroth* 8:4. Other evidence on Jewish polygamy is found in Justin Martyr, *Dialogue with Trypho,* chapter 134. Evidence for polygamy among non-Jews is not as extensive but is indicated in Herodotus (d. 420 B.C.) 1.135; 4.155; 2 Macc. 4:30 (about 170 B.C.); Tertullian, *Apology* 46.

does not specify a process of selection of elders, the immediately preceding context (1 Tim. 5:17–21) deals entirely with elders, and laying on of hands would be an appropriate ceremony for setting someone apart to the office of elder (note the laying on of hands to ordain or establish people in certain offices or tasks in Acts 6:6; 13:3; 1 Tim. 4:14). Therefore the setting apart of elders seems the most likely possibility for the action Paul has in mind. In this case he would be saying, "Do not be hasty in ordaining people as elders." This would be consistent with a process whereby deacons also are to be "tested first; then if they prove themselves blameless let them serve as deacons" (1 Tim. 3:10). Although Paul did ordain elders quite soon after the establishment of each church (Acts 14:23), here he cautions that such appointment should not be rushed, lest a mistake be made. And in the entire process, the church must be careful not to judge as the world judges, for "man looks on the outward appearance, but the LORD looks on the heart" (1 Sam. 16:7; cf. 2 Cor. 5:16). This necessity for evaluation of spiritual condition was also evident when the apostles encouraged the church at Jerusalem to pick out "seven men of good repute, *full of the Spirit and of wisdom,* whom we may appoint to this duty" (Acts 6:3). Among those chosen was "Stephen, a man full of faith and of the Holy Spirit" (Acts 6:5).

We should also note that the appointment of elders in Paul's early churches was accompanied by "prayer and fasting," perhaps in connection with the process of selection of the elders. (Note the example of Jesus who "went out to the mountain to pray; and all night he continued in prayer to God" before he chose his twelve disciples [Luke 6:12–13].)[22]

3. Deacon. The word *deacon* is a translation of the Greek word *diakonos,* which is the ordinary word for "servant" when it is used in contexts not dealing with church officers.

Deacons are mentioned clearly in Philippians 1:1: "To all the saints in Christ Jesus who are at Philippi, with the bishops and *deacons.*" But there is no specification of their function, other than to indicate that they are different from the bishops (elders). Deacons are also mentioned in 1 Timothy 3:8–13 in a more extensive passage:

> Deacons likewise must be serious, not double-tongued, not addicted to much wine, not greedy for gain; they must hold the mystery of the faith with a clear conscience. And let them also be tested first; then if they prove themselves blameless let them serve as deacons. The women [or 'wives'; the Greek can take either meaning] likewise must be serious, no slanderers, but temperate, faithful in all things. Let deacons be the husband of one wife, and let them manage their children and their households well; for those who serve well as deacons gain a good standing for themselves and also great confidence in the faith which is in Christ Jesus. (1 Tim. 3:8–13)

---

[22]We have not discussed the office held by Timothy and Titus under the category of apostle or under the category of elder. This is because Timothy and Titus, together with some of Paul's other co-workers, are not apostles, but neither are they elders or deacons. They seem to fall in an unusual category that we might call "apostolic assistants," for they had some delegated authority from the apostles to supervise early churches while they were being established. Since there is today no living apostle to whom people like this would be accountable and from whom they would derive their authority, we should not expect to have any apostolic assistants like this in the church today either.

The function of deacons is not spelled out here, but the qualifications for deacons suggest some functions. For instance, they seem to have had some responsibility in caring for the finances of the church, since they had to be people who were "not greedy for gain" (v. 8). They perhaps had some administrative responsibilities in other activities of the church as well, because they were to manage their children and their households well (v. 12). They may also have ministered to the physical needs of those in the church or community who needed help (see discussion of Acts 6 below). Moreover, if verse 11 speaks of their wives (as I think it does), then it would also be likely that they were involved in some house-to-house visitation and counseling, because the wives are to be "no slanderers." It would do no good for deacons if their wives (who would no doubt also be involved in prayer and counseling with the deacons) spread confidential matters around the church. But these are only suggestions of possible areas of responsibility hinted at in this passage.

The noun *deacon* is not itself used in Acts 6:1–6, but a related verb (Gk. *diakoneō*, "to serve") is found in verse 2: "It is not right that we should give up preaching the word of God to *serve* tables." Here the apostles who ruled over the Jerusalem church found it necessary to delegate some administrative responsibilities to others. In this case, the responsibilities included the distribution of food to widows who were in need. It seems appropriate to think of these seven men as "deacons" even though the name *deacon* had perhaps not yet come to be applied to them as they began this responsibility, for they seem to be given tasks which fit well with the responsibilities of deacons hinted at in 1 Timothy 3:8–12.

There are other texts in which it is difficult to know whether the New Testament is speaking about a deacon as a special church officer or is simply using the word to refer to a "servant" in a general sense. This is the difficulty in Romans 16:1, where Phoebe is called a "servant" or a "deaconess" or "deacon" (this type of Greek noun has the same form in both masculine and feminine genders, so it is simply a question of which English word is most appropriate) of the church at Cenchreae. Because Paul's requirement for deacons was that they be "the husband of one wife" (1 Tim. 3:12), the translation "servant" seems preferable in Romans 16:1 (*diakonos* takes this sense in Rom. 13:4; 15:8; and 1 Cor. 3:5).[23] In general, the verses on deacons show that they had recognized

---

[23]Some have argued that 1 Tim. 3:11 refers to women deacons: "The *women likewise* must be serious, no slanderers, but temperate, faithful in all things." However, if Timothy and the church at Ephesus knew that women could be deacons, it would seem very strange for Paul to have to add a separate verse that talked specifically about women deacons, and then specify nothing more about them than would have been required if the verse had not been there at all. Moreover, it would seem very odd for Paul to sandwich only one verse about women deacons in the middle of five verses (three preceding and two following) about men who are deacons. On the other hand, a verse referring to the wives of deacons in the middle of a list of qualifications for deacons would be very appropriate: Paul elsewhere includes family conduct as one aspect of the requirement for church office (1 Tim. 3:2, 4–5). It is true that Paul simply says "the

wives" rather than "their wives," but Greek frequently omits possessive adjectives when the person named (brother, sister, father, mother, etc.) would have an obvious relationship to the person being discussed in the immediate context.

For two views of this verse, and two views on whether women should be deacons today, see Thomas R. Schreiner, "The Valuable Ministries of Women in the Context of Male Leadership: A Survey of Old and New Testament Examples and Teaching," *Recovering Biblical Manhood and Womanhood*, ed. John Piper and Wayne Grudem (Wheaton, Ill.: Crossway, 1991), pp. 213–14, 219–221, and p. 505, n. 13; and, in the same volume, George W. Knight III, "The Family and the Church: How Should Biblical Manhood and Womanhood Work Out in Practice?" pp. 353–54.

offices to "serve" the church in various ways. Acts 6:1–6 suggests that they had some administrative responsibilities, but were nevertheless subject to the authority of those who had rule over the entire church.

It is significant that nowhere in the New Testament do deacons have ruling authority over the church as the elders do, nor are deacons ever required to be able to teach Scripture or sound doctrine.

4. Other Offices? In many churches today, there are other offices, such as treasurer, moderator (one responsible for chairing church business meetings), or trustees (in some forms of church government, these are people who have legal accountability for the property owned by the church). Moreover, churches with more than one paid staff member may have some staff members (such as music director, education director, youth worker, etc.) who are "publicly recognized as having the right and responsibility to perform certain functions in the church," and who thus fit our definition of church officer, and who may even be paid to perform such functions as a full-time occupation, but who may not be elders or deacons in the church.

There does not seem to be any reason to say that these should not be offices in the church as well, even though all of them could probably be put in the category of either elder or deacon (most of those mentioned above could be deacons with specific responsibilities, or the moderator could also be an elder who simply moderates church business meetings). Nevertheless, if these or other similar offices seem helpful for the functioning of the church, there seems to be no reason why they should not be established. Yet if they are established, it would be necessary to see that they not overshadow the importance of the offices specifically named in Scripture, and that they not have any authority that is not subject to the governing authority of those officers that are clearly named in Scripture. If significant influence or authority is gained by those who have offices not named in Scripture, then it is much less likely that people in the congregation or the office holders themselves will look to Scripture and find detailed descriptions of how they should act or how they should be chosen. This would tend to diminish the effective authority of Scripture to govern the church in the area of church leadership.

B. How Should Church Officers Be Chosen?

In the history of the church there have been two major types of process for the selection of church officers—selection by a higher authority, or selection by the local congregation. The Roman Catholic Church has its officers appointed by a higher authority: the Pope appoints cardinals and bishops, and the bishops appoint priests in local parishes. This is a "hierarchy" or system of government by a priesthood[24] that is distinct from the laypeople in the church. This system claims an unbroken line of descent from Christ and the apostles, and claims that the present priesthood stands as Christ's representatives in the church. Although the Church of England (the Episcopalian Church in the United

---

[24]The word *hierarchy* means "government by priests," and derives from the Greek words for "priest" (*hierus*) and "rule" (*archē*).

States) does not submit to government by the Pope or have cardinals, it does have some similarities to the hierarchical system of the Roman Catholic Church, since it is governed by bishops and archbishops, and its clergy are thought of as priests. It also claims direct succession from the apostles, and priests and bishops are appointed by a higher authority outside the local parish.[25]

In distinction from this system of appointment by higher authority, in most other Protestant groups church officers are chosen by the local church, or by some group within the local church, even though the form of church government may vary in other significant ways (see below). Since this is an area in which there is no absolutely decisive biblical text, we ought to be patient with some diversity among evangelicals on this issue. However, there are several reasons why it seems most appropriate that church officers (such as elder and deacon, and certainly including the "pastor") should be chosen or at least affirmed or recognized in some way by the whole congregation:

(1) In the New Testament, there are several examples where church officers were apparently chosen by the whole congregation. In Acts 6:3, the apostles do not themselves pick out the seven early deacons (if we see them as deacons), but say to the whole church, "*Pick out from among you* seven men of good repute, full of the Spirit and of wisdom, whom we may appoint to this duty." The initial selection of these men was done by the whole congregation. When a replacement was chosen for Judas to be numbered among the apostles, *the whole congregation of 120 persons* (see Acts 1:15) made the initial selection of two, from whom the Lord himself indicated which one he would appoint: "And *they* put forward two, Joseph called Barsabbas, who was surnamed Justus, and Matthias" (Acts 1:23). At the end of the Jerusalem council, the whole church had a part with the apostles and elders in choosing representatives to convey the decisions to the other churches, for the choosing and sending was done by "the apostles and elders, *with the whole church*" (Acts 15:22; cf. "in assembly," v. 25). Moreover, when some of the churches sent an offering with Paul to be taken to the Jerusalem church, the churches also sent a representative to accompany Paul, one who, according to Paul, "has been appointed *by the churches* to travel with us in this gracious work" (2 Cor. 8:19).[26]

It may be objected that Paul and Barnabas "*appointed*" elders in every church (Acts 14:23), and Paul also told Titus to "*appoint* elders in every town" (Titus 1:5). Does this not seem more like the Roman Catholic or Anglican system than a system of congregational choice? Yet even those verses need not imply that the apostles alone made the selection, but could certainly include congregational consultation and even consent before an official appointment or installation was made (as with the appointment in Acts 6:3, 6). The word *appoint* may also mean "install."[27]

(2) Another reason for congregational participation in the selection of church officers is that in the New Testament generally, final governing authority seems to rest not with any group outside the church or any group within the church, but with the church as

---

[25]The Methodist Church in the United States also has appointment of local clergy by bishops, and has some similarities to the Episcopal Church, from which it came.

[26]Of course, this church representative *may* have been appointed only by officers within the church, but there is no statement to that effect: Paul just says that he had been "appointed by the churches," and certainly does not mention any higher authority outside the churches.

[27]See BAGD, p. 881.

a whole. The final step in church discipline before excommunication is to *"tell it to the church"* (Matt. 18:17). Excommunication, or the act of excluding someone from the fellowship of the church, is done when the *whole congregation* is "assembled" (1 Cor. 5:4), and is therefore apparently done by the entire congregation. One other consideration that is suggestive, but not conclusive, is the fact that the epistles that are written to churches are not sent to the elders or some other group of leaders within the churches, but are all written to entire churches, and the whole congregation is encouraged to read and expected to give heed to these epistles (Rom. 1:7; 1 Cor. 1:2; 2 Cor. 1:1; cf. 2 Cor. 1:13; Col. 4:16; 1 Tim. 4:13). This means that the apostles relate directly to the congregations, not to the congregations through the officers.

There are also some practical reasons that can be mentioned:

(3) If the entire congregation selects the officers of the church, there is more accountability to the congregation. Paul assumed some level of accountability when he provided for the fact that "two or three witnesses" could bring a charge of wrongdoing against an elder (1 Tim. 5:19). This accountability provides an additional safeguard against temptations to sin and excessive lust for power.[28]

(4) Historically, false doctrine often seems to be adopted by the theologians of the church first, by the pastors second, and by the informed laity, who are daily reading their Bibles and walking with the Lord, last. Therefore, if the leadership begins to stray in doctrine or in life, and there is no election by the congregation, then the church as a whole has no practical means of getting hold of the situation and turning it around. But if officers are elected by the church, then there is a system of "checks and balances" whereby even the governing authority of the church has some accountability to the church as a whole.[29]

(5) Government works best when it has the consent of those governed (cf., in the Old Testament, Ex. 4:29–31; 1 Sam. 7:5–6; 10:24; 2 Sam. 2:4; 1 Kings 1:39–40; and note the mistake of Rehoboam in 1 Kings 12:1, 15).

These factors combine to indicate that although Scripture does not explicitly command one specific system of choosing church officers, it would seem most wise to have a system whereby the entire church has a significant role in the selection and recognition of the officers of the church—perhaps through a congregational vote, or through some other process whereby congregational recognition is required before church officers can assume office.[30]

Can anything else be said about the process of selecting officers? Some additional congregational checks against excessive use of authority might be built into the selection process. There is room for wide variation here, but provisions such as election to limited

---

[28]However, this situation also has a potential for abuse if a few influential members exert influence to keep the pastor from dealing with issues of sin in their own lives.

[29]I am not using the phrase "checks and balances" to reflect a preference for an American form of civil government at this point, but intend the phrase to be understood in a broader sense to mean safeguards that prevent excessive power from being concentrated in the hands of any one individual or group. (In fact, the system of plural elders which I see represented in the New Testament is very different from the concentration of power found in the office of the President of the United States.)

[30]When I mention a congregational vote I do not mean to suggest the idea of a competitive election such as is found in secular politics. It may simply involve a requirement that the congregation vote to ratify candidates who have been nominated by a mature group within the church (such as the present elders), or, on the other hand, it may involve a church-wide election, or other processes may be used. Scripture is silent regarding the actual process; therefore, God has decided to leave the matter to the wisdom of each congregation in its own setting.

terms of office, a requirement for a mandatory year off (except for full-time pastoral staff members who are elders) every few years, a requirement for periodic reaffirmation of election, and a provision in the nominating process whereby nominations can be made by the members of the congregation (even if most nominations come from the elders themselves), would all provide additional measures of accountability to the congregation without forfeiting any essential aspects of governing authority over the congregation once elders are elected.

These factors would also provide some arguments against a self-perpetuating group of elders which is not subject to election or periodic reconfirmation by the congregation, but once again it must be said that no specific directives are listed in Scripture and there is room for variation at this point.

C. Forms of Church Government

In discussing forms of church government there is some overlap with the previous section on the method of choosing church officers, for the selection of officers is one very important aspect of authority in the church. Different philosophies of church government will be reflected in different methods used for selecting officers of the church, as explained above.

This is evident in the fact that forms of church government can be broken down into three large categories, which we may term "episcopalian," "presbyterian," and "congregational." The *episcopalian* forms have a government by a distinct category of church officers known as a priesthood, and final authority for decision-making is found outside the local church.[31] The Episcopal Church system is the primary representative among Protestants of this form of government. The *presbyterian* forms have a government by elders, some of whom have authority not only over their local congregation, but also, through the presbytery and the general assembly, over all the churches in a region and then in the denomination as a whole. The *congregational* forms of church government all have final governing authority resting with the local congregation, although various degrees of self-rule are given up through denominational affiliation, and the actual form of local church government may vary considerably. We shall examine each of these forms of government in the following discussion.

1. Episcopalian. In the episcopalian system, an archbishop has authority over many bishops. They in turn have authority over a "diocese," which simply means the churches under the jurisdiction of a bishop. The officer in charge of a local parish is a rector (or sometimes a vicar, who is an "assistant" or one who substitutes for the rector). Archbishops, bishops, and rectors are all priests, since they have all at one time been ordained to the episcopalian priesthood (but in practice the rector is most often called the priest).[32]

---

[31]The Roman Catholic Church also has government by a priesthood, and is therefore "episcopalian" in form of government. Sometimes an episcopalian form of government is called a "hierarchical" government, especially when referring to the Roman Catholic Church.

[32]However, Episcopalians understand the English word

priest to be equivalent to the term *presbyter* (the Greek term for "elder"), while Roman Catholics understand the word *priest* differently, relating it to the Old Testament priesthood in its duty of offering sacrifices and representing the people to God and God to the people.

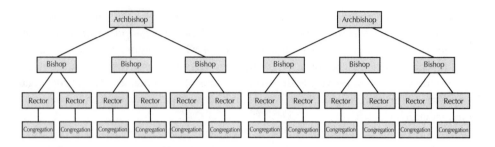

EPISCOPALIAN GOVERNMENT
Figure 5.1

The argument for the episcopalian system is not that it is found in the New Testament, but that it is a natural outgrowth of the development of the church which began in the New Testament, and it is not forbidden by the New Testament. E. A. Litton writes, "No order of Diocesan Bishops appears in the New Testament," but immediately adds:

> The evidence is in favour of the supposition that Episcopacy sprang from the Church itself, and by a natural process, and that it was sanctioned by Saint John, the last survivor of the Apostles. The Presbytery, when it assembled for consultation, would naturally elect a president to maintain order; first temporarily, but in time with permanent authority. . . . Thus it is probable that at an early period an informal episcopate had sprung up in each church. As the Apostles were one by one removed . . . the office would assume increased importance and become invested with greater powers.[33]

Moreover, since the office of bishop and the corresponding government structure found in the Episcopalian Church is both historical and beneficial, Litton argues that it should be preserved. Finally, the benefit of direct descent from the apostles is regarded as a strong reason in favor of the episcopalian system. Litton says, "The Apostles are the first link in the chain, and there is no reason why a succession, as regards to the external commission, should not proceed from age to age, the existing body of ministers handing down the official authority to their successors, and these latter in turn to theirs."[34]

But there are arguments that may be given on the other side of this question. (1) It is significant that the office of "bishop" is not a distinct office in the New Testament, but is simply a synonym for the name "elder," as Litton himself agrees.[35] There is no *single* bishop in the New Testament, but bishops (or overseers) are always plural in number. This should not be seen merely as an incidental fact, for even among the apostles Jesus did not leave one with superior authority over the others, but left a group of twelve who were equal in governing authority (and to whom others were later added, such as Paul). Though some apostles, such as Peter, James, and Paul, had prominence among

---

[33]Edward Arthur Litton, *Introduction to Dogmatic Theology,* ed. by Philip E. Hughes (London: James Clarke, 1960; first published in 2 vols., 1882, 1892), p. 401.

[34]Ibid., p. 390.
[35]Ibid., p. 400.

the group, they did not have any greater authority than the others, and even Peter was rebuked by Paul in Antioch (Gal. 2:11).[36] This may well reflect the wisdom of Christ in guarding against the abuse of power that inevitably comes when any one human being has too much power without sufficient checks and balances from others. Just as Jesus left a plurality of apostles to have ultimate (human) authority in the early church, so the apostles always appointed a plurality of elders in every church, never leaving only one person with governing authority.

(2) The theory of a group of bishops established to replace the apostles is not taught in the New Testament, nor is there an implication of a need for *physical* continuity of ordination through the laying on of hands by those who have been ordained in an unbroken chain of succession from the apostles. For example, in Acts 13:3, it was not the Jerusalem apostles who ordained Paul and Barnabas, but people in the church at Antioch who laid hands on them and sent them out. In fact, there is very little evidence that the apostles had any concern for a line of succession. Timothy apparently was ordained not simply by Paul but also by a "council of elders" (1 Tim. 4:14), though this may well have included Paul as well (see 2 Tim. 1:6). More importantly, ordaining is ultimately from the Lord himself (Acts 20:28; 1 Cor. 12:28; Eph. 4:11), and there is nothing in the nature of "ordaining" (when it is simply seen as public recognition of an office) that requires that it be done *only* by those previously ordained in *physical* descent from the apostles. If God has called an elder, he is to be recognized, and no concern about physical descent needs to be raised. In addition, if one is convinced that the local church should elect elders (see discussion above), then it would seem appropriate that the church that elected the elder—not an external bishop—should be the group to confer the outward recognition at election by installing the person in office or ordaining the pastor.[37]

(3) While it may be argued that the development of an episcopalian system with single bishops in authority over several churches was a beneficial development in the early church, one may also argue that it was a deviation from New Testament standards and a result of human dissatisfaction with the system of elected local elders that had been established by the apostles and that had apparently worked very well from A.D. 30 to 100 throughout all of the New Testament church. But one's evaluation of the historical data will of course depend on one's evaluation of earlier arguments for and against an episcopalian system.

2. Presbyterian. In this system, each local church elects elders to a session (E in figure 5.2 stands for elder, and the dotted lines indicate that the whole congregation elects the elders). The pastor of the church will be one of the elders in the session, equal in authority to the other elders. This session has governing authority over the local church. However, the members of the session (the elders) are also members of a presbytery, which has

[36]Roman Catholics argue that Peter had greater authority than the other apostles from the beginning, but the New Testament evidence does not bear this out. (On the "power of the keys" in Matt. 16:19, see chapter 4, section B.)

[37]Episcopalians, who favor appointment of officers by a bishop, would of course not agree with the premise of this last consideration.

authority over several churches in a region. This presbytery consists of some or all of the elders in the local churches over which it has authority. Moreover, some of the members of the presbytery are members of the "general assembly" which usually will have authority over all the presbyterian churches in a nation or region.[38]

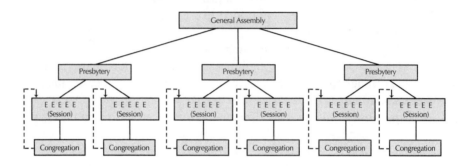

PRESBYTERIAN GOVERNMENT
Figure 5.2

The arguments in favor of this presbyterian system are: (1) that those who have wisdom and gifts for eldership should be called on to use their wisdom to govern more than just one local church, and (2) a national (or even worldwide) government of the church shows the unity of the body of Christ. Moreover (3) such a system is able to prevent an individual congregation from falling into doctrinal error much more effectively than any voluntary association of churches.[39]

The presbyterian system outlined above has many adherents among evangelical Christians today, and it certainly works effectively in many cases. However, some objections can be brought against this system: (1) Nowhere in Scripture do *elders* have regularly established authority over more than their own local church. The pattern is rather that elders are appointed in local churches and have authority over local churches. Against this claim the Jerusalem council in Acts 15 is often mentioned, but we should notice that this council was held in Jerusalem because of the presence of the apostles. Apparently the apostles and the elders in Jerusalem, with the representatives from Antioch (Acts 15:2), together sought God's wisdom on this matter. And there seems to have been some consultation with the whole church as well, for we read, at the conclusion of the discussion, "Then it seemed good to the apostles and the elders, *with the whole church,* to choose men from among them and send them to Antioch with Paul and Barnabas" (Acts 15:22). (If this narrative gives support to regional government by elders, it therefore also gives support to regional government by whole

---

[38]In the Christian Reformed Church, the form of government is similar to a presbyterian system, but the names of the governing bodies are different: the elders in a local church are called a *consistory* (instead of a session), the regional governing body is called a *classis* (instead of a *presbytery*), and the national governing assembly is called a *synod* (instead of a *general assembly*).

[39]A fuller defense of the presbyterian system of church government is found in Louis Berkhof, *Systematic Theology* (Grand Rapids: Eerdmans, 1939, 1941), pp. 581–92.

congregations!) This situation with the elders in Jerusalem is not a good pattern to defend a system whereby elders have authority over more than their local churches: the Jerusalem church did not send for all the elders in Judea, Samaria, and Galilee, and call a meeting of "the Judean presbytery" or a "general assembly." Although the apostles in Jerusalem certainly had authority over all the churches, there is no indication that elders by themselves, even in the Jerusalem church, had any such authority. And certainly there is no New Testament pattern for elders exercising authority over any other than their own local churches.[40]

(2) This system, in practice, results in much formal litigation, where doctrinal disputes are pursued year after year all the way to the level of the general assembly. One wonders if this should be characteristic of the church of Christ—perhaps so, but it seems to the present author to be a system that encourages such litigation far more than is necessary or edifying for the body of Christ.

(3) The effective power in church government seems, in practice, to be too removed from the final control of the laypeople in the church. Although Berkhof, who defends this system of government, affirms quite clearly that "the power of the church resides *primarily* in the governing body of the local church,"[41] he also admits that, "the more general the assembly, the more remote it is from the people."[42] Thus the system is very hard to turn around when it begins to go wrong since the laypersons who are not elders have no vote in the session or the presbytery or the general assembly, and the governing structure of the church is more removed from them than in other church government structures.

(4) Although in some cases it is true that a doctrinally sound denomination with a presbyterian system of government can keep a local church from going astray in its doctrine, in actuality very frequently the opposite has been true: the national leadership of a presbyterian denomination has adopted false doctrine and has put great pressure on local churches to conform to it.

(5) Although the presbyterian system does represent in one form the national or even worldwide unity of Christ's church, such unity can certainly be shown in other ways than through this system of government. The churches with more purely congregational forms of government do have voluntary associations that manifest this unity. In fact, these associations involve *all* the people in the churches, not just the elders or the clergy, as in a presbyterian system. The national meeting of a Baptist denomination, for example, where large numbers of ministers and laypersons (who are not necessarily elders or deacons, but just delegates from their churches) join together in fellowship might be seen as a better demonstration of the unity of Christ's body than a presbyterian general assembly where only elders are present.

---

[40]On the other hand, advocates of a presbyterian system could answer that nowhere in the New Testament do we find an example of an independent church—every church in the New Testament is subject to the worldwide governing authority of the apostles. Of course, a defender of independent churches might answer that we have no apostles today to exercise such authority. However, if we are looking to the New Testament for a pattern, the fact still remains that no independent churches are to be found there, and we would expect that something rather than nothing would replace a government by the apostles. This seems to me to indicate that some sort of denominational authority over local churches is still appropriate (though that will take different forms in different denominations).

[41]Berkhof, *Systematic Theology*, p. 584.

[42]Ibid., p. 591.

3. Congregational.

a. Single Elder (or Single Pastor): We can now look at five varieties of congregational government for the church. The first one, which is currently the most common among Baptist churches in the United States, is the "single elder" form of government. In this kind of government the pastor is seen as the only elder in the church, and there is an elected board of deacons who serve under his authority and give support to him (D in figure 5.3 stands for deacon).

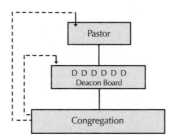

SINGLE-ELDER (SINGLE-PASTOR) GOVERNMENT
Figure 5.3

In this system, the congregation elects the pastor and also elects the deacons. The amount of authority the pastor has varies greatly from church to church, and will generally increase the longer a pastor remains in a church. The authority of the deacon board is often thought to be merely an advisory authority. In the way this system ordinarily functions, especially in smaller churches, many decisions must be brought before the congregation as a whole.

The arguments in favor of this system are clearly presented in A. H. Strong's *Systematic Theology*, a text that has been widely used in Baptist circles.[43] Strong gives the following arguments:

(1) The New Testament does not require a plurality of elders, but the pattern of plural elders seen in the New Testament was only due to the size of the churches at that time. He says:

> In certain of the New Testament churches there appears to have been a plurality of elders. . . . There is, however, no evidence that the number of elders was uniform, or that the plurality which frequently existed was due to any other cause than the size of the churches for which these elders cared. The New Testament example, while it permits the multiplication of assistant pastors according to need, does not require a plural eldership in every case.[44]

In this quotation Strong shows that he would regard additional pastors hired by a larger church to be elders as well, so that this system could be expanded beyond a single elder/

---

[43]A. H. Strong, *Systematic Theology* (Valley Forge, Pa.: Judson Press, 1907), pp. 914–17. Strong was President of Rochester Theological Seminary from 1872 to 1912.

[44]Ibid., pp. 915–16.

pastor to include two or more elder/pastors. But the crucial distinction is that *the governing authority of the office of elder is possessed only by the professional pastor(s) of the church,* and is not shared by any laypersons in the church. And we must realize that in practice, the vast majority of churches that follow this pattern today are relatively small churches with only one pastor; therefore, in actuality, this usually becomes a single elder form of government.[45]

(2) Strong adds that "James was the pastor or president of the church at Jerusalem," and cites Acts 12:17; 21:18; and Galatians 2:12 to show that this leadership by James was a pattern which could then be imitated by other churches.

(3) Strong notes that some passages have "bishop" in the singular but "deacons" in the plural, hinting at something similar to this common Baptist form of government. A literal translation of the Greek text shows a singular definite article modifying "bishop" in two verses: "*The bishop* therefore must be without reproach" (1 Tim. 3:2, literal translation) and that "*the bishop* must be blameless" (Titus 1:7, literal translation), but by contrast, we read, "*Deacons* likewise must be serious . . ." (1 Tim. 3:8).

(4) Finally, the "angel of the church" in Revelation 2:1, 8, 12, 18; 3:1, 7, 14, according to Strong, "is best interpreted as meaning the pastor of the church; and, if this be correct, it is clear that each church had, not many pastors, but one."[46]

(5) Another argument, not made by Strong, is found in recent literature on church growth. The argument is that churches need a strong single pastor in order to grow rapidly.[47]

Once again it must be said that this single elder form of government has also worked very successfully in many evangelical churches. However, there can be objections to the case presented by Strong and others.

(1) It seems inconsistent to argue that the New Testament falls short of giving a clear *command* that all churches should have a plurality of elders when the passages on qualifications of elders in 1 Timothy 3:1–7 and Titus 1:5–7 are used as scriptural *requirements* for church officers today. How can churches say that the *qualifications for elders* found in these verses are commanded for us today but the *system of plural elders* found in these very same verses is not commanded, but was required only in that time and in that society? Though it could be objected that these are commands written only to individual situations in Ephesus and Crete, much of the New Testament consists of apostolic commands written to individual churches on how they should conduct themselves. Yet we do not therefore say that we are free to disobey

---

[45]Another Baptist theologian, Millard Erickson, supports Strong's claim that the New Testament does not require plural elders in a church. He says that the New Testament examples of elders are "descriptive passages" that tell about a church order that already existed, but that "churches are not commanded to adopt a particular form of church order" (*Christian Theology,* p. 1084). Moreover, Erickson sees no one pattern of church government in the New Testament, but says, "There may well have been rather wide varieties of governmental arrangements. Each church adopted a pattern which fit its individual situation" (ibid.).

[46]Strong, *Systematic Theology,* p. 916.

[47]See, for example, C. Peter Wagner, *Leading Your Church to Growth* (Ventura, Calif.: Regal, 1984). He says, "The principal argument of this book is that if churches are going to maximize their growth potential they need pastors who are strong leaders. . . . Make no mistake about it: it is a rule" (p. 73). The book is filled with anecdotes and pronouncements from church growth experts telling the reader that leadership by a strong single pastor is essential to significant church growth.

these instructions in other parts of the epistles. In fact, 1 Timothy and Titus give us a great deal of material on the conduct of the local church, material which all believing churches seek to follow.

Moreover, it seems to be quite unwise to ignore a clear New Testament pattern which existed throughout all the churches for which we have evidence at the time the New Testament was written. When the New Testament shows us that *no* church was seen to have a single elder ("in *every* church," Acts 14:23; "in every town," Titus 1:5; "let him call for the *elders*," James 5:14; "I exhort the *elders* among you," 1 Peter 5:1), then it seems unpersuasive to say that smaller churches would have only had one elder. Even when Paul had just founded churches on his first missionary journey, there were *elders* appointed "in every church" (Acts 14:23). And "every town" on the island of Crete was to have elders, no matter how large or small the church was.

In addition, there is an inconsistency in Strong's argument when he says that the large churches were those which had plural elders, for then he claims that "the angel of the church in Ephesus" (Rev. 2:1) was a single pastor, according to this common Baptist pattern. Yet the church at Ephesus at that time was exceptionally large: Paul, in founding that church, had spent three years there (Acts 20:31), during which time *all the residents of Asia heard the word of the Lord,* both Jews and Greeks" (Acts 19:10). The population of Ephesus at that time was more than 250,000.[48]

We may ask, why should we follow Strong and adopt as the norm a pattern of church government which is *nowhere* found in the New Testament, and reject a pattern *everywhere* found in the New Testament?

(2) James may well have acted as moderator or presiding officer in the church in Jerusalem, for all churches will have some kind of designated leader like this in order to conduct meetings. But this does not imply that he was the "pastor" of the church in Jerusalem in a "single elder" sense. In fact, Acts 15:2 shows that there were *elders* (plural) in the church in Jerusalem, and James himself was probably numbered among the apostles (see Gal. 1:19) rather than the elders.

(3) In 1 Timothy 3:2 and Titus 1:7, the Greek definite article modifying "bishop" simply shows that Paul is speaking of general qualifications as they applied to any one example.[49] In fact, in both cases which Strong cites we know there were *elders* (plural) in the churches involved. 1 Timothy 3:2 is written to Timothy at Ephesus, and Acts 20:17 shows us that there were "elders" in the church at Ephesus. And even in 1 Timothy, Paul writes, "Let the *elders* who rule well be considered worthy of double honor, especially those who labor in preaching and teaching" (1 Tim. 5:17). With regard to Titus 1:7 we need only look to verse 5, where Paul directs Titus explicitly to "appoint *elders* in every town."

(4) The angels of the seven churches in Revelation 2–3 are unusual and rather weak evidence for single elders. "The angel of the church in Ephesus" (Rev. 2:1) can hardly

---

[48]Robert H. Mounce, *The Book of Revelation,* NIC (Grand Rapids: Eerdmans, 1977), p. 85.

[49]In terms of Greek grammar, the use of the definite article here is best understood as a "generic" use, which is defined as a use of the article "to select a normal or representative individual" (MHT 3, p. 180). Paul's use of the singular was natural after he said, "If *any one* aspires to the office of bishop, he desires a noble task" (1 Tim. 3:1), or "if *any man* is blameless . . ." (Titus 1:6).

The RSV gives a more appropriate translation for English readers, reflecting this generic use, at these two verses: "*a* bishop."

mean that there was only one elder in that church, since we know there were "elders" there in this very large church (Acts 20:17). The word "angel" used in the address to the seven churches in Revelation 2–3 may simply designate a special messenger to each church, perhaps even the human messenger who would take what John wrote to each church,[50] or it may represent "the prevailing spirit of the church" rather than the ruling official of the congregation,[51] or may even simply refer to an angel who was given special care over each congregation. Even if it did represent a presiding officer of some sort in each congregation, this "angel" is not shown to have any ruling authority or any functions equivalent to today's single pastor, or any functions equivalent to that of "elder" in the New Testament churches. This passage does not furnish strong enough evidence to dislodge the clear data throughout the New Testament showing plural elders in every church, even in the church in Ephesus.

It is interesting that all of the New Testament passages cited by Strong (Acts 15, Jerusalem; 1 Tim. 3:2, Ephesus; Titus 1:7, Crete; Rev. 2–3, the seven churches, including Ephesus) speak of situations in which the New Testament itself points quite clearly to a plurality of elders in authority in the churches mentioned.

(5) The argument from church growth studies does not really prove that government led by a single pastor is necessary, for at least three reasons: (a) We should not reject a pattern supported in Scripture and adopt a different one just because people tell us that the different pattern seems to work well in producing large churches—our role here, as in all of life, should rather be to obey Scripture as closely as we can and expect God to bring appropriate blessing as he wills. (b) There are many large churches with government by plural elders (both Presbyterian churches and independent churches), so the argument from pragmatic considerations is not conclusive. (c) C. Peter Wagner admits that strong leaders can be found in various forms of church government,[52] and we must agree that a system of plural elders in which all have equal authority does not prevent one elder (such as the pastor) from functioning as a sort of "first among equals" and having a significant leadership role among those elders.

(6) A common practical problem with a "single elder" system is either an excessive concentration of power in one person or excessive demands laid upon him. In either case, the temptations to sin are very great, and a lessened degree of accountability makes yielding to temptation more likely. As was mentioned above, it was never the pattern in the New Testament, even with the apostles, to concentrate ruling power in the hands of any one person.

Here it should be noted that the "single elder" view of church government really has no more New Testament support than the "single bishop" (episcopalian) view. Both seem to be attempts to justify what has already happened in the history of the church, not conclusions that have grown out of an inductive examination of the New Testament itself.

(7) Finally, it should be noted that in actual practice the "single elder" system can change and *function* more like a "plural elders" government, only those who function

---

[50]The word *angelos* ["angel"] in Rev. 2:1 et al. can mean not only "angel" but also just "messenger."

[51]So Robert Mounce, *The Book of Revelation*, p. 85.

[52]Wagner says at one point that a pastor can be a strong leader within a variety of kinds of church government (*Leading Your Church to Growth*, pp. 94–95). Therefore it is not appropriate to take his study as an argument that solely supports a single elder form of government.

as elders are instead called "deacons." This would happen if the deacons share the actual governing authority with the pastor, and the pastor and other deacons see themselves as accountable to the deacon board as a whole. The system then begins to look like figure 5.4.

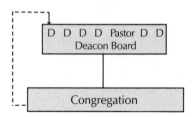

THE PASTOR AND DEACONS MAY GOVERN TOGETHER AND THUS
FUNCTION LIKE A GOVERNMENT OF PLURAL ELDERS
Figure 5.4

The problem with this arrangement is that it does not use biblical terminology to apply to the functions that people are carrying out, for "deacons" in the New Testament never had governing or teaching authority in the church. The result in such a situation is that people in the church (both the deacons and the other church members) will fail to read and apply scriptural passages on elders to those who are *in fact functioning as elders* in their church. Therefore these passages lose the direct relevance that they should have in the church. In this case however, the problem could be solved by changing the name "deacon" to "elder," and considering the pastor an elder along with the others.

b. Plural Local Elders: Is there any kind of church government that preserves the pattern of plural elders found in the New Testament and that avoids the expansion of elders' authority beyond the local congregation? Although such a system is not distinctive of any denomination today, it is found in many individual congregations. Using the conclusions reached to this point on the New Testament data, I would suggest figure 5.5 as a possible pattern.

Within such a system the elders govern the church and have authority to rule over it, authority which has been conferred by Christ himself, the head of the church, and by the Holy Spirit (Acts 20:28; Heb. 13:17). In this system of government, there is always more than one elder, a fact which distinguishes this form of government from the "single elder system" discussed above. In a contemporary congregation, the "pastor" (or "senior pastor") would be one among the elders in this system. He does not have authority over them, nor does he work for them as an employee. He has a somewhat distinct role in that he is engaged in the full-time work of "preaching and teaching" (1 Tim. 5:17), and derives part or all of his income from that work (1 Tim. 5:18). He also may frequently assume a leadership role (such as chairman) among the elders, which would fit with his leadership role among the congregation, but such a leadership role *among the elders* would not be necessary to the system. In addition, the pastor will ordinarily have considerable authority to make decisions and provide leadership in many areas of responsibility that have been delegated to him by the elder board as a whole. Such a system would allow a pastor to exercise strong leadership in the church while still having equal governing authority with the other elders.

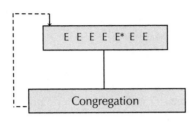

* Pastor

PLURAL LOCAL ELDER GOVERNMENT
Figure 5.5

The strength of this system of government is seen in the fact that the pastor does not have authority on his own over the congregation, but that authority belongs collectively to the entire group of elders (what may be called the elder board). Moreover, the pastor himself, like every other elder, is subject to the authority of the elder board as a whole. This can be a great benefit in keeping a pastor from making mistakes, and in supporting him in adversity and protecting him from attacks and opposition.[53]

In such a system, are there limitations that should be placed on the authority of the elders? In the section above on the manner of choosing church officers, several reasons were given to have some "checks and balances" that would put restrictions on the authority of the officers of a church.[54] Those arguments are also helpful here in indicating that, though elders have substantial governing authority over the church, it should not be unlimited authority. Examples of such limitations might be suggested, such as: (1) they may be elected rather than self-perpetuating; (2) they may have specific terms with a mandatory year off the board (except for the pastor, whose continuing leadership responsibilities

---

[53]If the church has more than one pastor who is paid for his work, these other associate or assistant pastors may or may not be viewed as elders (depending on the qualifications of each staff member and the policies of the church), but in either case, it would be entirely consistent with this form of government to have those associate pastors accountable to the senior pastor alone in their day-to-day work, and he accountable to the elder board with respect to his supervision of their activity.

[54]The arguments given above (pp. 99–100) for restrictions on the authority of church officers may be summarized as follows: (1) Church officers in the New Testament were apparently chosen by the whole congregation. (2) The final governing authority in New Testament churches seemed to rest with the whole church. (3) Accountability to the congregation provides a safeguard against temptations to sin. (4) Some degree of control by the entire congregation provides a safe-guard against the leadership falling into doctrinal error. (5) Government works best with the consent of those governed. In addition to those, there is another reason for restricting the authority of church officers: (6) The doctrine of the clarity of Scripture, and the doctrine of the priesthood of all believers (whereby the New Testament affirms that all Christians have access to God's throne in prayer and all share as members in a "royal priesthood" [1 Peter 2:9; cf. Heb. 10:19–25; 12:22–24]) combine to indicate that all Christians have some ability to interpret Scripture and some responsibility to seek God's wisdom in applying it to situations. All have access directly to God in order to seek to know his will. The New Testament allows for no special class of Christians who have greater access to God than others. Therefore, it is right to include all believers in some of the crucial decision-making processes of the church. "In an abundance of counselors there is safety" (Prov. 11:14).

require continuous participation as an elder); (3) some large decisions may be required to be brought to the whole church for approval. Regarding this third point, congregational approval is already a biblical requirement for church discipline in Matthew 18:17 and for excommunication in 1 Corinthians 5:4. The principle of congregational election of elders would imply that the decision to call any pastor would also have to be approved by the congregation as a whole. Major new directions in the ministry of the church, which will require large-scale congregational support, may be brought to the church as a whole for approval. Finally, it would seem wise to require congregational approval on such large financial decisions as an annual budget, the decision to purchase property, or the decision to borrow money for the church (if that is ever done), simply because the church as a whole will be asked to give generously to pay for these commitments.[55]

In fact, the reasons for placing some limitations on the authority of church officers may appear so strong that they would lead us to think that all decisions and all governing authority should rest with the congregation as a whole. (Some churches have adopted a system of almost pure democracy in governing the church, whereby everything must come to the congregation as a whole for approval.) However, this conclusion ignores the abundant New Testament evidence about the clear ruling and governing authority given to elders in New Testament churches. Therefore, while it is important to have *some recognized checks* on the authority of elders, and to rest ultimate governing authority with the congregation as a whole, it still is necessary, if we are to remain faithful to the New Testament pattern, to have a strong level of authority vested in the elders themselves.[56]

I have labeled this system one of "plural *local* elders" in order to distinguish it from a presbyterian system where elders, when gathered on the level of the presbytery or general assembly, have authority over more than their own local congregations. But in such a system of elected local elders, can there be any wider associations with churches beyond the local congregation? Yes, certainly. While churches with this system may choose to remain entirely independent, most will enter into voluntary associations with other churches of similar convictions in order to facilitate fellowship, pooling of resources for mission activity (and perhaps for other things such as Christian camps, publications, theological education, etc.). However, the only authority these larger associations would have over

---

[55]It should be noted that a church government system with a self-perpetuating group of elders, rather than one elected by the congregation, would be very similar in function to this system, but would not be as extensive in the checks and balances put on the authority of the elders. Such a church may still wish to have some mechanism whereby the congregation could remove elders who strayed from faithfulness to Scripture in serious ways.

[56]When this kind of system functions in a large church, it is important that a majority of the elder board be persons *who are not associate pastors in the church*. This is because the associate pastors are subject to the senior pastor in all of their church work (he usually hires and fires them and sets their pay, and they report to him). Therefore, if a majority of the elders consists of these associate pastors, the interpersonal dynamics involved will make it impossible for the senior pastor to be

subject to the authority of the elders as a group, and the system will in fact function as a (somewhat disguised) form of "single pastor" government, not as a plural elder government.

Someone may object that in a large church only full-time staff members know enough about the life of the church to be effective elders, but this is not a persuasive objection: Government by boards who are not closely involved in the everyday activities of those whom they govern works well in many realms of human activity, such as college and seminary boards, local school boards, boards of directors of corporations, and even state and national governments. All of these governing bodies direct policies and give guidance to full-time administrators, and they are able to obtain detailed information about specific situations when the need arises. (I realize that all these systems *can* work poorly, but my point is simply that they can work very well when the right people are put in leadership positions.)

the local congregation would be the authority to exclude an individual church from the association, not the authority to govern its individual affairs.

c. Corporate Board: The remaining three forms of congregational church government are not commonly used, but are sometimes found in evangelical churches. The first one is patterned after the example of a modern corporation, where the board of directors hires an executive officer who then has authority to run the business as he sees fit. This form of government could also be called the "you-work-for-us" structure. It is depicted in figure 5.6.

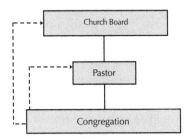

CORPORATE BOARD MODEL OF CHURCH GOVERNMENT
Figure 5.6

In favor of this structure it might be argued that this system in fact works well in contemporary businesses. However, there is no New Testament precedent or support for such a form of church government. It is simply the result of trying to run the church like a modern business, and it sees the pastor not as a spiritual leader, but merely as a paid employee.

Further objections to this structure are the fact that it deprives the pastor of sharing in the ruling authority that must be his if he is to carry out his eldership responsibilities effectively. Moreover, the members of the board are also members of the congregation over whom the pastor is supposed to have some authority, but that authority is seriously compromised if the leaders of the congregation are in fact his bosses.

d. Pure Democracy: This view, which takes congregational church government to its logical extreme, can be represented as in figure 5.7.

In this system *everything* must come to the congregational meeting. The result is that decisions are often argued endlessly, and, as the church grows, decision-making reaches a point of near paralysis. While this structure does attempt to do justice to some of the passages cited above regarding the need for final governing authority to rest with the congregation as a whole, it is unfaithful to the New Testament pattern of recognized and designated elders who have actual authority to rule the church in most situations.

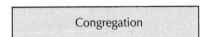

GOVERNMENT BY PURE DEMOCRACY
Figure 5.7

e. "No Government but the Holy Spirit": Some churches, particularly very new churches with more mystical or extremely pietistic tendencies, function with a church government that looks something like figure 5.8.

NO GOVERNMENT BUT THE HOLY SPIRIT
Figure 5.8

In this case, the church would deny that any form of government is needed, it would depend on all the members of the congregation being sensitive to the leading of the Holy Spirit in their own lives, and decisions would generally be made by consensus. This form of government never lasts very long. Not only is it unfaithful to the New Testament pattern of designated elders with governing authority in the church, but it is also subject to much abuse, because subjective feelings rather than wisdom and reason prevail in the decision-making process.

4. Conclusions. It must be made clear, in concluding this discussion of church government, that the form of government adopted by a church is not a major point of doctrine. Christians have lived comfortably and ministered very effectively within several different kinds of systems, and there are many evangelicals within each of the systems mentioned. Moreover, a number of different types of church government systems seem to work *fairly well*. Where there are weaknesses that appear to be inherent in the governing structure, individuals within the system generally recognize those weaknesses and attempt to compensate for them in whatever ways the system will allow.

Nevertheless, a church can be *more pure* or *less pure* on this point, as in other areas. As we are persuaded by Scripture concerning various aspects of church government, then we should continue to pray and work for the greater purity of the visible church in this area as well.

D. Should Women Be Church Officers?

Most systematic theologies have not included a section on the question of whether women can be church officers, because it has been assumed through the history of the church, with very few exceptions, that only men could be pastors or function as elders within a church.[57] But in recent years a major controversy has arisen within the evan-

---

[57]See William Weinrich, "Women in the History of the Church: Learned and Holy, But Not Pastors," in *Recovering* *Biblical Manhood and Womanhood: A Response to Evangelical Feminism*, ed. John Piper and Wayne Grudem (Wheaton,

gelical world: may women as well as men be pastors? May they share in all the offices of the church? I have treated this question much more extensively elsewhere[58] but a brief summary of the question can be given at this point.

We must affirm at the outset that the creation narrative in *Genesis 1:27 views men and women as equally created in the image of God.* Therefore, men and women have equal value to God, and should be seen by us as having absolutely equal value as persons, and equal value to the church. Moreover, Scripture assures men and women of equal access to all the blessings of salvation (see Acts 2:17–18; Gal. 3:28).[59] This is remarkably affirmed in the high dignity and respect which Jesus accorded to women in his earthly ministry.[60]

We must also admit that evangelical churches have often failed to recognize the full equality of men and women, and thereby have failed to count women equal in value to men. The result has been a tragic failure to recognize that God often gives women equal or greater spiritual gifts than men, a failure to encourage women to have full and free participation in the various ministries of the church, and a failure to take full account of the wisdom that God has given to women with respect to important decisions in the life of the church. If the present controversy over women's roles in the church can result in the eradication of some of these past abuses, then the church as a whole will benefit greatly.

Yet the question remains, should women be pastors or elders in churches? (Or should they fill roles equivalent to that of an elder in churches that have alternative forms of government?) My own conclusion on this issue is that the Bible does not permit women to function in the role of pastor or elder within a church. This has also been the conclusion of the vast majority of churches in various societies throughout history. The reasons that seem to me to be most persuasive in answering this question are the following:

1. 1 Timothy 2:11–14. The single passage in Scripture that addresses this question most directly is 1 Timothy 2:11–14:

> Let a woman learn in silence with all submissiveness. *I permit no woman to teach or to have authority over men;* she is to keep silent. For Adam was formed first, then Eve; and Adam was not deceived, but the woman was deceived and became a transgressor.

Here Paul is speaking about the church when it is assembled (see vv. 8–9). In such a setting, Paul says, "I permit no woman to *teach* or to *have authority* over men" (v. 12). These are the functions that are carried out by the elders of the church, and especially

Ill.: Crossway, 1991), pp. 263–79. See also Ruth A. Tucker and Walter L. Liefeld, *Daughters of the Church: Women and Ministry from New Testament Times to the Present* (Grand Rapids: Zondervan, 1987).

[58]See *Recovering Biblical Manhood and Womanhood*, ed. John Piper and Wayne Grudem. The position I have taken in the following paragraphs is consistent with the "Danvers Statement" issued in 1988 by the Council on Biblical Man-

hood and Womanhood, based in Louisville, Kentucky, USA.

[59]See also Raymond C. Ortlund, Jr., "Male-Female Equality and Male Headship: Gen. 1–3," in *Recovering Biblical Manhood and Womanhood*, pp. 95–112.

[60]See James A. Borland, "Women in the Life and Teachings of Jesus," in *Recovering Biblical Manhood and Womanhood*, pp. 113–23.

by what we know as a pastor in contemporary church situations.[61] It is specifically these functions unique to elders that Paul prohibits for women in the church.[62]

Several objections have been brought against this position:[63]

(a) It has been said that this passage applies only to a specific situation that Paul is addressing, probably one where women were teaching heretical doctrine within the church at Ephesus. But this objection is not persuasive, since there is no clear statement in 1 Timothy that says that women were actually *teaching* false doctrines. (1 Tim. 5:13 talks about women who are gossiping, but does not mention false doctrine.) Moreover, Paul does not simply tell certain women who are teaching false doctrine to be silent, but he says, "I permit *no woman* to teach or to have authority over men." And finally, the *reason* Paul gives for this prohibition is not the one proposed in this objection, but a far different one: the situation of Adam and Eve before the fall, and before there was any sin in the world (see v. 13), and the way in which a reversal in male and female roles occurred at the time of the fall (see v. 14). These reasons are not limited to one situation in the church at Ephesus, but have application to manhood and womanhood generally.

(b) Another objection is to say that Paul gave this prohibition because women were not well educated in the first century, and therefore were not qualified for teaching or governing roles in the church. But Paul does not give lack of education as a reason for saying that women cannot "teach or . . . have authority over men," but rather points back to creation (vv. 13–14). It is precarious to base an argument on a reason Paul did *not* give instead of the reason he *did* give.

In addition, this objection misunderstands the actual facts of the ancient church and the ancient world. Formal training in Scripture was not required for church leadership in the New Testament church, because several of the apostles did not have formal biblical training (see Acts 4:13). On the other hand, the skills of basic literacy and therefore the ability to read and study Scripture were available to men and women alike (note Acts 18:26; Rom. 16:1; 1 Tim. 2:11; Titus 2:3–4). There were many well-educated women in the ancient world, and particularly in a cultural center such as Ephesus.[64]

Finally, those who make such an argument are sometimes inconsistent in that elsewhere they point to women who had leadership positions in the ancient church, such as Priscilla. This point is especially relevant to 1 Timothy 2, because Paul was writing to Ephesus (1 Tim. 1:3), which was the home church of Priscilla and Aquila (see Acts 18:18–19, 21). It was in this very church at Ephesus that Priscilla knew Scripture well enough to help instruct Apollos in A.D. 51 (Acts 18:26). Then she had probably learned from Paul himself for another three years while he stayed at Ephesus teaching "the whole counsel of God" (Acts 20:27; cf. v. 31; also 1 Cor. 16:19). No doubt many other women in Ephesus had followed her example and also had learned from Paul. Although they later went to Rome, we find Aquila and Priscilla back in Ephesus at the end of Paul's life (2 Tim.

---

[61]See discussion in section A.2.c above regarding the teaching and ruling functions of elders in a church.

[62]For a more extensive treatment of this passage, see Douglas Moo, "What Does It Mean Not to Teach or Have Authority Over Men?: 1 Tim. 2:11–15," in *Recovering Biblical Manhood and Womanhood*, pp. 179–93.

[63]For more extensive statements of these objections see the books marked "Favors women as pastors" in the bibliography at the end of this chapter, especially the books by Mickelsen, Spencer, and Bilezikian.

[64]See Piper and Grudem, *Recovering Biblical Manhood and Womanhood*, p. 82.

4:19), about A.D. 67. Therefore, it is likely that they were in Ephesus in A.D. 65, about the time Paul wrote 1 Timothy (about *fourteen years after Priscilla had helped instruct Apollos*). Yet Paul does not allow even well-educated Priscilla or any other well-educated women at Ephesus to teach men in the public assembly of the church. The reason was not lack of education, but the order of creation which God established between men and women.

2. 1 Corinthians 14:33b–36. In a similar teaching, Paul says:

> As in all the churches of the saints, the women should keep silence in the churches. For they are not permitted to speak, but should be subordinate, as even the law says. If there is anything they desire to know, let them ask their husbands at home. For it is shameful for a woman to speak in church. What! Did the word of God originate with you, or are you the only ones it has reached? (1 Cor. 14:33b–36)

In this section Paul cannot be prohibiting all public speech by women in the church, for he clearly allows them to pray and prophesy in church in 1 Corinthians 11:5. There-fore, it is best to understand this passage as referring to speech that is in the category being discussed in the immediate context, namely, the spoken evaluation and judging of prophecies in the congregation (see v. 29: "Let two or three prophets speak, and *let the others weigh what is said*"). While Paul allows women to speak and give prophecies in the church meeting, he does not allow them to speak up and give evaluations or critiques of the prophecies that have been given, for this would be a ruling or governing function with respect to the whole church.[65] This understanding of the passage depends on our view of the gift of prophecy in the New Testament age, namely, that prophecy involves not authoritative Bible teaching, and not speaking words of God which are equal to Scripture, but rather reporting something which God spontaneously brings to mind.[66] In this way, Paul's teachings are quite consistent in 1 Corinthians 14 and 1 Timothy 2: in both cases he is concerned to preserve male leadership in the teaching and governing of the church.[67]

3. 1 Timothy 3:1–7 and Titus 1:5–9. Both 1 Timothy 3:1–7 and Titus 1:5–9 assume that elders are going to be men. An elder (or bishop/overseer) must be "the husband of

---

[65]For a fuller discussion of this question, see D. A. Carson, "'Silent in the Churches': On the Role of Women in 1 Cor. 14:33b–36," in *Recovering Biblical Manhood and Womanhood*, pp. 140–153. See also Wayne Grudem, *The Gift of Prophecy in the New Testament and Today*, pp. 217–24; also Wayne Grudem, "Prophecy—Yes, but Teaching—No: Paul's Consistent Advo-cacy of Women's Participation Without Governing Authority," *JETS* 30/1 (March 1987), pp. 11–23.

[66]This view of the gift of prophecy is explained more fully in chapter 11, section A.

[67]One recent evangelical objection to this conclusion on 1 Cor. 14:33–36 is simply to say that these verses were not writ-ten by Paul and do not belong in the text of 1 Corinthians, and are therefore not to be considered authoritative Scripture for us today: see Gordon Fee, *The First Epistle to the Corinthians*,

New International Commentary on the New Testament (Grand Rapids: Eerdmans, 1987), pp. 699–708. Fee's basic argument is that it is impossible to reconcile this passage with 1 Cor. 11:5, where Paul clearly allows women to speak in the church. (He also places much weight on the fact that vv. 34–35 are moved to the end of 1 Cor. 14 in some ancient manuscripts.) But Fee does not give adequate consideration to the view represented here, namely, that Paul is simply prohibiting women from the authoritative task of judging prophecies in the assembled church. Fee's position is surprising in light of the fact that no ancient manuscript of 1 Corinthians omits these verses. (The few manuscripts that place this section at the end of chapter 14 are far less reliable manuscripts that have frequent variations elsewhere in 1 Corinthians as well.)

one wife" (1 Tim. 3:2; also Titus 1:6), and "must manage his own household well, keeping his children submissive and respectful in every way" (1 Tim. 3:4).

Some may object that these were directions given only for the cultural situation in the ancient world, where women were not well educated, but the same response that was given above concerning 1 Timothy 2 would apply in this case as well.

4. The Relationship Between the Family and the Church. The New Testament makes frequent connections between the life of the family and the life of the church. Paul says, "If a man does not know how to manage his own household, how can he care for God's church?" (1 Tim. 3:5). He says to Timothy, "Do not rebuke an older man but exhort him as you would a *father;* treat younger men like *brothers,* older women like *mothers,* younger women like *sisters,* in all purity" (1 Tim. 5:1–2). Several other passages could be cited, but the close relationship between the family and the church should be clear.

Because of this connection, it is inevitable that leadership patterns in the family will reflect leadership patterns in the church, and vice versa. It is very appropriate that, as godly men fulfill their leadership responsibilities in the family, they should also fulfill leadership responsibilities in the church. Conversely, if patterns of female leadership are established in the church, it will inevitably bring pressures toward greater female leadership, and toward abdication of male leadership, within the family.[68]

5. The Example of the Apostles. While the apostles are not the same as elders in local churches, it is still important to realize that Jesus established a pattern of male leadership in the church when he appointed twelve men as apostles. It is simply not true that women have equal access to all offices in the church, for Jesus, the head of the church, is a man. And the twelve apostles who will sit on twelve thrones judging the twelve tribes of Israel (see Matt. 19:28), and whose names are written forever on the foundations of the heavenly city (Rev. 21:14), are all men. Therefore, *there will be no eternal modeling of equal roles for men and women at all levels of authority in the church.* Rather, there is a pattern of male leadership in the highest governing roles of the church, a pattern that will be evident to all believers for all eternity.

One objection brought against this argument is the claim that the culture at that time would not have allowed Jesus to choose six men and six women as apostles, or six husband-wife teams as apostles, and this is the reason he did not do so. But such an objection impugns Jesus' integrity and courage. Jesus was not afraid to break social customs when a moral principle was at stake: he criticized the Pharisees publicly, healed on the Sabbath, cleansed the temple, spoke with a Samaritan woman, ate with tax collectors and sinners, and ate with unwashed hands.[69] If Jesus had wanted to establish a principle of equal access to church leadership by both men and women, he certainly could have done so in the appointment of his apostles, and he would have done so, in spite of cul-

---

[68]For further discussion of this point, see Vern Poythress, "The Church as Family: Why Male Leadership in the Family Requires Male Leadership in the Church," in *Recovering Biblical Manhood and Womanhood,* pp. 233–47.

[69]This argument and the following one are taken from James Borland, "Women in the Life and Teachings of Jesus," in *Recovering Biblical Manhood and Womanhood,* pp. 120–22.

tural opposition, if it had been the pattern he wanted to establish in his church. But he did not.[70]

Another objection to this argument is to say that, if this is true, then only Jews can be leaders in our churches, since all twelve apostles were Jewish as well. But this objection is not persuasive because it fails to recognize that the church was entirely Jewish at its beginning. This was because it was God's plan to bring salvation through the Jews, and this led to twelve Jewish apostles. Yet within the pages of the New Testament, we see that the church soon expanded to include Gentiles (Matt. 28:19; Eph. 2:16) and Gentiles soon became elders and leaders in the New Testament church. A Gentile (Luke) wrote two books of the New Testament (Luke and Acts), and several Gentiles such as Titus and Epaphroditus were Paul's apostolic assistants and co-workers. In fact, God had progressively revealed from the time of Abraham (Gen. 12:3; 17:5) that it was his plan eventually to include countless Gentiles among his people.

So the Jewishness of the early apostles is not like their maleness. The church began as entirely Jewish, but soon became Jewish and Gentile as well. But the church did not begin all male, and only later include females as well. *Christ's followers were male and female from the beginning,* and both men and women were present at the beginning of the church at Pentecost. So this objection is not persuasive either.

6. The History of Male Teaching and Leadership Through the Whole Bible. Sometimes opponents of the view presented here have said it is based only on one text, 1 Timothy 2. Several of the foregoing arguments have demonstrated that this is not the case, but there is one further argument that can be made: throughout the history of the entire Bible, from Genesis to Revelation, there is a consistent pattern of male leadership among God's people. Though there are occasional examples of women having leadership in government positions such as queen (Athaliah did reign as sole monarch in 2 Kings 11:1–20, but she is hardly an example to imitate) or judge (note Deborah in Judg. 4–5), and though there were occasionally women such as Deborah and Huldah who were prophetesses (see Judg. 4–5; 2 Kings 22:14–20), we should note that these are rare exceptions in unusual circumstances. They occur in the midst of an overwhelming pattern of male leadership in teaching and governance, and, as such, they hardly serve as patterns for New Testament church office.[71] Moreover, *there is not one example in the entire Bible of a woman doing the kind of congregational Bible teaching that is expected of pastors/elders in the New Testament church.* In the Old Testament it was the priests who had teaching responsibilities for the people, and the priesthood was exclusively male; moreover, even the women

---

[70]Regarding "Junia" or "Junias" in Rom. 16:7, see p. 87.

[71]For further discussion of these narrative examples, see Thomas R. Schreiner, "The Valuable Ministries of Women in the Context of Male Leadership: A Survey of Old and New Testament Examples and Teaching," in *Recovering Biblical Manhood and Womanhood,* pp. 209–24. With reference to Deborah in particular, we must realize that the historical events narrated in the entire book of Judges require great care in interpretation before we can assume that they should be taken as models for us to imitate. And Deborah was different from other (male) prophets in that she did not prophesy in public, only in private (Jud. 4:5; Huldah does the same in 2 Kings 22:14–20); she handed over her leadership role to a man (Judg. 4:6–7); and, although God did bring blessing through her, it is interesting that there is no explicit affirmation of the fact that the LORD raised her up—making her unlike the other major judges such as Othniel (3:9), Ehud (3:15), Gideon (6:14), Jephthah (11:29), and Samson (13:25; 14:6), for whom there is explicit statement of their calling from God.

prophets Deborah and Huldah prophesied only privately, not publicly to a congregation of people.[72]

7. The History of the Church. As was mentioned above, the overwhelming pattern through the entire history of the church has been that the office of pastor/elder (or its equivalent) has been reserved for men. Although this does not demonstrate conclusively that such a position is correct, it should give us reason to reflect very seriously on the question before we rush ahead and declare that almost the entire church throughout its history has been wrong on this issue.[73]

8. Objections. Numerous objections have been brought against the position outlined here, only a few of which can be treated at this point.[74] It is objected that *ministry should be determined by gifts, not by gender.* But in response, it must be said that spiritual gifts have to be used within the guidelines given in Scripture. The Holy Spirit who empowers spiritual gifts is also the Holy Spirit who inspired the Bible, and he does not want us to use his gifts in disobedience to his words.

Another objection is to say that *if God has genuinely called a woman to be a pastor, she should not be prevented from acting as one.* The response to this objection is similar to the one given above: an individual claim to have experienced a call from God must always be tested by subjecting it to the words of God in Scripture. If the Bible teaches that God wills for men alone to bear the primary teaching and governing responsibilities of the pastorate, then by implication the Bible also teaches that God does not call women to be pastors. However, we should add that often what a woman discerns as a divine call to the pastorate may be indeed a call to full-time Christian ministry, but not to be a pastor/elder in a church. In fact, many opportunities for full-time occupational ministry exist within the local church and elsewhere, apart from being a teaching pastor or an elder—for example, church staff positions in counseling, women's ministries, Christian education, and children's ministries, as well as ministries of music and worship, campus student ministries, evangelistic ministries, ministries to the poor, and administrative responsibilities that do not involve functioning in the elder's role of government over the entire church.[75] This list could be expanded, but the point is that we should not make restrictions where Scripture itself does not place restrictions, but should allow and encourage full and free participation by women as well as men in all of these other areas.

Some object that *the New Testament emphasis is on servant leadership,* and therefore that we should not be so concerned about authority, since that is more a pagan than a

---

[72]See the previous footnote. Regarding the fact that women could prophesy in New Testament congregations, see the discussion under section 2 above.

[73]See footnote 57 above. A number of recent books have highlighted the neglected contributions that women have made to the church throughout its history: see especially Ruth Tucker and Walter Liefeld, *Daughters of the Church,* a book that is a treasure-house of information and provides extensive additional bibliography. But none of these studies overthrows the clear conclusion that the great majority of the church throughout its history has not accepted women as pastors.

[74]For further discussion, see *Recovering Biblical Manhood and Womanhood,* esp. pp. 60–92. Fuller statements of the objections listed here can be found in the books marked "Favors women as pastors" in the bibliography at the end of this chapter, esp. the volumes by Mickelsen, Spencer, and Bilezikian.

[75]For further discussion, see *Recovering Biblical Manhood and Womanhood,* pp. 54–59.

Christian concern. But this objection makes a false distinction between servanthood and authority. Certainly Jesus himself is the model of a servant leader, but Jesus also has authority—great authority! He is the Lord of our lives and the Lord of the church. By analogy, elders ought to follow Jesus' example of servant leadership (see 1 Peter 5:1–5) but that does not mean that they should neglect to govern with authority when the Bible itself gives them this responsibility (see 1 Tim. 5:17; Heb. 13:17; 1 Peter 5:5).[76]

Sometimes people object that, *just as the church finally realized that slavery was wrong, so the church today should recognize that male leadership is wrong,* and is an outdated cultural tradition that should be discarded. But this objection fails to realize the difference between the temporary cultural institution of slavery, which God certainly did not establish at creation, and the existence of a difference in male-female roles in marriage (and, by implication, in relationships within the church) which God established at creation. The seeds for the destruction of slavery were sown in the New Testament (see Philem. 16; Eph. 6:9; Col. 4:1; 1 Tim. 6:1–2), but no seeds for the destruction of marriage, or the destruction of male-female differences as created, are sown in the Bible. Moreover, the objection can be turned around: it is likely that a closer parallel to the Christian defenders of slavery in the nineteenth century is found in evangelical feminists who today use arguments from the Bible to justify conformity to some extremely strong pressures in contemporary society (in favor of slavery then, and women being pastors now).

It is sometimes objected that *Priscilla and Aquila together spoke to Apollos* and "expounded to him the way of God more accurately" (Acts 18:26). This is true, and it is helpful evidence showing that informal discussion of Scripture by men and women together, in which both men and women play a significant role in helping one another understand Scripture, is approved by the New Testament. Once again, an example such as this cautions us not to prohibit activities which are not prohibited by Scripture, yet it does not overturn the principle that the publicly recognized governing and teaching role within a church is restricted to men. Priscilla was not doing anything contrary to this restriction.

Sometimes it is objected that *it is inconsistent to allow women to vote in churches that have congregational government, but not to serve as elders.* But the authority of the church as a whole is not the same as the authority given to specific individuals within the church. When we say that the congregation as a whole has authority, we do not mean that each man and each woman in the congregation has the authority to speak or act for the congregation. Therefore, gender, as a part of individual personhood, is not significantly in view in corporate congregational decisions.

Another way of putting this is to say that the only question we are asking in this section is whether women can be officers within the church, and specifically whether they can be elders within the church. In any congregational system where the elders are elected by the congregation, it is evident to everyone in the church that the elders have a kind of delegated authority which other members of the congregation do not have—even though the other members of the congregation have voted for these people in the first place. It is the same in all systems of government where officials are elected: once the President

---

[76]See also the discussion of the authority of elders in section A.2.c above.

of the United States or the mayor of a city is elected, that person has a delegated authority over the people who elected him or her and it is an authority that is greater than the authority of any individual person who voted.[77]

At this point it is also appropriate to recognize that God has given much insight and wisdom to women as well as to men, and that any church leaders who neglect to draw on the wisdom that women have are really acting foolishly. Therefore, any group of elders or other male leaders who make decisions affecting the entire church should frequently have procedures within the church whereby the wisdom and insight of other members of the church, especially the wisdom and insight of women as well as men, can be drawn upon as an aid in making decisions.

9. What About Other Offices Within the Church? The entire discussion above has focused on the question of whether women should function as pastors or elders within the church. But what about other offices?

The biblical teaching regarding the office of *deacon* is much less extensive than that regarding the office of elder,[78] and what is involved in the office of deacon varies considerably from church to church. If deacons are actually functioning as elders and have the highest governing authority within a local church, then the arguments given above against women being elders would apply directly to this situation, and it would follow that Scripture does not permit women to be deacons in this sense. On the other hand, if deacons simply have delegated administrative responsibility for certain aspects of the ministry of the church, then there seems to be no good reason to prevent women from functioning as deacons. Regarding the question of women as deacons in 1 Timothy 3:8–13, it does not seem to the present author that this passage allows women to be deacons *in the way deacons are understood in that situation,* but there is a significant difference of viewpoint among evangelicals over the understanding of this passage,[79] and it is much less clear to us exactly what deacons did at that time than it is clear what elders did.[80]

With regard to other offices, such as treasurer, for example, or other staff positions such as youth minister or counseling director or children's minister, and so forth, the only question to be asked is whether these offices include the ruling and teaching functions reserved for elders in the New Testament. If not, then *all of these offices would be open to women as well as to men,* for we must be careful not to prohibit what the New Testament does not prohibit.

QUESTIONS FOR PERSONAL APPLICATION

1. No matter what kind of church government structure you currently find yourself in, are there ways in which you could be more encouraging and supportive to the current leaders in your church?

---

[77]See above, section B, for arguments in favor of participation by the entire congregation in some decision-making in the church, and especially in the selection of officers in the church.

[78]See above, section A.3, on the office of deacon.

[79]See footnote 23 above for information.

[80]Note that Acts 6:3 also requires that only men (Gk. *anēr*) be selected as the first deacons (if we understand that passage to be speaking of the office of deacon).

2. If you are currently an officer in your church, or if you someday would like to be one, is your pattern of life such that you would like to see it imitated by others in the church? If you have had a part in the process of selecting church leaders, have you tended to emphasize the character traits and spiritual qualifications talked about in Scripture, or have you emphasized other qualifications that the world would look for in selecting its leaders?

3. Do you think that the current governing structure of your church works quite well? How could it be improved, without changing the basic philosophy of church government to which it is committed? Whether or not your church has officers who are called "elders," who are the people who carry out the functions of elders in your church? Do you know if your own pastor would like to see some modifications in the government of your church, to enable him to carry out his task more effectively?

4. Before reading this chapter, what was your view on the question of women serving as teaching pastors or elders in a church? How has this chapter changed your view, if at all? Why do you think people's emotions are often very strong concerning this issue? Can you explain how you personally feel (emotionally) about the teaching presented in this chapter? Does it seem right to you, or not?

SPECIAL TERMS

apostle	local elders
bishop	officer
classis	overseer
congregational government	pastor
consistory	presbyterian government
deacon	presbytery
diocese	priest
elder	rector
episcopalian government	session
general assembly	synod
hierarchical government	vicar

BIBLIOGRAPHY

Babbage, S. B. "Church Officers." In *EDT,* pp. 243–45. (Contains a list of various titles for church officers used in different denominations today, with definitions.)

Bannerman, James. *The Church of Christ.* 2 vols. London: Banner of Truth, 1960. (First published in 1869.)

Baxter, Richard. *The Reformed Pastor.* Carlisle, Pa.: Banner of Truth, 1979. [Reprint.]

Bilezikian, Gilbert. *Beyond Sex Roles.* 2d ed. Grand Rapids: Baker, 1985. (Favors women as pastors.)

Burge, G. M. "Deacon, Deaconness." In *EDT*, pp. 295–96.

Carson, D. A. "Church, Authority in." In *EDT*, pp. 228–31.

Clark, Stephen B. *Man and Women in Christ*. Ann Arbor, Mich.: Servant, 1980. (Opposes women as pastors.)

Clowney, Edmund. *Called to the Ministry*. Chicago: InterVarsity Press, 1964.

_____. "Presbyterianism." In *EDT*, pp. 530–31.

Evans, Mary J. *Women in the Bible*. Exeter: Paternoster, and Downers Grove: InterVarsity Press, 1983. (Favors women as pastors.)

Foh, Susan. *Women and the Word of God: A Response to Biblical Feminism*. Philadelphia: Presbyterian and Reformed, 1980. (Opposes women as pastors.)

Fung, Ronald Y. K. "Ministry in the New Testament." In *The Church in the Bible and the World*. Ed. by D. A. Carson. Exeter: Paternoster, and Grand Rapids: Baker, 1987.

Gundry, Patricia. *Neither Slave nor Free: Helping Women Answer the Call to Church Leadership*. San Francisco: Harper and Row, 1987. (Favors women as pastors.)

_____. *Women Be Free! The Clear Message of Scripture*. Grand Rapids: Zondervan, 1988. (Favors women as pastors.)

Hodge, Charles. *Discussions in Church Polity*. New York: Charles Scribner's Sons, 1878.

Hort, F. J. A. *The Christian Ecclesia*. London: Macmillan, 1898.

House, H. Wayne. *The Role of Women in Ministry Today*. Nashville: Thomas Nelson, 1990. (Opposes women as pastors.)

Hurley, James B. *Man and Woman in Biblical Perspective*. Leicester: Inter-Varsity Press, and Grand Rapids: Zondervan, 1981. (Opposes women as pastors.)

Kirby, G. W. "Congregationalism." In *EDT*, pp. 159–61.

Knight, George W., III. *The Role Relationship of Men and Women*. Revised ed. Chicago: Moody, 1985. (Opposes women as pastors.)

Kroeger, Richard and Catherine. *I Suffer Not a Woman*. Grand Rapids: Baker, 1992. (Favors women as pastors.)

Macleod, D. "Church Government." In *NDT*, pp. 143–46.

Marshall, I. Howard. "Apostle." In *EDT*, p. 40.

Mickelsen, Alvera, ed. *Women, Authority, and the Bible*. Downers Grove, Ill.: InterVarsity Press, 1986. (A collection of essays by several authors, most of whom favor women as pastors.)

Morris, L. "Church Government." In *EDT*, pp. 238–41.

_____. *Ministers of God*. London: Inter-Varsity Press, 1964.

Piper, John, and Wayne Grudem, eds. *Recovering Biblical Manhood and Womanhood: A Response to Evangelical Feminism*. Wheaton, Ill.: Crossway, 1991. (A collection of twenty-eight essays by twenty-two authors; opposes women as pastors.)

Richards, Lawrence O. *A Theology of Church Leadership*. Grand Rapids: Zondervan, 1980.

Saucy, Robert L. "Authority in the Church." In *Walvoord: A Tribute*. Ed. by Donald K. Campbell. Chicago: Moody, 1982. pp. 219–37. (An extensive argument in favor of congregational government.)

_____. *The Church in God's Program*. Chicago: Moody, 1972.

Spencer, Aida Besancon. *Beyond the Curse: Women Called to Ministry*. Nashville: Thomas Nelson, 1985. (Favors women as pastors.)

Stott, John R. W. *The Preacher's Portrait.* Grand Rapids: Eerdmans, 1961.

Strauch, Alexander. *Biblical Eldership: An Urgent Call to Restore Biblical Church Leadership.* Littleton, Col.: Lewis and Roth, 1986.

Tiller, J. "Ministry." In *EDT,* pp. 430–33.

Toon, Peter. "Bishop." In *EDT,* pp. 157–58.

Tucker, Ruth A., and Walter L. Liefeld. *Daughters of the Church: Women and Ministry from New Testament Times to the Present.* Grand Rapids: Zondervan, 1987. (Favors women as pastors.)

Wallace, R. S. "Elder." In *EDT,* pp. 347–48.

SCRIPTURE MEMORY PASSAGE

1 Peter 5:1–4: *So I exhort the elders among you, as a fellow elder and a witness of the sufferings of Christ as well as a partaker in the glory that is to be revealed. Tend the flock of God that is your charge, not by constraint but willingly, not for shameful gain but eagerly, not as domineering over those in your charge but being examples to the flock. And when the chief Shepherd is manifested you will obtain the unfading crown of glory.*

HYMN

"Glorious Things of Thee Are Spoken"

There are not many hymns—if any—written about church government! I have put here a hymn which thanks God for the blessings of being a member of God's people in general, and therefore a citizen of the heavenly Mount Zion, the heavenly city where God's people dwell. But in the hymn the author also uses Old Testament imagery from the journey of God's people through the wilderness ("see the cloud and fire appear," v. 3), and the entire hymn can also be seen as one of thanks to God for the blessing of dwelling (spiritually) within the walls of the church today.

The author, John Newton, is also the author of the well-known hymn "Amazing Grace."

> Glorious things of thee are spoken, Zion, city of our God;
> He whose Word cannot be broken formed thee for his own abode:
> On the Rock of Ages founded, what can shake thy sure repose?
> With salvation's walls surrounded, thou may'st smile at all thy foes.
>
> See, the streams of living waters, springing from eternal love,
> Well supply thy sons and daughters, and all fear of want remove:
> Who can faint, while such a river ever flows their thirst t'assuage?
> Grace which, like the Lord, the giver, never fails from age to age.
>
> Round each habitation hov'ring, see the cloud and fire appear
> For a glory and cov'ring, showing that the Lord is near:

Thus deriving from their banner light by night and shade by day,
  Safe they feed upon the manna which he gives them when they
    pray.

Savior, if of Zion's city I, through grace, a member am,
  Let the world deride or pity, I will glory in thy name:
Fading is the worldling's pleasure, all his boasted pomp and show;
  Solid joys and lasting treasure none but Zion's children know.

AUTHOR: JOHN NEWTON, 1779

Chapter 6

MEANS OF GRACE WITHIN THE CHURCH

What are the different activities within the life of the church that God uses to bring blessing to us? What do we miss if we neglect involvement in a local church?

EXPLANATION AND SCRIPTURAL BASIS

A. How Many Means of Grace Are Available to Us?

All of the blessings we experience in this life are ultimately undeserved—they are all of *grace*. In fact, for Peter, the entire Christian life is lived by grace (1 Peter 5:12).

But are there any special *means* that God uses to give additional grace to us? Specifically, *within the fellowship of the church* are there certain means—that is, certain activities, ceremonies, or functions—that God uses to give more grace to us? Another way of formulating that question is to ask whether there are certain *means* through which the Holy Spirit works to convey blessings into the life of the believer. Of course, personal prayer, worship, and Bible study, and personal faith, are all means through which God works to bring grace to us as individual Christians. But in this chapter we are dealing with the doctrine of the church, and we are asking specifically *within the fellowship of the church* what the means of grace are that God uses to bring blessing to us.

We may define the means of grace as follows: *The means of grace are any activities within the fellowship of the church that God uses to give more grace to Christians.*

127

In the history of the discussion of "means of grace within the church," some theologians have restricted them to three: the preaching of the Word, and the two sacraments (baptism and the Lord's Supper).[1]

But is it wise to make such a short list of "means of grace"? If we wish to list and discuss all the means of receiving the Holy Spirit's blessing that come to believers specifically through the fellowship of the church, then it does not seem wise to limit the "means of grace" to three activities whose administration is restricted to the ordained clergy or officers of the church. There is wisdom, for example, in Charles Hodge's view that prayer is a fourth means of grace.[2]

But should we limit our discussion of the means of grace to these four activities only? It would seem more helpful to list all of the *many varied activities* within the church that God has given as special ways of receiving his "grace" day by day and week by week. Such a list may become quite long, and, depending on how it is organized, may include various numbers of elements. The following list may not be exhaustive, but it does include most of the means of grace that believers have access to within the fellowship of the church:

1. Teaching of the Word
2. Baptism
3. The Lord's Supper
4. Prayer for one another
5. Worship
6. Church discipline
7. Giving
8. Spiritual gifts
9. Fellowship
10. Evangelism
11. Personal ministry to individuals

All these are available to believers *within* the church. The Holy Spirit works through all of them to bring various kinds of blessing to individuals. Therefore, departing from the much shorter lists usually given in systematic theologies, I have decided to call all of these "means of grace" within the church.

The Roman Catholic Church has traditionally believed that God's "grace" comes to people only through the official ministry of the church, particularly through the

---

[1]This is the position of Louis Berkhof, *Systematic Theology* (Grand Rapids: Eerdmans, 1939, 1941), pp. 604–6. He calls these three means "objective channels which Christ has instituted in the church" (pp. 604–5), but the significant criterion in Berkhof's thinking appears to be the fact that these three are the special functions administered by the ordained clergy: Berkhof calls these "the *official* means of the church of Jesus Christ" (p. 605), and later says, "As the *official* means of grace placed at the disposal of the Church, both the Word and the sacraments *can only be administered by the lawful and properly qualified officers of the Church*" (p. 610). In this way, he clearly restricts the "means of grace" to those means administered by the ordained clergy.

Although those who follow Berkhof on this point could argue that this procedure is wise and serves the interest of maintaining good order in the church, we may ask whether in fact this restriction carries overtones of "sacerdotalism," the view of the Roman Catholic Church (and, to a lesser degree, the Anglican Church) that there is a special "priesthood" of ordained people within the church who have a special authority or ability to extend God's grace to people in the church.

(See chapter 7, p. 142, for a discussion of the use of the two terms *sacraments* and *ordinances* to refer to baptism and the Lord's Supper.)

[2]Hodge, *Systematic Theology*, 3 vols. (1871–73; reprint, Grand Rapids: Eerdmans, 1970), 3:692–709.

priests of the church. Therefore, when it specifies the means of grace (what it calls the "sacraments") that are available to people within the church, it has in view activities that are supervised and/or performed by only the priests of the church. The seven "sacraments" in Roman Catholic teaching are the following:

1. Baptism
2. Confirmation
3. Eucharist (the Lord's Supper as experienced in the mass)
4. Penance
5. Extreme unction (popularly known as the "last rites," the anointing with oil that is administered to a dying person)
6. Holy orders (ordination to the priesthood or diaconate)
7. Matrimony

There is not only a difference in the lists given by Catholics and Protestants; there is also a difference in fundamental meaning. Catholics view these as "means of salvation" that make people more fit to receive justification from God. But on a Protestant view, the means of grace are simply means of additional blessing within the Christian life, and do not add to our fitness to receive justification from God.[3] Catholics teach that the means of grace impart grace whether or not there is subjective faith on the part of the minister or the recipient,[4] while Protestants hold that God only imparts grace when there is faith on the part of the persons receiving these means. And while the Roman Catholic Church firmly restricts the administration of the sacraments to the clergy, our list of means of grace includes many activities that are carried out by all believers.

B. Discussion of Specific Means

1. Teaching of the Word. Even before people become Christians, the Word of God as preached and taught brings God's grace to them in that it is the instrument God uses to impart spiritual life to them and bring them to salvation. Paul says that the gospel is the "power of God for salvation" (Rom. 1:16) and that the preaching of Christ is "the power of God and the wisdom of God" (1 Cor. 1:24). God caused us to be born again or "brought . . . forth by the word of truth" (James 1:18) and Peter says, "You have been born anew, not of perishable seed but of imperishable, through the living and abiding word of God" (1 Peter 1:23). It is the written Word of God, the Bible, that is "able to instruct you for salvation through faith in Christ Jesus" (2 Tim. 3:15).

Moreover, once we have become Christians, Paul reminds us that it is the Word of God that is "able to build you up" (Acts 20:32). It is necessary for spiritual nourishment and for maintaining spiritual life, because we do not live on bread alone but on "every word that proceeds from the mouth of God" (Matt. 4:4). Moses speaks of the absolute necessity of the written Word of God when he tells the people, "It is no trifle for you, but it is your life, and thereby you shall live long in the land which you are going over the Jordan to possess" (Deut. 32:47).

---

[3]However, the Anglican Church teaches that baptism is "generally necessary" for salvation.

[4]See chapter 7, pp. 148–49, on the Roman Catholic view that the sacraments work *ex opere operato*.

It is the Word of God that convicts us of sin and turns us to righteousness, for it is profitable "for teaching, for reproof, for correction, and for training in righteousness" (2 Tim. 3:16). It gives direction and guidance as a "lamp" to our feet and a "light" to our path (Ps. 119:105). In the midst of an ungodly culture Scripture gives wisdom and guidance like "a lamp shining in a dark place" (2 Peter 1:19). Moreover, it is active in giving wisdom to all, even "making wise the simple" (Ps. 19:7). It gives hope to those who are in despair, because Paul says that it was written "that by steadfastness and by the encouragement of the scriptures we might have hope" (Rom. 15:4).

The Word of God is not weak or powerless in accomplishing these goals, for it speaks to us with the power of God and accomplishes God's purposes. The Lord says,

> For as the rain and the snow come down from heaven,
>> and return not thither but water the earth,
> making it bring forth and sprout,
>> giving seed to the sower and bread to the eater,
> so shall my word be that goes forth from my mouth;
>> it shall not return to me empty,
> but it shall accomplish that which I purpose,
>> and prosper in the thing for which I sent it. (Isa. 55:10–11)

God's Word is not weak but has his divine power accompanying it: "Is not my word *like fire,* says the LORD, and *like a hammer* which breaks the rock in pieces?" (Jer. 23:29). It is so sharp and powerful that it is the "*sword* of the Spirit" (Eph. 6:17), and it is so effective in speaking to people's needs that the author of Hebrews says, "the word of God is living and active, sharper than any *two-edged sword,* piercing to the division of soul and spirit, of joints and marrow, and discerning the thoughts and intentions of the heart" (Heb. 4:12).

So closely are the growth and strength of the church linked to the reign of the Word of God in people's lives that more than once the book of Acts can describe the growth of the church as the growth of the Word of God: "*And the word of God increased;* and the number of the disciples multiplied greatly in Jerusalem" (Acts 6:7); "But *the word of God grew and multiplied*" (Acts 12:24); "And *the word of the Lord spread* throughout all the region" (Acts 13:49).

So important is the Bible as the primary means of grace that God gives to his people that Charles Hodge reminds us that throughout history true Christianity has flourished "just in proportion to the degree in which the Bible is known, and its truths are diffused among the people." Moreover, he notes that there are no evidences of salvation or sanctification to be found where the Word of God is not known. "The nations where the Bible is unknown sit in darkness."[5]

It is appropriate that we list the teaching of the Word as the first and most important means of grace within the church. But we should add that such teaching includes not only officially recognized teaching by ordained clergy in the church, but also all the teaching that occurs in Bible studies, Sunday School classes, the reading of Christian books on Scripture, and even in personal Bible study.

---

[5]Hodge, *Systematic Theology,* 3:468–69.

2. Baptism. Since Jesus commanded his church to baptize (Matt. 28:19), we would expect that there would be a measure of blessing connected with baptism, because all obedience to God by Christians brings God's favor with it. This obedience is specifically a public act of confessing Jesus as Savior, an act which in itself brings joy and blessing to a believer. Moreover, it is a sign of the believer's death and resurrection with Christ (see Rom. 6:2–5; Col. 2:12), and it seems fitting that the Holy Spirit would work through such a sign to increase our faith, to increase our experiential realization of death to the power and love of sin in our lives, and to increase our experience of the power of new resurrection life in Christ that we have as believers. Since baptism is a physical symbol of the death and resurrection of Christ and our participation in them, it should also give additional assurance of union with Christ to all believers who are present. Finally, since water baptism is an outward symbol of inward spiritual baptism by the Holy Spirit, we may expect that the Holy Spirit will ordinarily work alongside the baptism, giving to believers an increasing realization of the benefits of the spiritual baptism to which it points.

When baptism very closely accompanies someone's initial profession of faith and is in fact the outward form that profession of faith takes, there is certainly a connection between baptism and receiving the gift of the Holy Spirit, for Peter says to his hearers at Pentecost, "Repent, and be baptized every one of you in the name of Jesus Christ for the forgiveness of your sins; and you shall receive the gift of the Holy Spirit" (Acts 2:38). Moreover, Paul says, "You were buried with him in baptism, in which you were also raised with him through faith in the working of God, who raised him from the dead" (Col. 2:12). The statement that it is "*through faith* in the working of God" that this happens reminds us that there is no magical property in the act of baptism itself, which causes a spiritual result to come about, yet the verse also indicates that when faith accompanies baptism there is genuine spiritual work in the life of the person being baptized. As we would expect, sometimes great spiritual joy follows upon baptism—a great joy in the Lord and in the salvation that baptism so vividly pictures (see Acts 8:39; 16:34).

Although we must avoid the Roman Catholic teaching that grace is imparted even *apart from* the faith of the person being baptized, we must not react so strongly to this error that we say that there is no spiritual benefit at all that comes from baptism, that the Holy Spirit *does not* work through it and that it is *merely symbolic.* It is better to say that where there is genuine faith on the part of the person being baptized, and where the faith of the church that watches the baptism is stirred up and encouraged by this ceremony, then the Holy Spirit certainly does work through baptism, and it becomes a "means of grace" through which the Holy Spirit brings blessing to the person being baptized and to the church as well. (Baptism will be more fully discussed in the next chapter.)

3. The Lord's Supper. In addition to baptism, the other ordinance or ceremony that Jesus commanded the church to carry out is participation in the Lord's Supper. Although this subject will be discussed more thoroughly in chapter 8, it is appropriate to note here that participation in the Lord's Supper is also very clearly a means of grace which the Holy Spirit uses to bring blessing to the church. The Lord's Supper is not simply an ordinary meal among human beings—it is a fellowship with Christ, in his presence and at his table.

Once again, we must avoid the idea that any automatic or magical benefit comes from sharing in the Lord's Supper, whether a person participates in faith or not.[6] But when a person participates in faith, renewing and strengthening his or her own trust in Christ for salvation, and believing that the Holy Spirit will bring spiritual blessing through such participation, then certainly additional blessing may be expected. We must be careful here, as with baptism, to avoid the mistake of overreacting to Roman Catholic teaching and maintaining that the Lord's Supper is *merely symbolic* and not a means of grace. Paul says, "The cup of blessing which we bless, is it not a *participation* (Gk. *koinōnia,* "sharing," "fellowship") in the blood of Christ? The bread which we break, is it not a *participation* [*koinōnia*] in the body of Christ?" (1 Cor. 10:16). Because there is such a sharing in the body and blood of Christ (apparently meaning a sharing in the benefits of Christ's body and blood given for us), the unity of believers is beautifully exhibited at the time of the Lord's Supper: "Because there is one bread, we who are many are one body, for we all partake of the one bread" (1 Cor. 10:17). And since we are participants at "the table of the Lord" (1 Cor. 10:21), Paul warns the Corinthians that they cannot participate in the Lord's table and also participate in idol worship: "You cannot partake in the table of the Lord and the table of demons" (1 Cor. 10:21). There is a spiritual union among believers and with the Lord that is strengthened and solidified at the Lord's Supper, and it is not to be taken lightly.

This is why the Corinthians were experiencing judgment for their abuse of the Lord's Supper (1 Cor. 11:29–30: "For any one who eats and drinks without discerning the body eats and drinks judgment upon himself. That is why many of you are weak and ill, and some have died"). But if Paul says there will be judgment for *wrong* participation in the Lord's Supper, then certainly we should expect *blessing* for right participation in the Lord's Supper. When we obey Jesus' command, "Take, eat" (Matt. 26:26), and go through the physical activity of eating and drinking at the Lord's table, our physical action *pictures* a corresponding spiritual nourishment, a nourishment of our souls that will occur when we participate in obedience and faith. Jesus says, "For my flesh is food indeed, and my blood is drink indeed. He who eats my flesh and drinks my blood abides in me, and I in him" (John 6:55–56; cf. vv. 52–54, 57–58; also vv. 27, 33–35, 48–51).

As with baptism, therefore, we should expect that the Lord would give spiritual blessing as we participate in the Lord's Supper in faith and in obedience to the directions laid down in Scripture, and in this way it is a "means of grace" which the Holy Spirit uses to convey blessing to us.

4. Prayer. We need to note here that corporate prayer within the church as it assembles, and prayer by church members for one another, are powerful means which the Holy Spirit uses daily to bring blessing to Christians within the church. Certainly we are to *pray together* as well as individually, following the example of the early church. When

---

[6]This view that there is blessing that comes automatically from participation in the Lord's Supper is the Roman Catholic doctrine of *ex opere operato* ("by the work performed"), which is discussed in chapter 8, section C.1; see also pp. 148–49.

they heard the threats of the Jewish leaders, "they lifted their voices *together* to God" in prayer (Acts 4:24–30), "And when they had prayed, the place in which they were gathered together was shaken; and they were all filled with the Holy Spirit and spoke the word of God with boldness" (Acts 4:31; cf. 2:42). When Peter was put in prison, "earnest prayer for him was made to God by the church" (Acts 12:5).

If prayer from the church is not simply the mouthing of words without heartfelt intention, but is the genuine expression of our hearts and the reflection of sincere faith, then we should expect that the Holy Spirit will bring a great blessing through it. Certainly when prayer is done "in the Spirit" (Eph. 6:18; cf. Jude 20: "pray in the Holy Spirit"), it involves fellowship with the Holy Spirit and therefore a ministry of the Holy Spirit to the people praying. And the author of Hebrews reminds us that as we "draw near" to God in prayer before the throne of grace, we do so "that we may receive mercy and find grace to help in time of need" (Heb. 4:16).

The more the genuine fellowship of a church increases, the more there ought to be continual prayer for one another within the church, and the more genuine spiritual blessing from the Holy Spirit may be expected to flow through the church.

5. Worship. Genuine worship is worship "in spirit" (John 4:23–24; Phil. 3:3), which probably means worship that is in the spiritual realm of activity (not merely the outward physical action of attendance at a worship service or singing of songs).[7] When we enter that spiritual realm of activity and minister to the Lord in worship, God also ministers to us. So, for example, in the church at Antioch, it was *While they were worshiping the Lord* and fasting" that "the Holy Spirit said, 'Set apart for me Barnabas and Saul for the work to which I have called them'" (Acts 13:2). This parallels the experience of the people of Israel in the Old Testament who knew the presence of God when they engaged in genuine worship:

> *When the song was raised,* with trumpets and cymbals and other musical instruments, *in praise to the LORD,* "For he is good, for his steadfast love endures forever," the house, the house of the LORD was filled with a cloud, so that the priests could not stand to minister because of the cloud; for *the glory of the LORD filled the house of God.* (2 Chron. 5:13–14)

When God's people worshiped, he came in a very visible way to dwell in their midst. Similarly in the New Testament, James promises, "Draw near to God and *he will draw near to you*" (James 4:8).

In fact, as God's people worshiped, he delivered them from their enemies (2 Chron. 20:18–23), or at other times gave them true spiritual insight into the nature of events around them (Ps. 73:17: "Until I went into the sanctuary of God; then I perceived their end").

If worship is genuinely an experience of drawing near to God, coming into his presence, and giving him the praise he deserves, then we certainly ought to count it one of the primary "means of grace" available to the church. Through genuine congregational

---

[7]See the discussion of worship "in spirit" in chapter 9, section D. (The whole of chapter 9 discusses worship in general.)

worship God will very often bring great blessing, both individually and corporately, to his people.

6. Church Discipline. Because church discipline is a means by which the purity of the church is advanced and holiness of life is encouraged, we certainly should count it as a "means of grace" as well. However, blessing is not automatically given: when the church disciplines, no spiritual good comes to the wrongdoer unless the Holy Spirit convicts him or her of sin and brings about a "godly grief" that "produces a repentance that leads to salvation and brings no regret" (2 Cor. 7:10), and no spiritual good comes to the church unless the Holy Spirit is active in the other members' lives when they become aware of the process. This is why the church is to carry out discipline with the knowledge that it is done in the presence of the Lord (1 Cor. 5:4; cf. 4:19–20), and with the assurance that it has heavenly sanction connected with it (Matt. 16:19; 18:18–20).[8]

It would be very healthy for the church to begin to think of church discipline not as an onerous burden placed upon it by the Lord, but as a genuine "means of grace" by which great blessing can come to the church—in reconciling believers to one another and to God, in restoring the erring brother or sister to walk in obedience, in warning all to "stand in fear" (1 Tim. 5:20), in increasing moral purity in the church, and in protecting and advancing Christ's honor. Though sorrow and pain are often connected with church discipline, when it is rightly done, with faith that the Lord is working through it, the sorrow will "bring no regret" (2 Cor. 7:10). When carried out in this way, church discipline should certainly be seen as a means of grace by which the Holy Spirit will bring blessing to his church.[9]

7. Giving. Giving is ordinarily done through the church as it receives and distributes gifts to the various ministries and needs cared for by the church. Once again, there is no automatic or mechanical bestowing of benefits on those who give. Simon the sorcerer was strongly rebuked for thinking that he "could obtain the gift of God with money" (Acts 8:20). But if giving is done in faith, out of commitment to Christ and love for his people, then certainly there will be great blessing in it. It is most pleasing to God when gifts of money are accompanied by an intensification of the giver's own personal commitment to God, as was the case among the Macedonians who "first . . . *gave themselves* to the Lord and to us by the will of God" (2 Cor. 8:5), and then gave to help the poor Christians in Jerusalem. When giving is carried out joyfully, "not reluctantly or under compulsion," there is the great reward of God's favor with it, "for God loves a cheerful giver" (2 Cor. 9:7).

Paul views the giving of money to the Lord's work as spiritual sowing that will lead to a harvest: "he who sows sparingly will also reap sparingly, and he who sows bountifully will also reap bountifully" (2 Cor. 9:6). And Paul expects that as the Corinthians give rightly God will bless them: "And God is able to make *all grace abound to you,* that always having all sufficiency in everything, you may have an abundance for every good deed" (2 Cor. 9:8 NASB). He tells them, "*You will be enriched in every way for great generosity,*

---

[8]See discussion of the "power of the keys" in chapter 4, section B.

[9]See chapter 4, section D, for a more full discussion of church discipline.

which through us will produce thanksgiving to God" (2 Cor. 9:11). Therefore giving blesses the *recipient* in that his or her needs are met and faith and thanksgiving for God's provision are increased; it blesses the *giver* because "God loves a cheerful giver" and will grant an abundant spiritual harvest, and brings blessing to *all who know about it* since it produces a harvest of "many thanksgivings to God" (2 Cor. 9:12). Rather than seeing giving as an unpleasant obligation, we would do well to view it as a rich means of grace within the church, and to expect that through it the Holy Spirit will bring blessing.

8. Spiritual Gifts. Peter views spiritual gifts as channels through which God's grace comes to the church because he says, "As each has received a gift, employ it for one another, *as good stewards of God's varied grace*" (1 Peter 4:10). When gifts are used for one another in the church, God's grace is thereby dispensed to those for whom God intended it. Great blessing will come to the church through proper use of spiritual gifts, as the church follows Paul's command to use the gifts to "strive to excel in building up the church" (1 Cor. 14:12; cf. Eph. 4:11–16).

If we listed all the spiritual gifts as separate means of grace, our list of the means of grace would be much longer than eleven items. But even if we contain them all in this one category, we should recognize that the different spiritual gifts in the church are all means by which the Holy Spirit brings blessing through individual Christians. This should remind us of the abundant favor that God has given us as undeserving sinners, and should also make us realize that many different Christians, with diverse gifts, can be the channels through which grace comes to us. In fact, in Peter's exhortation to use spiritual gifts as stewards of "God's *varied* grace" (1 Peter 4:10), the word translated "varied" (Gk. *poikilos*) means "having many facets or aspects; richly varied; having great diversity." Moreover, we should remember that these gifts are distributed not only to clergy or a limited number of Christians, but to all believers who have the Holy Spirit within them (1 Cor. 12:7, 11; 1 Peter 4:10).[10]

9. Fellowship. We should not neglect ordinary Christian fellowship as a valuable means of grace within the church. The early church "devoted themselves to the apostles' teaching *and fellowship,* to the breaking of bread and the prayers" (Acts 2:42). And the author of Hebrews reminds believers, "Let us consider how to stir up one another to love and good works, *not neglecting to meet together,* as is the habit of some, but encouraging one another, and all the more as you see the Day drawing near" (Heb. 10:24–25). In the fellowship of believers, ordinary friendship and affection for one another will grow, and Jesus' injunction that we "love one another" (John 15:12) will be fulfilled. Moreover, as believers care for one another, they will "Bear one another's burdens, and so fulfil the law of Christ" (Gal. 6:2).

An emphasis on the fellowship of believers with one another as a means of grace would also help to overcome an excessive focus on the ordained clergy as the primary dispensers of grace within the church, and particularly when the church as a whole is assembled. It would also be healthy for Christians to recognize that a measure of God's grace is

---

[10]See chapters 10 and 11 for a discussion of spiritual gifts.

experienced when Christians talk together and eat together, when they have times of work and play together, enjoying one another's fellowship. "And day by day, attending the temple together and breaking bread in their homes, they partook of food with glad and generous hearts, praising God and having favor with all the people" (Acts 2:46–47).

10. Evangelism. In Acts, there is a frequent connection between proclaiming the gospel (even in the face of opposition) and being filled with the Holy Spirit (see Acts 2:4 with vv. 14–36; 4:8, 31; 9:17 with v. 20; 13:9, 52). Evangelism is a means of grace, then, not only in the sense that it ministers saving grace to the unsaved, but also because those who evangelize experience more of the Holy Spirit's presence and blessing in their own lives. Sometimes evangelism is carried out by individuals, but at other times it is a corporate activity of the church (as in evangelistic campaigns). And even individual evangelism often involves other church members who will welcome an unbelieving visitor and give attention to his or her needs. So evangelism is rightly considered a means of grace in the church.

11. Personal Ministry to Individuals. Along with the previous ten "means of grace" within the church, it is appropriate to list one more specific means that the Holy Spirit very frequently uses to bring blessing to individual Christians. This means of grace operates when one or more Christians within the church take time to minister, in various ways, to very specific needs of another individual in the church.

Sometimes this ministry takes the form of *words of encouragement or exhortation or wise counsel*. We are to "teach and admonish one another in all wisdom" (Col. 3:16), and to speak words that "impart grace to those who hear" (Eph. 4:29). We are to attempt to bring back "a sinner from the error of his way" (James 5:20) and to "consider how to stir up one another to love and good works" and to be "encouraging one another" (Heb. 10:24–25). At other times such ministry involves *giving to assist the material needs of a brother or sister:* James rebukes those who merely say, "Go in peace, be warmed and filled," without "giving them the things needed for the body" (James 2:16). John warns us, "If any one has the world's goods and sees his brother in need, yet closes his heart against him, how does God's love abide in him?" (1 John 3:17). Therefore the early church gave readily to the needs of poor Christians, so that "There was not a needy person among them" (Acts 4:34). And Paul said that the leaders of the church in Jerusalem "would have us remember the poor, which very thing I was eager to do" (Gal. 2:10).

Another form this interpersonal ministry may take is the *anointing with oil* in conjunction with prayer for a sick person. Jesus' disciples "anointed with oil many that were sick and healed them" (Mark 6:13). Similarly, James says that a sick person should "call for the elders of the church, and let them pray over him, anointing him with oil in the name of the Lord" (James 5:14). In these cases the oil seems to have been a physical symbol of the healing power of the Holy Spirit coming to the sick person.

Finally, one more means of exercising personal ministry to individuals in the New Testament is the use of physical touch, particularly the *laying on of hands* in connection with prayer for someone in need. A survey of the New Testament may bring surprise to many modern Christians (as it did to the present author) when they see how frequently the laying on of hands and other kinds of physical touch are seen to function as a "means of grace" in the ministry of Jesus and the early church.

It seems that the laying on of hands was by far the most common method that Jesus used to pray for people. When crowds came bringing people "with various diseases" to him, "*he laid his hands on every one of them* and healed them" (Luke 4:40). Other passages specifically describe Jesus' placing his hands on people to heal them (Matt. 8:3; Mark 1:41; 6:5; 8:23–25; Luke 5:13; 13:13). But more significant than these individual passages is the fact that people who came to Jesus for healing would come specifically asking him to lay his hands on a sick person: "*Come and lay your hand on her,* and she will live" (Matt. 9:18), or "*Come and lay your hands on her,* so that she may be made well, and live" (Mark 5:23; cf. 7:32). The fact that people came with this request suggests that the laying on of hands was commonly recognized as the method Jesus usually used to heal people. In imitation of Jesus' method of healing, when the father of Publius was sick, "Paul visited him and prayed, and *putting his hands on him* healed him" (Acts 28:8).[11]

In other cases people sought more generally to touch Jesus, or asked that he would touch them, in order to be healed. "And some people brought to him a blind man, and begged him to *touch* him" (Mark 8:22). Similarly, people "brought to him all that were sick, and besought him that they might only touch the fringe of his garment; and as many as touched it were made well" (Matt. 14:35–36). This was because the power of the Holy Spirit was conveyed through Jesus' physical touch, and came forth and healed people. "All the crowd sought to *touch* him, for power came forth from him and healed them all" (Luke 6:19; cf. Matt. 9:20–22, 25; 20:34; Mark 1:31; 5:41; 9:27; Luke 7:14; 8:54; 22:51).

However, it was not simply to heal that Jesus and the early church laid on hands or touched people. When children came to Jesus "he took them in his arms and blessed them, laying his hands upon them" (Mark 10:16; cf. Matt. 19:13–15; Luke 18:15).

When Jesus so frequently touched people to bring healing or otherwise to bring blessing to them, it is not surprising that people would mention the miracles done by his hands: "What mighty works (Gk. *dynamis,* "miracle") are wrought *by his hands!*" (Mark 6:2).[12] Similarly, when Paul and Barnabas were on their first missionary journey, the Lord "bore witness to the word of his grace, granting signs and wonders to be done *by their hands*" (Acts 14:3).[13] In the same way, "God did extraordinary miracles by the *hands* of Paul" (Acts 19:11).[14] Since there was, as with the other means of grace, no automatic or magical power inherent in the hands of the early Christians, but healing and other kinds

---

[11]Although the longer ending of Mark is doubtful as part of Scripture, Mark 16:18 certainly does represent at least one stream of early tradition within the church as well: it says that those who believe in Jesus "will lay their hands on the sick, and they will recover."

[12]Because the gospels so frequently emphasize the fact that Jesus laid hands on people or touched them with his hands, this expression does not seem to be simply a metaphor meaning "What miracles are done by *him!*" but is better understood to be a reference to the specific way in which Jesus' hands were the means by which his miracles were very frequently brought about. Unfortunately, in this verse and several others mentioning miracles done by people's *hands,* the NIV has decided a literal translation is not important and has given the English

reader no mention of hands. For example, it simply translates Mark 6:2, "*He even does miracles!*" But the Greek text specifically says that miracles are done "*through his hands*" (*dia tōn cheirōn autou*). In the following section I have pointed out only some of the places where the NIV fails to translate the Greek word *cheir* ("hand"), but it is present in the Greek text in all the verses I quote, and readers who do not find it in their NIV translations should consult another translation, such as the RSV or NASB, that has a more literal translation policy.

[13]The NIV simply translates, "enabling *them* to do miraculous signs and wonders" (see previous footnote).

[14]The NIV simply says, "God did extraordinary miracles *through Paul*" (see previous two footnotes).

of blessing only came as God himself was pleased to work through the laying on of hands, it is not surprising that the early church prayed specifically that God would stretch forth *his hand* to heal. They prayed, "And now, Lord, look upon their threats, and grant to your servants to speak your word with all boldness, *while you stretch out your hand to heal"* (Acts 4:29 – 30). They realized that while they stretched forth their hands to touch those who were sick it would not be effective at all unless God's own mighty hand of power was working through their hands.

At other times the laying on of hands was done for some other purpose. Apparently it was done in connection with asking God to empower or equip people for some service or ministry. When the first deacons were appointed, the church brought them before the apostles, "and they prayed and *laid their hands upon them"* (Acts 6:6). Similarly, when the church at Antioch sent out Paul and Barnabas, "When they had fasted and prayed and *laid their hands on them,* they sent them away" (Acts 13:3 NASB).

When the gospel came to a new group of people, those who proclaimed the gospel would sometimes lay hands on the new believers in order that they might receive the new covenant power of the Holy Spirit. At Samaria, the apostles "laid their hands on them and they received the Holy Spirit" (Acts 8:17). Ananias laid his hands on Saul in order that he might regain his sight and "be filled with the Holy Spirit" (Acts 9:17). When Paul "laid his hands upon" the disciples at Ephesus who had just come to believe in Jesus, "the Holy Spirit came on them" (Acts 19:6).

In other cases the laying on of hands resulted in the impartation of some spiritual gift. In the incident just mentioned, the disciples at Ephesus also "spoke with tongues and prophesied" (Acts 19:6) after Paul laid his hands on them. Moreover, he reminds Timothy, "Do not neglect the gift you have, which was given you by prophetic utterance (literally, "through prophecy") when the council of elders laid their hands upon you" (1 Tim. 4:14). Paul may have been referring to the same event or a different one when he said later, "I remind you to rekindle the *gift* of God that is within you *through the laying on of my hands"* (2 Tim. 1:6). (In 1 Timothy 5:22, the statement "Do not be hasty in the laying on of hands" refers to the ordination of elders; see chapter 5, section A.2.f.)

If people in the early church were frequently praying for one another's needs, and if they imitated the example of Jesus and his disciples in the laying on of hands to pray for people for healing, for bringing blessing, for receiving the Holy Spirit at the time of conversion, for receiving spiritual gifts, or for empowering for ministry, then we would expect that instruction given to new Christians would have included the teaching that prayer for individual needs would ordinarily be accompanied by the placing of a hand or hands upon the person who was being prayed for. If this were so, then it would not be surprising that "the laying on of hands" would be classified as an "elementary" doctrine, something that belongs to the "foundation" of Christian instruction—which is in fact what we find in Hebrews 6:1 – 2. Although some have understood this to refer more narrowly to the laying on of hands that accompanies installation in some specific church office, that is only one small aspect of the pattern of situations in which laying on of hands is found in the New Testament. It seems much better to understand this phrase in Hebrews 6:2 to refer to elementary instruction about how to pray for others in various situations of need so that young Christians would immediately be able to begin ministering to others as well.

It seems appropriate, then, to count the laying on of hands as one other dimension of the rich diversity of "means of grace" that God has placed within the church to bring blessing to his people.

12. Should Footwashing Be Practiced As a Means of Grace Within the Church? From time to time some Christian groups have practiced a ceremony of washing one another's feet at a public meeting of the church. They have based this practice on Jesus's command, "If I then, your Lord and Teacher, have washed your feet, *you also ought to wash one another's feet*" (John 13:14). Those who advocate footwashing consider it a ceremony that Jesus commanded, similar to the ceremonies of baptism and the Lord's Supper.

However, there are several reasons why we should not think that in John 13:14 Jesus was establishing another ceremony for the church in addition to baptism and the Lord's Supper. (1) Baptism and the Lord's Supper explicitly symbolize the greatest event in the history of redemption, Christ's death and resurrection for us, but footwashing symbolizes no such redemptive-historical event. (2) Baptism and the Lord's Supper were clearly *symbolic* actions, but when Jesus washed the disciples' feet it was clearly *functional,* not merely symbolic, in that it met an ordinary human need of the day (dirty feet). (3) Baptism and the Lord's Supper are appropriate symbols of beginning and continuing in the Christian life,[15] but no such symbolism attaches to footwashing. (4) To make footwashing an ordinance like baptism and the Lord's Supper reduces it to a symbol—and if it is a symbol, then Jesus' words command us only to perform a symbol, and the real force of Jesus' command (to act in humility and love) is lost. (5) Whereas the epistles give evidence that baptism and the Lord's Supper were continuing ordinances observed by the New Testament churches, there is no evidence that the apostles or the early church observed footwashing as an ordinance. (6) There is a simple and straightforward explanation for Jesus' command: he is telling his disciples to take lowly tasks in serving one another. But if this is what the text means (and the vast majority of the church through history has understood it this way), then we need not look for an additional meaning (that Jesus is also instituting a new ceremony). By contrast, the New Testament texts about baptism and the Lord's Supper cannot be understood to command something *other* than a ceremony. Therefore, while all Christians would profit from pondering the application of Jesus' statement about footwashing to their present patterns of life, none should think that Jesus is encouraging them to practice a ceremony of footwashing.

C. Conclusions

At the end of this discussion of the means of grace within the church, we should realize first of all that when any of these are carried out in faith and obedience, we should eagerly expect and look for evidence that the Holy Spirit is actually ministering to people at the same time as these actions are being done. We as Christians ought not to neglect to "meet together" (Heb. 10:25), but ought to look forward eagerly to any

---

[15]See chapter 7, section A, on the symbolism of baptism, and chapter 8, section B, on the symbolism of the Lord's Supper.

assembly of believers in which any of these means would occur, expecting that God will bring blessing from each of these means!

On the other hand, we must realize that all of these means of grace occur within the fellowship of the church. Those who neglect the fellowship of the church willfully cut themselves off from all of these means of grace and thereby cut themselves off from most of the ordinary means that the Holy Spirit uses to bring blessing to his people.

These means of grace ought to give us great appreciation for the amazing privilege of being members of the body of Christ, the church.

QUESTIONS FOR PERSONAL APPLICATION

1. Before reading this chapter, did you think that it made very much difference if a Christian continued to be active in the fellowship of the church or not? How has this chapter changed your perspective on that question, if at all?

2. Which of the means of grace mentioned in this chapter has been most helpful to you in your own Christian life?

3. Which of the means of grace mentioned in this chapter do you think you appreciated least before reading the chapter? How has your appreciation for that means of grace increased? How do you think this will affect your actions from now on?

4. As you look over the list of means of grace, are there some areas in which people are not actually experiencing "grace" or blessing in your own church? What could be done to increase the effectiveness of these weak areas as means of grace in the life of your church?

5. Which of the means of grace are actually least helpful in your own life? Are there some that have become rather mechanical, and that you are performing only as an outward or physical activity, without any real participation in your heart? What could you do to increase the effectiveness of those means in your life?

6. As you look over the list of the means of grace again, name one or more in which you could begin to help the church be more effective in bringing blessing to its people.

SPECIAL TERMS

Eucharist	laying on of hands
extreme unction	means of grace
holy orders	sacrament

BIBLIOGRAPHY

Hughes, P. E. "Grace, Means of." In *EDT*, pp. 482–83.

Milne, Bruce. *We Belong Together: The Meaning of Fellowship.* Downers Grove, Ill.: Inter-Varsity Press, 1978.

SCRIPTURE MEMORY PASSAGE

Acts 2:41–42: *So those who received his word were baptized, and there were added that day about three thousand souls. And they devoted themselves to the apostles' teaching and fellowship, to the breaking of bread and the prayers.*

HYMN

"I Love Thy Kingdom, Lord"

This hymn expresses joy at the privilege of being in the church. In fact, the author exclaims, "Beyond my highest joy I prize her heavenly ways, /Her sweet communion, solemn vows, her hymns of love and praise." Here he is meditating on some of the means of grace within the church ("her heavenly ways"), particularly the fellowship or communion that comes within the church, the vows to God that are made there, and the hymns that are sung within it. Moreover, using the figure of Mount Zion to refer to the church, he says that "to Zion shall be given /The brightest glories earth can yield, and brighter bliss of heaven." When we sing this we can think of all the rich blessings that the Holy Spirit bestows on the church through the many means of grace.

The author of this hymn, Timothy Dwight, was President of Yale University from 1795 to 1817, during which time he reformed the administration and the curriculum and tripled the enrollment. He also was Professor of Divinity, and under his preaching a revival broke out in 1802, in which a third of the students were converted.

I love thy kingdom, Lord, the house of thine abode,
    The church our blest Redeemer saved with his own precious blood.

I love thy church, O God: her walls before thee stand,
    Dear as the apple of thine eye, and graven on thy hand.

For her my tears shall fall, for her my prayers ascend;
    To her my cares and toils be giv'n, till toils and cares shall end.

Beyond my highest joy I prize her heav'nly ways,
    Her sweet communion, solemn vows, her hymns of love and praise.

Jesus, thou Friend divine, our Savior and our King,
    Thy hand from ev'ry snare and foe shall great deliv'rance bring.

Sure as thy truth shall last, to Zion shall be giv'n
    The brightest glories earth can yield, and brighter bliss of heav'n.

AUTHOR: TIMOTHY DWIGHT, 1800

Chapter 7

BAPTISM

Who should be baptized? How should it be done? What does it mean?

EXPLANATION AND SCRIPTURAL BASIS

In this chapter and the next we treat baptism and the Lord's Supper, two ceremonies that Jesus commanded his church to perform. But before we begin consideration of either one of them we must note that there is disagreement among Protestants even over the general term that should be applied to them. Because the Roman Catholic Church calls these two ceremonies "sacraments," and because the Catholic Church teaches that these sacraments *in themselves* actually *convey grace* to people (without requiring faith from the persons participating in them), some Protestants (especially Baptists) have refused to refer to baptism and the Lord's Supper as "sacraments." They have preferred the word *ordinances* instead. This is thought to be an appropriate term because baptism and the Lord's Supper were "ordained" by Christ.[1] On the other hand, other Protestants such as those in the Anglican, Lutheran, and Reformed traditions, have been willing to use the word "sacraments" to refer to baptism and the Lord's Supper, without thereby endorsing the Roman Catholic position.

It does not seem that any significant point is at issue here in the question of whether to call baptism and the Lord's Supper "ordinances" or "sacraments." Since Protestants who use both words explain clearly what they mean by them, the argument is not really over doctrine but over the meaning of an English word. If we are willing to explain clearly

---

[1] A. H. Strong, *Systematic Theology* (Valley Forge, Pa.: Judson Press, 1907), says, "No ordinance is a sacrament in the Romanist sense of conferring grace" (p. 930). He also says, "The Romanist regards the ordinances as actually conferring grace and producing holiness" (ibid.).

what we mean, it does not seem to make any difference whether we use the word *sacrament* or not.[2] In this text, when referring to baptism and the Lord's Supper in Protestant teaching, I will use both "ordinances" and "sacraments" interchangeably, and regard them as synonymous in meaning.

Before beginning our discussion of baptism we must recognize that there has been historically, and is today, a strong difference of viewpoint among evangelical Christians regarding this subject. The position advocated in this book is that baptism is not a "major" doctrine that should be the basis of division among genuine Christians,[3] but it is nonetheless a matter of importance for ordinary church life, and it is appropriate that we give it full consideration.

The position advocated in this chapter is "Baptistic"—namely, that *baptism is appropriately administered only to those who give a believable profession of faith in Jesus Christ.* During the discussion, we shall interact particularly with the paedobaptist ("infant baptist") position as advocated by Louis Berkhof in his *Systematic Theology,* since this is a careful and responsible representation of the paedobaptist position, and it is in a widely used systematic theology text.

A. The Mode and Meaning of Baptism

The practice of baptism in the New Testament was carried out in one way: the person being baptized was *immersed* or put completely under the water and then brought back up again. Baptism *by immersion* is therefore the "mode" of baptism or the way in which baptism was carried out in the New Testament. This is evident for the following reasons:

(1) The Greek word *baptizō* means "to plunge, dip, immerse" something in water. This is the commonly recognized and standard meaning of the term in ancient Greek literature both inside and outside of the Bible.[4]

---

[2]The *American Heritage Dictionary* (Boston: Houghton Mifflin, 1981) allows a range of meanings, defining a sacrament as a rite considered as "a testament to inner grace *or* a channel that mediates grace" (p. 1141). Even the most conscientious Baptist would not object to calling baptism "a testament to inner grace" while Catholics would not object to calling baptism "a channel that mediates grace."

[3]Not all Christians agree with my view that this is a minor doctrine. Many Christians in previous generations were persecuted and even put to death because they differed with the official state church and its practice of infant baptism. For them, the issue was not merely a ceremony: it was the right to have a believers' church, one that did not automatically include all the people born in a geographical region. Viewed in this light, the controversy over baptism involves a larger difference over the nature of the church: does one become part of the church by birth into a believing family, or by voluntary profession of faith?

[4]So LSJ, p. 305: "plunge"; passive, "to be drowned." Similarly, BAGD, p. 131: "dip, immerse," and middle, "dip oneself,

wash (in non-Christian literature also 'plunge, sink, drench, overwhelm')." Also Albrecht Oepke, "*baptō, baptizō*, etc.," in *TDNT,* 1:530: "to immerse . . . to sink the ship"; passive, "to sink . . . to suffer shipwreck, to drown (the sense of 'to bathe' or 'to wash' is only occasionally found in Hellenism . . . the idea of going under or perishing is nearer the general usage)" (ibid.). A. H. Strong, *Systematic Theology,* pp. 933–35 gives much additional evidence to this effect.

Berkhof, *Systematic Theology* (Grand Rapids: Eerdmans, 1939, 1941), p. 630, objects and gives some counter-examples, but his evidence is unconvincing because he indiscriminately mixes examples of *baptizō* with a related but different word, *baptō.* (Passages that speak of "bathing" or washing [in the Septuagint, Judith 12:7, for example, and in the New Testament, Mark 7:4] would most likely involve covering one's body [or hands, in Mark 7:4] completely with water.)

If any New Testament author had wanted to indicate that people were sprinkled with water, a perfectly good Greek word meaning "to sprinkle" was available: *rhantizō* is used in this sense in Heb. 9:13, 19, 21; 10:22; see BAGD, p. 734.

(2) The sense "immerse" is appropriate and probably required for the word in several New Testament passages. In Mark 1:5, people were baptized by John "*in* the river Jordan" (the Greek text has *en*, "in," and not "beside" or "by" or "near" the river).[5] Mark also tells us that when Jesus had been baptized "he came up *out of the water*" (Mark 1:10). The Greek text specifies that he came "out of" (*ek*) the water, not that he came away from it (this would be expressed by Gk. *apo*). The fact that John and Jesus went into the river and came up out of it strongly suggests immersion, since sprinkling or pouring of water could much more readily have been done standing beside the river, particularly because multitudes of people were coming for baptism. John's gospel tells us, further, that John the Baptist "was baptizing at Aenon near Salim, because there was much water there" (John 3:23). Again, it would not take "much water" to baptize people by sprinkling, but it would take much water to baptize by immersion.

When Philip had shared the gospel with the Ethiopian eunuch, "as they went along the road they came to some water, and the eunuch said, 'See, here is water! What is to prevent my being baptized?'" (Acts 8:36). Apparently neither of them thought that sprinkling or pouring a handful of water from the container of drinking water that would have been carried in the chariot was enough to constitute baptism. Rather, they waited until there was a body of water near the road. Then "he commanded the chariot to stop, and they both went *down into the water*, Philip and the eunuch, and he baptized him. And when they came *up out of the water*, the Spirit of the Lord caught up Philip; and the eunuch saw him no more, and went on his way rejoicing" (Acts 8:38–39). As in the case of Jesus, this baptism occurred when Philip and the eunuch went down into a body of water, and after the baptism they came up out of that body of water. Once again baptism by immersion is the only satisfactory explanation of this narrative.[6]

(3) The symbolism of union with Christ in his death, burial, and resurrection seems to require baptism by immersion. Paul says,

> Do you not know that all of us who have been baptized into Christ Jesus were baptized into his death? We were buried therefore with him by baptism into death, so that as Christ was raised from the dead by the glory of the Father, we too might walk in newness of life. (Rom. 6:3–4)

Similarly, Paul tells the Colossians, "You were *buried with him in baptism,* in which you were also *raised with him* through faith in the working of God, who raised him from the dead" (Col. 2:12).

Now this truth is clearly symbolized in baptism by immersion. When the candidate for baptism goes down into the water it is a picture of going down into the grave and being buried. Coming up out of the water is then a picture of being raised with Christ to

---

[5]Berkhof asks, "Was John the Baptist capable of the enormous task of immersing the multitudes that flocked unto him at the river Jordan. . . ?" (p. 630). Certainly over a period of several days he would have been capable of immersing many hundreds of people, but it is also possible that his disciples (Matt. 9:14, et al.) assisted him with some of the baptisms.

[6]Berkhof (pp. 630–631) objects that in Acts 8:38 the Greek word *eis* can mean "to" and not necessarily "into." It is true that the word can take either meaning, but we must also note v. 39, where *ek* certainly means "out of," not "away from," which would be expressed by *apo*. And the going down and coming up (*katabainō* and *anabainō*) are not going down from the chariot and going back up into the chariot, but are specifically said to be going down *into the water* and coming up *out of the water*.

walk in newness of life. Baptism thus very clearly pictures death to one's old way of life and rising to a new kind of life in Christ. But baptism by sprinkling or pouring simply misses this symbolism.[7]

Sometimes it is objected that the essential thing symbolized in baptism is not death and resurrection with Christ but purification and cleansing from sins. Certainly it is true that water is an evident symbol of washing and cleansing, and the waters of baptism do symbolize washing and purification from sins as well as death and resurrection with Christ. Titus 3:5 speaks of "the washing of regeneration" and, even though the word *baptism* is not used in this text, it is certainly true that there is a cleansing from sin that occurs at the time of conversion. Ananias told Saul, "Rise and be baptized, and *wash away your sins,* calling on his name" (Acts 22:16).

But to say that washing away of sins is the only thing (or even the most essential thing) pictured in baptism does not faithfully represent New Testament teaching. Both washing and death and resurrection with Christ are symbolized in baptism, but Romans 6:1–11 and Colossians 2:11–12 place a clear emphasis on dying and rising with Christ. Even the washing is much more effectively symbolized by immersion than by sprinkling or pouring, and death and resurrection with Christ are symbolized only by immersion, not at all by sprinkling or pouring.

What then is the positive meaning of baptism? In all the discussion over the mode of baptism and the disputes over its meaning, it is easy for Christians to lose sight of the significance and beauty of baptism and to disregard the tremendous blessing that accompanies this ceremony. The amazing truths of passing through the waters of judgment safely, of dying and rising with Christ, and of having our sins washed away, are truths of momentous and eternal proportion and ought to be an occasion for giving great glory and praise to God. If churches would teach these truths more clearly, baptisms would be the occasion of much more blessing in the church.

---

[7]In fact, the waters of baptism have an even richer symbolism than simply the symbolism of the grave. The waters also remind us of the waters of God's judgment that came upon unbelievers at the time of the flood (Gen. 7:6–24), or the drowning of the Egyptians in the Exodus (Ex. 14:26–29). Similarly, when Jonah was thrown into the deep (Jonah 1:7–16), he was thrown down to the place of death because of God's judgment on his disobedience—even though he was miraculously rescued and thus became a sign of the resurrection. Therefore those who go down into the waters of baptism really are going down into the waters of judgment and death, death that they deserve from God for their sins. When they come back up out of the waters of baptism it shows that they have come safely through God's judgment only because of the merits of Jesus Christ, with whom they are united in his death and resurrection. This is why Peter can say in 1 Peter 3:21 that baptism "corresponds to" the saving of Noah and his family from the waters of judgment in the flood.

Douglas Moo, in Romans 1–8, *Wycliffe Exegetical Commentary* (Chicago: Moody Press, 1991), argues that baptism in Rom. 6 "functions as shorthand for the conversion experience as a whole. . . . It is not, then, that baptism is a symbol of dying and rising with Christ." (p. 371). He says that "there is no evidence in Romans 6, or in the NT, that the actual physical movements, immersion, and emersion, involved in baptism were accorded symbolical significance" (p. 379). While I agree that baptism in Rom. 6 functions as shorthand for the conversion experience as a whole, it does not seem to me that we can exclude the symbolism of dying and rising with Christ, for the following reasons: (1) The physical actions of going *down into* the water (where human beings cannot live for more than a few minutes) and coming *up out of* the water are so closely parallel to the actions of going down into the grave and coming up out of the grave that the connection is evident from the surface appearance of the actions, and no detailed explanation would be necessary. (2) The Old Testament background of being immersed by waters of God's judgment confirms this. (3) When Paul says, "You were buried with him in baptism, in which you were also raised with him through faith in the working of God, who raised him from the dead" (Col. 2:12), it is hard to imagine that any of Paul's readers, even children, would have missed the evident parallel between the actions of baptism and dying and rising with Christ. (This would be true even if, with Moo, we translate Col. 2:12 "*by means of* baptism.")

B. The Subjects of Baptism

The pattern revealed at several places in the New Testament is that only those who give a believable profession of faith should be baptized. This view is often called "believers' baptism," since it holds that only those who have themselves believed in Christ (or, more precisely, those who have given reasonable evidence of believing in Christ) should be baptized. This is because baptism, which is a *symbol of beginning the Christian life*, should only be given to those who have *in fact* begun the Christian life.

1. The Argument From the New Testament Narrative Passages on Baptism. The narrative examples of those who were baptized suggest that baptism was administered only to those who gave a believable profession of faith. After Peter's sermon at Pentecost we read, "*Those who received his word* were baptized" (Acts 2:41). The text specifies that baptism was administered to those who "received his word" and therefore trusted in Christ for salvation.[8] Similarly, when Philip preached the gospel in Samaria, we read, "*When they believed* Philip as he preached good news about the kingdom of God and the name of Jesus Christ, *they were baptized*, both men and women" (Acts 8:12). Likewise, when Peter preached to the Gentiles in Cornelius' household, he allowed baptism for those who had *heard* the Word and *received the Holy Spirit*—that is, for those who had given persuasive evidence of an internal work of regeneration. While Peter was preaching, "the Holy Spirit fell on all who heard the word" and Peter and his companions "heard them speaking in tongues and extolling God" (Acts 10:44–46). Peter's response was that baptism is appropriate for those who have received the regenerating work of the Holy Spirit: "Can any one forbid water for baptizing these people *who have received the Holy Spirit* just as we have?" Then Peter "commanded them to be baptized in the name of Jesus Christ" (Acts 10:47–48). The point of these three passages is that baptism is appropriately given to those who have received the gospel and trusted in Christ for salvation. There are other texts that indicate this as well—Acts 16:14–15 (Lydia and her household, after "the Lord opened her heart" to believe); Acts 16:32–33 (the family of the Philippian jailer, after Peter preached "the word of the Lord to him and to all that were in his house"); and 1 Corinthians 1:16 (the household of Stephanas), but these will be discussed more fully below when we look at the question of "household baptisms."

2. The Argument From the Meaning of Baptism. In addition to these indications from New Testament narratives that baptism always followed upon saving faith, there is a second consideration that argues for believers' baptism: the outward symbol of *beginning* the Christian life should only be given to those who *show evidence* of having begun the Christian life. The New Testament authors wrote as though they clearly assumed that everyone who was baptized had also personally trusted in Christ and experienced salvation. For

---

[8]Berkhof cautions against making too much of the silence of Scripture regarding infant baptism. Commenting on the fact that in some cases whole households were baptized, he says, "And if there were infants, it is morally certain that they were baptized along with the parents" (p. 634). But this is not what Acts 2:41 says: it specifies that "*those who received his word* were baptized," not those who did not receive his word but were infants belonging to the households of those who received his word.

example, Paul says, "As many of you as were baptized into Christ have put on Christ" (Gal. 3:27). Paul here assumes that baptism is the outward sign of inward regeneration. This simply would not have been true of infants—Paul could not have said, "As many *infants* as have been baptized into Christ have put on Christ," for infants have not yet come to saving faith or given any evidence of regeneration.[9]

Paul speaks the same way in Romans 6:3–4: "Do you not know that *all of us who have been baptized into Christ Jesus* were baptized into his death? We were buried therefore with him by baptism into death." Could Paul have said this of infants?[10] Could he have said that "all infants who have been baptized into Christ Jesus were baptized into his death" and "were buried therefore with him by baptism into death, so that as Christ was raised from the dead"? But if Paul could not have said those things about infants, then those who advocate infant baptism must say that baptism means something different for infants than what Paul says it means for "all of us who have been baptized into Christ Jesus." Those who argue for infant baptism at this point resort to what seems to the present author to be vague language about infants being adopted "into the covenant" or "into the covenant community," but the New Testament does not speak that way about baptism. Rather, it says that all of those who have been baptized have been buried with Christ, have been raised with him, and have put on Christ.

A similar argument can be made from Colossians 2:12: "You were buried with him in baptism, in which you were also raised with him through faith in the working of God, who raised him from the dead." But it could not be said of infants that they were buried with Christ, or were raised with him through faith, since they were not yet old enough to exercise faith for themselves.

3. Alternative #1: The Roman Catholic View. The Roman Catholic Church teaches that baptism should be administered to infants.[11] The reason for this is that the Catholic Church believes that baptism is *necessary* for salvation, and that the act of baptism itself *causes regeneration*. Therefore, in this view, baptism is a *means* whereby the church bestows saving grace on people. And if it is this kind of a channel of saving grace it should be given to all people.

Ludwig Ott, in his *Fundamentals of Catholic Dogma*[12] gives the following explanations:

> Baptism is that Sacrament in which man being washed with water in the name of the Three Divine Persons is spiritually reborn. (p. 350; Ott gives John 3:5; Titus 3:5; and Eph. 5:26 in support of this statement)

> Baptism, provided that the proper dispositions (Faith and sorrow for sin) are present, effects: a) the eradication of sins, both original sin and, in the case

---

[9]This is not to argue that *no* infants can be regenerated, but simply that Paul could have no theological basis for saying that *all* infants who have been baptized have begun the Christian life. He is talking in Gal. 3:27 of "as many of you as were baptized into Christ."

[10]See section 3 below for a response to the Roman Catholic

view that baptism causes regeneration.

[11]The act of baptizing an infant, including giving a name to the infant at that time, is sometimes called "christening," especially in Roman Catholic and Episcopalian churches.

[12]Trans. by Patrick Lynch, ed. by James Bastible, 4th ed. (Rockford, Ill.: TAN Books, 1960).

of adults, also personal, mortal or venial sins; b) inner sanctification by the infusion of sanctifying grace. (p. 354)

Even if it be unworthily received, valid Baptism imprints on the soul of the recipient an indelible spiritual mark, the Baptismal Character. . . . The baptized person is incorporated, by the Baptismal Character, into the Mystical Body of Christ. . . . Every validly baptized person, even one baptized outside the Catholic Church, becomes a member of the One Holy Catholic and Apostolic Church. (p. 355)

Ott goes on to explain that baptism is necessary for salvation and is to be performed only by priests:

Baptism by water . . . is, since the promulgation of the Gospel, necessary for all men without exception for salvation. (p. 356)[13]

Ott explains that, while baptism is ordinarily to be administered by a priest, in unusual circumstances (such as when a child is in danger of dying soon after birth) it may be performed by a deacon or a layperson. Even baptism performed by unbelievers is thought to be valid, for Ott says:

Yea, even a pagan or a heretic can baptise, provided he adheres to the form of the Church and has the intention of doing what the Church does. (p. 358)

Though infants cannot exercise saving faith themselves, the Roman Catholic Church teaches that the baptism of infants is valid:

Faith, as it is not the effective cause of justification . . . need not be present. The faith which infants lack is . . . replaced by the faith of the Church. (p. 359)

Essential to understanding the Roman Catholic view of baptism is the realization that Catholics hold that the sacraments work apart from the faith of the people participating in the sacrament. And if this is so, then it follows that baptism would confer grace even on infants who do not have the ability to exercise faith. Several statements in Ott's book make this clear:

The Catholic Church teaches that the Sacraments have an objective efficacy, that is, an efficacy independent of the subjective disposition of the recipient or of the minister. . . . The Sacraments confer grace immediately, that is, without the mediation of Fiducial faith. (pp. 328–29)

The Sacraments of the New Covenant contain the grace which they signify, and bestow it on those who do not hinder it. (p. 328)

The Sacraments work *ex opere operato*. . . . That is, the Sacraments operate by the power of the completed sacramental rite. (p. 329)[14]

---

[13]In extreme cases Ott and the teaching of the Catholic Church allow for baptism of desire (for one who sincerely longs to be baptized but cannot be) or baptism by blood (in martyrdom).

[14]The phrase *ex opere operato* represents an essential part of Roman Catholic teaching on the sacraments. This Latin phrase literally means "by work performed," and it means that the sacraments work in virtue of the actual activity done, and

The formula *"ex opere operato"* asserts, negatively, that the sacramental grace is not conferred by reason of the subjective activity of the recipient, and positively, that the sacramental grace is caused by the validly operated sacramental sign. (p. 330)

However, Ott is careful to explain that the Catholic teaching must not be interpreted "in the sense of mechanical or magical efficacy" (p. 330). He says,

On the contrary, in the case of the adult recipient faith is expressly demanded . . . nevertheless the subjective disposition of the recipient is not the cause of grace; it is merely an indispensable precondition of the communication of grace . . . The measure of the grace effected *ex opere operato* even depends on the grade of the subjective disposition. (p. 330)

In giving a response to this Roman Catholic teaching, we should remember that the Reformation centered upon this issue. Martin Luther's great concern was to teach that salvation depends on faith alone, not on faith *plus works.* But if baptism and participating in the other sacraments are *necessary for salvation* because they are *necessary* for receiving saving grace, then salvation really is based on faith plus works. In contrast to this, the clear New Testament message is that justification is by faith *alone.* "By grace you have been saved *through faith;* and this is not your own doing, it is the gift of God—*not because of works,* lest any man should boast" (Eph. 2:8–9). Moreover, "the *free gift* of God is eternal life in Christ Jesus our Lord" (Rom. 6:23).

The Roman Catholic argument that baptism is necessary for salvation is very similar to the argument of Paul's opponents in Galatia who said that circumcision was necessary for salvation. Paul's response is that those who require circumcision are preaching "a different gospel" (Gal. 1:6). He says that "all who rely on works of the law are under a curse" (Gal. 3:10), and speaks very severely to those who attempt to add any form of obedience as a requirement for justification: "You are severed from Christ, you who would be justified by the law; you have fallen away from grace" (Gal. 5:4). Therefore, we must conclude that no *work* is necessary for salvation. And therefore *baptism* is not necessary for salvation.

But what about John 3:5, "Unless one is *born of water* and the Spirit, he cannot enter the kingdom of God"? Although some have understood this as a reference to baptism, it is better understood against the background of the promise of the new covenant in Ezekiel 36:

I will sprinkle clean water upon you, and you shall be clean from all your uncleannesses, and from all your idols I will cleanse you. A new heart I will give you, and a new spirit I will put within you; and I will take out of your flesh the heart of stone and give you a heart of flesh. And I will put my spirit within you, and cause you to walk in my statutes and be careful to observe my ordinances. (Ezek. 36:25–27)

that the power of the sacraments does not depend on any subjective attitude of faith in the people participating in them.

Ezekiel here speaks of a "spiritual" washing that will come in the days of the new covenant when God puts his Spirit within his people. In the light of this, to be born of water and the Spirit is a "spiritual" washing that occurs when we are born again, just as we receive a spiritual, not a physical, "new heart" at that time as well.

Similarly, Titus 3:5 specifies not water baptism but "the washing of regeneration," explicitly stating that it is a *spiritual* giving of new life. Water baptism is simply not mentioned in this passage. A spiritual rather than literal washing is also referred to in Ephesians 5:26, where Paul says that Christ gave himself up for the church "that he might sanctify her, having cleansed her by the washing of water with the word." It is the Word of God that does the washing referred to here, not physical water.

As for the Roman Catholic view that baptism conveys grace apart from the subjective disposition of the recipient or the minister (a position that is consistent with baptizing infants, who do not exercise faith for themselves), we must recognize that no New Testament examples exist to prove this view, nor is there New Testament testimony to indicate this. Rather, the narrative accounts of those who were baptized indicate that they had first come to saving faith (see above). And when there are doctrinal statements about baptism they also indicate the need of saving faith. When Paul says, "You were buried with him in baptism, in which you were also raised with him," he immediately specifies "*through faith* in the working of God, who raised him from the dead" (Col. 2:12).

Finally, what about 1 Peter 3:21, where Peter says, "*Baptism . . . now saves you*"? Does this not give clear support to the Roman Catholic view that baptism itself brings saving grace to the recipient?[15] No, for when Peter uses this phrase he continues in the same sentence to explain exactly what he means by it. He says that baptism saves you "*not as a removal of dirt from the body*" (that is, not as an outward, physical act which washes dirt from the body—that is not the part which saves you), "*but as an appeal to God for a clear conscience*" (that is, as an inward, spiritual transaction between God and the individual, a transaction symbolized by the outward ceremony of baptism). We could paraphrase Peter's statement by saying, "Baptism now saves you—not the *outward* physical ceremony of baptism but the *inward* spiritual reality which baptism represents." In this way, Peter guards against any view of baptism that would attribute automatic saving power to the physical ceremony itself.

Peter's phrase, "an appeal to God for a clear conscience," is another way of saying "a request for forgiveness of sins and a new heart." When God gives a sinner a "clear conscience," that person has the assurance that every sin has been forgiven and that he or she stands in a right relationship with God (Heb. 9:14 and 10:22 speak this way about the cleansing of one's conscience through Christ). To be baptized rightly is to make such an "appeal" to God: it is to say, in effect, "Please, God, as I enter this baptism which will cleanse my body outwardly I am asking you to cleanse my heart inwardly, forgive my sins, and make me right before you." Understood in this way, baptism is an appropriate symbol for the beginning of the Christian life.[16]

---

[15]The next three paragraphs are adapted from Wayne Grudem, *The First Epistle of Peter,* TNTC (Leicester: IVP, and Grand Rapids: Eerdmans, 1988), pp. 163–65, and are used by permission.

[16]Some have argued that "pledge" is a better word than "appeal" in this verse. Thus, the NIV translates, "the *pledge* of a good conscience towards God." The data from other examples of the word is slim with regard to both meanings,

So 1 Peter 3:21 certainly does not teach that baptism saves people automatically or confers grace *ex opere operato*. It does not even teach that the act of baptism itself has saving power, but rather that salvation comes about through the inward exercise of faith that is represented by baptism (cf. Col. 2:12). In fact, Protestants who advocate believers' baptism might well see in 1 Peter 3:21 some support for their position: baptism, it might be argued, is appropriately administered to anyone who is old enough personally to make "an appeal to God for a clear conscience."[17]

In conclusion, the Roman Catholic teachings that baptism is necessary for salvation, that the act of baptism in itself confers saving grace, and that baptism is therefore appropriately administered to infants, are not persuasive in the light of New Testament teachings.

4. Alternative #2: The Protestant Paedobaptist View. In contrast both to the Baptist position defended in the earlier part of this chapter and to the Roman Catholic view just discussed, another important view is that baptism is rightly administered to *all infant children of believing parents*. This is a common view in many Protestant groups (especially Lutheran, Episcopalian, Methodist, and Presbyterian and Reformed churches). This view is sometimes known as the covenant argument for paedobaptism. It is called a "covenant" argument because it depends on seeing infants born to believers as part of the "covenant community" of God's people. The word "paedobaptism" means the practice of baptizing infants (the prefix *paedo-* means "child" and is derived from the Greek word *pais,* "child").[18] I will be interacting primarily with the arguments put forth by Louis Berkhof, who explains clearly and defends well the paedobaptist position.

The argument that infants of believers should be baptized depends primarily on the following three points:

a. Infants Were Circumcised in the Old Covenant: In the Old Testament, circumcision was the outward *sign* of entrance into the covenant community or the community of God's people. Circumcision was administered to all Israelite children (that is, male children) when they were eight days old.

---

and no conclusions can be drawn from an examination of other uses of the word alone (see discussion in W. Grudem, *1 Peter*, p. 164).

But much more significant is the fact that the translation "pledge" introduces a theological problem. If baptism is a "pledge to God" to maintain a good conscience (or a pledge to live an obedient life, which flows from a good conscience), then the emphasis is no longer on dependence on God to give salvation, but is rather on dependence on one's own effort or strength of resolve. And since this phrase in 1 Peter 3:21 is so clearly connected with the beginning of the Christian life and identified as the feature of baptism that "saves you," the translation "pledge" seems to be inconsistent with the New Testament teaching on salvation by faith alone; it would be the only place where a promise to be righteous is said to be the thing that "saves you." And since the lexical data are inconclusive for both senses (while suggesting that both senses are appar-

ently possible), it is better to adopt the translation "appeal" as a sense much more in accord with the doctrinal teaching of the rest of the New Testament.

[17]Col. 2:12 can be used in the same manner: Paul says that in baptism Christians were "raised with [Christ] *through faith* in the working of God, who raised him from the dead." This presupposes that those who were baptized were exercising faith when they were baptized—that is, that they were old enough to believe.

[18]Roman Catholics are also paedobaptists, but their supporting arguments are different, as explained above (they teach that baptism causes regeneration). In the material that follows, I will be comparing a Protestant defense of *paedobaptism* with a Protestant defense of *believers' baptism*. Therefore, I will use the term *paedobaptist* to refer to Protestant paedobaptists who hold to a covenant paedobaptist position.

b. Baptism Is Parallel to Circumcision: In the New Testament, the outward sign of entrance into the "covenant community" is baptism. Therefore baptism is the New Testament counterpart to circumcision. It follows that baptism should be administered to all infant children of believing parents. To deny them this benefit is to deprive them of a privilege and benefit that is rightfully theirs—the *sign* of belonging to the community of God's people, the "covenant community." The parallel between circumcision and baptism is seen quite clearly in Colossians 2:

> In him also *you were circumcised* with a circumcision made without hands, by putting off the body of flesh in the circumcision of Christ; and *you were buried with him in baptism,* in which you were also raised with him through faith in the working of God, who raised him from the dead. (Col. 2:11–12)

Here it is said that Paul makes an explicit connection between circumcision and baptism.

c. Household Baptisms: Further support for the practice of baptizing infants is found in the "household baptisms" reported in Acts and the epistles, particularly the baptism of the household of Lydia (Acts 16:15), the family of the Philippian jailer (Acts 16:33), and the household of Stephanas (1 Cor. 1:16). It is also claimed that Acts 2:39, which declares that the promised blessing of the gospel is "to you and to your children," supports this practice.

In response to these arguments for paedobaptism, the following points may be made:

(1) It is certainly true that baptism and circumcision are in many ways similar, but we must not forget that what they symbolize is also different in some important ways. The old covenant had a *physical, external means of entrance* into the "covenant community." One became a Jew by being born of Jewish parents. Therefore all Jewish males were circumcised. Circumcision was not restricted to people who had true inward spiritual life, but rather was given to *all who lived among the people of Israel.* God said:

> Every male among you shall be circumcised. . . . He that is eight days old among you shall be circumcised; every male throughout your generations, whether born in your house, or bought with your money from any foreigner who is not of your offspring, both *he that is born in your house and he that is bought with your money,* shall be circumcised. (Gen. 17:10–13)

It was not only the physical descendants of the people of Israel who were circumcised, but also those *servants* who were purchased by them and lived among them. The presence or absence of inward spiritual life made no difference whatsoever in the question of whether one was circumcised. So "Abraham took Ishmael his son *and all the slaves born in his house or bought with his money,* every male among the men of Abraham's house, and he circumcised the flesh of their foreskins that very day, as God had said to him" (Gen. 17:23; cf. Josh. 5:4).

We should realize that circumcision was given to every male living among the people of Israel even though *true circumcision* is something inward and spiritual: "Real circumcision is a matter of the heart, spiritual and not literal" (Rom. 2:29). Moreover, Paul in the New Testament explicitly states that "not all who are descended from Israel belong to Israel" (Rom. 9:6). But even though there was at the time of the Old Testament (and more fully in the time of the New Testament) a realization of the inward spiritual reality that circumcision was intended to represent, there was *no attempt* to restrict circumcision only to those whose hearts were *actually circumcised spiritually* and who had genuine saving faith. Even among the adult males, circumcision was applied to everyone, not just those who gave evidence of inward faith.

(2) But under the new covenant the situation is very different. The New Testament does not talk about a "covenant community" made up of believers *and* their unbelieving children and relatives and servants who happen to live among them. (In fact, in the discussion of baptism, the phrase "covenant community" as used by paedobaptists often tends to function as a broad and vague term that blurs the differences between the Old Testament and the New Testament on this matter.) In the New Testament church, the only question that matters is whether one has saving faith and has been spiritually incorporated into the body of Christ, the true church. The only "covenant community" discussed is *the church*, the fellowship of the redeemed.

But how does one become a member of the church? The means of entrance into the church is *voluntary, spiritual, and internal.* One becomes a member of the true church by being *born again* and by having *saving faith,* not by physical birth. It comes about not by an external act, but by internal faith in one's heart. It is certainly true that baptism is the sign of entrance into the church, but this means that it should only be given to those who *give evidence* of membership in the church, only to those who profess faith in Christ.[19]

We should not be surprised that there was a change from the way the covenant community was entered in the Old Testament (physical birth) to the way the church is entered in the New Testament (spiritual birth). There are many analogous changes between the old and new covenants in other areas as well. While the Israelites fed on physical manna in the wilderness, New Testament believers feed on Jesus Christ, the true bread that comes down from heaven (John 6:48–51). The Israelites drank physical water that gushed from the rock in the wilderness, but those who believe in Christ drink of the living water of eternal life that he gives (John 4:10–14). The old covenant had a physical temple to which Israel came for worship, but in the new covenant believers are built into a spiritual temple (1 Peter 2:5). Old covenant believers offered physical sacrifices of animals and crops upon an altar, but New Testament believers offer "spiritual sacrifices acceptable to God through Jesus Christ" (1 Peter 2:5; cf. Heb. 13:15–16). Old covenant believers received from God the physical land of Israel which he had promised to them, but New Testament believers receive "a better country, that is, a heavenly one" (Heb. 11:16). In the same way, in the old covenant those who were the physical seed or descendants of Abraham were

---

[19]At this point an advocate of paedobaptism may ask whether we should not have an idea of a "covenant community" in the New Testament church which is broader than the church and includes unbelieving children who belong to church families. But the New Testament speaks of no such community, nor does it give indication that unbelieving children of believing parents are members of the new covenant. And it certainly does not speak of baptism as a sign of entrance into such a broader group. Baptism symbolizes new birth and entrance into the church.

members of the people of Israel, but in the New Testament those who are the spiritual "seed" or descendants of Abraham by faith are members of the church (Gal. 3:29; cf. Rom. 4:11–12).

In all these contrasts we see the truth of the distinction that Paul emphasizes between the old covenant and the new covenant. The physical elements and activities of the old covenant were "only a shadow of what is to come," but the true reality, the "substance," is found in the new covenant relationship which we have in Christ (Col. 2:17). Therefore it is consistent with this change of systems that infant (male) children would automatically be circumcised in the old covenant, since their physical descent and physical presence in the community of Jewish people meant that they were members of that community in which faith was not an entrance requirement. But in the new covenant it is appropriate that infants *not* be baptized, and that baptism only be given to those who give evidence of genuine saving faith, because membership in the church is based on an internal spiritual reality, not on physical descent.

(3) The examples of household baptisms in the New Testament are really not decisive for one position or another. When we look at the actual examples more closely, we see that in a number of them there are indications of saving faith on the part of all of those baptized. For example, it is true that the family of the Philippian jailer was baptized (Acts 16:33), but it is also true that Paul and Silas "spoke the word of the Lord to him and *to all that were in his house*" (Acts 16:32). If the Word of the Lord was spoken to all in the house, there is an assumption that all were old enough to understand the word and believe it. Moreover, after the family had been baptized, we read that the Philippian jailer "*rejoiced with all his household* that he had believed in God" (Acts 16:34). So we have not only a household baptism but also a household reception of the Word of God and a household rejoicing in faith in God. These facts suggest quite strongly that the entire household had individually come to faith in Christ.

With regard to the fact that Paul baptized "the household of Stephanas" (1 Cor. 1:16), we must also note that Paul says at the end of 1 Corinthians that "the household of Stephanas were the first converts in Achaia, and they have devoted themselves to the service of the saints" (1 Cor. 16:15). So they were not only baptized; they were also converted and had worked at serving other believers. Once again the example of *household baptism* gives indication of *household faith*.

In fact, there are other instances where baptism is not mentioned but where we see explicit testimony to the fact that an entire household had come to faith. After Jesus healed the official's son, we read that the father "himself believed, *and all his household*" (John 4:53). Similarly, when Paul preached at Corinth, "Crispus, the ruler of the synagogue, *believed* in the Lord, *together with all his household*" (Acts 18:8).

This means that of all the examples of "household baptisms" in the New Testament, the only one that does not have some indication of household faith as well is Acts 16:14–15, speaking of Lydia: "The Lord opened her heart to give heed to what was said by Paul. And when she was baptized, with her household." The text simply does not contain any information about whether there were infants in her household or not. It is ambiguous and certainly not weighty evidence for infant baptism. It must be considered inconclusive in itself.

With regard to Peter's statement at Pentecost that "the promise is to you and to your children," we should note that the sentence continues as follows: "For the promise is to you and to your children and to all that are far off, *every one whom the Lord our God calls to him*" (Acts 2:39). Moreover, the same paragraph specifies not that believers and unbelieving children were baptized, but that "*those who received his word* were baptized, and there were added that day about three thousand souls" (Acts 2:41).

(4) A further argument in objection to the paedobaptist position can be made when we ask the simple question, "What does baptism *do?*" In other words, we might ask, "What does it actually accomplish? What benefit does it bring?"

Roman Catholics have a clear answer to this question: Baptism *causes* regeneration. And Baptists have a clear answer: Baptism *symbolizes* the fact that inward regeneration has occurred. But paedobaptists cannot adopt either of these answers. They do not want to say that baptism causes regeneration, nor are they able to say (with respect to infants) that it symbolizes a regeneration that has already occurred.[20] The only alternative seems to be to say that it symbolizes a regeneration that will occur in the future, when the infant is old enough to come to saving faith. But even that is not quite accurate, because it is not certain that the infant will be regenerated in the future—some infants who are baptized never come to saving faith later. So the most accurate paedobaptist explanation of what baptism symbolizes is that it symbolizes *probable future regeneration.*[21] It does not cause regeneration, nor does it symbolize actual regeneration; therefore it must be understood as symbolizing probable regeneration at some time in the future.

But at this point it seems apparent that the paedobaptist understanding of baptism is quite different from that of the New Testament. The New Testament never views baptism as something that symbolizes a probable future regeneration. The New Testament authors do not say, "Can anyone forbid water for baptizing those who will probably someday be saved?" (cf. Acts 10:47), or, "As many of you as were baptized into Christ will probably someday put on Christ" (cf. Gal. 3:27), or "Do you not know that all of us who have been baptized into Christ Jesus will probably someday be baptized into his death?" (cf. Rom. 6:3). This is simply not the way the New Testament speaks of baptism. Baptism in the New Testament is a sign of being born again, being cleansed from sin, and beginning the Christian life. It seems fitting to reserve this sign for those who give evidence that that is actually true in their lives.

One other perspective on the symbolism of baptism is given by Michael Green.[22] He says:

> Infant baptism stresses the objectivity of the gospel. It points to the solid achievement of Christ crucified and risen, whether or not we respond to it. . . .

---

[20]However, some Protestant paedobaptists will *presume* that regeneration has occurred (and the evidence will be seen later). Others, including many Episcopalians and Lutherans, would say that regeneration occurs at the time of baptism.

[21]This is not a quotation from any specific paedobaptist writer, but is my own conclusion from the logic of the paedobaptist position, which would seem to require this under-standing of what paedobaptism signifies with respect to regeneration.

[22]Michael Green, *Baptism: Its Purpose, Practice, and Power* (London: Hodder and Stoughton, and Downers Grove, Ill.: InterVarsity Press, 1987). This book contains an excellent statement of a paedobaptist position, and also contains much helpful analysis of the biblical teaching about baptism which both sides could endorse.

> Not that we gain anything from it unless we repent and believe. But it is the standing demonstration that our salvation does not depend on our own very fallible faith; it depends on what God has done for us. (p. 76)

He goes on to say:

> Infant baptism stresses the initiative of God in salvation. . . . Should it be attached primarily to man's response, or to God's initiative? That is the heart of the question. . . . For the Baptist, baptism primarily bears witness to what *we do* in responding to the grace of God. For the paedobaptist, it primarily bears witness to what *God has done* to make it all possible. (pp. 76–77, emphasis his)

But several points can be noted in response to Green. (a) His analysis at this point overlooks the fact that baptism does not *only* symbolize Christ's death and resurrection; as we have seen in the foregoing analysis of New Testament texts, it *also* symbolizes the application of redemption to us, as a result of our response of faith. Baptism pictures the fact that we have been united with Christ in his death and resurrection, and the washing with water symbolizes that we have been cleansed from our sins. In saying that the paedobaptist stresses God's initiative and the Baptist stresses man's response, Green has presented the reader with two incorrect alternatives from which to choose, because baptism pictures both of these and more. Baptism pictures (i) Christ's redemptive work, (ii) my response in faith (as I come to be baptized), and (iii) God's application of the benefits of redemption to my life. Believers' baptism pictures all three aspects (not just my faith, as Green suggests), but according to Green's view paedobaptism pictures only the first one. It is not a question of which is "primary"; it is a question of which view of baptism includes all that baptism stands for.

(b) When Green says that our salvation does not depend on our faith but on God's work, the expression "depend on" is capable of various interpretations. If "depend on" means "what we rely on," then of course both sides would agree that we rely on Christ's work, not on our faith. If "depend on" means that faith does not have any merit in itself whereby we can earn favor with God, then also both sides would agree. But if "depend on" means it makes no difference to our salvation whether we believe or not, then neither side would agree: Green himself says in the previous sentence that baptism does us no good unless we repent and believe. Therefore if baptism in any way represents the application of redemption to a person's life, then it is not enough to practice a form of baptism that *only* pictures Christ's death and resurrection; we should also picture our response in faith and the subsequent application of redemption to us. By contrast, on Green's view, there is a real danger of portraying a view (which Green would disagree with) that people will have salvation applied to them by God whether they believe or not.

(5) Finally, those who advocate believers' baptism often express concern about the practical consequences of paedobaptism. They argue that the practice of paedobaptism in actual church life frequently leads persons baptized in infancy to presume that they have been regenerated, and thereby they fail to feel the urgency of their need to come to personal faith in Christ. Over a period of years, this tendency is likely to result in more and more *unconverted* members of the "covenant community" — members who are not truly members of Christ's church. Of course, this would not make a paedobaptist church

a false church, but it would make it a less-pure church, and one that will frequently be fighting tendencies toward liberal doctrine or other kinds of unbelief that are brought in by the unregenerate sector of the membership.

C. The Effect of Baptism

We have argued above that baptism symbolizes regeneration or spiritual rebirth. But does it only symbolize? Or is there some way in which it is also a "means of grace," that is, a means that the Holy Spirit uses to bring blessing to people? We have already discussed this question in the previous chapter,[23] so here it only is necessary to say that when baptism is properly carried out then of course it brings some spiritual benefit to believers as well. There is the blessing of God's favor that comes with all obedience, as well as the joy that comes through public profession of one's faith, and the reassurance of having a clear physical picture of dying and rising with Christ and of washing away sins. Certainly the Lord gave us baptism to strengthen and encourage our faith—and it should do so for everyone who is baptized and for every believer who witnesses a baptism.

D. The Necessity of Baptism

While we recognize that Jesus commanded baptism (Matt. 28:19), as did the apostles (Acts 2:38), we should not say that baptism is *necessary* for salvation.[24] This question was discussed to some extent above under the response to the Roman Catholic view of baptism. To say that baptism or any other action is *necessary* for salvation is to say that we are not justified by faith alone, but by faith plus a certain "work," the work of baptism. The apostle Paul would have opposed the idea that baptism is necessary for salvation just as strongly as he opposed the similar idea that circumcision was necessary for salvation (see Gal. 5:1–12).

Those who argue that baptism is necessary for salvation often point to Mark 16:16: *"He who believes and is baptized will be saved; but he who does not believe will be condemned."* But the very evident answer to this is simply to say that the verse says nothing about those who *believe* and *are not baptized.* The verse is simply talking about general cases without making a pedantic qualification for the unusual case of someone who believes and is not baptized. But certainly the verse should not be pressed into service and made to speak of something it is not talking about.[25]

More to the point is Jesus' statement to the dying thief on the cross, "Today you will be with me in Paradise" (Luke 23:43). The thief could not be baptized before he died on the cross, but he was certainly saved that day. Moreover, the force of this point cannot be evaded by arguing that the thief was saved under the old covenant (under which baptism

---

[23]See chapter 6, section B.2.

[24]At this point I am differing not only with Roman Catholic teaching, but also with the teaching of several Protestant denominations that teach that, in some sense, baptism is necessary for salvation. Although there are different nuances in their teaching, such a position is held by many Episcopalians, many Lutherans, and by the Churches of Christ.

[25]Moreover, it is doubtful whether this verse should be used in support of a theological position at all, since there are many ancient manuscripts that do not have this verse (or Mark 16:9–20), and it seems most likely that this verse was not in the gospel as Mark originally wrote it.

was not necessary to salvation), because the new covenant took effect at the death of Jesus (see Heb. 9:17), and Jesus died *before* either of the two thieves who were crucified with him (see John 19:32–33).

Another reason why baptism is not necessary for salvation is that our justification from sins takes place at the point of saving faith, not at the point of water baptism, which usually occurs later. But if a person is already justified and has sins forgiven eternally at the point of saving faith, then baptism is not necessary for forgiveness of sins, or for the bestowal of new spiritual life.

Baptism, then, is not necessary for salvation. But it is necessary if we are to be obedient to Christ, for he commanded baptism for all who believe in him.

E. The Age for Baptism

Those who are convinced by the arguments for believers' baptism must then begin to ask, "How old should children be before they are baptized?"

The most direct answer is that they should be old enough to give a *believable* profession of faith. It is impossible to set a precise age that will apply to every child, but when parents see convincing evidence of genuine spiritual life, and also some degree of understanding regarding the meaning of trusting in Christ, then baptism is appropriate. Of course, this will require careful administration by the church, as well as a good explanation by parents in their homes. The exact age for baptism will vary from child to child, and somewhat from church to church as well.[26]

F. Remaining questions

1. Do Churches Need to Be Divided Over Baptism? In spite of many years of division over this question among Protestants, is there a way in which Christians who differ on baptism can demonstrate greater unity of fellowship? And is there a way that progress can be made in bringing the church closer to unity on this question?

Much progress in this regard has already been made. Christians who differ over baptism already demonstrate their unity in Christ through individual fellowship, Bible studies and prayer groups in their communities, occasional joint worship services, cooperation in city and regional evangelistic campaigns, joint support of many mission agencies and other parachurch groups, joint sponsorship of youth activities, pastors' fellowship groups, and so forth. Although baptism remains a difference, that difference does not generally lead to harmful divisions. In fact, most Christians seem to realize that baptism is not a major doctrine of the faith.[27]

---

[26]I participated in baptizing my own three children at a time when each was between seven and ten years old and showed a fair degree of understanding of the gospel together with genuine evidence of faith in Christ. In all three cases, I think they could have been baptized somewhat earlier, but we delayed out of deference to the ordinary pattern followed by the churches we were in, whereby children under seven were not usually baptized. (Among Baptists in the United Kingdom it is customary to wait until children are somewhat older than this, however.)

[27]I realize that some readers will object to this sentence and will say that baptism is *very important* because

of what the differing positions represent: differing views of the nature of the church. Many Baptists would argue that *practicing* infant baptism is inherently inconsistent with the idea of a church made up of believers only, and many paedobaptists would argue that *not practicing* infant baptism is inherently inconsistent with the idea of a covenant community that includes the children of believers.

I would encourage those who reason this way to consider how much they hold in common with evangelical believers on the other side of this issue—not necessarily with those far from them on other matters as well, but especially with those

A very few denominations have decided that they would allow both views of baptism to be taught and practiced within their denominations. The Evangelical Free Church of America (EFCA) does this, for example, as a result of a "compromise" reached in 1950 when the denomination was formed from two different groups that had different views on baptism. The EFCA allows ordination for pastors who hold to believer's baptism and for pastors who hold to infant baptism. And they allow into membership those who had been baptized as infants in a Christian church, without requiring them to be baptized as believers before joining the church. If some parents want to have their infant child baptized and the local pastor does not hold to infant baptism, the local church invites some other Evangelical Free Church pastor who holds to infant baptism to come and baptize the infant.

Although the Evangelical Free Church continues as a strong, healthy denomination today, there remain some difficulties inherent in this position. One is that there can be a tendency to minimize the importance of baptism: since members disagree on this topic, it is easier not to talk about it much or emphasize its importance.

But the most serious difficulty arises when people begin to think about what such a "compromise position" implies about the views of baptism held by the people who go along with this compromise. For people who hold to infant baptism, they have to be able to say that it is acceptable for believing parents not to baptize their infant children. But according to a paedobaptist view, this seems close to saying that it is acceptable for these parents to disobey a command of Scripture regarding the responsibility of parents to baptize their children. How can they really say this?

On the other side, those who hold to believer's baptism (as I do) would have to be willing to admit into church membership people who have been baptized as infants, and who did not make a personal profession of faith at the time they were baptized. But from a believer's baptism position, genuine baptism has to follow a personal profession of faith. So how can believer's baptism advocates in good conscience say that infant baptism is also a valid form of baptism? That contradicts what they believe about the essential nature of baptism—that it is an outward sign of an inward spiritual change, so that the apostle Paul could say, "As many of you as were baptized into Christ have put on Christ" (Gal. 3:27).

For someone who holds to believer's baptism, admitting to church membership someone who has not been baptized upon profession of faith, and telling the person that he or she never has to be baptized as a believer, is really giving up one's view on the proper nature of baptism. It is saying that infant baptism really is valid baptism! But then how could anyone who holds to this position tell anyone who had been baptized as an infant that he or she still needed to be baptized as a believer? This difficulty makes me think

---

on the other side who agree with them on most other aspects of the Christian life. Many Baptists *do* encourage and demonstrate a valued place for their children within their churches, and many paedobaptists *do* pray for the salvation of their *baptized* children with the same fervency with which Baptist parents pray for the salvation of their *unbaptized* children. Regarding church membership, evangelical paedobaptists *do* require a believable profession of faith before children can become full members of the church (their term is "communicant members";

that is, those who take Communion). They also require a believable profession of faith before any adults are allowed to join the church.

When these procedures are functioning well, both Baptists and paedobaptists use very similar procedures as they seek to have a church membership consisting of believers only, and both love and teach and pray for their children as most precious members of the larger church family who they hope will someday become true members of the body of Christ.

that some kind of "compromise" position on baptism is not very likely to be adopted by denominational groups in the future.

However, we should still be thankful that believers who differ on the issue of baptism can have wonderful fellowship with one another across denominational lines and can have respect for each other's sincerely held views.

2. Who Can Baptize? Finally, we may ask, "Who can perform the ceremony of baptism? Can only ordained clergy perform this ceremony?"

We should recognize here that Scripture simply does not specify any restrictions on who can perform the ceremony of baptism. Those churches that have a special priesthood through which certain actions (and blessings) come (such as Roman Catholics, and to some extent Anglicans) will wish to insist that only properly ordained clergy should baptize in ordinary circumstances (though exceptions could be made in unusual circumstances). But if we truly believe in the priesthood of all believers (see 1 Peter 2:4–10), then there seems to be no need *in principle* to restrict the right to perform baptism only to ordained clergy.

However, another consideration arises: Since baptism is the sign of entrance into the body of Christ, the church (cf. 1 Cor. 12:13 on inward spiritual baptism), then it seems appropriate that it be done *within the fellowship of the church* wherever possible, so that the church as a whole can rejoice with the person being baptized and so that the faith of all believers in that church might be built up.[28] Moreover, since baptism is a sign of beginning the Christian life and therefore of beginning life in the true church as well, it is fitting that the local church be assembled to give testimony to this fact and to give visible welcome to the baptized person. Also, in order that the people being baptized have a right understanding of what actually is happening, it is right for the church to safeguard the practice of baptism and keep it from abuse. Finally, if baptism is the sign of entering the fellowship of the visible church, then it seems appropriate that some officially designated representative or representatives of the church be selected to administer it. For these reasons it is usually the ordained clergy who baptize, but there seems to be no reason why the church from time to time, and where it deems it appropriate, might not call on other church officers or mature believers to baptize new converts. For example, someone effective in evangelism in a local church may be an appropriately designated person to baptize people who have come to Christ through the practice of that person's evangelistic ministry. (Note in Acts 8:12 that Philip preached the gospel in Samaria and then apparently baptized those who came to faith in Christ.)

QUESTIONS FOR PERSONAL APPLICATION

1. Have you been baptized? When? If you were baptized as a believer, what was the effect of the baptism on your Christian life (if any)? If you were baptized as an infant, what effect did the knowledge of your baptism have in your own thinking when you eventually learned that you had been baptized as an infant?

---

[28]The fact that baptism is an outward sign of *entrance* into the church, the body of Christ, would also make it appropriate to require baptism before someone is counted as a member of a local church.

2. What aspects of the meaning of baptism have you come to appreciate more as a result of reading this chapter (if any)? What aspects of the meaning of baptism would you like to see taught more clearly in your church?

3. When baptisms occur in your church, are they a time of rejoicing and praise to God? What do you think is happening to the person being baptized at that moment (if anything)? What do you think should be happening?

4. Have you modified your own view on the question of infant baptism versus believers' baptism as a result of reading this chapter? In what way?

5. What practical suggestions can you make for helping to overcome the differences among Christians on the question of baptism?

6. How can baptism be an effective help to evangelism in your church? Have you seen it function in this way?

SPECIAL TERMS

believable profession of faith   *ex opere operato*
believers' baptism   immersion
covenant community   paedobaptism

BIBLIOGRAPHY

Beasley-Murray, G. R. *Baptism in the New Testament.* Grand Rapids: Eerdmans, 1962.
_____. and R. F. G. Burnish. "Baptism." In *EDT,* pp. 69–73.
Berkouwer, G. C. *The Sacraments.* Trans. by Hugo Bekker. Grand Rapids: Eerdmans, 1969.
Bridge, Donald, and David Phypers. *The Water That Divides.* Downers Grove, Ill.: Inter-Varsity Press, 1977.
Bromiley, G. W. "Baptism." In *EDT,* pp. 112–14.
_____. *The Baptism of Infants.* London: Vine Books, 1955.
_____. *Children of Promise.* Grand Rapids: Eerdmans, 1979.
Brown, R. "Baptist Theology." In *EDT,* pp. 75–76.
Cottrell, Jack. *Baptism: A Biblical Study.* Joplin, Mo.: College Press, 1989. (Written from a Churches of Christ perspective, understanding baptism as necessary for salvation.)
Estep, William. *The Anabaptist Story.* Grand Rapids: Eerdmans, 1975.
Green, Michael. *Baptism: Its Purpose, Practice, and Power.* London: Hodder and Stoughton, and Downers Grove, Ill.: InterVarsity Press, 1987.
Jewett, Paul K. *Infant Baptism and the Covenant of Grace.* Grand Rapids: Eerdmans, 1978.
Kingdon, David. *Children of Abraham: A Reformed Baptist View of Baptism, the Covenant, and Children.* Haywards Heath, England: Carey Publications, 1973.
Marcel, Pierre Ch. *The Biblical Doctrine of Infant Baptism.* Trans. by Philip E. Hughes. London: J. Clarke, 1953.
Murray, John. *Christian Baptism.* Philadelphia: Presbyterian and Reformed, 1970.
Watson, T. E. *Baptism Not for Infants.* Worthing, England: Henry E. Walter, 1962.

SCRIPTURE MEMORY PASSAGE

Romans 6:3–4: *Do you not know that all of us who have been baptized into Christ Jesus were baptized into his death? We were buried therefore with him by baptism into death, so that as Christ was raised from the dead by the glory of the Father, we too might walk in newness of life.*

HYMN

"Up From the Grave He Arose"

There are few familiar hymns written specifically to be used during a baptismal service. It would be helpful for the church if more were written.

This hymn is appropriate for the topic of baptism, because it speaks triumphantly of Christ's resurrection. When we sing it, we should realize that Jesus not only triumphed over death and the grave for himself, but also for all of us who believe in him. This fact is vividly symbolized in the ceremony of baptism.

Alternative hymn: Most paedobaptist hymnals contain hymns to be sung at the baptism of infants, but I did not find any that were widely familiar.

Low in the grave he lay — Jesus, my Savior,
Waiting the coming day — Jesus, my Lord.

Refrain:
Up from the grave he arose,
    With a mighty triumph o'er his foes.
He arose a Victor from the dark domain,
    And he lives forever with his saints to reign.
He arose! He arose! Hallelujah! Christ arose!

Vainly they watch his bed — Jesus, my Savior;
Vainly they seal the dead — Jesus, my Lord.

Death cannot keep his prey — Jesus, my Savior;
He tore the bars away — Jesus, my Lord.

AUTHOR: ROBERT LOWREY, 1874.

Chapter 8

THE LORD'S SUPPER

What is the meaning of the Lord's Supper?
How should it be observed?

EXPLANATION AND SCRIPTURAL BASIS

The Lord Jesus instituted two ordinances (or sacraments) to be observed by the church. The previous chapter discussed *baptism*, an ordinance that is only observed once by each person, as a sign of the beginning of his or her Christian life. This chapter discusses *the Lord's Supper,* an ordinance that is to be observed repeatedly throughout our Christian lives, as a sign of continuing in fellowship with Christ.

A. Background in the History of Redemption

Jesus instituted the Lord's Supper in the following way:

> Now as they were eating, Jesus took bread, and blessed, and broke it, and gave it to the disciples and said, "Take, eat; this is my body." And he took a cup, and when he had given thanks he gave it to them, saying, "Drink of it, all of you; for this is my blood of the covenant, which is poured out for many for the forgiveness of sins. I tell you I shall not drink again of this fruit of the vine until that day when I drink it new with you in my Father's kingdom. (Matt. 26:26–29)

Paul adds the following sentences from the tradition he received (1 Cor. 11:23):

> This cup is the new covenant in my blood. Do this, as often as you drink it, in remembrance of me. (1 Cor. 11:25)

Is there a background to this ceremony in the Old Testament? It seems that there is, for there were instances of eating and drinking in the presence of God in the old covenant as well. For example, when the people of Israel were camped before Mount Sinai, just after God had given the Ten Commandments, God called the leaders of Israel up to the mountain to meet with him:

> Then Moses and Aaron, Nadab, and Abihu, and seventy of the elders of Israel went up, and they saw the God of Israel . . . *they beheld God, and ate and drank.* (Ex. 24:9–11)

Moreover, every year the people of Israel were to tithe (give one-tenth of) all their crops. Then the law of Moses specified,

> *Before the LORD your God,* in the place which he will choose, to make his name dwell there, *you shall eat the tithe of your grain, of your wine, and of your oil, and the firstlings of your herd and flock;* that you may learn to fear the LORD your God always. . . . *You shall eat there before the LORD your God and rejoice,* you and your household. (Deut. 14:23, 26)

But even earlier than that, God had put Adam and Eve in the Garden of Eden and given them all of its abundance to eat (except the fruit of the tree of the knowledge of good and evil). Since there was no sin in that situation, and since God had created them for fellowship with himself and to glorify himself, then every meal that Adam and Eve ate would have been a meal of feasting in the presence of the Lord.

When this fellowship in God's presence was later broken by sin, God still allowed some meals (such as the tithe of fruits mentioned above) that the people would eat in his presence. These meals were a partial restoration of the fellowship with God that Adam and Eve enjoyed before the Fall, even though it was marred by sin. But the fellowship of eating in the presence of the Lord that we find in the Lord's Supper is far better. The Old Testament sacrificial meals continually pointed to the fact that sins were not yet paid for, because the sacrifices in them were repeated year after year, and because they looked forward to the Messiah who was to come and take away sin (see Heb. 10:1–4). The Lord's Supper, however, reminds us that Jesus' payment for our sins has already been accomplished, so we now eat in the Lord's presence with great rejoicing.

Yet even the Lord's Supper looks forward to a more wonderful fellowship meal in God's presence in the future, when the fellowship of Eden will be restored and there will be even greater joy, because those who eat in God's presence will be forgiven sinners now confirmed in righteousness, never able to sin again. That future time of great rejoicing and eating in the presence of God is hinted at by Jesus when he says, "I tell you I shall not drink again of this fruit of the vine *until that day when I drink it new with you* in my Father's kingdom" (Matt. 26:29). We are told more explicitly in Revelation about the marriage supper of the Lamb: "And the angel said to me, 'Write this: Blessed are those who are invited to the marriage supper of the Lamb'" (Rev. 19:9). This will be a time of great rejoicing in the presence of the Lord, as well as a time of reverence and awe before him.

From Genesis to Revelation, then, God's aim has been to bring his people into fellowship with himself, and one of the great joys of experiencing that fellowship is the fact that we can eat and drink in the presence of the Lord. It would be healthy for the church today to recapture a more vivid sense of God's presence at the table of the Lord.

B. The Meaning of the Lord's Supper

The meaning of the Lord's Supper is complex, rich, and full. There are several things symbolized and affirmed in the Lord's Supper.

1. Christ's Death. When we participate in the Lord's supper we symbolize the death of Christ because our actions give a picture of his death for us. When the bread is broken it symbolizes the breaking of Christ's body, and when the cup is poured out it symbolizes the pouring out of Christ's blood for us. This is why participating in the Lord's Supper is also a kind of proclamation: "For as often as you eat this bread and drink the cup, *you proclaim the Lord's death* until he comes" (1 Cor. 11:26).

2. Our Participation in the Benefits of Christ's Death. Jesus commanded his disciples, "Take, eat; this is my body" (Matt. 26:26). As we individually reach out and take the cup for ourselves, each one of us is by that action proclaiming, "I am taking the benefits of Christ's death to myself." When we do this we give a symbol of the fact that we participate in or share in the benefits earned for us by the death of Jesus.

3. Spiritual Nourishment. Just as ordinary food nourishes our physical bodies, so the bread and wine of the Lord's Supper give nourishment to us. But they also picture the fact that there is spiritual nourishment and refreshment that Christ is giving to our souls—indeed, the ceremony that Jesus instituted is in its very nature designed to teach us this. Jesus said,

> Unless you eat the flesh of the Son of man and drink his blood, you have no life in you; he who eats my flesh and drinks my blood has eternal life, and I will raise him up at the last day. For my flesh is food indeed, and my blood is drink indeed. He who eats my flesh and drinks my blood abides in me, and I in him. As the living Father sent me, and I live because of the Father, so he who eats me will live because of me. (John 6:53–57)

Certainly Jesus is not speaking of a literal eating of his flesh and blood. But if he is not speaking of a literal eating and drinking, then he must have in mind a spiritual participation in the benefits of the redemption he earns. This spiritual nourishment, so necessary for our souls, is both symbolized and experienced in our participation in the Lord's Supper.

4. The Unity of Believers. When Christians participate in the Lord's Supper together they also give a clear sign of their unity with one another. In fact, Paul says, "Because there is one bread, we who are many are one body, for we all partake of the one bread" (1 Cor. 10:17).

When we put these four things together, we begin to realize some of the rich meaning of the Lord's Supper: when I participate I come into the presence of Christ; I remember that he died for me; I participate in the benefits of his death; I receive spiritual nourishment; and I am united with all other believers who participate in this Supper. What great cause for thanksgiving and joy is to be found in this Supper of the Lord!

But in addition to these truths visibly portrayed by the Lord's Supper, the fact that Christ has instituted this ceremony for us means that by it he is also promising or affirming certain things to us as well. When we participate in the Lord's Supper, we should be reminded again and again of the following affirmations that Christ is making to us:

5. Christ Affirms His Love for Me. The fact that I am able to participate in the Lord's Supper—indeed, that Jesus *invites me* to come—is a vivid reminder and visual reassurance that Jesus Christ loves *me,* individually and personally. When I come to take of the Lord's Supper I thereby find reassurance again and again of Christ's personal love for me.

6. Christ Affirms That All the Blessings of Salvation Are Reserved for Me. When I come at Christ's invitation to the Lord's Supper, the fact that he has invited me into his presence assures me that he has abundant blessings for me. In this Supper I am actually eating and drinking at a foretaste of the great banquet table of the King. I come to his table as a member of his *eternal* family. When the Lord welcomes me to this table, he assures me that he will welcome me to all the other blessings of earth and heaven as well, and especially to the great marriage supper of the Lamb, at which a place has been reserved for me.

7. I Affirm My Faith in Christ. Finally, as I take the bread and cup for myself, by my actions I am proclaiming, "I need you and trust you, Lord Jesus, to forgive my sins and give life and health to my soul, for only by your broken body and shed blood can I be saved." In fact, as I partake in the breaking of the bread when I eat it and the pouring out of the cup when I drink from it, I proclaim again and again that *my sins* were part of the cause of Jesus' suffering and death. In this way sorrow, joy, thanksgiving, and deep love for Christ are richly intermingled in the beauty of the Lord's Supper.

C. How Is Christ Present in the Lord's Supper?

1. The Roman Catholic View: Transubstantiation. According to the teaching of the Roman Catholic Church, the bread and wine *actually become* the body and blood of Christ. This happens at the moment the priest says, "This is my body" during the celebration of the mass. At the same time as the priest says this, the bread is raised up (elevated) and adored. This action of elevating the bread and pronouncing it to be Christ's body can only be performed by a priest.

When this happens, according to Roman Catholic teaching, grace is imparted to those present *ex opere operato,* that is, "by the work performed,"[1] but the amount of grace dispensed is in proportion to the subjective disposition of the recipient of grace.[2] Moreover, every time the mass is celebrated, the sacrifice of Christ is repeated (in some sense), and the Catholic church is careful to affirm that this is a real sacrifice, even though it is not the same as the sacrifice that Christ paid on the cross.

So Ludwig Ott's *Fundamentals of Catholic Dogma* teaches as follows:

> Christ becomes present in the Sacrament of the Altar by the transformation of the whole substance of the bread into His Body and of the whole substance of the wine into His Blood. . . . This transformation is called Transubstantiation. (p. 379)

> The power of consecration resides in a validly consecrated priest only. (p. 397)

> The Worship of Adoration (Latria) must be given to Christ present in the Eucharist. . . . It follows from the wholeness and permanence of the Real Presence that the absolute worship of adoration (Cultus Latriae) is due to Christ present in the Eucharist. (p. 387)[3]

In Catholic teaching, because the elements of bread and wine literally become the body and blood of Christ, the church for many centuries did not allow the laypeople to drink from the cup of the Lord's Supper (for fear that the blood of Christ would be spilled) but only to eat the bread.[4] Ott's textbook tells us,

> Communion under two forms is not necessary for any individual member of the Faithful, either by reason of Divine precept or as a means of salvation. . . . The reason is that Christ is whole and entire under each species. . . . The abolition of the reception from the chalice in the Middle Ages (12th and 13th centuries) was enjoined for practical reasons, particularly danger of profanation of the Sacrament. (p. 397)

With respect to the actual sacrifice of Christ in the mass, Ott's textbook says,

> The Holy Mass is a true and proper Sacrifice. (p. 402)

> In the Sacrifice of the Mass and in the Sacrifice of the Cross the Sacrificial Gift and the Primary Sacrificing Priest are identical; only the nature and mode of the

---

[1]See discussion of the term *ex opere operato* in relationship to baptism in chapter 7 above, pp. 148–49.

[2]Ludwig Ott, *Fundamentals of Catholic Dogma* (Rockford, Ill.: TAN Books, 1960), says, "Since the measure of the grace conferred *ex opere operato* is in proportion to the subjective disposition of the recipient, the reception of Holy Communion should be preceded by a good preparation, and an appropriate thanksgiving should follow it. . . . An unworthy Communion is a sacrilege" (p. 399).

[3]The word *eucharist* simply means the Lord's Supper. (It is derived from the Greek word *eucharistia*, "giving of thanks."

The related verb *eucharisteō,* "to give thanks," is found in the biblical records of the Last Supper in Matt. 26:27; Mark 14:23; Luke 22:19; and 1 Cor. 11:24: "when he had *given thanks.*") The term *eucharist* is often used by Roman Catholics and frequently by Episcopalians as well. Among many Protestant churches the term *Communion* is commonly used to refer to the Lord's Supper.

[4]However, since the Vatican II council (1962–65), administration of both the bread and the wine to laypersons has been allowed, but it is not always practiced.

offering are different. . . . The Sacrificial Gift is the Body and Blood of Christ. . . . The Primary Sacrificing Priest is Jesus Christ, who utilizes the human priest as His servant and representative and fulfills the consecration through him. According to the Thomistic view, *in every Mass Christ also performs an actual immediate sacrificial activity* which, however, must not be conceived as a totality of many successive acts but as one single uninterrupted sacrificial act of the Transfigured Christ.

The purpose of the Sacrifice is the same in the Sacrifice of the Mass as in the Sacrifice of the Cross; primarily the glorification of God, secondarily atonement, thanksgiving and appeal. (p. 408)

As a propitiatory sacrifice . . . the Sacrifice of the Mass effects the remission of sins and the punishment for sins; as a sacrifice of appeal . . . it brings about the conferring of supernatural and natural gifts. The Eucharistic Sacrifice of propitiation can, as the Council of Trent expressly asserted, be offered, not merely for the living, but also for the poor souls in Purgatory. (pp. 412–13)

In response to the Roman Catholic teaching on the Lord's Supper, it must be said that it first fails to recognize the symbolic character of Jesus' statements when he declared, "This is my body," or, "This is my blood." Jesus spoke in symbolic ways many times when speaking of himself. He said, for example, *"I am the true vine"* (John 15:1), or *"I am the door; if any one enters by me, he will be saved"* (John 10:9), or "I am the bread which came down from heaven" (John 6:41). In a similar way, when Jesus says, "This is my body," he means it in a symbolic way, not in an actual, literal, physical way. In fact, as he was sitting with his disciples holding the bread, the bread was in his hand but it was distinct from his body, and that was, of course, evident to the disciples. None of the disciples present would have thought that the loaf of bread that Jesus held in his hand was actually his physical body, for they could see his body before their eyes. They would have naturally understood Jesus' statement in a symbolic way. Similarly, when Jesus said, *"This cup* which is poured out for you *is the new covenant* in my blood" (Luke 22:20), he certainly did not mean that the cup was actually the new covenant, but that the cup *represented* the new covenant.

Moreover, the Roman Catholic view fails to recognize the clear New Testament teaching on the *finality* and *completeness* of Christ's sacrifice once for all time for our sins: the book of Hebrews emphasizes this many times, as when it says, *"Nor was it to offer himself repeatedly,* as the high priest enters the Holy Place yearly with blood not his own; for then he would have had to suffer repeatedly since the foundation of the world. But as it is, he has appeared *once* for all at the end of the age to put away sin by the sacrifice of himself . . . Christ, having been offered *once* to bear the sins of many" (Heb. 9:25–28). To say that Christ's sacrifice continues or is repeated in the mass has been, since the Reformation, one of the most objectionable Roman Catholic doctrines from the standpoint of Protestants. When we realize that Christ's sacrifice for our sins is finished and completed (*"It is finished,"* John 19:30; cf. Heb. 1:3), it gives great assurance to us that our sins are all paid for, and there remains no sacrifice yet to be paid. But the idea of a continuation of Christ's sacrifice destroys our assurance that the payment has been made by Christ and accepted by God the Father, and that there is "no condemnation" (Rom. 8:1) now remaining for us.

For Protestants the idea that the mass is in any sense a repetition of the death of Christ seems to mark a return to the repeated sacrifices of the old covenant, which were "a reminder of sin year after year" (Heb. 10:3). Instead of the assurance of complete forgiveness of sins through the once for all sacrifice of Christ (Heb. 10:12), the idea that the mass is a repeated sacrifice gives a constant reminder of sins and remaining guilt to be atoned for week after week.[5]

With regard to the teaching that only priests can officiate at the Lord's Supper, the New Testament gives no instructions at all that place restrictions on the people who can preside at Communion. And since Scripture places no such restrictions on us, it would not seem to be justified to say that only priests can dispense the elements of the Lord's Supper. More-over, since the New Testament teaches that all believers are priests and members of a "royal priesthood" (1 Peter 2:9; cf. Heb. 4:16; 10:19–22), we should not specify a certain class of people who have the rights of priests, as in the old covenant, but we should emphasize that all believers share the great spiritual privilege of coming near to God.

Finally, any continuation of the restriction that will not allow laypersons to drink of the cup of the Lord's Supper would be arguing from caution and tradition to justify disobedience to Jesus' direct commands, not only the command to his disciples where he said, "Drink of it, *all of you*" (Matt. 26:27), but also the direction Paul recorded, in which Jesus said, "Do this, as often as *you drink it*, in remembrance of me" (1 Cor. 11:25).

2. The Lutheran View: "In, With, and Under." Martin Luther rejected the Roman Catholic view of the Lord's Supper, yet he insisted that the phrase "This is my body" had to be taken in some sense as a literal statement. His conclusion was not that the bread actually *becomes* the physical body of Christ, but that the physical body of Christ *is present* "in, with, and under" the bread of the Lord's Supper. The example sometimes given is to say that Christ's body is present in the bread as water is present in a sponge—the water is not the sponge, but is present "in, with, and under" a sponge, and is present wherever the sponge is present. Other examples given are that of magnetism in a magnet or a soul in the body.

The Lutheran understanding of the Lord's Supper is found in the textbook of Francis Pieper, *Christian Dogmatics*.[6] He quotes Luther's Small Catechism: "What is the Sacrament of the Altar? It is the true body and blood of our Lord Jesus Christ, under the bread and wine, for us Christians to eat and to drink, instituted by Christ Himself."[7] Similarly, the Augsburg Confession, Article X, says, "Of the Supper of the Lord they teach that the Body and Blood of Christ are truly present, and are distributed to those who eat in the Supper of the Lord."[8]

---

[5]This is why that many Protestants have felt that they could readily partake of the Lord's Supper in any other Protestant church, even in high church Anglican services that in form appear quite similar to Roman Catholic services, but could not in good conscience participate in a Roman Catholic mass, because of the Roman Catholic teaching on the nature of the mass itself.

[6]Francis Pieper, *Christian Dogmatics,* 4 vols. (St. Louis: Concordia, 1950–57).

[7]Ibid., 3:296.

[8]Ibid. John Theodore Mueller says Lutherans reject the term "consubstantiation" to describe their views (*Christian Dogmatics* [St. Louis: Concordia, 1934], p. 528).

One passage that may be thought to give support to this position is 1 Corinthians 10:16, "The bread which we break, is it not a participation in the body of Christ?"

However, in order to affirm this doctrine, Luther had to answer an important question: How can Christ's physical body, or more generally Christ's human nature, be everywhere present? Is it not true that Jesus in his human nature ascended into heaven and remains there until his return? Did he not say that he was leaving the earth and would no longer be in the world but was going to the Father (John 16:28; 17:11)? In answer to this problem Luther taught the *ubiquity* of Christ's human nature after his ascension—that is, that Christ's human nature was present everywhere ("ubiquitous"). But theologians ever since Luther's time have suspected that he taught the ubiquity of Christ's human nature, not because it is found anywhere in Scripture, but because he needed it to explain how his view of consubstantiation could be true.

In response to the Lutheran view, it can be said that it too fails to realize that Jesus is speaking of a *spiritual* reality but using *physical* objects to teach us when he says, "This is my body." We should take this no more literally than we take the corresponding sentence, "*This cup* which is poured out for you *is the new covenant* in my blood" (Luke 22:20). In fact, Luther does not really do justice to Jesus' words in a literal sense at all. Louis Berkhof rightly objects that Luther really makes the words of Jesus mean, "This accompanies my body."[9] In this matter it would help to read again John 6:27–59, where the context shows that Jesus is talking in literal, physical terms about bread, but he is continually explaining it in terms of spiritual reality.

3. The Rest of Protestantism: A Symbolic and Spiritual Presence of Christ. In distinction from Martin Luther, John Calvin and other Reformers argued that the bread and wine of the Lord's Supper did not change into the body and blood of Christ, nor did they somehow contain the body and blood of Christ. Rather, the bread and wine *symbolized* the body and blood of Christ, and they gave a visible sign of the fact that Christ himself was truly present.[10] Calvin said:

> By the showing of the symbol the thing itself is also shown. For unless a man means to call God a deceiver, he would never dare assert that an empty symbol is set forth by him. . . . And the godly ought by all means to keep this rule: whenever they see symbols appointed by the Lord, to think and be persuaded that the truth of the thing signified is surely present there. For why would the Lord put in your hand the symbol of his body, except to assure you of a true participation in it? (*Institutes*, 4.17.10; p. 1371)

Yet Calvin was careful to differ both with Roman Catholic teaching (which said that the bread became Christ's body) and with Lutheran teaching (which said that the bread contained Christ's body).

---

[9]Louis Berkhof, *Systematic Theology* (Grand Rapids: Eerdmans, 1939, 1941), p. 653.

[10]There was some difference between Calvin and another Swiss Reformer, Ulrich Zwingli (1484–1531) on the nature of the presence of Christ in the Lord's supper, both agreeing that Christ was present in a symbolic way, but Zwingli being much more hesitant about affirming a real spiritual presence of Christ. However, the actual teaching of Zwingli in this regard is a matter of some difference among historians.

> But we must establish such a presence of Christ in the Supper as may neither fasten him to the element of bread, nor enclose him in bread, nor circumscribe him in any way (all which things, it is clear, detract from his heavenly glory). (*Institutes*, 4.17.19; p. 1381)

Today most Protestants would say, in addition to the fact that the bread and wine symbolize the body and blood of Christ, that Christ is also *spiritually present* in a special way as we partake of the bread and wine. Indeed, Jesus promised to be present whenever believers worship: "Where two or three are gathered in my name, there am I in the midst of them" (Matt. 18:20).[11] And if he is especially present when Christians gather to worship, then we would expect that he will be present in a special way in the Lord's Supper:[12] We meet him at *his* table, to which he comes to give himself to us. As we receive the elements of bread and wine in the presence of Christ, so we partake of him and all his benefits. We "feed upon him in our hearts" with thanksgiving. Indeed, even a child who knows Christ will understand this without being told and will expect to receive a special blessing from the Lord during this ceremony, because the meaning of it is so inherent in the very actions of eating and drinking. Yet we must not say that Christ is present apart from our personal faith, but only meets and blesses us there in accordance with our faith in him.

In what way is Christ present then? Certainly there is a symbolic presence of Christ, but it is also a genuine spiritual presence and there is genuine spiritual blessing in this ceremony.

D. Who Should Participate in the Lord's Supper?

Despite differences over some aspects of the Lord's Supper, most Protestants would agree, first, that *only those who believe in Christ* should participate in it, because it is a sign of being a Christian and continuing in the Christian life.[13] Paul warns that those who eat and drink unworthily face serious consequences: "For any one who eats and drinks without discerning the body eats and drinks judgment upon himself. That is why many of you are weak and ill, and some have died" (1 Cor. 11:29–30).

Second, many Protestants would argue from the meaning of baptism and the meaning of the Lord's Supper that, ordinarily, *only those who have been baptized* should participate in the Lord's Supper. This is because baptism is so clearly a symbol of *beginning* the Christian life, while the Lord's Supper is clearly a symbol of *continuing* the Christian

---

[11]It is true that this sentence is spoken in a context that applies specifically to church discipline (vv. 15–19), but it is a statement of a general truth used here to support a specific application, and there is no good reason to restrict its application to occasions of church discipline. It tells us that Jesus is always present when believers gather in his name.

[12]Sometimes Protestants have become so concerned to deny the Roman Catholic view of the "real presence" of Christ in the elements that they have wrongly denied even any spiritual presence. Millard Erickson notes the humorous situation that results: "Out of a zeal to avoid the conception that Jesus is present in some sort of magical way, certain Baptists among others have sometimes gone to such extremes as to give the impression that the one place where Jesus most assuredly is not to be found is the Lord's supper. This is what one Baptist leader termed 'the doctrine of the real absence' of Jesus Christ" (*Christian Theology,* [Grand Rapids: Baker, 1983–85], p. 1123).

[13]However, some in the Church of England and elsewhere have recently begun to allow young children to participate in the Lord's Supper, reasoning that if they have been given the sign of baptism it is wrong to deny them the sign of the Supper.

life. Therefore if someone is taking the Lord's Supper and thereby giving public proclamation that he or she is continuing in the Christian life, then that person should be asked, "Wouldn't it be good to be baptized now and thereby give a symbol that you are beginning the Christian life?"

But others, including the present author, would object to such a restriction as follows: A different problem arises if someone who is a genuine believer, but not yet baptized, is *not* allowed to participate in the Lord's Supper when Christians get together. In that case the person's nonparticipation symbolizes that he or she is *not* a member of the body of Christ which is coming together to observe the Lord's Supper in a unified fellowship (see 1 Cor. 10:17: "Because there is one bread, we who are many are one body, for we all partake of the one bread"). Therefore churches may think it best to allow non-baptized believers to participate in the Lord's Supper but to urge them to be baptized as soon as possible. For if they are willing to participate in one outward symbol of being a Christian, there seems no reason why they should not be willing to participate in the other, a symbol that appropriately comes first.

Of course, the problems that arise in both situations (when unbaptized believers take Communion and when they do not) can all be avoided if new Christians are regularly baptized shortly after coming to faith. And, whichever position a church takes on the question of whether unbaptized believers should take Communion, in the teaching ministry of the church, it would seem wise to teach that the ideal situation is for new believers first to be baptized and then to partake of the Lord's Supper.

The third qualification for participation is that *self-examination:*

> Whoever, therefore, eats the bread or drinks the cup of the Lord in an unworthy manner will be guilty of profaning the body and blood of the Lord. *Let a man examine himself, and so eat of the bread and drink of the cup.* For any one who eats and drinks without discerning the body eats and drinks judgment upon himself. (1 Cor. 11:27–29)

In the context of 1 Corinthians 11 Paul is rebuking the Corinthians for their selfish and inconsiderate conduct when they come together as a church: "When you meet together, it is not the Lord's supper that you eat. For in eating, each one goes ahead with his own meal, and one is hungry and another is drunk" (1 Cor. 11:20–21). This helps us understand what Paul means when he talks about those who eat and drink "without discerning the body" (1 Cor. 11:29). The problem at Corinth was *not* a failure to understand that the bread and cup represented the body and blood of the Lord—they certainly knew that. The problem rather was their selfish, inconsiderate conduct toward each other while they were at the Lord's table. They were not understanding or "discerning" the true nature of the church *as one body*. This interpretation of "without discerning the body" is supported by Paul's mention of the church as the body of Christ just a bit earlier, in 1 Corinthians 10:17: "Because there is one bread, we who are many *are one* body, for we all partake of the one bread."[14] So the phrase "not discerning the *body*" means "not understanding the

---

[14]Moreover, from this very brief mention of the idea of one body we may rightly suppose that it was not a new idea, but that Paul had taught them this idea while staying in Corinth for two years when he founded the church there.

unity and interdependence of people in the church, which is the body of Christ." It means not taking thought for our brothers and sisters when we come to the *Lord's* Supper, at which we ought to reflect his character.[15]

What does it mean, then, to eat or drink "in an unworthy manner" (1 Cor. 11:27)? We might at first think the words apply rather narrowly and pertain only to the way we conduct ourselves when we actually eat and drink the bread and wine. But when Paul explains that unworthy participation involves "not discerning the body," he indicates that we are to take thought for all of our relationships within the body of Christ: are we acting in ways that vividly portray not the unity of the one bread and one body, but disunity? Are we conducting ourselves in ways that proclaim not the self-giving sacrifice of our Lord, but enmity and selfishness? In a broad sense, then, "Let a man examine himself" means that we ought to ask whether our relationships in the body of Christ are in fact reflecting the character of the Lord whom we meet there and whom we represent.

In this connection, Jesus' teaching about coming to worship in general should also be mentioned:

> So if you are offering your gift at the altar, and there remember that your brother has something against you, leave your gift there before the altar and go; first be reconciled to your brother, and then come and offer your gift. (Matt. 5:23–24)

Jesus here tells us that whenever we come to worship we should be sure that our relationships with others are right, and if they are not, we should act quickly to make them right and then come to worship God. This admonition ought to be especially true when we come to the Lord's Supper.

Of course, no pastor or church leader will know whether people are examining themselves or not (except in cases where clearly offensive or sinful conduct becomes evident to others). For the most part, the church must depend on the pastors and teachers to explain clearly the meaning of the Lord's Supper and to warn of the dangers of participating unworthily. Then people will have the responsibility to examine their own lives, in accordance with what Paul says. Indeed, Paul does not say that the pastors should examine everyone else's lives, but encourages individual self-examination instead: "Let a man examine himself" (1 Cor. 11:28).[16]

---

[15]Two other reasons for this interpretation are: (1) Paul only says "not discerning the body," and he does not say "not discerning the body and blood of the Lord," which he more likely would have done if he had meant "not understanding that the bread and cup represent the body and blood of the Lord." (2) In addition, Paul says, "Let a man examine *himself*" (and this would no doubt include examining his relationships with others in the church), but Paul does not say, "Let him see if he understands what the bread and wine stand for."

[16]In cases of church discipline or in cases where outward behavior gives clear evidence that a person is straying from Christ, the leaders of the church may wish to give a strong and clear verbal warning against participation in the Lord's Supper, so that the erring brother or sister does not eat and drink judgment upon himself or herself. But these cases should be rare, and we must also avoid the mistake of some churches that have been so strict in administration of the Lord's Supper that many true believers have been kept away and thus the unity of the true body of Christ has not been represented, nor have believers had access to the spiritual blessings that should rightly be theirs in Christ in participating in this ordinance and thereby obeying their Lord.

E. Other Questions

Who should administer the Lord's Supper? Scripture gives no explicit teaching on this question, so we are left simply to decide what is wise and appropriate for the benefit of the believers in the church. In order to guard against abuse of the Lord's Supper, a responsible leader ought to be in charge of administering it, but it does not seem that Scripture requires that only ordained clergy or selected church officers could do this. In ordinary situations, of course, the pastor or other leader who ordinarily officiates at the worship services of the church would appropriately officiate at Communion as well. But beyond this, there would seem to be no reason why only officers or only leaders, or only men, should distribute the elements. Would it not speak much more clearly of our unity and spiritual equality in Christ if both men and women, for example, assisted in distributing the elements of the Lord's Supper?[17]

How often should the Lord's Supper be celebrated? Scripture does not tell us. Jesus simply said, "As often as you eat this bread and drink the cup . . ." (1 Cor. 11:26). Paul's directive here regarding worship services would also be appropriate to consider: "Let all things be done for edification" (1 Cor. 14:26). In actuality it has been the practice of most of the church throughout its history to celebrate the Lord's Supper every week when believers gather. However, in many Protestant groups since the Reformation, there has been a less frequent celebration of the Lord's Supper—sometimes once a month or twice a month, or, in many Reformed churches, only four times a year. If the Lord's Supper is planned and explained and carried out in such a way that it is a time of self-examination, confession, and thanksgiving and praise, then it does not seem that celebrating it once a week would be too often, however, and it certainly could be observed that frequently "for edification."

QUESTIONS FOR PERSONAL APPLICATION

1. What things symbolized by the Lord's Supper have received new emphasis in your thinking as a result of reading this chapter? Do you feel more eager to participate in the Lord's Supper now than before you read the chapter? Why?

2. In what ways (if any) will you approach the Lord's Supper differently now? Which of the things symbolized in the Lord's Supper is most encouraging to your Christian life right now?

3. What view of the nature of Christ's presence in the Lord's Supper have you been taught in your church previously? What is your own view now?

---

[17]Of course, where distribution of the Lord's Supper is thought to be a priestly function (as in Anglican churches), churches may decide that another approach to this question is more consistent with their own teachings. Moreover, in a church where only the leading officers of the church have assisted in serving Communion for many years, the church may decide that allowing anyone else to participate in distrib-uting the elements would be symbolizing the participation of those people in the leadership and governing of the church, and they may wish to delay making a change at least until some clear teaching could be given. Other churches may feel that the leadership function of the church is so clearly tied up with the distribution of the elements that they would wish to continue with that restriction on their practice.

4. Are there any broken personal relationships that you need to make right before you come to the Lord's Supper again?

5. Are there areas in which your church needs to do more teaching about the nature of the Lord's Supper? What are they?

SPECIAL TERMS

Communion	spiritual presence
consubstantiation	symbolic presence
Eucharist	transubstantiation
not discerning the body	ubiquity of Christ's human nature

BIBLIOGRAPHY

Beckwith, Roger T. "Eucharist." In *EDT*, pp. 236–38.
Berkouwer, G. C. *The Sacraments*. Trans. by Hugo Bekker. Grand Rapids: Eerdmans, 1969.
Bridge, D., and D. Phypers. *Communion: The Meal That Unites?* London: Hodder and Stoughton, 1981.
Marshall, I. Howard. *Last Supper and Lord's Supper*. Grand Rapids: Eerdmans, 1980.
Osterhaven, M. E. "Lord's Supper, Views of." In *EDT*, pp. 653–56.
Wallace, R. S. "Lord's Supper." In *EDT*, pp. 651–53.

SCRIPTURE MEMORY PASSAGE

1 Corinthians 11:23–26: *For I received from the Lord what I also delivered to you, that the Lord Jesus on the night when he was betrayed took bread, and when he had given thanks, he broke it, and said, "This is my body which is for you. Do this in remembrance of me." In the same way also the cup, after supper, saying, "This cup is the new covenant in my blood. Do this, as often as you drink it, in remembrance of me." For as often as you eat this bread and drink the cup, you proclaim the Lord's death until he comes.*

HYMN

"Here, O My Lord, I See Thee Face to Face"

This beautiful hymn is not frequently sung, but it speaks so directly to Jesus himself and speaks so clearly of the spiritual reality that we need to remember in the Lord's supper that it is one of the greatest hymns ever written regarding this doctrine. It conveys an attitude of reverence in the Lord's presence, joy in salvation, and genuine repentance for sin as well. The sweet beauty of spirit that Horatius Bonar exemplified in this hymn is matched by very few hymns in the history of the church.

Tune: "Spirit of God, Descend Upon My Heart"

Here, O my Lord, I see thee face to face;
　Here would I touch and handle things unseen,
Here grasp with firmer hand th' eternal grace,
　And all my weariness upon thee lean.

Here would I feed upon the bread of God,
　Here drink with thee the royal wine of heaven;
Here would I lay aside each earthly load,
　Here taste afresh the calm of sin forgiven.

This is the hour of banquet and of song;
　This is the heav'nly table spread for me:
Here let me feast, and, feasting, still prolong
　The brief, bright hour of fellowship with thee.

I have no help but thine, nor do I need
　Another arm save thine to lean upon:
It is enough, my Lord, enough indeed;
　My strength is in thy might, thy might alone.

Mine is the sin, but thine the righteousness;
　Mine is the guilt, but thine the cleansing blood;
Here is my robe, my refuge, and my peace,
　Thy blood, thy righteousness, O Lord my God.

AUTHOR: HORATIUS BONAR, 1855

WORSHIP

How can our worship fulfill its great purpose in the New Testament age? What does it mean to worship "in spirit and in truth"?

EXPLANATION AND SCRIPTURAL BASIS

The term *worship* is sometimes applied to all of a Christian's life, and it is rightly said that everything in our life should be an act of worship, and everything the church does should be considered worship, for everything we do should glorify God. However, in this chapter I am not using the word in that broad sense. Rather, I am using *worship* in a more specific sense to refer to the music and words that Christians direct to God in praise, together with the heart attitudes that accompany that praise, especially when Christians assemble together.

A. Definition and Purpose of Worship

Worship is the activity of glorifying God in his presence with our voices and hearts.

In this definition we note that worship is an act of glorifying God. Yet all aspects of our lives are supposed to glorify God, so this definition specifies that worship is something we do especially when we come into God's presence, when we are conscious of adoration of him in our hearts, and when we praise him with our voices and speak about him so others may hear. Paul encourages the Christians in Colossae, "Let the word of Christ dwell in you richly, *teach and admonish one another* in all wisdom, and *sing psalms and hymns and spiritual songs with thankfulness in your hearts to God*" (Col. 3:16).

In fact, the primary reason that God called us into the assembly of the church is that as a corporate assembly we might worship him. Edmund Clowney wisely says:

God had demanded of Pharaoh, "Let my people go, *so that they may worship me in the desert*" (Ex. 7:16b). . . . God brings them out that he might bring them in, into his assembly, to the great company of those who stand before his face. . . . *God's assembly at Sinai is therefore the immediate goal of the exodus. God brings his people into his presence that they might hear his voice and worship him.*

But Clowney explains that the worshiping assembly at Mount Sinai could not remain in session before God forever. Therefore God established other festivals in which the whole nation would assemble before him three times a year. He says that "Israelites are a nation formed for worship, called to assemble in the courts of the Lord, and to praise together the name of the Most High."[1]

Yet Clowney points out that, rather than worshiping God in a unified, holy assembly, the people turned aside to serving idols and, rather than assembling the people to worship before him, "in judgment God scattered the people in exile."[2]

But God promised that his purposes for his people would yet be fulfilled, that there would someday be a great assembly not just of Israel but of all nations before his throne (Isa. 2:2–4; 25:6–8; 49:22; 66:18–21; cf. Jer. 48:47; 49:6, 39). Clowney notes that the fulfillment of that promise began only when Jesus started to build his church:

> Pentecost was the time of the firstfruits, the beginning of the great harvest of redemption. Peter preached the fulfillment of the prophecy of Joel. The Spirit had been poured out, *the worship of the new age had been ushered in. The church, the assembly for worship, was praising God.* . . . Now the ingathering had begun.
>
> The gospel call is a call to worship, to turn from sin and call upon the name of the Lord. . . . The picture of the church as a worshiping assembly is nowhere more powerfully presented than by the author of the Epistle to the Hebrews (12:18–29). . . . In our worship in Christ's church we approach the throne of God the judge of all. *We enter the festival assembly of the saints and the angels.* We gather in spirit with the spirits of just men made perfect. We enter the assembly of glory through Christ our mediator, and the blood of his atoning death. . . .
>
> *Reverent corporate worship*, then, is not optional for the church of God. . . . Rather, it *brings to expression the very being of the church.* It manifests on earth the reality of the heavenly assembly.[3]

Worship is therefore a *direct* expression of our ultimate purpose for living, "to glorify God and fully to enjoy him forever."[4] God speaks of his "sons" and "daughters" as "every one who is called by my name, whom I created *for my glory,* whom I formed and made"

---

[1] Edmund Clowney, "The Biblical Theology of the Church" in *The Church in the Bible and the World,* ed. D. A. Carson (Grand Rapids: Baker, 1987), pp. 17–19 (italics mine).
[2] Ibid.
[3] Ibid., pp. 20–22.

[4] This familiar phrase has been widely used in Christian teachings. It is found in the *Westminster Larger Catechism,* Question One: *"What is the chief and highest end of man? Answer:* Man's chief and highest end is to glorify God, and fully to enjoy him forever."

(Isa. 43:6–7). And Paul uses similar language when he says that "we who first hoped in Christ have been destined and appointed *to live for the praise of his glory*" (Eph. 1:12). Scripture is clear here and in many other passages that God created us to glorify him.

When we reflect on the purpose of worship it also reminds us that *God is worthy of worship and we are not.* Even the apostle John had to be told that he should not worship any creature, not even a powerful angel in heaven. When he "fell down to worship" at the feet of the angel who showed him marvelous visions in heaven, the angel said to him, "You must not do that! . . . Worship God" (Rev. 22:8–9).

This is because God is jealous for his own honor and he rightly seeks his own honor. He says, "I the Lord your God am a jealous God" (Ex. 20:5) and "My glory I will not give to another" (Isa. 48:11). Something within us should tremble and rejoice at this fact. We should tremble with fear lest we rob God's glory from him. And we should rejoice that it is *right* that God seek his own honor and be jealous for his own honor, for he, infinitely more than anything he has made, is *worthy* of honor. The twenty-four elders in heaven feel this reverence and joy, for they fall down before God's throne and cast their crowns before him singing, "You are worthy, our Lord and God, to receive glory and honor and power, for you created all things, and by your will they existed and were created" (Rev. 4:11). When we feel the absolute *rightness* of this deep within ourselves we then have the appropriate heart attitude for genuine worship.

Because God is worthy of worship and seeks to be worshiped, everything in our worship services should be designed and carried out not to call attention to ourselves or bring glory to ourselves, but to call attention to God and to cause people to think about him. It would be appropriate for us frequently to re-evaluate the various elements in our Sunday services—the preaching, public prayer, leading of worship, special music, celebration of the Lord's Supper, and even the announcements and the offering. Are they really bringing glory to God in the way they are done?[5] Peter says that spiritual gifts are to be used in such a way that "in everything God may be glorified through Jesus Christ" (1 Peter 4:11).

B. The Results of Genuine Worship

When we worship God in the sense described above, truly giving him glory in our hearts and with our voices, several things happen as a result:

1. We Delight in God. God created us not only to glorify him but also to enjoy him and delight in his excellence.[6] We probably experience delight in God more fully in worship than in any other activity in this life. David confesses that the "one thing" that he will seek for above all else is "that I may dwell in the house of the Lord all the days of my life, to behold the beauty of the Lord, and to inquire in his temple" (Ps. 27:4). He also says, "*In your presence there is fulness of joy,* in your right hand are pleasures for evermore"

---

[5]Few things destroy an atmosphere of worship more quickly than a soloist or choir who enjoy drawing attention to themselves, or a preacher who parades his own intelligence or skill in speaking. "God opposes the proud, but gives grace to the humble" (1 Peter 5:5).

[6]See the excellent discussion of living all of life by delighting in God in John Piper, *Desiring God* (Portland, Ore.: Multnomah, 1986); also his analysis of God's delight in himself and what reflects his excellence, in John Piper, *The Pleasures of God* (Portland, Ore.: Multnomah, 1991).

(Ps. 16:11). Similarly, Asaph knows that God alone is the fulfillment of all his hopes and desires: *"Whom have I in heaven but you? And there is nothing upon earth that I desire besides you"* (Ps. 73:25). And the sons of Korah say:

> How lovely is your dwelling place,
> O LORD of hosts!
> My soul longs, yea, faints
> for the courts of the LORD;
>
> My heart and flesh sing for joy
> to the living God . . .
> Blessed are those who dwell in your house,
> ever singing your praise! . . .
>
> For a day in your courts is better
> than a thousand elsewhere. (Ps. 84:1–2, 4, 10)

The early church knew such joy in worship, for "day by day, attending the temple together and breaking bread in their homes, they partook of food with glad and generous hearts, *praising God* and having favor with all the people" (Acts 2:46). In fact, immediately after Jesus' ascension into heaven, the disciples "returned to Jerusalem with great joy, *and were continually in the temple blessing God"* (Luke 24:52–53).

Of course, such activity of continual praise cannot last forever in this age, for living in a fallen world requires that we give time to many other responsibilities as well. But extended praise does give us a foretaste of the atmosphere of heaven, where the four living creatures "never cease to sing, 'Holy, holy, holy, is the Lord God Almighty, who was and is and is to come!'" (Rev. 4:8), and the other heavenly creatures and the redeemed who have died join in that heavenly worship and extol "the Lamb who was slain" (Rev. 5:12).

2. God Delights in Us. What does God do when we worship him? The amazing truth of Scripture is that as the creation glorifies God, he also takes delight in it. When God first made the universe, he looked on all of it with delight, and saw that "it was very good" (Gen. 1:31). God takes special delight in human beings whom he has created and redeemed. Isaiah reminded the people of the Lord,

> You shall be a crown of beauty in the hand of the LORD . . .
> you shall be called My delight is in her . . .
> for the LORD delights in you . . .
> as the bridegroom rejoices over the bride,
> so shall your God rejoice over you. (Isa. 62:3–5)

Zephaniah echoes the same theme when he says,

> The LORD, your God, is in your midst,
> a warrior who gives victory;
> he will rejoice over you with gladness,
> he will renew you in his love;
> he will exult over you with loud singing. (Zeph. 3:17)

This truth should bring great encouragement to us, for as we love God and praise him we realize that we are bringing joy and delight to his heart. And the deepest joy of love is the joy of bringing delight to the heart of the one you love.

3. We Draw Near to God: The Amazing Unseen Reality of New Covenant Worship.
In the old covenant believers could only draw near to God in a limited way through the temple ceremonies; indeed, most of the people of Israel could not enter into the temple itself, but had to remain in the courtyard. Even the priests could only go into the outer court of the temple, the "Holy Place," when it was their appointed duty. But into the inner room of the temple, the "Holy of Holies," no one could go except the high priest, and he only once a year (Heb. 9:1–7).

Now, under the new covenant, believers have the amazing privilege of being able to enter directly into the holy of holies in heaven when they worship. "We have confidence to enter the Most Holy Place by the blood of Jesus" (Heb. 10:19 NIV).[7] Since we have that confidence to enter into the very presence of God, the author of Hebrews encourages us, "*Let us draw near* with a true heart in full assurance of faith" (Heb. 10:22). Worship in the New Testament church is not simply practice for some later heavenly experience of genuine worship, nor is it simply pretending, or going through some outward activities. It is *genuine worship* in the presence of God himself, and when we worship we enter before his throne.

This reality is expressed more fully by the author of Hebrews in chapter 12, when he tells Christians that they have not come to a place like the earthly Mount Sinai where the people of Israel received the Ten Commandments from God, but they have come to something far better, the heavenly Jerusalem:

> For *you have not come* to what may be touched, a blazing fire, and darkness, and gloom, and a tempest, and the sound of a trumpet, and a voice whose words made the hearers entreat that no further messages be spoken to them. . . . *But you have come to Mount Zion and to the city of the living God,* the heavenly Jerusalem, and to innumerable angels in festal gathering, and to the assembly of the first-born who are enrolled in heaven, and to a judge who is God of all, and to the spirits of just men made perfect, and to Jesus, the mediator of a new covenant, and to the sprinkled blood that speaks more graciously than the blood of Abel. (Heb. 12:18–24)

This is the reality of new covenant worship: it actually *is* worship in the presence of God, though we do not now see him with our physical eyes, nor do we see the angels gathered around his throne or the spirits of believers who have gone before and are now worshiping in God's presence. But it is all there, and it is all real, more real and more permanent than the physical creation that we see around us, which will someday be destroyed in the final judgment. And if we believe Scripture to be true, then we must also believe it

---

[7]The Greek text literally says that we "have confidence into the entrance of *the holy places,*" because the plural *tōn hagiōn* is used elsewhere in Hebrews to refer to the holy place and the holy of holies together as "the holy places" (Heb. 8:2; 9:8, 25; 13:11). The RSV regularly renders this expression by "the sanctuary," but that translation obscures the fact that it is referring both to the holy place and to the holy of holies. (The NASB renders these plurals as singulars, an uncommon departure from its ordinary tendency to translate more literally.)

to be actually true that *we ourselves* come to that place and join *our* voices with those already worshiping in heaven whenever we come to God in worship. Our only appropriate response is this: "Let us offer to God acceptable worship, with reverence and awe; for our God is a consuming fire" (Heb. 12:28–29).

4. God Draws Near to Us. James tells us, "Draw near to God and he will draw near to you" (James 4:8). This has been the pattern of God's dealings with his people throughout the Bible, and we should be confident that it will be true also today.

In the Old Testament, when God's people began to praise him at the dedication of the temple, he descended and made himself known in their midst:

> *When the song was raised,* with trumpets and cymbals and other musical instruments, in praise to the LORD, "For he is good, for his steadfast love endures for ever," the house, *the house of the LORD, was filled with a cloud,* so that the priests could not stand to minister because of the cloud; *for the glory of the LORD filled the house of God.* (2 Chron. 5:13–14)

Though this only speaks of one specific incident, it does not seem wrong to suppose that God will also make his presence known at other times among his people, whenever he is pleased with the praise they offer (even if he does not come in the form of a visible cloud). David says, "Yet you are holy, enthroned on the praises of Israel" (Ps. 22:3).

5. God Ministers to Us. Although the primary purpose of worship is to glorify God, the Scriptures teach that in worship something also happens to us: we ourselves are built up or edified. To some extent this happens, of course, when we learn from the Bible teachings that are given or the words of encouragement that others speak to us—Paul says, "Let all things be done for edification" (1 Cor. 14:26), and he says that we are to "teach and admonish one another in all wisdom" (Col. 3:16), and to be "addressing one another in psalms and hymns and spiritual songs" (Eph. 5:19; cf. Heb. 10:24–25).

But in addition to the edification that comes from growth in understanding the Bible and hearing words of encouragement from others, there is another kind of edification that occurs in worship: when we worship God he meets with us and directly ministers to us, strengthening our faith, intensifying our awareness of his presence, and granting refreshment to our spirits. Peter says that as Christians are continually coming to Christ (in worship and prayer and faith), they are then "*being built up* as a spiritual house for a holy priesthood, to offer up spiritual sacrifices acceptable to God through Jesus Christ" (1 Peter 2:5 NASB). When we come to worship we come into God's presence in a special way, and we may expect that he will meet us there and minister to us: as we "draw near to the throne of grace" we will "receive mercy and find grace to help in time of need" (Heb. 4:16).[8] During genuine worship we will often experience an intensification of the sanctifying work of the Holy Spirit, who is at work continually changing us into the likeness of Christ "from one degree of glory to another" (2 Cor. 3:18).[9]

---

[8]See also Ps. 34:4–5, 8; 37:4.

[9]Somehow, the more we see of God the more we become like him. That is evident especially when we enter the age to come, for John says, "When he appears we shall be like him, *for we shall see him as he is*" (1 John 3:2). But it is also true to some degree in this life, as we run the race that is set before us,

CHAPTER 9 · WORSHIP

6. The Lord's Enemies Flee. When the people of Israel began to worship, God at times would fight for them against their enemies. For example, when the Moabites, Edomites, and Syrians came against Judah, King Jehoshaphat sent out the choir praising God in front of the army:

> He appointed those who were to sing to the LORD and praise him in holy array, as they went *before the army.* . . . And *when they began to sing and praise,* the LORD set an ambush against the men of Ammon, Moab, and Mount Seir, who had come against Judah, so that they were routed. (2 Chron. 20:21–22)

Similarly, when God's people offer him worship today, we may expect that the Lord will battle against demonic forces that oppose the gospel and cause them to flee.

7. Unbelievers Know They Are in God's Presence. Though Scripture does not emphasize evangelism as a primary purpose when the church meets for worship, Paul does tell the Corinthians to take thought for unbelievers and outsiders who come to their services, to be sure that the Christians speak in understandable ways (see 1 Cor. 14:23). He also tells them that if the gift of prophecy is functioning properly, unbelievers will from time to time have the secrets of their heart disclosed, and they will fall on their face and *"worship God and declare that God is really among you"* (1 Cor. 14:25; cf. Acts 2:11). But evangelism is not seen as a primary purpose when the church assembles for worship, and it would therefore not be right to have the only weekly gathering of believers designed primarily with an evangelistic purpose. Paul's concern is rather that visitors understand what is going on (and not think that Christians are "mad," 1 Cor. 14:23), and that they recognize that "God is really among you" (1 Cor. 14:25).

C. The Eternal Value of Worship

Because worship glorifies God and fulfills the purpose for which God created us, it is an activity of eternal significance and great value. When Paul cautions the Ephesians not to waste their time but to use it well, he puts it in the context of living as those who are wise: "Look carefully then how you walk, not as unwise men but as wise, *making the most of the time,* because the days are evil" (Eph. 5:15–16).

Paul then explains what it is to be wise and to make the most of the time:

> Therefore do not be foolish, but understand what the will of the Lord is. And do not get drunk with wine, for that is debauchery; but be filled with the Spirit, addressing one another in psalms and hymns and spiritual songs, *singing and making melody to the Lord with all your heart,* always and for everything giving thanks in the name of our Lord Jesus Christ to God the Father. (Eph. 5:17–20)

"looking to Jesus the pioneer and perfecter of our faith" (Heb. 12:2). At times the presence of the Lord and the accompanying working of the Holy Spirit in our hearts will be so evident that we will recognize that God is doing something within us—as the disciples certainly did when Jesus walked with them on the Emmaus road, for later they said, "Did not our hearts burn within us while he talked to us on the road, while he opened to us the scriptures?" (Luke 24:32).

Therefore in the context of using time wisely and making the most of the time, Paul includes both singing of spiritual psalms to one another and singing to the Lord with our hearts.

This means that *worship is doing the will of God!* Worship is the result of understanding "what the will of the Lord is." It is "making the most of the time." Moreover, because God is eternal and omniscient, the praise that we give him will never fade from his consciousness but will continue to bring delight to his heart for all eternity (cf. Jude 25: "To the only God, our Savior through Jesus Christ our Lord, be glory, majesty, dominion, and authority, before all time and now *and for ever*").

The fact that worship is an activity of great significance and eternal value is also evident in the fact that it is the primary activity carried on by those who are already in heaven (cf. Rev. 4:8–11; 5:11–14).

D. How Can We Enter Into Genuine Worship?

Ultimately, worship is a spiritual activity and it must be empowered by the Holy Spirit working within us. This means that we must pray that the Holy Spirit will enable us to worship rightly.

The fact that genuine worship is to be carried on in the unseen, spiritual realm is evident in Jesus' words:

> The hour is coming, and now is, when the true worshipers will worship the Father *in spirit and truth,* for such the Father seeks to worship him. God is spirit, and those who worship him must worship in spirit and truth. (John 4:23–24)

To worship "in spirit and truth" is best understood to mean not "in the Holy Spirit," but rather "*in the spiritual realm, in the realm of spiritual activity.*"[10] This means that true worship involves not only our physical bodies but also our spirits, the immaterial aspect of our existence that primarily acts in the unseen realm. Mary knew she was worshiping in that way, for she exclaimed, "*My soul* magnifies the Lord, and *my spirit* rejoices in God my Savior" (Luke 1:46–47).

We should realize also that God continually "seeks" (John 4:23) those who will worship him in the spiritual realm and therefore those whose spirit as well as body and mind is worshiping God. Such worship is not optional because those who worship God "*must* worship in spirit and truth" (v. 24). Unless our spirits are worshiping God we are not truly worshiping him.

An attitude of worship comes upon us when we begin to see God as he is and then respond to his presence. Even in heaven the seraphim who behold God's glory cry out, "Holy, holy, holy is the LORD of hosts; the whole earth is full of his glory" (Isa. 6:3).

---

[10]This is because (1) the discussion that Jesus is having with the woman at the well in this context is a discussion about the *location* of worship (see vv. 20–21)—should it be in Samaria or in Jerusalem? Jesus' answer would fit this inquiry much better if he were speaking about the spiritual realm in which we worship, as opposed to the physical location of Jerusalem or Samaria. (2) In the Greek text the word *en* ("in") of the phrase "in spirit and truth" corresponds to the same word (*en*) used in v. 21 to speak of (literally) "in this mountain" and "in Jerusalem." Once again the contrast is in terms of location "in" which one is to worship. (3) The word *truth* refers to a quality of worship, not to a person. The parallel would be more understandable if "in spirit" likewise referred not to a person but to some quality of the worship, such as the realm in which it is to be done.

When the disciples saw Jesus walking on the water, and then saw the wind cease when he got into the boat, "those in the boat *worshiped him,* saying, 'Truly you are the Son of God'" (Matt. 14:33). The author of Hebrews knows that when we come into the presence of God (Heb. 12:18–24), the proper response is to "offer to God acceptable worship, with reverence and awe; for our God is a consuming fire" (Heb. 12:28–29). Therefore genuine worship is not something that is self-generated or that can be worked up within ourselves. It must rather be the outpouring of our hearts *in response* to a realization of who God is.

It is appropriate to ask whether there is much genuine, deep, heartfelt worship in our churches. In many evangelical churches people do not truly worship God in their hearts until the last hymn, after the sermon has focused their attention on who God is so that they begin to rejoice in God with a heart full of praise. But then, just when heartfelt worship has begun, the service abruptly ends. It should be just beginning! If genuine worship is lacking in our churches, we should ask how we can bring ourselves to experience much more of the depth and richness of worship, which is the natural response of the believing heart to a clear awareness of God's presence and character.[11]

Is there anything else we can do to make worship more effective? We must remember that worship is a spiritual matter (John 4:21–24), and the primary solutions will therefore be spiritual ones. There will need to be much prayer in preparation for worship, especially on the part of those in leadership, asking that God will bless the worship times and make himself known to us. Also, congregations will need teaching about the spiritual nature of worship and the New Testament understanding of worship in God's presence (see Heb. 12:22–24). In addition, Christians need to be encouraged to make right any broken interpersonal relationships. Paul says that men are to lift holy hands "without anger or quarreling" (1 Tim. 2:8), and Jesus reminds us that we are first to "be reconciled" to our brother, and then come before God's altar and offer a gift (Matt. 5:24). In fact, John says that anyone who says, "I love God" but hates his brother "is a liar" (1 John 4:20). Husbands particularly need to make sure they are living "considerately" with their wives, and honoring them, in order that their prayers "may not be hindered" (1 Peter 3:7). And the entire church is responsible to watch "that no 'root of bitterness' spring up and cause trouble, and by it the many become defiled" (Heb. 12:15) — an indication that sin and broken relationships among a few can spread to many and result in the withholding of God's blessing from the whole congregation.

Moreover, if we are truly to draw near to God in worship, there must be a striving for personal holiness of life. The author of Hebrews reminds believers to strive for "the holiness without which no one will see the Lord" (Heb. 12:14), and Jesus says that it is the "pure in heart" who shall "see God" (Matt. 5:8) — a promise that is fulfilled partially in this life and completely in the age to come. Specifically in connection with prayer, John says, "If our hearts do not condemn us, we have confidence before God" (1 John 3:21), but this principle certainly applies to worship as well, as we have boldness to come into God's presence to offer him praise. James indicates a similar concern

---

[11]Of course, God's character can be revealed not only through the preaching of the Word, but also through the words of the hymns that are sung, through prayer, and through the reading of Bible passages even without comment.

when, immediately after saying, "Draw near to God and he will draw near to you," he adds, "*Cleanse* your hands, you sinners, and *purify* your hearts, you men of double mind" (James 4:8).[12]

Yet the physical setting and the structure of worship services do matter, for there are indications that Jesus thought that the atmosphere of worship was very important. He "entered the temple of God and drove out all who sold and bought in the temple, and he overturned the tables of the money-changers and the seats of those who sold pigeons." In explanation of this action, Jesus insisted that the temple was to be a house of prayer, for he said, "It is written, 'My house shall be called a house of prayer'; but you make it a den of robbers" (Matt. 21:12 – 13). He also told believers, "When you pray, *go into your room and shut the door* and pray to your Father who is in secret" (Matt. 6:6), not only because in our rooms we will not be seen by men, and will not pray so as to receive glory from men, but also because the knowledge that others are watching us in our prayers so easily distracts our attention, so that then we pray in part to be heard by others or at least so as not to offend them. This does not mean that corporate worship and prayer are forbidden (for both are very evident in both the Old Testament and New Testament), but it is to say that we should choose a *setting* for prayer or for worship that avoids distractions as much as possible. This is consistent with the fact that worship is to be done in an orderly way, for "God is not a God of confusion but of peace" (1 Cor. 14:33; cf. v. 40). The atmosphere and mood of worship are important, because we are to "offer to God acceptable worship, with reverence and awe" (Heb. 12:28). This means that it is appropriate to come together as a church in a setting that is conducive to worship, one that is ordinarily private and free from distractions, giving opportunity to focus attention on the Lord.[13]

Singing is especially important to worship in both Old and New Testaments. In our day there has been quite a change in both the standard English that is spoken by people and the musical forms that people are familiar with, and churches need to talk and plan openly and honestly in order to find a mix of songs that can be sung well by the whole congregation, and that people can genuinely identify with as a vehicle for expressing their praise to God. Songs that address God directly in the second person (that is, speaking to God as "you" rather than speaking about him as "he") will often be especially effective as worship songs—though the Psalms show that both kinds of songs are pleasing to God.

In addition, it is important to allow enough time for the various aspects of corporate worship. Genuine prayer can certainly take time (see Luke 6:12; 22:39 – 46; Acts 12:12; 13:2).

---

[12]Other Scripture passages indicate a connection between personal holiness and worship of God: see Prov. 15:8: "The sacrifice of the wicked is an abomination to the LORD, but the prayer of the upright is his delight." See also Prov. 15:29; 28:9; also Ps. 34:15 – 18; 66:18.

[13]The practical considerations discussed in this section can be applied to many different forms of worship, but I have not discussed the actual forms that worship will take. Those will vary widely, from the extensive structured liturgies of Episcopalian services to the unstructured spontaneity of charismatic services. Since Scripture does not prescribe any one form, the major principle to use is Paul's directive, "Let all things be done for edification" (1 Cor. 14:26). Evangelicals need to be cautious, however, that they do not too quickly dismiss unfamiliar forms of worship: people in liturgical churches should realize that spontaneity can be managed in an orderly way, and people in charismatic groups should realize that edification and genuine worship can occur within a detailed structure. (Regarding the unison reading of a liturgy, if Christians can worship and pray by *singing* words in unison, there is nothing to prevent them from genuinely worshiping and praying by *reading* words aloud in unison!) Yet any one form that is used excessively can become a meaningless routine for most participants.

Solid Bible teaching can often take a long time as well (Matt. 15:32; Acts 20:7–11). Moreover, genuine, heartfelt worship and praise will also take quite a bit of time if it is to be effective.

This is true in part because different aspects of a worship service require different attitudes and states of mind. Listening to Bible teaching requires attentiveness to the text and the teacher. Praise requires joy and a focus on the Lord and his excellence. Prayers of petition require a focus on needs and a deep concern for others. Times when offerings are given require a focus on sacrificing ourselves to the Lord as well as giving to him from our means and trusting him to provide for our needs. The Lord's Supper requires a time of reflection, self-examination, and perhaps repentance, along with thanksgiving. But we cannot have all of these attitudes at once, for we are finite. Different attitudes of mind require time to attain and dwell in. For that reason it is impossible to fulfill all the tasks necessary for an assembled congregation simply in one hour on Sunday morning, and it is harmful even to try. Those who do try to do everything crowd too much into a brief time and fail to do anything well.[14] If congregations are to fulfill the various purposes for which God wants them to assemble together, and especially to have extended times of reverent worship, they will probably need to find creative solutions that enable them to meet for longer periods of time, and omit or reschedule some activities that have become habitual or traditional on Sunday mornings but are really not necessary.

QUESTIONS FOR PERSONAL APPLICATION

1. Do you experience genuine, fulfilling worship in your church each Sunday? How much time is specifically allotted to worship (narrowly defined) — that is, to times of praise and thanksgiving to God? Would you like the time to be longer? What aspects of the worship time do you find most meaningful? Which aspects are least meaningful? How could your church take steps to strengthen and deepen its experience of worship (if that is needed)?

2. Have you ever felt a strong sense of the presence of God in corporate worship? When was this? Can you describe it? Do you know what factors contributed to this sense?

3. During times of worship, can you describe the emotions that are most prominent in your consciousness? Is this experience similar to other experiences in daily life, or are these feelings unique to times of worship? Have you ever sensed that God is ministering to you while you are worshiping him? What made you aware of that?

---

[14]Unfortunately, pastors who try to officiate at a service into which too many activities are crowded begin to resemble the master of ceremonies at a three-ring circus who shouts, "Look here! Look there!" at one act after another. In a similar way the pastor exhorts, "Praise God! Be generous! Think about Scripture! Pray! Shake hands with your neighbor! Say hello to your friends! Examine yourselves! Repent of your sins! Sing to the Lord! Amen? Amen!" In a situation like this people's emotions are jerked back and forth so quickly that they are unable to respond as whole persons, and the result is that they withdraw emotionally and do not respond from the heart. They will leave the service feeling frustrated and disappointed because the need of their hearts to experience genuine worship, prayer, and learning from Scripture has not been satisfied.

For most human beings, focused attention is slowly attained and easily lost. Because of this, I personally find that a worship leader who talks to the congregation between songs usually distracts my attention away from the Lord and onto himself, and my attitude of worship is greatly diminished.

4. Do you think there is enough genuine worship in a typical week in your life? If not, what are the hindrances to such worship?

5. How do you feel about the fact that God is jealous for his own honor and seeks his honor? Can you think of anything in the universe that would be more right than for God to seek his own honor? Can you think of anything other than worship of God that would make you feel more deeply that you are doing the thing for which you were created?

SPECIAL TERMS

worship

BIBLIOGRAPHY

Allen, Ronald, and Gordon Borror. *Worship: Rediscovering the Missing Jewel.* Portland, Ore.: Multnomah, 1982.

Carson, Herbert M. *Hallelujah! Christian Worship.* Welwyn, Hertfordshire, England: Evangelical Press, 1980.

Engle, Paul E. *Discovering the Fullness of Worship.* Philadelphia: Great Commission, 1978.

Harrison, E. F. "Worship." In *EDT.* pp. 1192–1193.

Kraueter, Tom. *Keys to Becoming an Effective Worship Leader.* Available from Psalmist Resources, 9820 E. Watson Rd., St. Louis, MO 63126. 1991.

Manson, P. D. "Worship." In *EDT,* pp. 730–32.

Martin, Ralph P. *Worship in the Early Church.* Westwood, N.J.: Revell, 1964.

_____. *The Worship of God.* Grand Rapids: Eerdmans, 1982.

Moule, C. F. D. *Worship in the New Testament.* Richmond, Va.: John Knox, 1961.

Peterson, David. *Engaging With God: A Biblical Theology of Worship.* Leicester: Inter-Varsity Press, and Grand Rapids: Eerdmans, 1992.

Rayburn, Robert G. *O Come, Let Us Worship.* Grand Rapids: Baker, 1980.

Taylor, Jack R. *The Hallelujah Factor.* Nashville, Tenn.: Broadman, 1983.

Wainwright, Geoffrey. *Doxology: The Praise of God in Worship, Doctrine, and Life.* New York: Oxford University Press, 1980.

Webber, Robert E. *Worship Old and New.* Grand Rapids: Zondervan, 1982.

SCRIPTURE MEMORY PASSAGE

Revelation 4:11:   *You are worthy, our Lord and God,*
to receive glory and honor and power,
for you created all things,
and by your will they existed and were created.

HYMN

"Thou Art Worthy"

Thou art worthy, thou art worthy, thou art worthy, O Lord.
To receive glory, glory and honor, glory and honor and power.
For thou hast created, hast all things created, thou hast created all things;
And for thy pleasure, they are created, thou art worthy, O Lord.

AUTHOR: PAULINE MICHAEL MILLS (FROM REV. 4:11)
COPYRIGHT © FRED BOCK MUSIC, 1963, 1975.
USED BY PERMISSION.

Chapter 10

GIFTS OF THE HOLY SPIRIT: (PART 1) GENERAL QUESTIONS

What are spiritual gifts? How many are there? Have some gifts ceased? Seeking and using spiritual gifts.

EXPLANATION AND SCRIPTURAL BASIS

A. Questions Regarding Spiritual Gifts in General

In previous generations, systematic theologies did not have chapters on spiritual gifts, for there were few questions regarding the nature and use of spiritual gifts in the church. But the twentieth century has seen a remarkable increase in interest in spiritual gifts, primarily because of the influence of the Pentecostal and charismatic movements within the church. In this chapter we will first look at some general questions regarding spiritual gifts, then examine the specific question of whether some (miraculous) gifts have ceased. In the next chapter we shall analyze the New Testament teaching about particular gifts.

Before beginning the discussion, however, we may define spiritual gifts as follows: *A spiritual gift is any ability that is empowered by the Holy Spirit and used in any ministry of the church.* This broad definition includes both gifts that are related to natural abilities (such as teaching, showing mercy, or administration) and gifts that seem to be more "miraculous" and less related to natural abilities (such as prophecy, healing, or distinguishing between spirits). The reason for this is that when Paul lists spiritual gifts (in Rom. 12:6–8; 1 Cor. 7:7; 12:8–10, 28; and Eph. 4:11) he includes both kinds of gifts.

Yet not every natural ability that people have is included here, because Paul is clear that all spiritual gifts must be empowered "by one and the same Spirit" (1 Cor. 12:11), that they are given "for the common good" (1 Cor. 12:7), and that they are all to be used for "edification" (1 Cor. 14:26), or for building up the church.[1]

1. Spiritual Gifts in the History of Redemption. Certainly the Holy Spirit was at work in the Old Testament, bringing people to faith and working in remarkable ways in a few individuals such as Moses or Samuel, David or Elijah. But in general there was *less powerful* activity of the Holy Spirit in the lives of most believers. Effective evangelism of the nations was very uncommon, casting out of demons[2] was unknown, miraculous healing was uncommon (though it did happen, especially in the ministries of Elijah and Elisha), prophecy was restricted to a few prophets or small bands of prophets, and "resurrection power" over sin in the sense of Romans 6:1–14 and Philippians 3:10 was rarely experienced.

But at several points the Old Testament looks forward to a time when there would be a greater empowering of the Holy Spirit that would reach to all of God's people. Moses said, "Would that all the LORD's people were prophets, that the LORD would put his spirit upon them!" (Num. 11:29). And the LORD prophesied through Joel:

> And it shall come to pass afterward,
> that I will pour out my spirit on all flesh;
> your sons and your daughters shall prophesy,
> your old men shall dream dreams,
> and your young men shall see visions.
> Even upon the menservants and maidservants
> in those days, I will pour out my spirit. (Joel 2:28–29)

John the Baptist heightens people's expectations of the fulfillment of Joel's prophecy when he announces that someone is coming after him who "will baptize you with the Holy Spirit and with fire" (Matt. 3:11; cf. Mark 1:8; Luke 3:16; John 1:33; Acts 1:5).

When Jesus begins his ministry he comes bringing the fullness and power of the Holy Spirit in his person. Luke writes, "And Jesus returned *in the power of the Spirit* into Galilee" (Luke 4:14). The result is that he teaches with great power (Luke 4:15–22) and he heals and casts out demons from all who are oppressed (Luke 4:31–41). Clearly, Jesus has come in the *greater new covenant power of the Holy Spirit,* and he has come to *conquer* Satan's kingdom.

---

[1]When seemingly natural gifts (such as teaching, helps, administration, or musical gifts) are empowered by the Holy Spirit, they will generally show increased effectiveness and power in their use. Paul says the Corinthians were "enriched" in all their speech and knowledge as spiritual gifts came to them (1 Cor. 1:5–7). Any pastor who has preached for a time knows the difference between preaching in his own "natural" ability and preaching the same sermon under the anointing or empowering of the Holy Spirit.

[2]The only thing that comes close to casting out of demons in the Old Testament is the fact that when David played the lyre for King Saul, "Saul was refreshed, and was well, and the evil spirit departed from him" (1 Sam. 16:23), but David had to do this "whenever the evil spirit from God was upon Saul" (ibid.), indicating that there was no permanent relief from the demonic oppression that Saul experienced.

In fact, he says that the power of the Holy Spirit at work in him enabling him to cast out demons is an indication that the kingdom of God has come in power: "If it is by the Spirit of God that I cast out demons, then the kingdom of God has come upon you" (Matt. 12:28). Looking back on Jesus' life and ministry, John tells us, "The reason the Son of God appeared was to destroy the works of the devil" (1 John 3:8).

But this new covenant power of the Holy Spirit is not limited to the ministry of Jesus alone. He sent his disciples out, saying, "The kingdom of heaven is at hand" and told them, "Heal the sick, raise the dead, cleanse lepers, cast out demons" (Matt. 10:7–8). Nevertheless, this new covenant power of the Holy Spirit is not yet distributed to all who believed in Jesus or followed him, but only to his twelve disciples or to the seventy disciples (Luke 10:1–12).

The pouring out of the Holy Spirit in new covenant fullness and power in the church occurred at Pentecost. Before Jesus ascended into heaven he commanded his apostles "not to depart from Jerusalem, but to wait for the promise of the Father," and the content of that promise was, "Before many days you shall be baptized with the Holy Spirit" (Acts 1:4–5). He promised them, *"You shall receive power when the Holy Spirit has come upon you"* (Acts 1:8). When the Spirit was poured out on the church at Pentecost Peter recognized that Joel's prophecy was being fulfilled, for he said, "this is what was spoken by the prophet Joel" (Acts 2:16), and he then quoted Joel's prophecy (vv. 17–21). Peter recognized that the new covenant empowering of the Holy Spirit had come to God's people and the new covenant age had begun as a direct result of the activity of Jesus in heaven, for Peter said,

> This Jesus God raised up, and of that we are all witnesses. Being therefore exalted at the right hand of God, and *having received from the Father the promise of the Holy Spirit, he has poured out this which you see and hear.* (Acts 2:32–33)

Against the background of Jesus' ministry and the earlier ministry of the disciples with Jesus, the disciples present at Pentecost would rightly have expected that powerful evangelistic preaching, deliverance from demonic oppression, physical healing, and perhaps also prophecy, dreams, and visions would all begin and continue among those who believe in Christ, and that these things would be *characteristic* of the new covenant age that began at Pentecost. A further characteristic of this outpouring of the Holy Spirit was a widespread distribution of spiritual gifts to all people—sons and daughters, young men and old men, menservants and maidservants, in the words of Joel—*all* received a new covenant empowering of the Holy Spirit, and it would also be expected that all would receive gifts of the Holy Spirit then as well. In fact, that is what happened in the early church (see 1 Cor. 12–14; Gal. 3:5; James 5:14–15). As B. B. Warfield said:

> We are justified in considering it characteristic of the Apostolic churches that such miraculous gifts should be displayed in them. The exception would be, not a church with, but a church without, such gifts. . . . *The Apostolic Church was characteristically a miracle-working church.*[3]

---

[3]B. B. Warfield, *Counterfeit Miracles* (1918; reprint, Edinburgh: Banner of Truth, 1972), p. 5.

(This is true regardless of what view one takes about the continuation of miraculous gifts after the time of the apostles.)

2. The Purpose of Spiritual Gifts in the New Testament Age. Spiritual gifts are given *to equip the church to carry out its ministry until Christ returns.* Paul tells the Corinthians, *"You are not lacking in any spiritual gift, as you wait for the revealing of our Lord Jesus Christ"* (1 Cor. 1:7). Here he connects the possession of spiritual gifts and their situation in the history of redemption (waiting for Christ's return), suggesting that gifts are given to the church for the period between Christ's ascension and his return. Similarly, Paul looks forward to the time of Christ's return and says, "When the perfect comes, the imperfect will pass away" (1 Cor. 13:10), indicating also that these "imperfect" gifts (mentioned in vv. 8–9) will be in operation until Christ returns, when they will be superseded by something far greater.[4] Indeed, the pouring out of the Holy Spirit in "power" at Pentecost (Acts 1:8) was to equip the church to preach the gospel (Acts 1:8) — something that will continue until Christ returns. And Paul reminds believers that in their use of spiritual gifts they are to "strive to excel in *building up* the church" (1 Cor. 14:12). Finally, in writing to the Ephesians, Paul specifies that when Christ ascended into heaven he gave gifts "to *equip* the saints for the work of ministry, for building up the body of Christ" (Eph. 4:12).

But spiritual gifts not only equip the church for the time until Christ returns, they also *give a foretaste of the age to come.* Paul reminds the Corinthians that they were *"enriched"* in all their speech and all their knowledge, and that the result of this enriching was that they were "not lacking in any spiritual gift" (1 Cor. 1:5, 7). Of course, this *enrichment* in their speech and knowledge did not give them the perfect speech or the perfect knowledge that would be theirs in heaven, but only a foretaste or down payment of that heavenly perfection. Similarly, Paul reminds the Corinthians that spiritual gifts are "imperfect" but when the "perfect" way of knowing comes at the Lord's return, then these gifts will pass away (1 Cor. 13:10). Just as the Holy Spirit himself is in this age a "down payment" (2 Cor. 1:22 NASB mg.; cf. 2 Cor. 5:5; Eph. 1:14) of the fuller work of the Holy Spirit within us in the age to come, so the gifts the Holy Spirit gives us are *partial foretastes* of the fuller working of the Holy Spirit that will be ours in the age to come.

In this way, gifts of insight and discernment prefigure the much greater discernment we will have when Christ returns. Gifts of knowledge and wisdom prefigure the much greater wisdom that will be ours when we "know as we are known" (cf. 1 Cor. 13:12). Gifts of healing give a foretaste of the perfect health that will be ours when Christ grants to us resurrection bodies. Similar parallels could be found with all the New Testament gifts. Even the diversity of gifts should lead to greater unity and interdependence in the church (see 1 Cor. 12:12–13, 24–25; Eph. 4:13), and this diversity in unity will itself be a foretaste of the unity that believers will have in heaven.

3. How Many Gifts Are There? The New Testament epistles list specific spiritual gifts in six different passages. Consider the table on the next page.

---

[4]This interpretation of 1 Cor. 13:10 is defended at greater length in section B below.

What is obvious is that these lists are all quite different. No one list has all these gifts, and no gift except prophecy is mentioned on all the lists (prophecy is not mentioned in 1 Cor. 7:7, where only the subject of marriage and celibacy is under discussion, but it is certainly included in the "whoever speaks" of 1 Peter 4:11). In fact, 1 Corinthians 7:7 mentions two gifts that are not on any other list: in the context of speaking of marriage and celibacy, Paul says, "Each has his own special *gift*[5] from God, one of one kind and one of another."

These facts indicate that Paul was not attempting to construct exhaustive lists of gifts when he specified the ones he did. Although there is sometimes an indication of some order (he puts apostles first, prophets second, and teachers third, but tongues last in 1 Cor. 12:28), it seems that in general Paul was almost randomly listing a series of different examples of gifts as they came to mind.

1 Corinthians 12:28	**Ephesians 4:11**[7]	**1 Peter 4:11**
1. apostle[6]	(1) apostle	Whoever speaks (covering several gifts)
2. prophet	(2) prophet	
3. teacher	14. evangelist	Whoever renders service
4. miracles	15. pastor-teacher	(covering several gifts)
5. kinds of healings		
6. helps	**Romans 12:6-8**	
7. administration	(2) prophecy	
8. tongues	16. serving	
	(3) teaching	
1 Corinthians 12:8-10	17. encouraging	
9. word of wisdom	18. contributing	
10. word of knowledge	19. leadership	
11. faith	20. mercy	
(5) gifts of healing		
(4) miracles	**1 Corinthians 7:7**	
(2) prophecy	21. marriage	
12. distinguishing between spirits	22. celibacy	
(8) tongues		
13. interpretation of tongues		

Moreover, there is some degree of overlap among the gifts listed at various places. No doubt the gift of administration (*kybernēsis*, 1 Cor. 12:28) is similar to the gift of leadership (*ho proistamenos*, Rom. 12:8), and both terms could probably be applied to many who have the office of pastor-teacher (Eph. 4:11). Moreover, in some cases Paul lists an activity and in other cases lists the related noun that describes the person

---

[5]The Greek term for "gift" here is *charisma*, the same term Paul uses in 1 Cor. 12–14 to talk about spiritual gifts.

[6]Strictly speaking, to be an apostle is an office, not a gift (see chapter 5, section A.1, on the office of apostle).

[7]This list gives four kinds of persons in terms of offices or functions, not, strictly speaking, four gifts. For three of the functions on the list, the corresponding gifts would be prophecy, evangelism, and teaching.

(such as "prophecy" in Rom. 12:6 and 1 Cor. 12:10, but "prophet" in 1 Cor. 12:28 and Eph. 4:11).[8]

Another reason for thinking that Paul could have made much longer lists if he had wanted to is the fact that some of the gifts listed will have many different expressions as they are found in different people. Certainly the gift of serving (Rom. 12:6) or helps (1 Cor. 12:28) will take many different forms in different situations and among different people. Some may serve or help by giving wise counsel, others by cooking meals, others by caring for children or befriending an older person, others by giving specialized legal or medical or financial advice when needed within the church. These gifts differ greatly. Among those who possess the gift of evangelism, some will be good at personal evangelism within a neighborhood, others at evangelism through writing of tracts and Christian literature, and others at evangelism through large campaigns and public meetings. Still others will be good at evangelism through radio and television. Not all of these evangelistic gifts are the same, even though they fall under the broad category of "evangelism." The same could be said about gifts of teaching or administration.[9] All of this simply means that no two people's gifts are exactly alike.

How many different gifts are there then? It simply depends on how specific we wish to be. We can make a very short list of only two gifts as Peter does in 1 Peter 4:11: "whoever *speaks*" and "whoever *renders service*." In this list of only two items Peter includes all the gifts mentioned in any other list because all of them fit in one of these two categories. On the other hand, we could take the Old Testament offices of prophet, priest, and king, and have a list of three kinds of gifts: *prophetic* gifts (in this broad sense) would include anything that involves teaching, encouraging, exhorting, or rebuking others. *Priestly* gifts would include anything that involves showing mercy and care for those in need or involve interceding before God (such as praying in tongues). The *kingly* gifts would involve anything having to do with administration or government or order in the church.

---

[8]Something can be said at this point about the relationship between gifts and offices in the church. As we look at these lists, it is evident that in some cases Paul names the specific gift (such as gifts of healing or administration or tongues), and in other cases he names the *persons* who have those gifts (such as apostles, prophets, or evangelists). Some lists name only the gifts themselves (such as 1 Cor. 12:8–10), while other lists name only the people who possess those gifts (such as Eph. 4:11 or 1 Peter 4:11). And some lists are mixed, naming some gifts and some persons who have the gifts (such as Rom. 12:6–8 and 1 Cor. 12:28).

In addition to that, another distinction should be made: In cases where Paul names *persons,* he sometimes gives a name that refers to an officially recognized *office* in the church (such as "apostles" or "pastor-teachers"). We would expect that such people would begin to function in those offices after they had received formal recognition by the church as a whole (this would be called "ordination" or "installation in office" for the office of pastor [or elder] for example). But in other cases, though the person is named, it is not necessary to think there was any official recognition or establishment in office in front of the entire church. This would be the case, for example, for "he who encourages" and "he who contributes" and "he who does acts of mercy" in Rom. 12:6–8. Similarly, the New Testament does not clearly indicate that prophets or evangelists were established in any formally recognized offices in the early church, and the word "prophet" probably just refers to one who prophesied regularly and with evident blessing in the church. "Evangelist" could similarly refer to those who regularly functioned effectively in the work of evangelism, and "teachers" could include both those who had formally recognized teaching functions in the church, perhaps in connection with the office of elder, and those who had teaching functions in less-formal capacities in the church but regularly taught with effectiveness in informal or smaller group settings.

For convenience, we will continue to refer to these lists as lists of "spiritual gifts," although, to be more precise, we should realize that they include both spiritual gifts and persons who exercise those gifts. Since both the gifts and the persons are given to the church by Jesus Christ, it is appropriate that both are named in various parts of these lists.

[9]See the excellent discussion in John R. W. Stott, *Baptism and Fullness: The Work of the Holy Spirit Today* (Downers Grove, Ill. InterVarsity Press, 1964), pp. 88–89.

Other classifications of gifts are gifts of *knowledge* (such as distinguishing between spirits, word of wisdom, and word of knowledge), gifts of *power* (such as healing, miracles, and faith), and gifts of *speech* (tongues, interpretation, and prophecy).[10] Then again we could make a much longer list, such as the list of twenty-two gifts enumerated above. But even that list does not include all the possible gifts (no list includes a gift of intercessory prayer, for instance, which may be related to a gift of faith but is not the same as a gift of faith; no musical gifts are included on any list either, and neither is any gift of casting out demons, even though Paul must have known that some Christians were more effective in that area than others). And if we wished to divide up *different kinds* of service or administration or evangelism or teaching, then we could quite easily have a list that included fifty or even a hundred items.[11]

The point of all of this is simply to say that God gives the church an amazing variety of spiritual gifts, and they are all tokens of his varied grace. In fact, Peter says as much: "As each has received a gift, employ it for one another, as good stewards of God's *varied grace*" (1 Peter 4:10; the word "varied" here is *poikilos,* which means "having many facets or aspects; having rich diversity").

The practical outcome of this discussion is that we should be willing to recognize and appreciate people who have gifts that differ from ours and whose gifts may differ from our expectations of what certain gifts should look like. Moreover, a healthy church will have a great diversity of gifts, and this diversity should not lead to fragmentation but to greater unity among believers in the church. Paul's whole point in the analogy of the body with many members (1 Cor. 12:12–26) is to say that God has put us in the body with these differences *so that we might depend on each other.* "The eye cannot say to the hand, 'I have no need of you,' nor again the head to the feet, 'I have no need of you.' On the contrary, the parts of the body which seem to be weaker are indispensable" (1 Cor. 12:21–22; cf. vv. 4–6). It runs counter to the world's way of thinking to say that we will enjoy greater unity when we join closely together with those who are different from us, but that is precisely the point that Paul makes in 1 Corinthians 12, demonstrating the glory of God's wisdom in not allowing anyone to have all the necessary gifts for the church, but in requiring us to depend upon each other for the proper functioning of the church.

4. Gifts May Vary in Strength. Paul says that if we have the gift of prophecy, we should use it *"in proportion to our faith"* (Rom. 12:6), indicating that the gift can be more or less strongly developed in different individuals, or in the same individual over a period of time. This is why Paul can remind Timothy, "Do not neglect the gift you have" (1 Tim. 4:14), and can say, "I remind you to *rekindle* the gift of God that is within you" (2 Tim. 1:6). It was possible for Timothy to allow his gift to weaken, apparently through infrequent use, and Paul reminds him to stir it up by using it and thereby strengthening it. This should not be surprising, for we realize that many gifts increase

---

[10]This classification is from Dennis and Rita Bennett, *The Holy Spirit and You* (Plainfield, N.J.: Logos International, 1971), p. 83. The Bennetts' actual categorization is gifts of revelation, gifts of power, and inspirational or fellowship gifts, and they list them in reverse order to what I have given here.

[11]This variety of ways of classifying gifts allows us to say that many types of classification are possible for teaching purposes, but we should beware of any claim that a certain way of classifying or listing gifts is the only valid one, for Scripture does not limit us to any one scheme of classification.

in strength and effectiveness as they are used, whether evangelism, teaching, encouraging, administration, or faith. Apollos had a strong gift of preaching and teaching, for we read that he was "mighty (or "powerful," Gk. *dynatos*) in the Scriptures" (Acts 18:24 NASB). And Paul apparently had a frequently used and very effective gift of speaking in tongues because he says, "I thank God that I speak in tongues more than you all" (1 Cor. 14:18).[12]

All of these texts indicate that *spiritual gifts may vary in strength*. If we think of any gift, whether teaching or evangelism on the one hand, or prophecy or healing on the other, we should realize that within any congregation there will likely be people who are very effective in the use of that gift (perhaps through long use and experience), others who are moderately strong in that gift, and others who probably have the gift but are just beginning to use it. This variation in strength in spiritual gifts depends on a combination of divine and human influence. The divine influence is the sovereign working of the Holy Spirit as he "apportions to each one individually as he wills" (1 Cor. 12:11). The human influence comes from experience, training, wisdom, and natural ability in the use of that gift. It is usually not possible to know in what proportion the divine and human influences combine at any one time, nor is it really necessary to know, for even the abilities we think to be "natural" are from God (1 Cor. 4:7) and under his sovereign control.

But this leads to an interesting question: how strong does an ability have to be before it can be called a spiritual gift? How much teaching ability does someone need before he or she could be said to have a gift of teaching, for example? Or how effective in evangelism would someone need to be before we would recognize a gift of evangelism? Or how frequently would someone have to see prayers for healing answered before he or she could be said to have a gift of healing?

Scripture does not directly answer this question, but the fact that Paul speaks of these gifts as useful for the building up of the church (1 Cor. 14:12), and the fact that Peter likewise says that each person who has received a gift should remember to employ it "for one another" (1 Peter 4:10), suggest that both Paul and Peter thought of gifts as abilities that were *strong enough to function for the benefit of the church*, whether for the assembled congregation (as in prophecy or teaching), or for individuals at various times in the congregation (as helps or encouragement).

Probably no definite line can be drawn in this matter, but Paul does remind us that *not all have every gift or any one gift*. He is quite clear in this in a set of questions that expect the answer no at each point: "Are all apostles? Are all prophets? Are all teachers? Do all work miracles? Do all possess gifts of healing? Do all speak with tongues? Do all interpret?" (1 Cor. 12:29–30). The Greek text (with the particle *mē* before each question) clearly expects the answer no to every question. Therefore, not all are teachers, for example, nor do all possess gifts of healing, nor do all speak in tongues.

But even though not all have the gift of teaching, it is true that all people "teach" *in some sense* of the word *teach*. Even people who would never dream of teaching a Sunday school class will read Bible stories to their own children and explain the meaning to them—indeed, Moses commanded the Israelites to do this very thing with their children

[12]See also 1 Cor. 13:1–3 where Paul gives examples of some gifts developed to the highest imaginable degree, examples which he uses to show that even such gifts without love would bring no benefit.

(Deut. 6:7), explaining God's words to them as they sat in their house or walked on the road. So we must say on the one hand that not everyone has the *gift* of teaching. But on the other hand we must say that there is *some general ability* related to the gift of teaching that all Christians have. Another way of saying this would be to say that there is no spiritual gift that all believers have, yet there is some general ability similar to every gift that all Christians have.

We can see this with a number of gifts. Not all Christians have a gift of evangelism, but all Christians have the ability to share the gospel with their neighbors. Not all Christians have gifts of healing (in fact, as we shall see below, some people say that no one today has genuine gifts of healing), but nevertheless every Christian can and does pray for God to heal friends or relatives who are ill. Not every Christian has the gift of faith, but every believer has some degree of faith, and we would expect it to be growing in the life of an ordinary Christian.

We can even say that other gifts, such as prophecy and speaking in tongues, not only vary in strength among those who have the gift, but also find a counterpart in some general abilities that are found in the life of every Christian. For example, if we understand prophecy (according to the definition given in chapter 11)[13] to be "reporting something that God spontaneously brings to mind," then it is true that not everyone experiences this as a gift, for not everyone experiences God spontaneously bringing things to mind with such clarity and force that he or she feels free to speak about them among an assembled group of Christians. But probably every believer has at one time or another had a sense that God was bringing to mind the need to pray for a distant friend or to write or phone a word of encouragement to someone distant, and later has found that that was exactly the thing that was needed at the moment. Few would deny that God sovereignly brought that need to mind in a spontaneous way, and, though this would not be called a gift of prophecy, it is a general ability to receive special direction or guidance from God that is similar to what happens in the gift of prophecy, although it is functioning at a weaker level.

We can even consider the gift of speaking in tongues from this perspective. If we think of speaking in tongues as prayer in syllables not understood by the speaker (see 1 Cor. 14:2, 14),[14] then it is true that not every Christian has the gift of speaking in tongues (and once again it must be said that some Christians would argue that no one has that gift today, since the age of the apostles has ended). But on the other hand we must recognize that every Christian has times of prayer in which his or her prayer is expressed not only in intelligible words and syllables, but also in terms of sighs, groans, or weeping that we know is understood and heard by the Lord, and that expresses needs and concerns of our hearts that we cannot fully put into words (cf. Rom. 8:26–27). Once again we should not call this a gift of speaking in tongues, but it does seem to be a general ability in our Christian lives that is somewhat related to the gift of speaking in tongues, in that it gives expression to prayer in syllables that we do not fully understand, but that the Holy Spirit nonetheless makes into effective prayer that is heard by God.

[13]See chapter 13, section A, for a definition of the gift of prophecy in the church.

[14]See also the discussion of the gift of speaking in tongues in chapter 13, section E.

The point of this whole discussion is simply to say that spiritual gifts are not as mysterious and "other worldly" as people sometimes make them out to be. Many of them are only intensifications or highly developed instances of phenomena that most Christians experience in their own lives. The other important point to be drawn from this discussion is that even though we have been given gifts by God, we are still responsible to use them effectively, and to seek to grow in their use that the church may receive more benefit from the gifts of which God has allowed us to be stewards.

Finally, the fact that gifts may vary in strength allows us to recognize that a certain person's gift (such as teaching or administration, for example) may not be strong enough to function for the benefit of the entire church in a large church where many people already have that gift developed to a very high degree. But that same person, moving to a younger, smaller church where few have gifts of teaching or administration, may find that his or her gifts are very much in demand and able to function for the benefit of the entire congregation. (In this sense, something that is only considered a general ability in one setting might rightly be considered a spiritual gift in another setting.)

5. Do Christians Possess Gifts Temporarily or Permanently? In most cases, it seems that the New Testament pictures a *permanent* possession of spiritual gifts. The analogy of the parts of the body in 1 Corinthians 12:12–26 fits this, in that the eye does not become a hand, nor does the ear become a foot, but various parts exist in the body permanently.[15] Moreover, Paul says that some people have titles that describe a continuing function. Some people can be called "prophets" or "teachers" (1 Cor. 12:29) or "evangelists" (Eph. 4:11). We would expect that those people have a permanent possession of the gifts of prophecy, teaching, and evangelism, unless some unusual circumstance would come along which would take that gift away. Similarly, Paul talks in terms of possessing spiritual gifts when he says, "If I *have* the gift of prophecy" (1 Cor. 13:2 NIV). And when Paul requires that there be an interpreter present for anyone to speak in tongues (1 Cor. 14:28), he assumes that the church will know whether someone who has the gift of interpretation is present, which implies that that gift would be possessed by someone over time. When he says, "If any one thinks that he is a prophet" (1 Cor. 14:37), he realizes that some at Corinth will have functioned with the gift of prophecy frequently enough to think of themselves as "prophets." All of these verses point in the direction of a permanent, or at least abiding and continuing, possession of spiritual gifts.

Indeed, in Romans 12, Paul begins his sentence, "*Having gifts* that differ according to the grace given to us" (Rom. 12:6). And he tells Timothy, "Do not neglect the gift *that is in you*" (1 Tim. 4:14, literal translation), again indicating that Timothy had had that gift over a period of time. Therefore it seems that in general the New Testament indicates that people have spiritual gifts given to them and, once they have them, they are usually able to continue to use them over the course of their Christian life.

---

[15]We should not press the metaphor of the body too far, of course, for people *do* receive other gifts, and Paul even encourages people to seek additional spiritual gifts (1 Cor. 14:1). But the metaphor does suggest *some* degree of stability or permanence in the possession of gifts.

However, some important qualifications must be made, because there are some senses in which gifts are *not permanent*. There are some gifts that are non-permanent by their very nature, such as the gifts of marriage and celibacy (1 Cor. 7:7). Though Paul calls them gifts, in the lives of most believers there will be times at which they are unmarried, and times at which they are married. Moreover, some gifts, though perhaps exercised fairly frequently, still cannot be exercised at will. Effectiveness in the gift of healing, for example, depends on God's sovereign will in answering prayer for healing. Similarly, prophecy depends on the giving of a spontaneous "revelation" (1 Cor. 14:30) from God, and simply cannot be exercised at will. The same could even be said about the gift of evangelism: It is ultimately the work of the Holy Spirit to bring regeneration and enable someone to believe, so the evangelist may pray and preach, but only God can give the harvest of souls.

In other cases, some particular gift may be given for a unique need or event. Though it is not, strictly speaking, a spiritual gift in the New Testament sense, the return of Samson's strength one last time at the end of his life (Judg. 16:28) was given temporarily for one final moment in his life. And, in the New Testament, the remarkable revelation of heaven Stephen had when he, "full of the Holy Spirit, gazed into heaven and saw the glory of God, and Jesus standing at the right hand of God" (Acts 7:55) was a manifestation of the Spirit given to him only for that specific moment.

Another sense in which a gift may be non-permanent is if a person neglects his or her gift, and perhaps grieves the Holy Spirit or falls into serious doctrinal or moral error (as Samson did in the Old Testament, for example). In such a case the gift may be withdrawn. Certainly Paul warned Timothy, "Do not neglect the gift you have" (1 Tim. 4:14), and we may perhaps also learn from the parable of the talents, in which Jesus says that "to every one who has will more be given, and he will have abundance; but from him who has not, even what he has will be taken away" (Matt. 25:29).[16]

Moreover, we must remember that *the Holy Spirit is still sovereign in distributing gifts:* he "apportions to each one individually *as he wills*" (1 Cor. 12:11). The word here translated "apportions" is a present participle, which indicates continuing activity over time, and we could paraphrase, "The Holy Spirit *is always continuing to distribute or apportion gifts* to each person individually just as he wills to do." This means that, although it is *ordinarily* the custom of the Holy Spirit to continue to empower the same gift or gifts in people over time, nonetheless, there is a continual willing and deciding of the Holy Spirit to do this or not, and he may for his own reasons withdraw a gift for a time, or cause it to be much stronger or much weaker than it was.

Finally, 1 Corinthians 13:8–13 (to be discussed below) indicates that the present spiritual gifts which we have are only for this age, and will be superseded by something far greater. Therefore in that sense no gift is "permanent" since every gift will be rendered useless at the time of the Lord's return.

Within this discussion of the question of whether spiritual gifts are temporary or permanent, sometimes Romans 11:29 is mentioned: "For the gifts and the call of God

---

[16]Although the primary point of this parable has to do with rewards at the final judgment, it nonetheless encourages faithfulness in stewardship with what one has been given, and it is not unreasonable to expect that God would act toward us in that way, at least in principle, in this life as well.

are irrevocable." It does not seem to be appropriate to use the verse in the context of this discussion, however, for in this case Paul is talking about the status of the Jewish people, including their calling as God's people and the gifts or blessings bestowed on them as a result of that status. Here Paul is arguing that God still has a purpose for his people Israel, but the question of gifts of the Holy Spirit in the sense of 1 Corinthians 12–14 is not in view at all in Romans 11:29. And certainly in any case this sentence would not be true as a totally unrestricted statement concerning spiritual gifts, for it is evident that through misuse, neglect, or grieving of the Holy Spirit, people can have their gifts diminished or removed by God's sovereign choice.

6. Are Gifts Miraculous or Nonmiraculous? The answer to this question really depends on the definition of the word *miracle*. If we define *miracle* as "a direct activity of God in the world," then all the spiritual gifts are miraculous because they are all empowered by the Holy Spirit (1 Cor. 12:11; cf. vv. 4–6). But in that sense *everything* that happens in the world might be said to be miraculous, because all of it is brought about by God's providential work in creation (see Eph. 1:11; Dan. 4:35; Matt. 5:45). Therefore the word *miracle* loses its usefulness, because it is difficult for us to find something that happens in the world that is *not* miraculous in this sense.

It is better to define *miracle* in a narrower sense: "A miracle is a less common activity of God in which he arouses people's awe and wonder and bears witness to himself." In terms of this definition, only some gifts are "miraculous": namely, those gifts that people think to be miraculous because they are amazed at the activity of God operating in them. Certainly we would include in this category prophecy (note the amazement of the unbeliever in 1 Cor. 14:24–25), healing (similarly, note the response of people in Acts 3:10 et al.), casting out of demons (see Acts 19:11–13, 17), or speaking in tongues when it is an actual foreign language and understood by others (see the description of Pentecost in Acts 2:7). Probably other remarkable phenomena would be included in the gift of miracles (1 Cor. 12:10) as well.

On the other hand, in this definition, some gifts would be thought of as nonmiraculous. Gifts of serving, teaching, encouraging, contributing, and doing acts of mercy (in Rom. 12:7–8) would fall in this category, as would the gifts of those who act as helpers and administrators (1 Cor. 12:28). But it is still the same Holy Spirit who gives them and works through them.

The point of this analysis is to caution us against making a supernatural/natural distinction in our minds whereby we think that some gifts are "supernatural" and some gifts are simply "natural." The Bible makes no such distinction, and the danger of doing this is that we may tend to think that some gifts (which we think to be "supernatural") are more important or more clearly from the Lord, and we may tend to devalue or deemphasize the gifts which we think to be "natural." If we do this we will fail to see God's hand in the working of all the gifts and fail to thank him for all of them.

On the other hand, the misleading supernatural/natural distinction could also cause us to be very suspicious about those which we think to be "supernatural," or could lead us to think that they are very unlikely to happen in our own experience. In that case, we would tend to emphasize the gifts we thought to be "natural" and have a very low degree of expectation or faith regarding anything which we thought to be "supernatural."

In contrast to this perspective, Scripture says that "all" the gifts are worked in us by the same Holy Spirit, the same Lord, and the same God (1 Cor. 12:4–6). The worldview of Scripture is one of continuity and continual interaction between the *visible world* that we can see and touch and the *invisible world* that Scripture tells us is there and is real. God works in both, and we do ourselves and the church a great disservice by separating these aspects of creation into "supernatural" and "natural."

Finally, should we seek the more unusual or miraculous gifts, or should we seek the more ordinary gifts? Once again, Scripture does not make this kind of distinction when it tells us what kind of gifts to seek. Paul says to the Corinthians, "Since you are eager for manifestations of the Spirit, *strive to excel in building up the church*" (1 Cor. 14:12). This means that we should learn which gifts are most needed in the church we attend, and then pray that God would give those gifts to ourselves or to others. Whether those gifts are thought to be miraculous or non-miraculous really is not the important point at all.

7. Discovering and Seeking Spiritual Gifts. Paul seems to assume that believers will know what their spiritual gifts are. He simply tells those in the church at Rome to use their gifts in various ways: "if prophecy, in proportion to our faith . . . he who contributes, in liberality; he who gives aid, with zeal; he who does acts of mercy, with cheerfulness" (Rom. 12:6–8). Similarly, Peter simply tells his readers how to use their gifts, but does not say anything about discovering what they are: "*As each has received a gift*, employ it for one another, as good stewards of God's varied grace" (1 Peter 4:10).

But what if many members in a church do not know what spiritual gift or gifts God has given to them? In such a case, the leaders of the church need to ask whether they are providing sufficient opportunities for varieties of gifts to be used. Though the lists of gifts given in the New Testament are not exhaustive, they certainly provide a good starting point for churches to ask whether at least there is opportunity for *these gifts* to be used. If God has placed people with certain gifts in a church when these gifts are not encouraged or perhaps not allowed to be used, they will feel frustrated and unfulfilled in their Christian ministries, and will perhaps move to another church where their gifts can function for the benefit of the church.

In the case of individuals who do not know what their gifts are, they can begin by asking what the needs and opportunities for ministry are in their church. Specifically, they can ask what gifts are most needed for the building up of the church at that point. In addition, each individual believer who does not know what his or her gifts are should do some self-examination. What interests and desires and abilities does he or she have? Can others give advice or encouragement pointing in the direction of specific gifts? Moreover, has there been blessing in the past in ministering in a particular kind of service? In all of this, the person seeking to discover his or her gifts should pray and ask God for wisdom, confident that it will be given according to his promise, "If any of you lacks wisdom, let him ask God, who gives to all men generously and without reproaching, and it will be given him. But let him ask in faith, with no doubting" (James 1:5–6). Sometimes God will grant this wisdom in terms of more accurate insight into one's own abilities. At other times it may come through advice from others or through seeing increased blessing in one area of ministry. And Paul indicates that in some cases there may be prophecy that gives indication of a specific gift, for he says to Timothy, "*Do not neglect the gift you have, which was given you through prophecy* with the laying on of hands of the council of elders" (1 Tim. 4:14, author's translation).

Finally, the person wondering what his or her spiritual gifts are should simply begin to try ministering in various areas and see where God brings blessing. Teaching a Sunday school class or home Bible study is an excellent way to begin using the gift of teaching. Every community has opportunities for greater use of the gift of evangelism. People who think they may have a gift of healing could ask their elders for opportunities to accompany them when they go to pray for the sick. People who think they may have a gift of faith or a gift of intercessory prayer could begin to ask some Christian friends for specific needs about which to pray. In all of this, churches can give encouragement and opportunities for people to try out using various gifts, and can also give teaching and practical training in the proper methods of using various gifts. In addition, churches should continually be praying that God would allow people to find what their gifts are and then to be able to use them. In all of this the goal is that the body of Christ in each location grow up to maturity, until "the whole body, joined and knit together by every joint with which it is supplied, *when each part is working properly,* makes bodily growth and upbuilds itself in love" (Eph. 4:16).

Beyond the question of discovering what gifts one has is the question of seeking additional spiritual gifts. Paul commands Christians, "*Earnestly desire the higher gifts*" (1 Cor. 12:31), and says later, "Make love your aim, and *earnestly desire the spiritual gifts,* especially that you may prophesy" (1 Cor. 14:1). In this context, Paul defines what he means by "higher gifts" or "greater gifts" because in 1 Corinthians 14:5 he repeats the word he used in 12:31 for "higher" (Gk. *meizōn*) when he says, "He who prophesies is *greater* than he who speaks in tongues, unless someone interprets, *so that the church may be edified*" (1 Cor. 14:5). Here the "greater" gifts are those that most edify the church. This is consistent with Paul's statement a few verses later, when he says, "since you are eager for manifestations of the Spirit, strive to excel in building up the church" (1 Cor. 14:12). The *higher gifts* are *those that build up the church more and bring more benefit to others.*

But how do we seek more spiritual gifts? First, we should *ask God for them.* Paul says directly that "he who speaks in a tongue *should pray for the power to interpret*" (1 Cor. 14:13; cf. James 1:5, where James tells people that they should ask God for wisdom). Next, people who seek additional spiritual gifts should *have right motives.* If spiritual gifts are sought only so that the person may be more prominent or have more influence or power, this certainly is wrong in God's eyes. This was the motivation of Simon the Sorcerer in Acts 8:19, when he said, "Give me also this power, that any one on whom I lay my hands may receive the Holy Spirit" (see Peter's rebuke in vv. 21–22). Similarly, Ananias and Sapphira sought glory for themselves when they purported to be giving the entire proceeds of the sale of their land to the church, but it was not true, and both lost their lives (Acts 5:1–11). It is a fearful thing to want spiritual gifts or prominence in the church only for our own glory, not for the glory of God and for the help of others.

Therefore those who seek spiritual gifts must first ask if they are seeking them out of love for others and a concern to be able to minister to their needs, because those who have great spiritual gifts but "have not love" are "nothing" in God's sight (cf. 1 Cor. 13:1–3). This is why Paul says, *"Make love your aim,"* and only after that adds, "and earnestly desire the spiritual gifts" (1 Cor. 14:1). He repeats the same theme again when he says, "since you are eager for manifestations of the Spirit, *strive to excel in building up the church"* (1 Cor. 14:12). Every person asking God for an additional spiritual gift should search his or her own heart frequently, asking why this particular gift is desired. Is it really out of a love for others and a desire to build up the church and to see God glorified?

After that, it is appropriate to *seek opportunities to try the gift,* just as in the case of a person trying to discover his or her gift, as explained above. Small group Bible studies or prayer meetings in homes often provide a good setting in which people can try gifts of teaching or intercessory prayer or encouragement or prophecy or healing, for example.

Finally, those who are seeking additional spiritual gifts should *continue to use the gifts they now have,* and should *be content* if God chooses not to give them more. The master approved of the servant whose pound had "made ten pounds more," but condemned the one who hid his pound in a napkin and did nothing with it (Luke 19:16–17, 20–23)—certainly showing us that we have responsibility to *use* and *attempt to increase* whatever talents or abilities God has given to us as his stewards.

To balance this emphasis on seeking and growing in spiritual gifts we must also remember that Paul clearly says that spiritual gifts are apportioned to each person individually by the Holy Spirit *"as he wills"* (1 Cor. 12:11), and that "God arranged the organs in the body, each one of them, *as he chose"* (1 Cor. 12:18). He says that God has put various gifts in the church and not all are apostles or prophets or teachers (1 Cor. 12:28–30). In this way he reminds the Corinthians that ultimately the distribution of gifts is a matter of God's sovereign will, and it is for the good of the church and for our good that none of us have all of the gifts, and that we will need continually to depend on others who have gifts differing from ours. These considerations should make us content if God chooses not to give us the other gifts that we seek.

8. Gifts Are Tools for Ministry, and Not Necessarily Related to Christian Maturity. We must recognize that spiritual gifts are given to *every* believer (1 Cor. 12:7, 11; 1 Peter 4:10). Even immature Christians receive spiritual gifts from the Lord—this was certainly evident in the Corinthian church, which had an abundance of spiritual gifts (1 Cor. 1:7), but was still very immature in many areas of doctrine and conduct. Paul says, "But I, brethren, could not address you as spiritual men, but as men of the flesh, as babes in Christ" (1 Cor. 3:1). So spiritual gifts are not necessarily a sign of spiritual maturity. It is possible to have remarkable spiritual gifts in one area or another but still be quite immature in doctrinal understanding or in Christian conduct, as was the case at Corinth. Indeed, on occasion even *unbelievers* are able to prophesy and cast out demons and do miracles, for Jesus says that at the last day many will say to him, "Lord, Lord, did we not prophesy in your name, and cast out demons in your name, and do many mighty works in your name?" But Jesus will declare to them, "I *never* knew you;

depart from me, you evildoers" (Matt. 7:22–23). It is not that Jesus knew them once and later did not know them; he says, "I never knew you." They were never Christians, yet they performed many remarkable works. So *we must not evaluate spiritual maturity on the basis of spiritual gifting.* Maturity comes through a close walk with Jesus, and results in obedience to his commands in everyday life: "He who says he abides in him ought to walk in the same way in which he walked" (1 John 2:6).

Why then does the Holy Spirit give us spiritual gifts? They are given for the work of ministry and are *simply tools* to be used for that end. They should never be a source of personal pride on the part of those who possess them, nor should they be thought of as a mark of maturity. We should strive simply to excel in loving others, caring for their needs, building up the church, and living a life of conformity to the pattern of Christ's life. If we do that, and if God chooses to give us spiritual gifts that equip us for those tasks, then we should thank him for that, and pray that he would keep us from pride over gifts that have been freely and graciously given, and which we did not earn.

B. Have Some Gifts Ceased? The Cessationist Debate

Within the evangelical world today there are differing positions over the question, "Are all the gifts mentioned in the New Testament valid for use in the church today?" Some would say yes.[17] Others would say no, and would argue that some of the more miraculous gifts (such as prophecy, tongues plus interpretation, and perhaps healing and casting out of demons) were given only during the time of the apostles, as "signs" to authenticate the apostles during the early preaching of the gospel. They state that these gifts are no longer needed as signs today, and that they ceased at the end of the apostolic age, probably at the end of the first century or beginning of the second century A.D.

We should also realize that there is a large "middle" group with respect to this question, a group of "mainstream evangelicals" who are neither charismatics or Pentecostals on the one hand, nor "cessationists"[18] on the other hand, but are simply undecided, and unsure if this question can be decided from Scripture.[19]

1. Does 1 Corinthians 13:8–13 Tell Us When Miraculous Gifts Will Cease? Paul says:

Love never ends; as for prophecies, they will pass away; as for tongues, they will cease; as for knowledge, it will pass away. For our knowledge is imperfect and our prophecy is imperfect; but *when the perfect comes, the imperfect will pass away.* When I was a child, I spoke like a child, I thought like a child, I reasoned like a child; when I became a man, I gave up childish ways. For now we see in a mirror dimly, but then face to face. Now I know in part; then I shall understand

---

[17]Many who say yes, such as the present author, would add the qualification that "apostle" is an office, not a gift, and that the office of apostle does not continue today (see chapter 5, section A.1, for this argument).

[18]*Cessationist* refers to someone who thinks that certain miraculous spiritual gifts *ceased* long ago, when the apostles died and Scripture was complete.

[19]The discussion in the remainder of this section on the cessationist debate is adapted from Wayne Grudem, *The Gift of Prophecy in the New Testament and Today* (Eastbourne: Kingsway, and Westchester, Ill.: Crossway, 1988), pp. 227–52, and is used by permission.

fully, even as I have been fully understood. So faith, hope, love abide, these three; but the greatest of these is love. (1 Cor. 13:8–13)

This passage is important to the discussion because in it Paul mentions the gift of prophecy as something that is "imperfect," and then says that what is "imperfect" will "pass away" (1 Cor. 13:10). He even says when this will happen: "when the perfect comes." But when is that? And even if we can determine when it is, does that mean that Paul had in mind something that would answer this "cessation" question for the church today? Can the gift of prophecy in this passage be representative of miraculous gifts in general in the church age?

a. The Purpose of 1 Corinthians 13:8–13: Paul interrupts his discussion of spiritual gifts with chapter 13 of 1 Corinthians, in which he intends to put the entire discussion of gifts in proper perspective. It is not enough simply to "seek the greater gifts" (12:31a, author's translation). One must also "seek after love" (14:1, author's translation), thus coupling proper goals with proper motives. Without love, the gifts are without value (13:1–3). In fact, Paul argues, love is superior to all the gifts and therefore it is more important to act in love than to have any of the gifts.

In order to show the superiority of love, Paul argues that it lasts forever, whereas the gifts are all temporary (13:8). Verses 9–12 further explain why the gifts are temporary. Our present knowledge and prophesying are partial and imperfect (v. 9), but someday something perfect will come to replace them (v. 10). This is explained by the analogy of a child who gives up childish thought and speech for the thought and speech of an adult (v. 11). Paul then elaborates further on verses 9–10 by explaining that our present perception and knowledge are indirect and imperfect, but that someday they will be direct and perfect (v. 12).

In this argument Paul connects the function of prophecy with the time of its cessation. It fills a certain need now, but does so only imperfectly. When "the perfect" comes, that function will be better fulfilled by something else, and prophecy will cease because it will be made obsolete or useless (this is the probable nuance of the Greek term used here, *katargeō*, "pass away" in vv. 8, 10). So the overall function of 1 Corinthians 13:8–13 is to show that love is superior to gifts like prophecy because those gifts will pass away but love will not pass away.

b. 1 Corinthians 13:10: The Cessation of Prophecy When Christ Returns: Paul writes in verse 10, "But *when the perfect comes,* the imperfect will pass away." The phrase "the imperfect" (Gk. *ek merous*, "partial, imperfect") refers most clearly to knowing and prophesying, the two activities that are said to be done "partially, imperfectly" in verse 9 (also using in both cases the same Greek phrase, *ek merous*). To bring out this connection, we could translate,

Love never fails. Whether there be prophecies, they will *pass away;* whether there be tongues, they will cease; whether there be knowledge, it will *pass away.* This is because we know *imperfectly* and we prophesy *imperfectly*—but when the perfect comes, the imperfect will *pass away.*

Thus, the strong links between the statements are made clear by the repetition of two key terms, "pass away" and "imperfect."

No doubt Paul also intended tongues to be included in the sense of verse 9 as among those activities that are "imperfect," but omitted overly pedantic repetition for stylistic reasons. Yet tongues must be understood as part of the sense of verse 9, for verse 9 is the reason for verse 8, as the word "for" (Gk. *gar*) shows. Thus verse 9 must give the reason why tongues, as well as knowledge and prophecy, will cease. In fact, the repeated "if . . . if . . . if" in verse 8 suggests that Paul could have listed more gifts here (wisdom, healing, interpretation?) if he had wished.

So 1 Corinthians 13:10 could be paraphrased, "When the perfect is come, *prophecy and tongues and other imperfect gifts* will pass away." The only remaining problem is to determine what time is meant by the word "when." Several factors argue that the time of the Lord's return is what Paul has in mind.

(1) First, the meaning of verse 12 seems to require that verse 10 is talking about the time of the Lord's return. The word "then" (Gk. *tote*) in verse 12 refers to the time "when the perfect comes" in verse 10. This is evident from looking at verse 12: "For now we see in a mirror dimly, but then face to face. Now I know in part; *then* I shall know even as I have been known" (author's translation).

When shall we see "face to face"? When shall we know "even as we have been known"? These events can only happen when the Lord returns.

The phrase "see face to face" is several times used in the Old Testament to refer to see-ing God personally[20] — not fully or exhaustively, for no finite creature can ever do that, but personally and truly nonetheless. So when Paul says, "but then face to face" he clearly means, "but then *we shall see God* face to face." Indeed, that will be the greatest blessing of heaven and our greatest joy for all eternity (Rev. 22:4: "They shall see his face").

The second half of verse 12 says, "Now I know in part; then I shall know even as I have been known." The second and third word for "know" — the one used for "Then I shall *know* even as I have been *known*" — is a somewhat stronger word for knowing (Gk. *epiginōskō*), but certainly does not imply infinite knowledge or omniscience. Paul does not expect to know all things, and he does not say, "Then I shall know all things," which would have been easy to say in Greek.[21] Rather, he means that when the Lord returns Paul expects to be freed from the misconceptions and inabilities to understand (especially to understand God and his work) which are part of this present life. His knowledge will resemble God's present knowledge of him because it will contain no false impressions and will not be limited to what is able to be perceived in this age. But such knowledge will only occur when the Lord returns.

Now what is the word "then" in verse 12 referring to? Paul says, "For now we see in a mirror dimly, but *then* we shall see face to face. Now I know in part; but *then* I shall know even as I have been known" (author's translation). His word "then" has to refer back to something in the previous verses that he has been explaining. We look first to verse 11, but

---

[20]See, for example, Gen. 32:30 and Judg. 6:22 (exactly the same Greek wording as 1 Cor. 13:12); Deut. 5:4; 34:10; Ezek. 20:35 (very similar wording); Ex. 33:11 (the same concept, and the same wording as some of the preceding passages in Hebrew, but different wording this time in the Greek translation of the Septuagint).

[21]Greek *epignōsomai ta panta* would say, "I shall know all things."

see that nothing in verse 11 can be a future time Paul refers to as "then": "When I was a child, I spoke like a child, I thought like a child, I reasoned like a child; when I became a man, I gave up childish ways." All of this refers to the past, not the future. It speaks of past events in Paul's life by way of providing a natural human illustration of what he has said in verse 10. But nothing in the verse speaks of a future time when something *will* happen.

So we look back to verse 10: "but when the perfect comes, the imperfect will pass away." Here is a statement about the future. At some point in the future, Paul says that "the perfect" *will* come, and "the imperfect" *will* pass away, *will* be "made useless." When will this happen? This is what is explained by verse 12. *Then,* at the time the perfect comes, we shall see "face to face" and know "even as we are known."

This means that the time when "the perfect" comes must be the time of Christ's return.[22] Therefore, we can paraphrase verse 10: "But *when Christ returns,* the imperfect will pass away."[23] Or, to use our conclusion above that "the imperfect" included prophecy and tongues, we can paraphrase, "But *when Christ returns, prophecy and tongues (and other imperfect gifts) will pass away.*" Thus we have in 1 Corinthians 13:10 a definite statement about the time of the cessation of imperfect gifts like prophecy: they will "be made useless" or "pass away" *when Christ returns.* And this would imply that they will continue to exist and be useful for the church, throughout the church age, including today, and right up to the day when Christ returns.

(2) Another reason why the time when "the perfect" comes is the time when Christ returns is also evident from the purpose of the passage: Paul is attempting to emphasize the greatness of love, and in so doing he wants to establish that "Love never ends" (1 Cor. 13:8). To prove his point he argues that it will last beyond the time when the Lord returns, unlike present spiritual gifts. This makes a convincing argument: love is so fundamental to God's plans for the universe that it will last beyond the transition from this age to the age to come at Christ's return—it will continue for eternity.

(3) A third reason why this passage refers to the time of the Lord's return can be found in a more general statement from Paul about the purpose of spiritual gifts in the New Testament age. In 1 Corinthians 1:7 Paul ties the possession of spiritual gifts (Gk. *charismata*) to the activity of waiting for the Lord's return: "you are not lacking in any spiritual gift, as you wait for the revealing of our Lord Jesus Christ."

This suggests that Paul saw the gifts as a temporary provision made to equip believers for ministry *until the Lord returned.* So this verse provides a close parallel to the thought of 1 Corinthians 13:8–13, where prophecy and knowledge (and no doubt tongues) are seen, similarly, as useful until Christ's return but unnecessary beyond that time.

---

[22]I have stated it this way because, more precisely, "the perfect" in 1 Cor. 13:10 is not Christ himself, but is a method of acquiring knowledge which is so superior to present knowledge and prophecy that it makes these two obsolete. For when this "perfect" comes it renders the imperfect useless. But only the kind of knowledge Paul expected in the final consummation of all things could be so qualitatively different from present knowledge that it could provide this kind of contrast and be called "the perfect" as opposed to "the imperfect."

[23]D. A. Carson, *Showing the Spirit: A Theological Exposition of 1 Corinthians 12–14* (Grand Rapids: Baker, 1987), pp.

70–72, gives several similar reasons why the time "when the perfect comes" must be the time of Christ's return (with references to other views, and to the relevant literature).

Among "cessationists" (those who hold that gifts such as prophecy have "ceased" and are not valid for today), some, but not all, agree that the time "when the perfect comes" must be the time of Christ's return: see John F. MacArthur, Jr., *The Charismatics: A Doctrinal Perspective* (Grand Rapids: Zondervan, 1978), pp. 165–66, and Richard B. Gaffin, *Perspectives on Pentecost* (Phillipsburg, N.J.: Presbyterian and Reformed, 1979), p. 109.

1 Corinthians 13:10, therefore, refers to the time of Christ's return and says that these spiritual gifts will last among believers until that time. This means that we have a clear biblical statement that Paul expected these gifts to continue through the entire church age and to function for the benefit of the church until the Lord returns.

c. Objections: Various objections to this conclusion have been raised, usually by those who hold that these gifts have ceased in the church and should no longer be used.

(1) This Passage Does Not Specify When the Gifts Will Cease: The first objection to our conclusion above comes from Richard Gaffin's thoughtful study, *Perspectives on Pentecost*. While Dr. Gaffin agrees that "when the perfect comes" refers to the time of Christ's return, he does not think that this verse specifies the time of the cessation of certain gifts. He thinks, rather, that Paul is just viewing "the entire period until Christ's return, without regard to whether or not discontinuities may intervene during the course of this period."[24]

In fact, Gaffin argues, Paul's overall purpose is to emphasize the enduring qualities of faith, hope, and love, especially love, and not to specify the time in which certain gifts will cease. He says:

> Paul is not intending to specify the time when any particular mode will cease. What he does affirm is the termination of the believer's present, fragmentary knowledge . . . when "the perfect" comes. The time of the cessation of prophecy and tongues is an open question so far as this passage is concerned and will have to be decided on the basis of other passages and considerations.[25]

He also says that, in addition to prophecy, tongues, and knowledge, Paul might just as well have added "inscripturation," too — and if he had done this, the list would then have included an element that ceased long before Christ's return. (Inscripturation is the process of writing Scripture.) So, Gaffin concludes, it might be true of some of the others in the list as well.

In response to this objection it must be said that it does not do justice to the actual words of the text. Evangelicals have rightly insisted (and I know that Dr. Gaffin agrees with this) that passages of Scripture are true not only in the main point of each passage, but also in the minor details that are affirmed as well. The main point of the passage may well be that love lasts forever, but another point, and certainly an important one as well, is that verse 10 affirms not just that these imperfect gifts will cease sometime, but that they will cease "*when* the perfect comes." Paul specifies a certain time: "*When the perfect comes,* the imperfect will pass away." But Dr. Gaffin seems to claim that Paul is not actually saying this. Yet the force of the words cannot be avoided by affirming that the overall theme of the larger context is something else.

In addition, Dr. Gaffin's suggestion does not seem to fit with the logic of the passage. Paul's argument is that it is specifically the coming of "the perfect," which does away with prophecy, tongues, and knowledge, because then there is a new, far-superior way of learning and knowing things "even as I have been known." But *until* that time, the new and

---

[24]Richard B. Gaffin, *Perspectives on Pentecost*, pp. 109–10.   [25]Ibid., p. 111.

superior way of knowing has not come, and therefore these imperfect gifts are still valid and useful. Finally, it is precarious to put much weight on something we think Paul might have said but in fact did not say. To say that Paul might have included "inscripturation" in this list means that Paul might have written, "When Christ returns, inscripturation will cease." But I cannot believe at all that Paul could have written such a statement, for it would have been false—indeed, a "false prophecy" in the words of Scripture. For "inscripturation" ceased long ago, when the book of Revelation was written by the apostle John.

So Dr. Gaffin's objections do not seem to overturn our conclusions on 1 Corinthians 13:10. If "the perfect" refers to the time of Christ's return, then Paul says that gifts such as prophecy and tongues will cease at that time, and implies therefore that they continue through the church age.

(2) "When the Perfect Comes" in 1 Corinthians 13:10 Refers to a Time Earlier Than the Time of the Lord's Return: Those who make this second objection argue that "when the perfect comes" means one of several different things, such as "when the church is mature" or "when Scripture is complete" or "when the Gentiles are included in the church." Probably the most careful statement of this view is found in the book by Robert L. Reymond, *What About Continuing Revelations and Miracles in the Presbyterian Church Today?*[26] but another clear statement of a similar position is found in Walter Chantry's book, *Signs of the Apostles.*[27]

Chantry's argument depends on the fact that elsewhere in 1 Corinthians the word here translated "perfect" (Gk. *teleios*) is used to refer to human maturity (1 Cor. 14:20, "in thinking be mature") or to maturity in the Christian life (as in 1 Cor. 2:6). Yet here again we must note that a word does not have to be used to refer to the same thing every time it is used in Scripture—in some cases *teleios* may refer to "mature" or "perfect" manhood, in other cases some other kind of "completeness" or "perfection." The word *teleios* is used in Hebrews 9:11, for example, to refer to the "more perfect tent"—yet we would not therefore conclude that "perfect" in 1 Corinthians 13:10 must refer to a perfect tent. The precise referent of the word must be determined by the individual context, and there, as we have seen, the context indicates that "when the perfect comes" refers to the time of Christ's return.

Dr. Reymond's argument is somewhat different. He reasons as follows (p. 34):

(a) "The imperfect" things mentioned in verses 9–10—prophecy, tongues, and knowledge—are incomplete means of revelation, "all relating to God's making his will known to his church."

(b) "The perfect" in this context must refer to something in the same category as the "imperfect" things.

(c) Therefore "the perfect" in this context must refer to a means of revelation, but a completed one. And this completed means of God's making his will known to his church is Scripture.

---

[26]Robert L. Reymond, *What About Continuing Revelations and Miracles in the Presbyterian Church Today?* (Phillipsburg, N.J.: Presbyterian and Reformed, 1977), pp. 32–34. Kenneth L. Gentry, Jr., *The Charismatic Gift of Prophecy: A Reformed Analysis* (Memphis, Tenn.: Whitefield Seminary Press, 1986), pp. 31–33, lists both this view and the view of Dr. Gaffin (see objection 1, above) as acceptable options. See also the entries under Robert Thomas, Victor Budgen, and Thomas Edgar in the bibliography to chapter 11.

[27]Walter J. Chantry, *Signs of the Apostles,* 2d ed. (Carlisle, Pa.: Banner of Truth, 1976), pp. 50–52.

(d) Conclusion: "When the perfect comes" refers to the time when the canon of Scripture will be complete.

Reymond notes that he is not saying that "the perfect" refers exactly to the canon of Scripture, but rather to "the completed revelatory process" that resulted in Scripture (p. 32). And in response to the objection that "then we shall see face to face" in verse 12 refers to seeing God face to face, he answers that it may not mean this, but may simply mean seeing "plainly" as opposed to "obscurely" (p. 32).

In response, it may be said that this argument, while careful and consistent in itself, still depends on one prior assumption which is really the point at issue in this whole discussion: the authority of New Testament prophecy and related gifts. Once Reymond assumes that prophecy (and tongues and the kind of "knowledge" mentioned here) are Scripture-quality revelation, the whole argument falls into place. The argument could be recast as follows:

(a) Prophecy and tongues are Scripture-quality revelation.

(b) Therefore this whole passage is about Scripture-quality revelation.

(c) Therefore "the perfect" refers to the perfection or completion of Scripture-quality revelation, or the completion of Scripture.

In such an argument the initial assumption determines the conclusion. However, before this assumption can be made, it needs to be demonstrated from an inductive analysis of the New Testament texts on prophecy.[28] Yet, to my knowledge, no such inductive demonstration of the Scripture-quality authority of New Testament congregational prophecy has been made.

Moreover, there are some other factors in the text of 1 Corinthians 13:8–13 that are hard to reconcile with Reymond's position. The regular Old Testament usage of seeing "face to face" as an expression not just for seeing clearly but for *personally* seeing God (see above) remains unexplained. And the fact that Paul includes himself in the expressions "Then *we* shall see face to face" and "Then I shall know even as I have been known" make it difficult to view these as references to the time of the completion of Scripture. Does Paul really think that when the other apostles finally finish their contributions to the New Testament he will suddenly gain such a remarkable change in his knowledge that he will know as he has been known, and will go from seeing in a mirror dimly to seeing face to face?

In addition to the views of Reymond and Chantry, there have been other attempts to see "when the perfect comes" as some time before Christ's return, but we will not treat them in detail here. Such views all break down at verse 12, where Paul implies that believers will see God "face to face" "when the perfect comes." This cannot be said about the time suggested in any of these other proposals.

The proposal about the completion of the canon of New Testament Scripture (the group of writings that came to be included in the New Testament) also fails to fit Paul's purpose in the context. If we take A.D. 90 as the approximate date of the writing of Revelation, the last New Testament book written, then the end of the writing of Scripture came about thirty-five years after Paul wrote 1 Corinthians (about A.D. 55). But would it be

---

[28]See chapter 11, section A, for a fuller discussion of the gift of prophecy; also Grudem, *The Gift of Prophecy in the New Testament and Today.*

persuasive to argue as follows: "We can be sure that love will never end, for we know that it will last more than thirty-five years"? This would hardly be a convincing argument. The context requires rather that Paul be contrasting this age with the age to come, and saying that love will endure into eternity.[29] In fact, we see a similar procedure elsewhere in 1 Corinthians. When Paul wants to demonstrate the eternal value of something, he does this by arguing that it will last beyond the day of the Lord's return (cf, 1 Cor. 3:13–15; 15:51–58). By contrast, prophecy and other gifts will not last beyond that day.

Finally, these proposals fail to find any support in the immediate context. Whereas Christ's return is mentioned clearly in verse 12, no verse in this section mentions anything about the completion of Scripture or a collection of the books of the New Testament or the inclusion of the Gentiles in the church or the "maturity" of the church (whatever that means—is the church really mature even today?). All of these suggestions bring in new elements not found in the context to replace the one element—Christ's return—which clearly is right there in the context already. In fact, Richard Gaffin, who himself holds that the gift of prophecy is not valid for today, nevertheless says that the "perfect" in verse 10 and the "then" in verse 12 "no doubt refer to the time of Christ's return. The view that they describe the point at which the New Testament canon is completed cannot be made credible exegetically."[30]

Dr. D. Martyn Lloyd-Jones observes that the view that makes "when the perfect comes" equal the time of the completion of the New Testament encounters another difficulty:

> It means that you and I, who have the Scriptures open before us, know much more than the apostle Paul of God's truth. . . . It means that we are altogether superior . . . even to the apostles themselves, including the apostle Paul! It means that we are now in a position in which . . . "we know, even as also we are known" by God . . . indeed, there is only one word to describe such a view, it is nonsense.[31]

John Calvin, referring to 1 Corinthians 13:8–13, says, "It is stupid of people to make the whole of this discussion apply to the intervening time."[32]

2. Would the Continuation of Prophecy Today Challenge the Sufficiency of Scripture?

a. The Authority of the Gift of Prophecy: Those who take a "cessationist" view argue that once the last New Testament book was written (probably the book of Revelation

---

[29]Some argue that faith and hope will not endure in heaven, so 1 Cor. 13:13 only means that faith and hope last until, not beyond, Christ's return. However, if faith is dependence on God and trust in him, and if hope is a confident expectation of future blessings to be received from God, then there is no reason to think that we will cease to have faith and hope in heaven. (See Carson's good discussion of faith, hope, and love as "eternally permanent virtues" in *Showing the Spirit,* pp. 74–75.)

[30]Gaffin, *Perspectives on Pentecost,* p. 109; cf. Max Turner, "Spiritual Gifts Then and Now," *Vox Evangelica* 15 (1985), p. 38.

[31]D. Martyn Lloyd-Jones, *Prove All Things,* ed. by Christopher Catherwood (Eastbourne, England: Kingsway, 1985), pp. 32–33.

[32]John Calvin, *The First Epistle of Paul the Apostle to the Corinthians,* trans. by J. W. Fraser, ed. by D. W. Torrance and T. F. Torrance (Grand Rapids: Eerdmans, 1960), p. 281 (on 1 Cor. 13:10).

around A.D. 90), there were to be no more "words of God" spoken or written in the church. This is especially relevant for the gift of prophecy, according to the cessationist position, because from that point on *Scripture* was the complete and sufficient source of God's words for his people. To add any more words from continuing prophetic utterances would be, in effect, either to add to Scripture or to compete with Scripture. In both cases, the sufficiency of Scripture itself would be challenged, and, in practice, its unique authority in our lives compromised.

Now *if* New Testament congregational prophecy was like Old Testament prophecy and New Testament apostolic words in its authority, then this cessationist objection would indeed be true. *If* prophets today, for example, spoke words that we knew were the very words of God, then these words *would be* equal to Scripture in authority, and we *would be* obligated to write them down and add them to our Bibles whenever we heard them. But if we are convinced that God stopped causing Scripture to be written when the book of Revelation was completed, then we have to say that *this* kind of speech, uttering the very words of God, cannot happen today. And any claims to have "new" Scripture, "new" words of God, must be rejected as false.

This question is very important, because the claim that New Testament congregational prophecy had authority equal to Scripture is the basis of many cessationist arguments. Yet it must be noted that noncessationists themselves do not seem to view prophecy that way. George Mallone writes, "To my knowledge no noncessationist in the mainstream of Christianity claims that revelation today is equal with Scripture."[33] Perhaps it would be good for those arguing against continuing prophecy today to give a more sympathetic hearing to the most responsible charismatic writers, simply for the purpose of being able to respond to something that charismatics *actually believe* (even if not always expressed in theologically precise form), instead of responding to something that cessationists say that charismatics believe or say that charismatics should believe.

Furthermore, aside from the question of current practice or belief, I have argued extensively elsewhere that ordinary congregational prophecy in New Testament churches did *not* have the authority of Scripture.[34] It was not spoken in words that were the very words of God, but rather in merely human words. And because it has this lesser authority, there is no reason to think that it will not continue in the church until Christ returns. It does not threaten or compete with Scripture in authority but is subject to Scripture, as well as to the mature judgment of the congregation.

b. The Question of Guidance: Another objection is sometimes raised at this point. Some will argue that even if those who use the gift of prophecy today *say* that it does not equal Scripture in authority, *in fact* it functions in their lives to compete with or even replace Scripture in giving guidance concerning God's will. Thus, prophecy today, it is said, challenges the doctrine of the sufficiency of Scripture for guidance in our lives.

[33]George Mallone, ed., *Those Controversial Gifts* (Downers Grove, Ill.: InterVarsity Press, 1983), p. 21.

[34]For further discussion of the authority of the gift of prophecy, see chapter 11, section A. See also Wayne Grudem, *The Gift of Prophecy in 1 Corinthians;* Wayne Grudem, *The Gift of Prophecy in the New Testament and Today;* D. A. Carson, *Showing the Spirit: A Theological Exposition of 1 Corinthians 12–14,* pp. 91–100; Graham Houston, *Prophecy: A Gift For Today?* (Downers Grove, Ill.: InterVarsity Press, 1989). (Alternative views are noted in the discussion in chapter 11; see esp. the book by Richard Gaffin, *Perspectives on Pentecost.*)

Here it must be admitted that many mistakes have been made in the history of the church. John MacArthur points to the way in which the idea of further revelations has given rise to many heretical movements in the church.[35]

But here the question must be, Are abuses *necessary* to the functioning of the gift of prophecy? If we are to argue that mistakes and abuses of a gift make the gift itself invalid, then we would have to reject Bible teaching too (for many Bible teachers have taught error and started cults), and church administration as well (for many church leaders have led people astray), and so forth. The *abuse* of a gift does not mean that we must prohibit the *proper use* of the gift, unless it can be shown that there cannot be proper use—that *all* use has to be abuse.[36]

Moreover, specifically with respect to guidance, it is good to note how cautious many in the charismatic movement are about the use of prophecy to give specific guidance. Several quotations will illustrate this point.

Michael Harper (Church of England):

> Prophecies which tell other people what they are to do—are to be regarded with great suspicion.[37]

Dennis and Rita Bennett (American Episcopalians):

> We should also be careful of personal, directive prophecy, especially outside the ministry of a mature and submitted man of God. Unrestrained "personal prophecy" did much to undermine the movement of the Holy Spirit which began at the turn of the century.... Christians are certainly given words for one another "in the Lord"... and such words can be most refreshing and helpful, but there must be a witness of the Spirit on the part of the person receiving the words, and extreme caution should be used in receiving any alleged directive or predictive prophecy. Never undertake any project simply because you were told to by presumed prophetic utterance or interpretation of tongues, or by a

[35]John F. MacArthur, Jr., *The Charismatics: A Doctrinal Perspective,* chapters 2–6; see esp. pp. 27ff. MacArthur has expanded his criticisms in an updated edition, *Charismatic Chaos* (Grand Rapids: Zondervan, 1992), pp. 47–84. A thoughtful and extensive critique of MacArthur is found in Rich Nathan, *A Response to Charismatic Chaos* (Anaheim, Calif.: Association of Vineyard Churches, 1993).

[36]Some may object that prophecy has more potential for abuse than other gifts because the idea that God can reveal things to people today (in prophecies) inevitably leads to competition with the authority of Scripture. In response, three points can be made: (1) Teaching on the fallible nature of all contemporary prophecies has not been as extensive as needed to prevent abuse, especially at the popular level, among groups that allow prophecy today. Therefore there has been more misuse of prophecy than there should have been. Even where strong cautions have been proclaimed, there has seldom been an explanation of how prophecy can be from God but still not equal to God's words in authority—that is, very few Pentecostal or charismatic writers have explained prophecy as a *human* report of something that God has spontaneously brought to mind (the view which I defend in chapter 11, section A.). (However, see the helpful cautions from several charismatic writers in the following paragraphs in the text above.) (2) It is simply not true that teaching a congregation that prophecy must always be *subject* to Scripture inevitably leads people to exalt prophecies *above* Scripture. This will happen where such teaching is neglected, not where it is propagated. (3) If the Bible indeed teaches that prophecy can be expected to continue today in a form that does not challenge scriptural authority, then we are not free to reject it because we recognize a potential for abuse. (Other gifts have potential for abuse in other areas.) Rather, we should encourage the gift and do our best to guard against abuse.

[37]Michael Harper, *Prophecy: A Gift for the Body of Christ* (Plainhill, N.J.: Logos, 1964), p. 26.

presumed word of wisdom, or knowledge. Never do something just because a friend comes to you and says: "The Lord told me to tell you to do thus and thus." If the Lord has instructions for you, He will give you a witness in your own heart, in which case the words coming from a friend . . . will be a confirmation to what God *has already been* showing you. Your guidance must also agree with Scripture. . . .[38]

Donald Gee (Assemblies of God):

[There are] grave problems raised by the habit of giving and receiving personal "messages" of guidance through the gifts of the Spirit. . . . The Bible gives a place for such direction from the Holy Spirit. . . . But it must be kept in proportion. An examination of the Scriptures will show us that as a matter of fact the early Christians did *not* continually receive such voices from heaven. In most cases they made their decisions by the use of what we often call "sanctified common-sense" and lived quite normal lives. Many of our errors where spiritual gifts are concerned arise when we want the extraordinary and exceptional to be made the frequent and habitual. Let all who develop excessive desire for "messages" through the gifts take warning from the wreckage of past generations as well as of contemporaries. . . . The Holy Scriptures are a lamp unto our feet and a light unto our path.[39]

On the other hand, even among very Reformed cessationists, there is a willingness to admit some kind of continuing "illumination" by the Holy Spirit in believers' lives. For example, Westminster Seminary professor Richard Gaffin says,

Often, too, what is seen as prophecy is actually a spontaneous, Spirit-worked application of Scripture, a more or less sudden grasp of the bearing that biblical teaching has on a particular situation or problem. All Christians need to be open to these more spontaneous workings of the Spirit.[40]

And Robert Reymond defines *illumination* as "the Holy Spirit's enabling of Christians generally to understand, to recall to mind, and to apply the Scriptures they have studied."[41]

But if these writers will allow for the present activity of the Holy Spirit enabling Christians to "understand" or "recall to mind" or "apply" or "grasp" the teachings of Scripture, then there does not seem to be such a great difference in principle between what they are *saying* and what many in the charismatic movement are *doing* (even though there will probably be some remaining differences over the precise way guidance functions—yet this is not so much a difference about prophecy as about guidance generally, and particularly the way guidance from Scripture relates to guidance from advice, counsel, conscience, circumstances, sermons, etc.). The larger point is

---

[38]Dennis and Rita Bennett, *The Holy Spirit and You*, p. 107.
[39]Donald Gee, *Spiritual Gifts in the Work of Ministry Today* (Springfield, Mo.: Gospel Publishing House, 1963), pp. 51–52.

[40]Gaffin, *Perspectives on Pentecost*, p. 120.
[41]Reymond, *What About . . . ?* pp. 28–29.

that what Gaffin and Reymond here call "illumination," the New Testament seems to call a "revelation," and what they would call a spoken report of such illumination, the New Testament seems to call a "prophecy."

So I wonder if there may be room for more joint theological reflection in this area. Charismatics need to realize that cessationists are skeptical about the scope and frequency of such "illumination," whether it is right to call it New Testament prophecy, whether it really does have value for the church, and whether it should be sought after. And cessationists need to realize that their own highly developed and carefully formulated doctrine of the sufficiency of Scripture in guidance is not usually shared or even understood by much of evangelicalism, including those in the charismatic movement. Nevertheless, perhaps the Reformed idea of "illumination" allows for what is happening in prophecy today, and may provide a way of understanding it that is not seen as challenging the sufficiency of Scripture.

What shall we conclude then about the relationship between the gift of prophecy and the sufficiency of Scripture? We must say that we appreciate the desire of the cessationists to protect the uniqueness of Scripture and not to allow anything to compete with the authority of Scripture in our lives. We also must be thankful for the desire of cessationists that Christians understand and follow sound principles of guidance in their daily lives, and not get off into an area of excessive subjectivism that does not have the controls of Scripture attached to it. On the other hand, there is certainly a danger that comes with the cessationist viewpoint if it is wrong here. It is the very real danger of opposing something that God is doing in the church today and failing to give him glory for that work. God is jealous for his works and seeks glory from them for himself, and we must continually pray not only that he would keep us from endorsing error, but also that he would keep us from opposing something that is genuinely from him.

3. Were Miraculous Gifts Limited to the Apostles and Their Companions? Another cessationist argument is that miraculous gifts were limited to the apostles and their close companions.

4. Did Miraculous Gifts Only Accompany the Giving of New Scripture? Another objection is to say that miraculous gifts accompanied the giving of Scripture, and since there is no new Scripture given today, we should expect no new miracles today.

But in response to that it must be said that this is not the only purpose for miraculous gifts. Miracles have several other purposes in Scripture: (1) they authenticate the gospel message throughout the church age; (2) they give help to those in need, and thereby demonstrate God's mercy and love; (3) they equip people for ministry; and (4) they glorify God.

We should also note that not all miracles accompany the giving of additional Scripture. For example, the ministries of Elijah and Elisha were marked by several miracles in the Old Testament, but they wrote no books or sections of the Bible. In the New Testament, there were many occurrences of miracles that were not accompanied by the giving of Scripture. Both Stephen and Philip in the book of Acts worked miracles but wrote no Scripture. There were prophets who wrote no Scripture in Caesarea (Acts 21:4) and Tyre

(Acts 21:9–11) and Rome (Rom. 12:6) and Thessalonica (1 Thess. 5:20–21) and Ephesus (Eph. 4:11) and the communities to which 1 John was written (1 John 4:1–6). There
were apparently many miracles in the churches of Galatia (Gal. 3:5). There were many
miraculous things occurring at Corinth (1 Cor. 12:8–10), but in 1 Corinthians 14:36
Paul denies that any Scripture has come forth from the Corinthian church.[42] And James
expects that healing will occur at the hands of the elders in all the churches to which he
writes (see James 5:14–16).

**5. Is It a Historical Fact That Miraculous Gifts Ceased Early in the History of the
Church?** Some cessationists have argued that miraculous gifts in fact ceased when the
apostles died, because the purpose of miracles was to give authentication to the apostles.
For this reason, it is argued, there should be no miraculous gifts today. B. B. Warfield
argued this extensively in his book, *Counterfeit Miracles.*[43]

In response, it must be said first that the premise just stated is very doubtful on historical grounds. There is increasing historical evidence[44] that miraculous gifts were
occurring throughout the history of the church in greater or lesser degree, even when
exaggerated or evidently spurious claims are discounted. Healings and other kinds of
miraculous answers to prayer are often recorded. There were also people claiming to be
prophets throughout the history of the early church—the problem was that too often
they misunderstood their gift, or others misunderstood it, so that their utterances were
(mistakenly) treated like actual words of God. Sometimes they would be tolerated, and

---

[42]See chapter 11, section A.3.d, for a discussion of 1 Cor.
14:36.

[43]London: Banner of Truth, 1972 (reprint of 1918 edition).
It should be noted that Warfield's argument, though frequently quoted, is really a historical survey, not an analysis of
biblical texts. Moreover, Warfield's purpose was not to refute
any use of spiritual gifts among Christians like those in much
of the charismatic movement today, whose doctrine (on all
matters other than spiritual gifts) and whose church affiliation put them in the mainstream of evangelical Protestantism.
Warfield rather was refuting the spurious claims to miracles
which had come from some branches of Roman Catholicism at
various periods in the history of the church, and from various
heretical sects (Warfield includes discussion of the followers of
Edward Irving [1792–1834], who strayed into eccentric teachings and was excommunicated from the Church of Scotland
in 1833). It is open to question whether modern-day cessationists are right to claim Warfield's support when opposing
something which is far different in doctrine and life from that
which Warfield himself opposed.

[44]Warfield's position has come in for criticism from recent
evangelical studies: see Max Turner, "Spiritual Gifts Then and
Now," *Vox Evangelica* 15 (1985), pp. 41–43, with notes to other
literature; Donald Bridge, *Signs and Wonders Today* (Leicester:
Inter-Varsity Press, 1985), pp. 166–77; and Ronald A. Kydd,
Charismatic Gifts in the Early Church (Peabody, Mass.: Hen-
driksen, 1984). Significant evidence of miraculous gifts in
early church history is found in Eusebius A. Stephanou, "The

Charismata in the Early Church Fathers," *The Greek Orthodox Theological Review* 21:2 (Summer, 1976), pp. 125–46.

A broad-ranging but popularly written study of the history
of miraculous gifts in the church is found in Paul Thigpen,
"Did the Power of the Spirit Ever Leave the Church?" *Charisma* 18:2 (Sept. 1992), pp. 20–28. Most recently, see Jon
Ruthven, *On the Cessation of the Charismata: The Protestant
Polemic on Post-Biblical Miracles* (Sheffield: Sheffield University Academic Press, 1993); this is a revision and expansion of
the author's Ph.D. dissertation responding to the arguments of
cessationists from Warfield to the present.

The argument from church history can be turned the other
way by an analysis of events from about 1970 to the present.
Church growth analysts tell us that Pentecostal and charismatic churches, which encourage miraculous gifts, are experiencing growth unprecedented in the history of the church.
Fuller Seminary professor C. Peter Wagner says, "While back
in 1945 Pentecostals/charismatics could count only sixteen
million members worldwide, by 1975 they had grown to
ninety-six million and then ten years later in 1985 they numbered an astounding 247 million. I am not aware of any non-
political, non-militaristic voluntary association which has
grown at that rate in all of human history" ("Exploring the
Supernatural Dimensions of Church Growth," *Global Church
Growth* [Oct.-Dec., 1988], p. 3). (By way of comparison, if the
world population was 5 billion, the 1985 figure of 247 million
constituted 5 percent of the population of the world.)

sometimes they were too much of a threat to the established leadership of the churches and they would begin splinter groups—tragically, no longer under the restraining and evaluating authority of the established churches. Then too, others may have had "revelations" given to them which they then did not express, or simply included without comment in a prayer, or in a sermon or word of exhortation, or in the writing of a hymn or some devotional literature.[45]

It should also be clear that when Paul said, "When the perfect comes, the imperfect will pass away" (1 Cor. 13:10), he was not saying anything about the relative *frequency* of miraculous gifts in the history of the church. That would be subject to much variation depending on the spiritual maturity and vitality of the church in various periods, the degree to which these gifts were sought as a blessing or rejected as a heresy, the frequency with which the meetings of the church normally made provision for the exercise of these gifts, the degree to which the nature of these gifts was correctly understood, and, over all of this, the Holy Spirit's sovereign work in distributing gifts to the church.

What Paul is speaking about, however, is the total and final abolition of these gifts that is to be brought about by divine initiative at the return of Christ. And he is saying that he thinks that until the time of the return of Christ these gifts will at least to some extent remain available for use, and the Holy Spirit will continue to distribute these gifts to people. Calvin notes the abundance of spiritual gifts in Paul's day and then comments (on 1 Cor. 14:32):

> Today we see our own slender resources, our poverty in fact; but this is undoubtedly the punishment we deserve, as the reward for our ingratitude. For God's riches are not exhausted, nor has His liberality grown less; but we are not worthy of His largess, or capable of receiving all that He generously gives.[46]

6. Are Miraculous Gifts Today the Same As the Miraculous Gifts in Scripture? Yet another objection to the continuation of miracles today is to say that the alleged miracles today are not like the miracles in Scripture because they are far weaker and often are only partially effective. In response to this objection we must ask whether it really matters whether the miracles today are exactly as powerful as those that occurred at the time of the New Testament. For one thing, we have very little information about the kind of miracles done by ordinary Christians in various congregations, such as the Christians at

---

[45]We must realize that unless people understand prophecy as the fallible report of something that God spontaneously brings to mind, it will be very difficult for the church to encourage or even tolerate it. If prophecy is indeed based on something God suddenly brings to mind, it would eventually be very easy for Christian prophets, whether for good or ill motives, to begin to claim not only that they had received a "revelation" from God or Christ, but also that they spoke with a divine authority like that of Scripture. This apparently happened, at least in Montanism (second century A.D.) and probably in many other cases as well. Of course, if these prophets began to promote heretical ideas, the reaction of the rest of the

church would eventually be to drive them out altogether: someone who claims absolute divine authority would eventually be accepted or rejected; he could not be merely tolerated.

But along with this rejection of prophets who misunderstood their status there was perhaps also a rejection of the gift of prophecy altogether, so that a failure on the part of the church itself to understand the nature of the gift of prophecy might have been the cause of a fairly complete suppression of at least the public expression of the gift of prophecy in the church.

[46]John Calvin, *The First Epistle of Paul the Apostle to the Corinthians*, p. 305.

Corinth or in the churches in Galatia. Moreover, although remarkable miracles done by Jesus are recorded in the gospels, when Jesus healed "every disease and every infirmity" (Matt. 9:35) this must have included many with less serious diseases. We must also ask what the expected benefit is for the objection that miracles today are not as powerful as those in Scripture. If today only three hundred are converted at an evangelistic meeting instead of the three thousand converted on the day of Pentecost (Acts 2:41), shall we say that the speaker does not really have the gift of evangelism, since the gift did not operate as powerfully as it did with the apostles? Or if only 30 percent of the people we pray for regarding physical illness are fully healed instead of 100 percent in the life of Jesus or of the apostles, shall we say this is not the New Testament gift of healing?[47] We must remember that gifts can vary in strength and no gift is perfect in this age. But does that mean that we should stop using these gifts altogether, or oppose them where we see them functioning with some degree of effectiveness? Shall we not praise God if 300 are converted rather than three thousand, or if 30 percent are healed rather than 100 percent of those for whom we pray? Is not the work of the Lord being done? If the quantity is not as great as in New Testament times, then we may ask the Lord for more grace or mercy, but it does not seem appropriate to give up on the use of these gifts or to oppose those who do use them.

7. Is It Dangerous for a Church to Allow for the Possibility of Miraculous Gifts Today?

A final objection from the cessationist position is to say that a church that emphasizes the use of miraculous gifts is in danger of becoming imbalanced, and will likely neglect other important things such as evangelism, sound doctrine, and moral purity of life.

To say that the use of miraculous gifts is "dangerous" is not by itself an adequate criticism, because some things that are right are dangerous, at least in some sense. Missionary work is dangerous. Driving a car is dangerous. If we define dangerous to mean "something might go wrong," then we can criticize anything that anybody might do as "dangerous," and this just becomes an all-purpose criticism when there is no specific abuse to point to. A better approach with respect to spiritual gifts is to ask, "Are they

[47]The figure of 30 percent is simply an example for illustrative purposes, but it is close to two recent tabulations concerning people who received prayer for healing. One tabulation is found in David C. Lewis, *Healing: Fiction, Fantasy, or Fact?* (London: Hodder and Stoughton, 1989), an academic investigation of 1,890 people who attended one of John Wimber's conferences in Harrogate, England, in 1986. The author is a social anthropologist who prepared a detailed questionnaire that people filled out during the conference, and then followed up some randomly selected cases several months later. Of 862 cases of prayer for physical healing, 32 percent (or 279) reported a "great deal" of healing or "total healing." Another 26 percent (or 222) reported a "fair amount" of healing. The remaining 42 percent (or 366) reported "little" or "no healing" (pp. 21–22). Many case studies are reported in detail, in several instances with medical reports quoted at length. All the physical problems prayed for are listed in a detailed appendix (pp. 276–83). (These physical problems are distinguished from prayer for spiritual problems such as inner healing and deliverance, which are tabulated separately by Lewis.) The other tabulation is found in John Wimber with Kevin Springer (San Francisco: Harper & Row, 1987), p. 188, who says that, of people who received extended prayer for healing at his church, "During 1986 thirty-two percent of all people prayed for were completely healed, while overall eighty-six percent showed evidence of some significant healing." (D. A. Carson, *How Long, O Lord?* [Grand Rapids: Baker, 1990], p. 124, says, "Wimber is quite candid: he estimates that his 'success rate' is about 2 percent," but Carson gives no documentation for this statement, and it is apparently incorrect in light of what Wimber has actually written.)

being used in accordance with Scripture?" and "Are adequate steps being taken to guard against the dangers of abuse?"

Of course it is true that churches can become imbalanced, and some in fact have done so. But not all will, nor do they have to do so. Furthermore, since this argument is one based on actual results in the life of a church, it is also appropriate to ask, "Which churches in the world today have the most effective evangelism? Which have the most sacrificial giving among their members? Which in fact have the most emphasis on purity of life? Which have the deepest love for the Lord and for his Word?" It seems to me that it is difficult to answer these questions clearly, but I do not think that we can fairly say that those churches in the charismatic and Pentecostal movements *by and large* are *weaker* in these areas than other evangelical churches. In fact, in some cases they may be stronger in these areas. The point is simply that any argument that says that churches emphasizing miraculous gifts *will* become imbalanced is simply not proven in actual practice.

8. A Final Note: Cessationists and Charismatics Need Each Other. Finally, it can be argued that those in the charismatic and Pentecostal camps, and those in the cessationist camp (primarily Reformed and dispensational Christians) really need each other, and they would do well to appreciate each other more. The former tend to have more practical experience in the use of spiritual gifts and in vitality in worship that cessationists could benefit from, if they were willing to learn. On the other hand, Reformed and dispensational groups have traditionally been very strong in understanding of Christian doctrine and in deep and accurate understanding of the teachings of Scripture. Charismatic and Pentecostal groups could learn much from them if they would be willing to do so. But it certainly is not helpful to the church as a whole for both sides to think they can learn nothing from the other, or that they can gain no benefit from fellowship with each other.

QUESTIONS FOR PERSONAL APPLICATION

1. Before reading this chapter, what spiritual gift or gifts did you think you had? Has your understanding of your own spiritual gift(s) changed after studying this chapter? In what way?

2. Explain how each of the spiritual gifts that you understand yourself to have is greater than what would have been known to most old covenant believers. Explain how each gift is a foretaste of some knowledge or ability you will have after Christ returns.

3. What can you do to stir up or strengthen those spiritual gifts in you that need strengthening? Are there some gifts that you have been given but have neglected? Why do you think you have neglected them? What could be done to stir up or rekindle them in you?

4. As you think about your own church, which spiritual gifts do you think are most effectively functioning at the present time? Which are most needed in your church? Is there anything you can do to help meet those needs?

5. What do you think could be done to help churches avoid having controversies, and even divisions, over the question of spiritual gifts? Are there tensions in your own church with regard to these questions today? If so, what can you do to help alleviate these tensions?

6. Do you think that some spiritual gifts mentioned in the New Testament ceased early in the history of the church, and are no longer valid for today? Has your opinion on this question changed as a result of reading this chapter?

7. In your viewpoint, would a church be healthier and more unified if it concentrated on a few gifts and used them carefully and well, or if it encouraged a multiplicity of different gifts, and allowed them to be used at many different times by many different people? If you answered with the latter option, what things might your church do to include a greater diversity and distribution in the use of spiritual gifts? What are some of the dangers that might accompany such widespread use, and how can they be guarded against?

SPECIAL TERMS

See the list at the end of the next chapter.

BIBLIOGRAPHY

See the list at the end of the next chapter.

SCRIPTURE MEMORY PASSAGE

1 Peter 4:10–11: *As each has received a gift, employ it for one another, as good stewards of God's varied grace: whoever speaks, as one who utters oracles of God; whoever renders service, as one who renders it by the strength which God supplies; in order that in everything God may be glorified through Jesus Christ. To him belong glory and dominion for ever and ever. Amen.*

HYMN

"Come, Thou Almighty King"

This is a trinitarian hymn in which the first verse is addressed to God the Father, the second to God the Son, and the third to God the Holy Spirit. The third verse is a request that the Holy Spirit would come and rule in our hearts, be ever-present among us, and dwell among us as the "Spirit of power." The final verse is a hymn of praise to God "the great One in Three." In the midst of a long discussion on spiritual gifts, it is good to refocus our attention on God himself, who is the giver of all good gifts, and whose glory is the goal of the use of every gift.

> Come, thou almighty King, Help us thy name to sing,
> Help us to praise:
> Father, all glorious, O'er all victorious,
> Come, and reign over us, Ancient of Days.
>
> Come, thou incarnate Word, Gird on thy mighty sword,
> Our prayer attend:
> Come, and thy people bless, And give thy Word success;
> Spirit of holiness, on us descend.
>
> Come, holy Comforter, Thy sacred witness bear
> In this glad hour:
> Thou who almighty art, Now rule in every heart,
> And ne'er from us depart, Spirit of pow'r.
>
> To the great One in Three, Eternal praises be,
> Hence evermore.
> His sovereign majesty May we in glory see,
> And to eternity love and adore.

AUTHOR: ANON., 1757

Chapter **11**

GIFTS OF THE HOLY SPIRIT: (PART 2) SPECIFIC GIFTS

How should we understand and use specific spiritual gifts?

EXPLANATION AND SCRIPTURAL BASIS

In this chapter we will build on the general discussion about spiritual gifts in the previous chapter and examine several specific gifts in more detail. We will not consider every gift mentioned in the New Testament, but will focus on several gifts that are not well understood or whose use has aroused some controversy today. Therefore we will not examine gifts whose meaning and use are self-evident from the term involved (such as serving, encouraging, contributing, showing leadership, or showing mercy), but will rather concentrate on those in the following list, primarily taken from 1 Corinthians 12:28 and 12:8–10:

1. prophecy
2. teaching
3. miracles
4. healing
5. tongues and interpretation
6. word of wisdom/word of knowledge
7. distinguishing between spirits

A. Prophecy

Although several definitions have been given for the gift of prophecy, a fresh examination of the New Testament teaching on this gift will show that it should be defined not as "predicting the future," nor as "proclaiming a word from the Lord," nor as "powerful preaching"—but rather as *telling something that God has sponta-neously brought to mind.*" The first four points in the following material support this conclusion; the remaining points deal with other considerations regarding this gift.[1]

1. The New Testament Counterparts to Old Testament Prophets Are New Testament Apostles. Old Testament prophets had an amazing responsibility—they were able to speak and write words that had absolute divine authority. They could say, "Thus says the Lord," and the words that followed were the very words of God. The Old Testament prophets wrote their words as God's words in Scripture for all time (see Num. 22:38; Deut. 18:18–20; Jer. 1:9; Ezek. 2:7, et al.). Therefore, to disbelieve or disobey a prophet's words was to disbelieve or disobey God (see Deut. 18:19; 1 Sam. 8:7; 1 Kings 20:36; and many other passages).

In the New Testament there were also people who spoke and wrote God's very words and had them recorded in Scripture, but we may be surprised to find that Jesus no longer calls them "prophets" but uses a new term, "apostles." The apostles are the New Testament counterpart to the Old Testament prophets (see 1 Cor. 2:13; 2 Cor. 13:3; Gal. 1:8–9, 11–12; 1 Thess. 2:13; 4:8, 15; 2 Peter 3:2). It is the apostles, not the prophets, who have authority to write the words of New Testament Scripture.

When the apostles want to establish their unique authority they never appeal to the title "prophet" but rather call themselves "apostles" (Rom. 1:1; 1 Cor. 1:1; 9:1–2; 2 Cor. 1:1; 11:12–13; 12:11–12; Gal. 1:1; Eph. 1:1; 1 Peter 1:1; 2 Peter 1:1; 3:2, et al.).

2. The Meaning of the Word *Prophet* in the Time of the New Testament. Why did Jesus choose the new term *apostle* to designate those who had the authority to write Scripture? It was probably because the Greek word *prophētēs* ("prophet") at the time of the New Testament had a very broad range of meanings. It generally did not have the sense "one who speaks God's very words" but rather "one who speaks on the basis of some external influence" (often a spiritual influence of some kind). Titus 1:12 uses the word in this sense, where Paul quotes the pagan Greek poet Epimenides: "One of themselves, a *prophet* of their own, said, 'Cretans are always liars, evil beasts, lazy gluttons.'" The soldiers who mock Jesus also seem to use the word *prophesy* in this way, when they blindfold Jesus and cruelly demand, "Prophesy! Who is it that struck you?" (Luke 22:64). They do not

[1]For a more extensive development of all of the following points about the gift of prophecy, see Wayne Grudem, *The Gift of Prophecy in 1 Corinthians,* (Lanham, Md.: University Press of America, 1982), and Wayne Grudem, *The Gift of Prophecy in the New Testament and Today.* (Westchester, Ill.: Crossway, 1988). (The first book is more technical, with much more interaction with the scholarly literature.)

Much of the following material on prophecy is adapted from my article, "Why Christians Can Still Prophesy," in *CT* (Sept. 16, 1988), pp. 29–35, and is used by permission; see also my articles, "What Should Be the Relationship Between Prophet and Pastor?" in *Equipping the Saints* (Fall 1990), pp. 7–9, 21–22; and "Does God Still Give Revelation Today?" in *Charisma* (Sept. 1992), pp. 38–42.

Several writers have differed with my understanding of the gift of prophecy. For alternative views to the position presented in this chapter, see Richard Gaffin, *Perspectives on Pentecost* (Phillipsburg, N. J.: Presbyterian and Reformed, 1979), and the bibliography entries at the end of the chapter under Victor Budgen, F. David Farnell, Kenneth L. Gentry, Jr., Robert Saucy, Robert L. Thomas, and R. Fowler White. On the other hand, the studies listed in the bibliography by D. A. Carson, Roy Clements, Graham Houston, Charles Hummel, and M. M. B. Turner, along with several book reviews, have expressed substantial agreement with the position I advocated in my 1982 and 1988 books.

mean, "Speak words of absolute divine authority," but, "Tell us something that has been revealed to you" (cf. John 4:19).

Many writings outside the Bible use the word *prophet* (Gk. *prophētēs*) in this way, without signifying any divine authority in the words of one called a "prophet." In fact, by the time of the New Testament the term *prophet* in everyday use often simply meant "one who has supernatural knowledge" or "one who predicts the future"—or even just "spokesman" (without any connotations of divine authority). Several examples near the time of the New Testament are given in Helmut Krämer's article in *Theological Dictionary of the New Testament:*[2]

> A philosopher is called "a *prophet* of immortal nature" (Dio Chrysostom, A.D. 40–120)
>
> A teacher (Diogenes) wants to be "a *prophet* of truth and candor" (Lucian of Samosata, A.D. 120–180)
>
> Those who advocate Epicurean philosophy are called "*prophets* of Epicurus" (Plutarch, A.D. 50–120)
>
> Written history is called "the *prophetess* of truth" (Diodorus Siculus, wrote c. 60–30 B.C.)
>
> A "specialist" in botany is called a "*prophet*" (Dioscurides of Cilicia, first century A.D.)
>
> A "quack" in medicine is called a "*prophet*" (Galen of Pergamum, A.D. 129–199)

Krämer concludes that the Greek word for "prophet" (*prophētēs*) "simply expresses the formal function of declaring, proclaiming, making known." Yet, because "every prophet declares something which is not his own," the Greek word for "herald" (*kēryx*) "is the closest synonym."[3]

Of course, the words *prophet* and *prophecy* were *sometimes used of the apostles* in contexts that emphasized the external spiritual influence (from the Holy Spirit) under which they spoke (so Rev. 1:3; 22:7; and Eph. 2:20; 3:5),[4] but this was not the ordinary terminology used for the apostles, nor did the terms *prophet* and *prophecy* in themselves

---

[2]The following examples are taken from *TDNT* 6, p. 794.

[3]Ibid., p. 795.

[4]I have a long discussion of Eph. 2:20 in *The Gift of Prophecy in the New Testament and Today,* pp. 45–63, in which I argue that Paul says that the church is "built up on the foundation of the apostle-prophets" (or "apostles who are also prophets"). This is a grammatically acceptable translation of the phrase *tōn apostolōn kai prophetōn.* As such, the passage refers to the apostles, to whom the mystery of Gentile inclusion in the church was revealed (see Eph. 3:5, which specifies that this mystery "has now been revealed to his holy apostles and prophets [or "apostle-prophets" or, "apostles who are also prophets"] by the Spirit").

I do not think that Eph. 2:20 has much relevance to the entire discussion of the nature of the gift of prophecy.

Whether we see one group here as I do (apostle-prophets) or two groups, as Richard Gaffin and several others do (apostles and prophets), we all agree that *these* prophets are ones who provided the foundation of the church, and therefore these are prophets who spoke infallible words of God. Where we disagree is on the question of whether this verse describes the character of *all who had the gift of prophecy* in the New Testament churches. I see no convincing evidence that it describes all who prophesied in the early church. Rather, the context clearly indicates a very limited group of prophets who were (a) part of the very foundation of the church, (b) closely connected with the apostles, and (c) recipients of the revelation from God that the Gentiles were equal members with Jews in the church (Eph. 3:5). Whether we say this group was only the apostles, or was a small group of prophets closely associated

imply divine authority for their speech or writing. Much more commonly, the words *prophet* and *prophecy* were used of ordinary Christians who spoke not with absolute divine authority, but simply to report something that God had laid on their hearts or brought to their minds. There are many indications in the New Testament that this ordinary gift of prophecy had authority less than that of the Bible, and even less than that of recognized Bible teaching in the early church, as is evident from the following section.

3. Indications That "Prophets" Did Not Speak With Authority Equal to the Words of Scripture.

a. Acts 21:4: In Acts 21:4, we read of the disciples at Tyre: "Through the Spirit they told Paul not to go on to Jerusalem." This seems to be a reference to prophecy directed towards Paul, but Paul disobeyed it! He never would have done this if this prophecy contained God's very words and had authority equal to Scripture.

b. Acts 21:10–11: Then in Acts 21:10–11, Agabus prophesied that the Jews at Jerusalem would bind Paul and "deliver him into the hands of the Gentiles," a prediction that was nearly correct but not quite: the Romans, not the Jews, bound Paul (v. 33; also 22:29),[5] and the Jews, rather than delivering him voluntarily, tried to kill him and he had to be rescued by force (v. 32).[6] The prediction was not far off, but it had inaccuracies in detail that would have called into question the validity of any Old Testament prophet. On the other hand, this text could be perfectly well explained by supposing that Agabus had had a vision of Paul as a prisoner of the Romans in Jerusalem, surrounded by an angry mob of Jews. His own interpretation of such a "vision" or "revelation" from the Holy Spirit would be that the Jews had bound Paul and handed him over to the Romans, and that is what Agabus would (somewhat erroneously) prophesy. This is exactly the kind of fallible prophecy that would fit the definition of New Testament congregational prophecy proposed above—reporting in one's own words something that God has spontaneously brought to mind.

One objection to this view is to say that Agabus' prophecy was in fact fulfilled, and that Paul even reports that in Acts 28:17: "I was delivered prisoner from Jerusalem into the hands of the Romans."[7]

---

with the apostles who spoke Scripture-quality words, we are still left with a picture of a very small and unique group of people who provide this foundation for the church universal.

My friend Dan Wallace, for whom I have great respect, incorrectly says that my view of the grammar of Eph. 2:20 is "essential to [Grudem's] view of NT prophecy" (Daniel Wallace, *Greek Grammar Beyond the Basics* [Grand Rapids: Zondervan, 1996], p. 284). But as I point out above, it is not essential at all, for whether someone understands one group (apostle-prophets) or two groups (apostles and prophets), the context shows this to be a limited group, not to all who had the gift of prophecy at the time of the NT. (See also Rom. 16:7 and Col. 1:2, each of which includes a plural noun in a similar construction used to refer to one group.) For further discussion see Wayne Grudem, *The Gift of Prophecy in the New Testa-*

ment and Today, Revised Edition (Wheaton: Crossway, 2000), pp. 345-346.

[5]In both verses Luke uses the same Greek verb (*deō*) that Agabus had used to predict that the Jews would bind Paul.

[6]The verb that Agabus used (*paradidōmi*, "to deliver, hand over") requires the sense of voluntarily, consciously, deliberately giving over or handing over something to someone else. That is the sense it has in all 119 other instances of the word in the New Testament. But that sense is not true with respect to the treatment of Paul by the Jews: they did not voluntarily hand Paul over to the Romans!

[7]This is the view of Gaffin, *Perspectives*, pp. 65–66, and F. David Farnell, "The Gift of Prophecy in the Old and New Testaments," *BibSac* 149:596 (Oct.–Dec. 1992), p. 395, both of whom refer to Acts 28:17 for support.

But the verse itself will not support that interpretation. The Greek text of Acts 28:17 explicitly refers to Paul's transfer *out of* Jerusalem as *a prisoner*.[8] Therefore Paul's statement describes his transfer out of the Jewish judicial system (the Jews were seeking to bring him again to be examined by the Sanhedrin in Acts 23:15, 20) and *into* the Roman judicial system at Caesarea (Acts 23:23–35). Therefore Paul correctly says in Acts 28:18 that the same Romans into whose hands he had been delivered as a prisoner (v. 17) were the ones who (Gk. *hoitines,* v. 18), "When they had examined me . . . wished to set me at liberty, because there was no reason for the death penalty in my case" (Acts 28:18; cf. 23:29; also 25:11, 18–19; 26:31–32). Then Paul adds that when the Jews objected he was compelled "to appeal to Caesar" (Acts 28:19; cf. 25:11). This whole narrative in Acts 28:17–19 refers to Paul's transfer out of Jerusalem to Caesarea in Acts 23:12–35, and explains to the Jews in Rome why Paul is in Roman custody. The narrative does not refer to Acts 21:27–36 and the mob scene near the Jerusalem temple at all. So this objection is not persuasive. The verse does not point to a fulfillment of either half of Agabus' prophecy: it does not mention any binding by the Jews, nor does it mention that the Jews handed Paul over to the Romans. In fact, in the scene it refers to (Acts 23:12–35), once again Paul had just been taken from the Jews "by force" (Acts 23:10), and, far from seeking to hand him over to the Romans, they were waiting in an ambush to kill him (Acts 23:13–15).

Another objection to my understanding of Acts 21:10–11 is to say that the Jews did not really have to bind Paul and deliver him into the hands of the Gentiles for the prophecy of Agabus to be true, because the Jews were *responsible* for these activities even if they did not carry them out. Robert Thomas says, "It is common to speak of the responsible party or parties as performing an act even though he or they may not have been the immediate agent(s)."[9] Thomas cites similar examples from Acts 2:23 (where Peter says that the Jews crucified Christ, whereas the Romans actually did it) and John 19:1 (we read that Pilate scourged Jesus, whereas his soldiers no doubt carried out the action). Thomas concludes, therefore, "the Jews were the ones who put Paul in chains just as Agabus predicted."[10]

In response, I agree that Scripture can speak of someone as doing an act that is carried out by that person's agent. But *in every case* the person who is said to do the action both *wills* the act to be done and *gives directions* to others to do it. Pilate directed his soldiers to scourge Jesus. The Jews actively demanded that the Romans would crucify Christ. By contrast, in the situation of Paul's capture in Jerusalem, there is no such parallel. The Jews did not order him to be bound but the Roman tribune did it: "Then the tribune came up and arrested him, and ordered him to be bound with two chains" (Acts 21:33). And in fact the parallel form of speech is found here, because, although the tribune *ordered* Paul to be bound, later we read that "the tribune also was afraid, for he realized that Paul was a Roman citizen and that *he had bound him*" (Acts 22:29). So this narrative does speak

---

[8]The NIV translation, "I was arrested *in* Jerusalem and handed over to the Romans," completely misses the idea (which the Greek text requires) of being delivered *out of* (*ex*) Jerusalem, and removes the idea that he was delivered as a prisoner (Gk. *desmios*), adding rather the idea that he was arrested in Jerusalem, an event that is not mentioned here in the Greek text.

[9]Robert L. Thomas, "Prophecy Rediscovered? A Review of The Gift of Prophecy in the New Testament and Today," *BibSac* 149:593 (Jan.–Mar. 1992), p. 91. The same argument is made by Kenneth L. Gentry, Jr. *The Charismatic Gift of Prophecy: A Reformed Response to Wayne Grudem,* 2d ed. (Memphis, Tenn.: Footstool Publications, 1989), p. 43.

[10]Thomas, "Prophecy Rediscovered?" p. 91.

of the binding as done either by the responsible agent or by the people who carried it out, but in both cases these are Romans, not Jews. In summary, this objection says that the Jews put Paul in chains. But Acts says twice that the Romans bound him. This objection says that the Jews turned Paul over to the Gentiles. But Acts says that they violently refused to turn him over, so that he had to be taken from them by force. The objection does not fit the words of the text.[11]

c. 1 Thessalonians 5:19–21: Paul tells the Thessalonians, "do not despise prophesying, but test everything; hold fast what is good" (1 Thess. 5:20–21). If the Thessalonians had thought that prophecy equaled God's Word in authority, he would never have had to tell the Thessalonians not to despise it—they "received" and "accepted" God's Word "with joy from the Holy Spirit" (1 Thess. 1:6; 2:13; cf. 4:15). But when Paul tells them to "test everything" it must include at least the prophecies he mentioned in the previous phrase. He implies that prophecies contain some things that are good and some things that are not good when he encourages them to "hold fast *what is good.*" This is something that could never have been said of the words of an Old Testament prophet, or the authoritative teachings of a New Testament apostle.

d. 1 Corinthians 14:29–38: More extensive evidence on New Testament prophecy is found in 1 Corinthians 14. When Paul says, "Let two or three prophets speak, and *let the others weigh what is said*" (1 Cor. 14:29), he suggests that they should listen carefully and sift the good from the bad, accepting some and rejecting the rest (for this is the implication of the Greek word *diakrinō,* here translated "weigh what is said"). We cannot imagine that an Old Testament prophet like Isaiah would have said, "Listen to what I say and weigh what is said—sort the good from the bad, what you accept from what you should not accept"! If prophecy had absolute divine authority, it would be sin to do this. But here Paul commands that it be done, suggesting that New Testament prophecy did not have the authority of God's very words.[12]

In 1 Corinthians 14:30, Paul allows one prophet to interrupt another one: "If a revelation is made to another sitting by, let the first be silent. For you can all prophesy one by one." Again, if prophets had been speaking God's very words, equal in value to Scripture, it is hard to imagine that Paul would say they should be interrupted and not be allowed to finish their message. But that is what Paul commands.

Paul suggests that no one at Corinth, a church that had much prophecy, was able to speak God's very words. He says in 1 Corinthians 14:36, "What! *Did the word of God come forth from you,* or are you the only ones it has reached?" (author's translation).[13]

---

[11]See below, section 4, on the question of Agabus' introductory phrase, "Thus says the Holy Spirit."

[12]Paul's instructions are different from those in the early Christian document known as the *Didache,* which tells people, "Do not test or examine any prophet who is speaking in a spirit (or: in the Spirit)" (chapter 11). But the *Didache* says several things that are contrary to New Testament doctrine (see Grudem, *The Gift of Prophecy in the New Testament and Today,* pp. 106–8).

[13]The RSV translates, "Did the word of God *originate* with you?" but there is no need to make the Greek verb here (the aorist of *exerchomai,* "to go out") speak so specifically of the origin of the gospel message: Paul does not say, "Did the word of God *first* go forth from you?" but simply, "Did the word of God go forth from you?" He realizes they must admit that the Word of God *has not* come forth from them—therefore, their prophets cannot have been speaking words of God equal to Scripture in authority.

Then in verses 37 and 38, he claims authority far greater than any prophet at Corinth: "If any one thinks that he is a prophet, or spiritual, he should acknowledge that what I am writing to you is a command of the Lord. If any one does not recognize this, he is not recognized."

All these passages indicate that the common idea that prophets spoke "words of the Lord" when the apostles were not present in the early churches is simply incorrect.

e. Apostolic Preparations for Their Absence: In addition to the verses we have considered so far, one other type of evidence suggests that New Testament congregational prophets spoke with less authority than New Testament apostles or Scripture: the problem of successors to the apostles is solved not by encouraging Christians to listen to the *prophets* (even though there were prophets around) but by pointing to the *Scriptures*.[14]

So Paul, at the end of his life, emphasizes "rightly handling the word of truth" (2 Tim. 2:15), and the "God-breathed" character of "scripture" for "teaching, for reproof, for correction, and for training in righteousness" (2 Tim. 3:16). Jude urges his readers to "contend for the faith which was once for all delivered to the saints" (Jude 3). Peter, at the end of his life, encourages his readers to "pay attention" to Scripture, which is like "a lamp shining in a dark place" (2 Peter 1:19–20), and reminds them of the teaching of the apostle Paul "in all his letters" (2 Peter 3:16). In no case do we read exhortations to "give heed to the prophets in your churches" or to "obey the words of the Lord through your prophets," etc. Yet there certainly were prophets prophesying in many local congregations after the death of the apostles. It seems that they did not have authority equal to the apostles, and the authors of Scripture knew that. The conclusion is that prophecies today are not "the words of God" either.

4. How Should We Speak About the Authority of Prophecy Today? So prophecies in the church today should be considered merely human words, not God's words, and not equal to God's words in authority. But does this conclusion conflict with current charismatic teaching or practice? I think it conflicts with much charismatic practice, but not with most charismatic teaching.

Most charismatic teachers today would agree that contemporary prophecy is not equal to Scripture in authority. Though some will speak of prophecy as being the "word of God" for today, there is almost uniform testimony from all sections of the charismatic movement that prophecy is imperfect and impure, and will contain elements that are not to be obeyed or trusted. For example, Bruce Yocum, the author of a widely used charismatic book on prophecy, writes, "Prophecy can be impure—our own thoughts or ideas can get mixed into the message we receive—whether we receive the words directly or only receive a sense of the message."[15]

But it must be said that in actual practice much confusion results from the habit of prefacing prophecies with the common Old Testament phrase, "Thus says the Lord"

---

[14]I have taken this idea from the very helpful booklet by Roy Clements, *Word and Spirit: The Bible and the Gift of Prophecy Today* (Leicester: UCCF Booklets, 1986), p. 24; cf. D. A. Carson, *Showing the Spirit: A Theological Exposition of 1 Corinthians* 12–14 (Grand Rapids: Baker, 1987), p. 96.

[15]See Bruce Yokum, *Prophecy* (Ann Arbor: Word of Life, 1976), p. 79.

(a phrase nowhere spoken in the New Testament by any prophets in New Testament churches). This is unfortunate, because it gives the impression that the words that follow are God's very words, whereas the New Testament does not justify that position and, when pressed, most responsible charismatic spokesmen would not want to claim it for every part of their prophecies anyway. So there would be much gain and no loss if that introductory phrase were dropped.

Now it is true that Agabus uses a similar phrase ("Thus says the Holy Spirit") in Acts 21:11, but the same words (Gk. *tade legei*) are used by Christian writers just after the time of the New Testament to introduce very general paraphrases or greatly expanded interpretations of what is being reported (so Ignatius, *Epistle to the Philadelphians* 7:1–2 [about A.D. 108] and *Epistle of Barnabas* 6:8; 9:2, 5 [A.D. 70–100]). The phrase can apparently mean, "This is generally (or approximately) what the Holy Spirit is saying to us."

If someone really does think God is bringing something to mind which should be reported in the congregation, there is nothing wrong with saying, "*I think* the Lord is putting on my mind that . . ." or "*It seems to me that* the Lord is showing us . . ." or some similar expression. Of course that does not sound as "forceful" as "Thus says the Lord," but if the message is really from God, the Holy Spirit will cause it to speak with great power to the hearts of those who need to hear.

5. A Spontaneous "Revelation" Made Prophecy Different From Other Gifts. If prophecy does not contain God's very words, then what is it? In what sense is it from God?

Paul indicates that God could bring something spontaneously to mind so that the person prophesying would report it in his or her own words. Paul calls this a "revelation": "If a revelation is made to another sitting by, let the first be silent. For you can all prophesy one by one, so that all may learn and all be encouraged" (1 Cor. 14:30–31). Here he uses the word *revelation* in a broader sense than the technical way theologians have used it to speak of the words of Scripture—but the New Testament elsewhere uses the terms *reveal* and *revelation* in this broader sense of communication from God that does not result in written Scripture or words equal to written Scripture in authority (see Phil. 3:15; Rom. 1:18; Eph. 1:17; Matt. 11:27).

Paul is simply referring to something that God may suddenly bring to mind, or something that God may impress on someone's consciousness in such a way that the person has a sense that it is from God. It may be that the thought brought to mind is surprisingly distinct from the person's own train of thought, or that it is accompanied by a sense of vividness or urgency or persistence, or in some other way gives the person a rather clear sense that it is from the Lord.[16]

Figure 11.1 illustrates the idea of a revelation from God that is reported in the prophet's own (merely human) words.

Thus, if a stranger comes in and all prophesy, "the secrets of his heart are disclosed; and so, falling on his face, he will worship God and declare that God is really among

---

[16]Although we argued above that the *authority* of prophecy in the New Testament church is far different from the authority of Old Testament canonical prophecy, this does not mean that everything about New Testament prophecy has to be different. With respect to *the form in which the revelation comes* to the prophet, there may be not only words or ideas that come to mind, but also mental pictures (or "visions," Acts 2:17) and dreams (Acts 2:17) as well.

you" (1 Cor. 14:25). I have heard a report of this happening in a clearly noncharismatic Baptist church in America. A missionary speaker paused in the middle of his message and said something like this: "I didn't plan to say this, but it seems the Lord is indicating that someone in this church has just walked out on his wife and family. If that is so, let me tell you that God wants you to return to them and learn to follow God's pattern for family life." The missionary did not know it, but in the unlit balcony sat a man who had entered the church moments before for the first time in his life. The description fit him exactly, and he made himself known, acknowledged his sin, and began to seek after God.

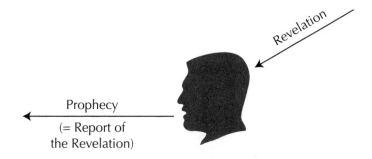

PROPHECY OCCURS WHEN A REVELATION FROM GOD IS REPORTED
IN THE PROPHET'S OWN (MERELY HUMAN) WORDS
Figure 11.1

In this way, prophecy serves as a "sign" for believers (1 Cor. 14:22) — it is a clear demonstration that God is definitely at work in their midst, a "sign" of God's hand of blessing on the congregation. And since it will work for the conversion of unbelievers as well, Paul encourages this gift to be used when "unbelievers or outsiders enter" (1 Cor. 14:23).

Many Christians in all periods of the church have experienced or heard of similar events — for example, an unplanned but urgent request may have been given to pray for certain missionaries in Nigeria. Then much later those who prayed discovered that just at that time the missionaries had been in an auto accident or at a point of intense spiritual conflict, and had needed those prayers. Paul would call the sense or intuition of those things a "revelation," and the report to the assembled church of that prompting from God would be called a "prophecy." It may have elements of the speaker's own understanding or interpretation in it and it certainly needs evaluation and testing, yet it has a valuable function in the church nonetheless.[17]

---

[17]We must caution people, however, that the mere fact of a "revelation" that seems supernatural (and that even may contain some surprisingly accurate information) does not guarantee that a message is a true prophecy from God, for false prophets can "prophesy" under demonic influence. Demons can know about hidden activities or private conversations in our lives, even though they cannot know the future or read our thoughts.

John warns that "many false prophets have gone out into the world" (1 John 4:1), and he gives tests of true doctrine to discern them (vv. 1–6), and says "The world listens to them" (v. 5). Other marks of false prophets can be found in 2 John 7–9 (denying the incarnation and not abiding in the doctrine of Christ); Matt. 7:15–20 ("You will know them by their fruits," v. 16); Matt. 24:11 (leading many astray); and Matt. 24:24 (showing signs and wonders for the purpose of leading astray the elect). On the other hand, 1 Cor. 12:3 seems to tell us that we should not think that genuine Christians will

6. The Difference Between Prophecy and Teaching. As far as we can tell, all New Testament "prophecy" was based on this kind of spontaneous prompting from the Holy Spirit (cf. Acts 11:28; 21:4, 10–11; and note the ideas of prophecy represented in Luke 7:39; 23:63–64; John 4:19; 11:51). Unless a person receives a spontaneous "revelation" from God, there is no prophecy.

By contrast, no human speech act that is called a "teaching" or done by a "teacher," or described by the verb "teach," is ever said to be based on a "revelation" in the New Testament. Rather, "teaching" is often simply an explanation or application of Scripture (Acts 15:35; 18:11, 24–28; Rom. 2:21; 15:4; Col. 3:16; Heb. 5:12) or a repetition and explanation of apostolic instructions (Rom. 16:17; 2 Tim. 2:2; 3:10, et al.). It is what we would call "Bible teaching" or "preaching" today.

So prophecy has less authority than "teaching," and prophecies in the church are always to be subject to the authoritative teaching of Scripture. Timothy was not told to *prophesy* Paul's instructions in the church; he was to *teach* them (1 Tim. 4:11; 6:2). Paul did not *prophesy* his lifestyle in Christ in every church; he *taught* it (1 Cor. 4:17). The Thessalonians were not told to hold firm to the traditions that were "prophesied" to them but to the traditions that they were "taught" by Paul (2 Thess. 2:15). Contrary to some views, it was teachers, not prophets, who gave leadership and direction to the early churches.

Among the elders, therefore, were "those who labor in preaching and teaching" (1 Tim. 5:17), and an elder was to be "an apt teacher" (1 Tim. 3:2; cf. Titus 1:9)—but nothing is said about any elders whose work was prophesying, nor is it ever said that an elder has to be "an apt prophet" or that elders should be "holding firm to sound prophecies." In his leadership function Timothy was to take heed to himself and to his "teaching" (1 Tim. 4:16), but he is never told to take heed to his prophesying. James warned that those who teach, not those who prophesy, will be judged with greater strictness (James 3:1).

The task of interpreting and applying Scripture, then, is called "teaching" in the New Testament. Although a few people have claimed that the prophets in New Testament churches gave "charismatically inspired" interpretations of Old Testament Scripture, that claim has hardly been persuasive, primarily because it is hard to find in the New Testament any convincing examples where the "prophet" word group is used to refer to someone engaged in this kind of activity.

So the distinction is quite clear: if a message is the result of conscious reflection on the text of Scripture, containing interpretation of the text and application to life, then it is (in New Testament terms) a teaching. But if a message is the report of something God brings suddenly to mind, then it is a prophecy. And of course, even prepared teachings can be interrupted by unplanned additional material that the Bible teacher suddenly felt God was bringing to his mind—in that case, it would be a "teaching" with an element of prophecy mixed in.

7. Objection: This Makes Prophecy "Too Subjective." At this point some have objected that waiting for such "promptings" from God is "just too subjective" a process. But in

---

be false prophets, speaking by the power of demons (see the discussion of 1 Cor. 12:3 below in section E.2.h), and 1 John 4:4 reassures Christians that "he who is in you is greater than he who is in the world."

response, it may be said that, for the health of the church, it is often the people who make this objection who need this subjective process most in their own Christian lives! This gift requires waiting on the Lord, listening for him, hearing his prompting in our hearts. For Christians who are completely evangelical, doctrinally sound, intellectual, and "objective," probably what is needed most is the strong balancing influence of a more vital "subjective" relationship with the Lord in everyday life. And these people are also those who have the least likelihood of being led into error, for they already place great emphasis on solid grounding in the Word of God.

Yet there is an opposite danger of excessive reliance on subjective impressions for guidance, and that must be clearly guarded against. People who continually seek subjective "messages" from God to guide their lives must be cautioned that subjective personal guidance is not a primary function of New Testament prophecy. They need to place much more emphasis on Scripture and seeking God's sure wisdom written there.

Many charismatic writers would agree with this caution, as the following quotations indicate:

Michael Harper (Anglican charismatic pastor):

> Prophecies which tell other people what they are to do — are to be regarded with great suspicion.[18]

Donald Gee (Assemblies of God):

> Many of our errors where spiritual gifts are concerned arise when we want the extraordinary and exceptional to be made the frequent and habitual. Let all who develop excessive desire for "messages" through the gifts take warning from the wreckage of past generations as well as of contemporaries. . . . The Holy Scriptures are a lamp unto our feet and a light unto our path.[19]

Donald Bridge (British charismatic pastor):

> The illuminist constantly finds that "God tells him" to do things. . . . Illuminists are often very sincere, very dedicated, and possessed of a commitment to obey God that shames more cautious Christians. Nevertheless they are treading a dangerous path. Their ancestors have trodden it before, and always with disastrous results in the long run. Inner feelings and special promptings are by their very nature subjective. The Bible provides our objective guide.[20]

8. Prophecies Could Include Any Edifying Content. The examples of prophecies in the New Testament mentioned above show that the idea of prophecy as only "predicting the future" is certainly wrong. There were some predictions (Acts 11:28; 21:11), but there was also the disclosure of sins (1 Cor. 14:25). In fact, anything that edified could have been included, for Paul says, "He who prophesies speaks to men *for their upbuilding and encouragement and consolation*" (1 Cor. 14:3). Another indication of

[18]*Prophecy: A Gift for the Body of Christ* (Plainfield, N.J.: Logos, 1964), p. 26.
[19]*Spiritual Gifts in the Work of Ministry Today* (Springfield, Mo.: Gospel Publishing House, 1963), pp. 51–52.
[20]*Signs and Wonders Today* (Leicester: Inter-Varsity Press, 1985), p. 183.

the value of prophecy was that it could speak to the needs of people's hearts in a spontaneous, direct way.

9. Many People in the Congregation Can Prophesy. Another great benefit of prophecy is that it provides opportunity for participation by everyone in the congregation, not just those who are skilled speakers or who have gifts of teaching. Paul says that he wants "all" the Corinthians to prophesy (1 Cor. 14:5), and he says, "You can all prophesy one by one, so that all may learn and all be encouraged" (1 Cor. 14:31).[21] This does not mean that every believer will actually be able to prophesy, for Paul says, "Not all are prophets, are they?" (1 Cor. 12:29, author's translation). But it does mean that anyone who receives a "revelation" from God has permission to prophesy (within Paul's guidelines), and it suggests that many will.[22] Because of this, greater openness to the gift of prophecy could help overcome the situation where many who attend our churches are merely spectators and not participants. Perhaps we are contributing to the problem of "spectator Christianity" by quenching the work of the spirit in this area.

10. We Should "Earnestly Desire" Prophecy. Paul valued this gift so highly that he told the Corinthians, "Make love your aim, and earnestly desire the spiritual gifts *especially that you may prophesy*" (1 Cor. 14:1). Then at the end of his discussion of spiritual gifts he said again, "So, my brethren, *earnestly desire to prophesy*" (1 Cor. 14:39). And he said, "He who prophesies edifies the church" (1 Cor. 14:4).

If Paul was eager for the gift of prophecy to function at Corinth, troubled as the church was by immaturity, selfishness, divisions, and other problems, then should we not also actively seek this valuable gift in our congregations today? We evangelicals who profess to believe and obey all that Scripture says, should we not also believe and obey this? And might a greater openness to the gift of prophecy perhaps help to correct a dangerous imbalance in church life, an imbalance that comes because we are too exclusively intellectual, objective, and narrowly doctrinal?

11. Encouraging and Regulating Prophecy in the Local Church. Finally, if a church begins to encourage the use of prophecy where it has not been used before, what should it do? How can it encourage this gift without falling into abuse?

For all Christians, and especially for pastors and others who have teaching responsibilities in the church, several steps would be both appropriate and pastorally wise: (1) Pray seriously for the Lord's wisdom on how and when to approach this subject in the church. (2) There should be teaching on this subject in the regular Bible teaching times the church already provides. (3) The church should be patient and proceed slowly—church leaders should not be "domineering" (or "pushy") (1 Peter 5:3), and a patient approach will avoid frightening people away or alienating them unnecessarily. (4) The church should recognize and encourage the gift of prophecy in ways it

---

[21]Here Paul's meaning is that all who receive a revelation in the sense just mentioned in v. 29 will be able to take turns and prophesy one at a time. He does not mean that every single Christian at Corinth had the gift of prophecy.

[22]In a large church, only few would be able to speak when the whole church assembled, for Paul says, "Let two or three prophets speak" (1 Cor. 14:29). But many more would find opportunities to prophesy in smaller gatherings in homes.

has already been functioning in the church—at church prayer meetings, for example, when someone has felt unusually "led" by the Holy Spirit to pray for something, or when it has seemed that the Holy Spirit was bringing to mind a hymn or Scripture passage, or when giving a common sense of the tone or the specific focus of a time of group worship or prayer. Even Christians in churches not open to the gift of prophecy can at least be sensitive to promptings from the Holy Spirit regarding what to pray for in church prayer meetings, and can then express those promptings in the form of a prayer (what might be called a "prophetic prayer") to the Lord.

(5) If the first four steps have been followed, and if the congregation and its leadership will accept it, some opportunities for the gift of prophecy to be used might be made in the less formal worship services of the church, or in smaller home groups. If this is allowed, those who prophesy should be kept within scriptural guidelines (1 Cor. 14:29–36), should genuinely seek the edification of the church and not their own prestige (1 Cor. 14:12, 26), and should not dominate the meeting or be overly dramatic or emotional in their speech (and thus attract attention to themselves rather than to the Lord). Prophecies should certainly be evaluated according to the teachings of Scripture (1 Cor. 14:29–36; 1 Thess. 5:19–21).

(6) If the gift of prophecy begins to be used in a church, the church should place even more emphasis on the vastly superior value of Scripture as the source to which Christians can always go to hear the voice of the living God. Prophecy is a valuable gift, as are many other gifts, but it is in Scripture that God and only God speaks to us his very words, even today, and throughout our lives. Rather than hoping at every worship service that the highlight would be some word of prophecy, those who use the gift of prophecy need to be reminded that we should find our focus of joy, our expectation, and our delight in God himself as he speaks to us through the Bible. There we have a treasure of infinite worth: the actual words of our Creator speaking to us in language we can understand. And rather than seeking frequent guidance through prophecy, we should emphasize that it is in Scripture that we are to find guidance for our lives. In Scripture is our source of direction, our focus when seeking God's will, our sufficient and completely reliable standard. It is of God's words in Scripture that we can with confidence say, "Your word is a lamp to my feet and a light to my path" (Ps. 119:105).

B. Teaching

The gift of teaching in the New Testament is *the ability to explain Scripture and apply it to people's lives.* This is evident from a number of passages. In Acts 15:35, Paul and Barnabas and "many others" are in Antioch "*teaching* and preaching the word of the Lord." At Corinth, Paul stayed one and a half years "*teaching* the word of God among them" (Acts 18:11). And the readers of the epistle to the Hebrews, though they ought to have been teachers, needed rather to have someone to teach them again "the first principles of God's word" (Heb. 5:12). Paul tells the Romans that the words of the Old Testament Scriptures "were written for our instruction (or "teaching," Gk. *didaskalia*)" (Rom. 15:4), and writes to Timothy that "all scripture" is "profitable for teaching [*didaskalia*]" (2 Tim. 3:16).

Of course, if "teaching" in the early church was so often based on Old Testament Scripture, it is not surprising that it could also be based on something equal to Scripture in authority, namely, a received body of apostolic instructions. So Timothy was to take the teaching he had received from Paul and commit it to faithful men who would be able to "teach others also" (2 Tim. 2:2). And the Thessalonians were to "hold firm to the traditions" they were "taught" by Paul (2 Thess. 2:15). Far from being based on a spontaneous revelation that came during the worship service of the church (as prophecy was), this kind of "teaching" was the repetition and explanation of authentic apostolic teaching. To teach contrary to Paul's instructions was to teach different or heretical doctrine (*heterodidaskalō*) and to fail to give heed to "the sound words of our Lord Jesus Christ and the *teaching* that accords with godliness" (1 Tim. 6:3). In fact, Paul said that Timothy was to remind the Corinthians of Paul's ways "as I *teach* them everywhere in every church" (1 Cor. 4:17). Similarly, Timothy was to "command and teach" (1 Tim. 4:11) and to "teach and urge" (1 Tim. 6:2) Paul's instructions to the Ephesian church. Thus it was not prophecy but teaching which in a primary sense (from the apostles) first provided the doctrinal and ethical norms by which the church was regulated. And as those who learned from the apostles also taught, their teaching guided and directed the local churches.[23]

So teaching in terms of the New Testament epistles consisted of repeating and explaining the words of Scripture (or the equally authoritative teachings of Jesus and of the apostles) and applying them to the hearers. In the New Testament epistles, "teaching" is something very much like what is described by our phrase "Bible teaching" today.

C. Miracles

Just after apostles, prophets and teachers, Paul says "then miracles" (1 Cor. 12:28). Although many of the miracles seen in the New Testament were specifically miracles of healing, Paul here lists healing as a separate gift. Therefore in this context he must have something other than physical healing in view.

We should realize that the English word *miracles* may not give a very close approximation to what Paul intended, since the Greek word is simply the plural form of the word *dynamis*, "power."[24] This means that the term may refer to any kind of activity where God's mighty power is evident. It may include answers to prayer for deliverance from physical danger (as in the deliverance of the apostles from prison in Acts 5:19–20 or 12:6–11), or powerful works of judgment on the enemies of the gospel or those who require discipline within the church (see Acts 5:1–11; 13:9–12), or miraculous deliverance from injury (as with Paul and the viper in Acts 28:3–6). But such acts of spiritual power may also include power to triumph over demonic opposition (as in Acts 16:18; cf. Luke 10:17).

Since Paul does not define "works of miracles" any more specifically than this, we can say that the gift of miracles may include the working of divine power in deliverance from danger, in intervention to meet special needs in the physical world (as in the case of Elijah in 1 Kings 17:1–16), in judgment on those who irrationally and violently

---

[23]See also the discussion in section A.6 above, on the differences between prophecy and teaching.

[24]The NIV translates this word "miraculous powers" at 1 Cor. 12:10, and the NASB mg. translates "works of power" in both places.

oppose the gospel message, in vanquishing the demonic forces that wage war against the church, and in any other way in which God's power is manifested in an evident way to further God's purposes in a situation. All of these would be works of "power" in which the church would be helped and God's glory would be made evident.

D. Healing

1. Introduction: Sickness and Health in the History of Redemption. We must realize at the outset that physical sickness came as a result of the fall of Adam, and illness and disease are simply part of the outworking of the curse after the fall, and will eventually lead toward physical death. However, Christ redeemed us from that curse when he died on the cross: "Surely *he took up our infirmities* and carried our sorrows . . . *by his wounds we are healed*" (Isa. 53:4–5 NIV). This passage refers to both physical and spiritual healing that Christ purchased for us, for Peter quotes it to refer to our salvation: "He himself *bore our sins* in his body on the tree, that we might die to sin and live to righteousness. *By his wounds you have been healed*" (1 Peter 2:24).

But Matthew quotes the same passage from Isaiah with reference to the physical healings Jesus performed: "and he cast out the spirits with a word, and *healed all who were sick. This was to fulfill what was spoken by the prophet Isaiah, 'He took our infirmities and bore our diseases'*" (Matt. 8:16–17).

All Christians would probably agree that in the atonement Christ has purchased for us not only complete freedom from sin but also complete freedom from physical weakness and infirmity in his work of redemption. And all Christians would also no doubt agree that our full and complete possession of all the benefits that Christ earned for us will not come until Christ returns: it is only "at his coming" (1 Cor. 15:23) that we receive our perfect resurrection bodies. So it is with physical healing and redemption from the physical sickness that came as a result of the curse in Genesis 3: our complete possession of redemption from physical illness will not be ours until Christ returns and we receive resurrection bodies.[25]

But the question that confronts us with respect to the gift of healing is whether God may from time to time grant us a foretaste or a down payment of the physical healing which he will grant us fully in the future.[26] The healing miracles of Jesus certainly demonstrate that at times God is willing to grant a partial foretaste of the perfect health that will be ours for eternity. And the ministry of healing seen in the lives of the apostles and others in the early church also indicates that this was part of the ministry of the new covenant age. As such, it fits the larger pattern of blessings in the new covenant, many or all of which give partial foretastes of the blessings that will be ours when Christ returns.

---

[25]When people say that complete healing is "in the atonement," the statement is true in an ultimate sense, but it really does not tell us anything about when we will receive "complete healing" (or any part of it).

[26]For two very helpful treatments of this question, and of the gift of healing in general, see John Wimber with Kevin Springer, *Power Healing* (San Francisco: Harper & Row, 1987),

and Ken Blue, *Authority to Heal* (Downers Grove, Ill.: InterVarsity Press, 1987). See also the excellent discussion in Jack Deere, *Surprised by the Power of the Holy Spirit* (Grand Rapids: Zondervan, 1993). Several scholarly defenses of a ministry of healing today are found in Gary Greig and Kevin Springer, eds., *The Kingdom and the Power* (Ventura, Calif.: Gospel Light, 1993).

We "already" possess some of the blessings of the kingdom, but those blessings are "not yet" fully ours.

2. The Purposes of Healing. As with other spiritual gifts, healing has several purposes. Certainly it functions as a "sign" to authenticate the gospel message, and show that the kingdom of God has come. Then also healing brings comfort and health to those who are ill, and thereby demonstrates God's attribute of mercy toward those in distress. Third, healing equips people for service, as physical impediments to ministry are removed. Fourth, healing provides opportunity for God to be glorified as people see physical evidence of his goodness, love, power, wisdom, and presence.

3. What About the Use of Medicine? What is the relationship between prayer for healing and the use of medicine and the skill of a physician? Certainly we should use medicine if it is available because God has also created substances in the earth that can be made into medicine with healing properties. Medicines thus should be considered part of the whole creation that God considered "very good" (Gen. 1:31). We should willingly use medicine with thankfulness to the Lord, for "The earth is the LORD's and the fulness thereof" (Ps. 24:1). In fact, when medicine is available and we refuse to use it (in cases where it would put ourselves or others in danger), then it seems that we are wrongly "forcing a test" on the Lord our God (cf. Luke 4:12): this is similar to the case of Satan tempting Jesus to jump from the temple rather than walking down the steps. Where ordinary means of getting down from the temple (the steps) are available, it is "forcing a test" on God to jump and thereby demand that he perform a miracle at that exact moment. To refuse to use effective medicine, insisting that God perform a miracle of healing instead of healing through the medicine, is very similar to this.

Of course, it is wrong to rely on doctors or medicine *instead* of relying on the Lord, a mistake tragically made by King Asa:

> In the thirty-ninth year of his reign Asa was diseased in his feet, and his disease became severe; yet even in his disease he did not seek the LORD, but sought help from physicians. And Asa slept with his fathers, dying in the forty-first year of his reign. (2 Chron. 16:12–13)

But if medicine is used in connection with prayer, then we should expect God to bless and often multiply the effectiveness of the medicine.[27] Even when Isaiah had received from the Lord a promise of healing for King Hezekiah, he told Hezekiah's servants to bring a cake of figs and apply it (as a medical remedy) to a boil that Hezekiah suffered from: "And Isaiah said, 'Bring a cake of figs. And let them take and lay it on the boil, that he may recover'" (2 Kings 20:7).

However, sometimes there is no appropriate medicine available, or the medicine does not work. Certainly we must remember that God can heal where doctors and medicine cannot heal (and it may amaze us to realize how frequently doctors cannot heal, even in

---

[27]Note Paul's recommendation of a use of wine for health purposes in 1 Tim. 5:23: "No longer drink only water, but use a little wine for the sake of your stomach and your frequent ailments."

the most medically advanced countries). Moreover, there may be many times when an illness is not putting us or others in immediate danger, and we decide to ask God to heal our sickness without the use of medicine, simply because we wish for another opportunity to exercise our faith and give him glory, and perhaps because we wish to avoid spending the time or money to use medical means, or we wish to avoid the side-effects that some medicines have. In all of these cases, it is simply a matter of personal choice and would not seem to be "forcing a test" on God. (However, a decision not to use medicine in these cases should be a personal choice and not one that is forced on others.)

We see Jesus healing explicitly where medical means have failed, when "a woman who had had a flow of blood for twelve years and *could not be healed by any one*" then "came up behind him, and touched the fringe of his garment; and immediately her flow of blood ceased" (Luke 8:43–44). There were no doubt many people beyond the help of physicians who came whenever Jesus was teaching and healing, yet we read that "*all* those who had *any* that were sick with various diseases brought them to him; and he laid his hands on *every one of them* and healed them" (Luke 4:40). There was no disease that Jesus was unable to heal.

4. Does the New Testament Show Common Methods Used in Healing? The methods used by Jesus and the disciples to bring healing varied from case to case, but most frequently they included laying on of hands.[28] In the verse just quoted, Jesus no doubt could have spoken a powerful word of command and healed everyone in the large crowd instantly, but instead, "*he laid his hands on every one of them* and healed them" (Luke 4:40). Laying on of hands seems to have been the primary means Jesus used to heal, because when people came and asked him for healing they did not simply ask for prayer but said, for example, "come and lay your hand on her, and she will live" (Matt. 9:18).[29]

Another physical symbol of the Holy Spirit's power coming for healing was anointing with oil. Jesus' disciples "*anointed with oil* many that were sick and healed them" (Mark 6:13). And James tells the elders of the church to anoint the sick person with oil when they pray: "Is any among you sick? Let him call for the elders of the church, and let them pray over him, *anointing him with oil* in the name of the Lord; and the prayer of faith will save the sick man, and the Lord will raise him up; and if he has committed sins, he will be forgiven" (James 5:14–15).[30]

The New Testament often emphasizes the role of faith in the healing process—sometimes the faith of the sick person (Luke 8:48; 17:19), but at other times the faith of others who bring the sick person for healing. In James 5:15 it is the elders who pray, and James says it is "the prayer of faith" that saves the sick person—this then must be the faith of

---

[28]See the discussion of laying on of hands in chapter 6, section B.11.

[29]See also Luke 5:13; 13:13; Acts 28:8; also Mark 6:2, and several other verses in the gospels that mention laying on of hands. Jesus did not always heal in this way, however.

[30]The anointing with oil in James 5:14 should be understood as a symbol of the power of the Holy Spirit, not simply as medicinal, because oil would not be appropriate as a medicine for all diseases. Moreover, if its use were just medicinal, it is hard to see why only the elders should apply it. Oil is frequently a symbol of the Holy Spirit in the Old Testament (see Ex. 29:7; 1 Sam. 16:13; cf. Ps. 45:7), and this seems to be the case here as well. (See the thorough discussion in Douglas J. Moo, *The Letter of James*, TNTC [Downers Grove, Ill.: InterVarsity Press, 1985], pp. 177–81.)

the elders praying,[31] not the faith of the one who is sick. When the four men let down a paralytic through a hole in the roof where Jesus was preaching, we read, "And when Jesus saw *their* faith . . ." (Mark 2:5). At other times Jesus mentions the faith of the Canaanite woman regarding the healing of her daughter (Matt. 15:28), or of the centurion for the healing of his servant (Matt. 8:10, 13).[32]

5. How Then Should We Pray for Healing? How then should we pray regarding physical illness? Certainly it is right to ask God for healing, for Jesus tells us to pray, "Deliver us from evil" (Matt. 6:13), and the apostle John writes to Gaius, "I pray that all may go well with you and *that you may be in health*" (3 John 2). Moreover, Jesus frequently healed *all* who were brought to him, and he never sent people away, telling them it would be good for them to remain ill for a longer time! In addition to this, whenever we take any kind of medicine or seek any medical help for an illness, *by those actions we admit that we think it to be God's will that we seek to be well.* If we thought that God wanted us to continue in our illness, we would never seek medical means for healing! So when we pray it seems right that our first assumption, unless we have specific reason to think otherwise, should be that God would be pleased to heal the person we are praying for—as far as we can tell from Scripture, this is God's revealed will.[33]

Ken Blue has a helpful observation here. He argues that if we want to understand God's attitude toward physical healing we should look at Jesus' life and ministry. Blue says, "If Jesus truly reveals the character of God to us, then we may cease speculating about and arguing over God's will in sickness and healing. Jesus healed people because he loved them. Very simply, he had compassion for them; he was on their side; he wanted to solve their problems."[34] This is a strong argument, especially when coupled with the realization that Jesus came to inaugurate the presence of the kingdom of God among us and to show us what the kingdom of God would be like.

How then should we pray? Certainly it is right to ask God for healing, and we should go to him with the simple request that he give physical healing in time of need. James warns us that simple unbelief can lead to prayerlessness and failure to receive answers from God: "You do not have, because you do not ask" (James 4:2). But when we pray for healing we should remember that we must pray for God to be glorified in the situation, whether he chooses to heal or not. And we also ought to pray out of the same compassion of heart that Jesus felt for those whom he healed. When we pray this way, God will sometimes—and perhaps often—grant answers to our prayers.

---

[31]We may wonder why it is the elders who are called to come and pray for healing in James 5:14–15. Although James does not give a reason, it may be because they had responsibilities for pastoral care, maturity and wisdom in dealing with the possible sin involved (see vv. 15–16), and a measure of spiritual authority that accompanied their office. They would certainly be able to bring others with gifts of healing if they wished. Moreover, James broadens his directions to include all Christians in v. 16: "Therefore confess your sins to one another, and *pray for one another, that you may be healed.*"

[32]By contrast, we can note that when the disciples could not cast out a demon, Jesus says it was "because of your little faith" (Matt. 17:20).

[33]Of course we realize that God's *secret* will, unknown to us in any specifics, is that not all will be healed, just as it is his secret will that not all will be saved. But in both situations we should pray for what we see in Scripture to be God's revealed will: to save sinners and to heal those who are ill.

[34]Blue, *Authority to Heal*, pp. 72, 78.

Someone may object at this point that, from a pastoral standpoint, much harm is done when people are encouraged to believe that a miracle of healing will occur and then nothing happens—disappointment with the church and anger at God may result. Those who pray for people to be healed today need to hear this objection and use wisdom in what they tell people who are ill.

But we also need to realize that there is more than one kind of mistake to make: (1) *Not praying for healing at all* is not a correct solution, for it involves disobedience to James 5. (2) Telling people that *God seldom heals today* and that they should expect nothing to happen is not a correct solution either, for it does not provide an atmosphere conducive to faith and is inconsistent with the pattern we see in the ministry of Jesus and the early church in the New Testament. (3) Telling people that *God always heals today* if we have enough faith is a cruel teaching not supported by Scripture (see section 6 below).

The pastorally wise solution, it seems, lies between (2) and (3) above. We can tell people that God frequently heals today (if we believe that is true), and that it is very possible that they will be healed,[35] but that we are still living in an age when the kingdom of God is "already" here but "not yet" fully here. Therefore Christians in this life will experience healing (and many other answers to prayer), but they will also experience continuing illness and eventual death. In each individual case it is God's sovereign wisdom that decides the outcome, and our role is simply to ask him and wait for him to answer (whether "yes" or "no" or "keep praying and wait").

Those with "gifts of healings" (a literal translation of the plurals in 1 Cor. 12:9, 28) will be those people who find that their prayers for healing are answered more frequently and more thoroughly than others. When that becomes evident, a church would be wise to encourage them in this ministry and give them more opportunities to pray for others who are ill. We should also realize that gifts of healing could include ministry not only in terms of physical healing, but also in terms of emotional healing. And it may at times include the ability to set people free from demonic attack, for this is also called "healing" sometimes in Scripture (see Luke 6:18; Acts 10:38). Perhaps the gifts of being able to pray effectively in different kinds of situations and for different kinds of needs are what Paul referred to when he used the plural expression, *"gifts of healings."*

6. But What if God Does Not Heal? Nonetheless, we must realize that not all prayers for healing will be answered in this age. Sometimes God will not grant the special "faith" (James 5:15) that healing will occur, and at times God will choose not to heal, because of his own sovereign purposes. In these cases we must remember that Romans 8:28 is still true: though we experience the "sufferings of this present time," and though we "groan inwardly as we wait for . . . the redemption of our bodies" (Rom. 8:18, 23), nonetheless, "we know that in everything God works for good with those who love him, who are called

---

[35]Sometimes God may grant a strong subjective assurance of faith, something like what James calls "the prayer of faith" (James 5:15), and Heb. 11:1 calls "the assurance of things hoped for," and Mark 11:24 calls believing "that you have received it." In those cases the person praying may feel confidence to say that it is probable or even very likely that someone will be healed. But I do not think that God gives anyone warrant to promise or "guarantee" healing in this age, for his written Word makes no such guarantee, and our subjective sense of his will is always subject to some degree of uncertainty and some measure of error in this life.

according to his purpose" (Rom. 8:28). This includes working in our circumstances of suffering and illness as well.

Whatever Paul's "thorn in the flesh" was (and centuries of work by Bible-believing interpreters have failed to turn up a definitive answer), Paul realized that God allowed it to remain with him "to keep me from being too elated" (2 Cor. 12:7), that is, to keep Paul humble before the Lord.[36] So the Lord told him, "My grace is sufficient for you, for my power is made perfect in weakness" (2 Cor. 12:9). There are indications in the early church that even in the presence of the apostles not all people were healed. Paul recognized that "our outer nature is wasting away" (2 Cor. 4:16), and sometimes disease and illness will not be healed. When Epaphroditus came to visit Paul, he had an illness that brought him "near to death" (Phil. 2:27). Paul indicates in the narrative of Philippians 2 that it appeared as though Epaphroditus were going to die—that God did not heal him immediately when he became ill. But eventually God did heal (Phil. 2:27) in answer to prayer. Paul told Timothy that he should drink a little wine "for the sake of your stomach and your frequent ailments" (1 Tim. 5:23). He said, "Trophimus I left *ill* at Miletus" (2 Tim. 4:20). And both Peter (1 Peter 1:6–7; 4:19) and James (James 1:2–4) have words of encouragement and counsel for those who are suffering trials of various kinds:[37]

> Count it all joy, my brethren, when you meet various trials, for you know that the testing of your faith produces steadfastness. And let steadfastness have its full effect, that you may be perfect and complete, lacking in nothing. (James 1:2–4)

When God chooses not to heal, even though we ask him for it, then it is right that we "give thanks in all circumstances" (1 Thess. 5:18) and realize that God can use sickness to draw us closer to himself and to increase in us obedience to his will. So the psalmist can say, "*It is good for me that I was afflicted,* that I might learn your statutes" (Ps. 119:71), and, "Before I was afflicted I went astray; but now I keep your word" (Ps. 119:67).

---

[36]After some study of 2 Cor. 12:7, my own conclusion at this point is that there is not enough information in the text to decide what Paul's thorn in the flesh was. There are reasons that can be given in support of all three main possibilities: (1) a physical ailment of some kind; (2) a demon that was harassing him; or (3) Jewish persecutors. The fact that we are unable to decide conclusively has some benefits, however: it means that we can apply this text to all of these kinds of situations in our own lives, when the Lord in his sovereign wisdom decides not to remove them from us.

[37]Some have attempted to establish a difference between sickness and other kinds of suffering, and to say that the passages in Scripture that tell Christians they should expect to suffer have to do with *other* kinds of suffering, such as persecution, but do not include physical sickness.

This argument seems unconvincing to me for two reasons: first, Scripture talks about "*various trials*" (James 1:2; also 1 Peter 1:6), and the intention of the authors in both cases seems to be to speak of *all* the kinds of trials that we

experience in this life, including physical illness and affliction. Did James and Peter *not* want Christians who were ill to apply those passages to their own situations? This is hardly likely. (These are both general epistles written to thousands of Christians.)

Second, unless the Lord returns, we will all know the progressive aging and deterioration of our physical bodies, and eventually we will die. Paul says, "Our outer nature is wasting away" (2 Cor. 4:16). Almost inevitably this aging process includes various kinds of physical ailments.

It seems best to conclude that the sufferings which God allows us to experience from time to time in this life may at times include physical illness, which God in his sovereign wisdom decides not to heal. There may in fact be many cases when, for various reasons, we do not feel freedom to ask in faith for God to heal. Yet even in these cases the heart of faith will take God's Word as true and believe that this also has come into our lives "for good" (Rom. 8:28), and that God will bring good to us from it.

Therefore God can bring increased sanctification to us through illness and suffering—just as he can bring sanctification and growth in faith through miraculous healing. But the emphasis of the New Testament, both in Jesus' ministry and in the ministry of the disciples in Acts, seems to be one that encourages us in most cases eagerly and earnestly to seek God for healing, and then to continue to trust him to bring good out of the situation, whether he grants the physical healing or not. The point is that in everything God should receive glory and our joy and trust in him should increase.

E. Tongues and Interpretation

It should be said at the outset that the Greek word *glōssa,* translated "tongue," is used not only to mean the physical tongue in a person's mouth, but also to mean "language." In the New Testament passages where speaking in tongues is discussed, the meaning "languages" is certainly in view. It is unfortunate, therefore, that English translations have continued to use the phrase "speaking in tongues," which is an expression not otherwise used in ordinary English and which gives the impression of a strange experience, something completely foreign to ordinary human life. But if English translations were to use the expression "speaking in languages," it would not seem nearly as strange, and would give the reader a sense much closer to what first century Greek speaking readers would have heard in the phrase when they read it in Acts or 1 Corinthians.[38] However, because current usage of the phrase "speaking in tongues" is so widely established, we will continue to use it in this discussion.

1. Tongues in the History of Redemption. The phenomenon of speaking in tongues is unique to the new covenant age. Before Adam and Eve fell into sin, there was no need to speak in other languages, because they spoke the *same language* and were *united in service of God* and in fellowship with him. After the fall people spoke the *same language* but eventually became *united in opposition to God,* and "the wickedness of man was great in the earth" and "every imagination of the thoughts of his heart was only evil continually" (Gen. 6:5). This unified language used in rebellion against God culminated in the building of the tower of Babel at a time when "the whole earth had one language and few words" (Gen. 11:1). In order to stop this united rebellion against him, God at Babel "confused the language of all the earth" and scattered people abroad over the face of the earth (Gen. 11:9).

When God called Abraham to himself (Gen. 12:1), he promised to make of Abraham a "great nation" (Gen. 12:2), and the nation of Israel that resulted from this call had one language that God wanted them to use in service for him. Yet this language was not spoken by the rest of the nations of the world, and they remained outside the reach of God's plan of redemption. So the situation was improved somewhat, for *one language out of all the languages of the world was used in service of God,* whereas in Genesis 11 God was not praised with any language.

---

[38]The NIV margin does translate "or *languages*" or *"other languages"* in Acts 2:4, 11; 10:46; 19:6, and throughout 1 Cor. 12–14. This is a preferable translation, for reasons mentioned above.

Now if we pass over the age of the New Testament church and look at eternity future, we see that once again unity of language will be restored, but this time everyone will once again speak the *same language in service of God,* and in praise to him (Rev. 7:9–12; cf. Zeph. 3:9; 1 Cor. 13:8; perhaps Isa. 19:18).

In the New Testament church, there is something of a foretaste of the unity of language that will exist in heaven, but it is given only at some times, and only in a partial way. At Pentecost, which was the point at which the gospel began to go to all nations, it was appropriate that the disciples gathered in Jerusalem "began to speak in other tongues, as the Spirit gave them utterance" (Acts 2:4).[39] The result was that Jewish visitors to Jerusalem from various nations all heard in their own languages a proclamation of "the mighty works of God" (Acts 2:11). This was a remarkable symbol of the fact that the gospel message was about to go forth to all the nations of the world.[40] Such a symbolic action would have been inappropriate in the Old Testament, for there the evangelistic message was one of inviting people from other nations to come and join themselves to the Jewish people and become Jews, and thereby worship God. But here the message is about to go to each nation in its own language, inviting people in every place to turn to Christ and be saved.[41]

Moreover, within the context of the worship service of the church, speaking in tongues plus interpretation gives further indication of a promise that one day the differences in languages that originated at Babel will be overcome. If this gift is operating in a church, no matter what language a word of prayer or praise is given in, once there is an interpretation, everyone can understand it. This is, of course, a two-step process that is "imperfect," as are all gifts in this age (1 Cor. 13:9), but it is still an improvement on the situation from Babel to Pentecost when there was no provision to enable people to understand a message in a language they did not know.

Finally, prayer in tongues in a private setting is another form of prayer to God. Paul says, "If I pray in a tongue, *my spirit prays* but my mind is unfruitful" (1 Cor. 14:14). In the overall context of the history of redemption, this also may be seen as one more partial solution to the results of the fall, whereby we were cut off from fellowship with God. Of course, this does not mean that people's spirits can *only* have fellowship with God when they speak in tongues—for Paul affirms that he prays and sings both in tongues and in his own language (1 Cor. 14:15). However, Paul does see prayer in tongues as an additional means of fellowship directly with God in prayer and worship. Once again, this aspect of the gift of speaking in tongues was not operative, so far as we know, before the new covenant age.

2. What Is Speaking in Tongues? We may define this gift as follows: *Speaking in tongues is prayer or praise spoken in syllables not understood by the speaker.*

---

[39]This verse shows that the miracle was one of speaking, not of hearing. The disciples "began to *speak* in other tongues (or languages)."

[40]The speaking in tongues at Pentecost was unusual in that it was accompanied by "tongues as of fire, distributed and resting on each one of them" (Acts 2:3). Since fire in Scripture is often a symbol of God's purifying judgment, the presence of fire here may be a symbol of the fact that God was purifying language for use in his service.

[41]It is true that the first hearers of this message were still only Jews in Jerusalem (Acts 2:5), not Gentiles, but the symbolism of the gospel being proclaimed in many languages did give an indication of the worldwide evangelistic effort that would soon follow.

a. Words of Prayer or Praise Spoken to God: This definition indicates that speaking in tongues is primarily speech directed toward God (that is, prayer or praise). Therefore it is unlike the gift of prophecy, which frequently consists of messages directed *from* God toward people in the church. Paul says, "one who speaks in a tongue speaks not to men but *to God*" (1 Cor. 14:2), and if there is no interpreter present at the church service, Paul says that someone who has a gift of speaking in tongues should "keep silence in church and speak to himself and *to God*" (1 Cor. 14:28).

What kind of speech is this that is directed toward God? Paul says, "If I *pray* in a tongue, *my spirit prays* but my mind is unfruitful" (1 Cor. 14:14; cf. vv. 14–17, where Paul categorizes speech in tongues as praying and giving thanks, and v. 28). Therefore speaking in tongues apparently is prayer or praise directed to God, and it comes from the "spirit" of the person who is speaking. This is not inconsistent with the narrative in Acts 2, because the crowd said, "we hear them telling in our own tongues the mighty works of God" (Acts 2:11), a description that certainly could mean that the disciples were all glorifying God and proclaiming his mighty works in worship, and the crowd began to listen to this as it occurred in various languages. In fact, there is no indication that the disciples themselves were speaking to the crowd until Acts 2:14, when Peter then stands and addresses the crowd directly, presumably in Greek.[42]

b. Not Understood by the Speaker: Paul says that "one who speaks in a tongue speaks not to men but to God; *for no one understands him,* but he utters mysteries in the Spirit" (1 Cor. 14:2). Similarly, he says that if there is speaking in tongues without interpretation no meaning will be communicated: "I shall be a foreigner to the speaker and the speaker a foreigner to me" (1 Cor. 14:11). Moreover, the entire paragraph of 1 Corinthians 14:13–19 assumes that speech in tongues in the congregation, when it is not accompanied by interpretation, is not understood by those who hear:

> Therefore, he who speaks in a tongue should pray for the power to interpret. For if I pray in a tongue, my spirit prays but my mind is unfruitful. What am I to do? I will pray with the spirit and I will pray with the mind also; I will sing with the spirit and I will sing with the mind also. Otherwise, if you bless with the spirit, how can any one in the position of an outsider say the "Amen" to your thanksgiving when he does not know what you are saying? For you may give thanks well enough, but the other man is not edified. I thank God that I speak in tongues more than you all; nevertheless, in church I would rather speak five words with my mind, *in order to instruct others,* than ten thousand words in a tongue.

---

[42]In Acts 10:46 the people at Cornelius' household began "speaking in tongues and extolling God." Again, this either means that the speech consisted of praise to God or was very closely connected with it—grammatically one cannot tell from the text itself.

I do not want to rule out the possibility that speaking in tongues could sometimes include speech directed to people, not to God, because it is just possible that Paul's statement in 1 Cor. 14:2 is a generalization that is not intended to cover every instance, and, in any case, the main point of the verse is that only God can *understand* uninterpreted tongues, not that God is the only one to whom speech in tongues can be addressed. In fact, speech to men might be what is happening in Acts 2. Nevertheless, the evidence that we do have in 1 Cor. 14 indicates speech directed toward God, and it seems safe to say that that is generally what speaking in tongues will be.

Now at Pentecost speech in tongues was in known languages that were understood by those who heard: "each one heard them speaking *in his own language*" (Acts 2:6). But once again the speech was not understood by the speakers, for what caused the amazement was that Galileans were speaking all these different languages (v. 7). It seems, therefore, that *at times* speaking in tongues may involve speech in actual human languages, sometimes even languages that are understood by some of those who hear. But at other times—and Paul assumes that this will ordinarily be the case—the speech will be in a language that "no one understands" (1 Cor. 14:2).

Some have objected that speaking in tongues must always consist of speech in *known* human languages, since that is what happened at Pentecost. But the fact that speaking in tongues occurred in known human languages *once* in Scripture does not require that it *always* happen with known languages, especially when another description of speaking in tongues (1 Cor. 14) indicates exactly the opposite. Paul does not say that foreign visitors to Corinth will understand the speaker, but he says that when someone speaks in tongues *"no one"* will understand and the outsider will not know what the person is saying (1 Cor. 14:2, 16).[43] In fact, Paul explicitly says that quite the opposite of the phenomenon at Pentecost will happen in the ordinary conduct of church life: if "all speak in tongues" and "outsiders or unbelievers enter," far from understanding the message, they will say "that you are mad" (1 Cor. 14:23). Moreover, we must realize that 1 Corinthians 14 is Paul's general instruction based on a wide experience of tongues-speaking in many different churches, whereas Acts 2 simply describes one unique event at a significant turning point in the history of redemption (Acts 2 is historical narrative while 1 Cor. 14 is doctrinal instruction). Therefore it would seem appropriate to take 1 Corinthians 14 as the passage that most closely describes the ordinary experience of New Testament churches, and to take Paul's instructions there as the standard by which God intends churches to regulate the use of this gift.[44]

Are tongues known human languages then? Sometimes this gift may result in speaking in a human language that the speaker has not learned, but ordinarily it seems that it will involve speech in a language that no one understands, whether that be a human language or not.[45]

---

[43]Robertson and Plummer note that 1 Cor. 14:18, "I thank God that I speak in tongues more than you all," is "strong evidence that Tongues are not foreign languages" (A. Robertson and A. Plummer, *A Critical and Exegetical Commentary on the First Epistle of St. Paul to the Corinthians,* ICC [Edinburgh: T. & T. Clark, 1914], p. 314). If they were known foreign languages that foreigners could understand, as at Pentecost, why would Paul speak more than all the Corinthians in private, where no one would understand, rather than in church where foreign visitors could understand?

[44]Note that at Pentecost this speaking in tongues had another characteristic that was not shared by any later speech in tongues: there were tongues of fire appearing over the heads of those who spoke (Acts 2:3). But this is not a paradigm for all later experiences of speaking in tongues, not even for those found later in Acts.

[45]Paul does say, "If I speak in the tongues of men *and of angels*" (1 Cor. 13:1), suggesting that he sees the possibility that speaking in tongues may include more than merely human speech. Whether he thinks this is only a hypothetical possibility or a real one is difficult to say, but we certainly cannot rule out the idea that angelic languages would be involved with this speech as well.

Some have objected that since *glōssa* elsewhere in Greek (outside the New Testament) refers to *known* human languages, it must refer to known languages in the New Testament as well. But this objection is not convincing, since there was no other word in Greek better suited to refer to this phenomenon, even if it involved talking to God in languages that were not human languages or not fully developed languages of any sort, so long as some content or information was conveyed by the speech. I am not here arguing that speaking in tongues

c. Prayer With the Spirit, Not With the Mind: Paul says: "If I pray in a tongue, *my spirit prays* but my *mind is unfruitful.* What am I to do? I will pray with the spirit and I will pray with the mind also; I will sing with the spirit and I will sing with the mind also" (1 Cor. 14:14–15).

Paul is not here talking about the Holy Spirit praying through us. The contrast between "my spirit" and "my mind" in verse 14 indicates that it is Paul's own human spirit that he is talking about, the nonmaterial aspect of his being. As he uses this gift, his spirit speaks directly to God, even though his mind does not have to formulate words and sentences and decide what to pray for.[46] Paul sees this kind of prayer as an activity that occurs in the spiritual realm, whereby our spirits speak directly to God but our mind is somehow bypassed and does not understand what we are praying.

We may wonder why God would give the church a gift that operates in the unseen, spiritual realm and that is not understood by our minds. One reason may be to keep us humble, and to help prevent intellectual pride. Another reason may be to remind us that God is greater than our understanding and that he works in ways that transcend our understanding. Finally, it is characteristic of much that God does in the new covenant age that it is done in the unseen, spiritual realm: regeneration, genuine prayer, worship "in spirit and in truth," the spiritual blessings that come through the Lord's Supper, spiritual warfare, laying up treasures in heaven, setting our minds on things above, where Christ is—all these and many more elements of the Christian life involve activities that occur in the unseen, spiritual realm, activities that we do not see or fully understand. In that light, speaking in tongues is simply another activity that occurs in the unseen spiritual realm, an activity we believe is effective because Scripture tells us it is, not because we can comprehend it with our minds (cf. 1 Cor. 14:5).

d. Not Ecstatic but Self-controlled: The New English Bible translated the phrase "speaking in tongues" as "ecstatic speech," thus giving further support to the idea that those who speak in tongues lose awareness of their surroundings or lose self-control or are forced to speak against their will. Moreover, some of the extreme elements in the Pentecostal movement have allowed frenzied and disorderly conduct at worship services, and this has, in the minds of some, perpetuated the notion that speaking in tongues is a kind of ecstatic speech.

---

in Acts 2 was a different phenomenon from the speaking in tongues that Paul discusses in 1 Cor. 14. I am simply saying that the phrase "speaking in tongues" in Acts 2 and 1 Cor. 14 refers to speech in syllables not understood by the speaker but understood by God, to whom this speech is directed. In Acts 2 this happened to be speech in known human languages that had not been learned by the speakers, whereas in 1 Cor. 14 the speech may have been in unknown human languages, or in angelic languages, or in some specialized kind of language given by the Holy Spirit to various speakers individually. The expression is broad enough to include a wide variety of phenomena.

[46]The phrase "pray in the Holy Spirit" in Jude 20 is not the same expression, since it is specifically the "Holy Spirit"

who is designated. Jude is simply saying that Christians should pray in conformity to the character and leading of the Holy Spirit, and that may certainly include prayer in tongues, but it would include any other kind of prayer in an understandable language as well. Similarly, "Pray at all times *in the Spirit,* with all prayer and supplication" (Eph. 6:18) is specifically a statement that claims to cover all prayer that is made at all times. It refers to prayer in conformity to the character of the Holy Spirit and sensitive to the leading of the Holy Spirit, but it should not be restricted to speaking in tongues. Once again, it may include speaking in tongues, but should include all other types of prayer as well.

But this is not the picture given in the New Testament. Even when the Holy Spirit came with overwhelming power at Pentecost, the disciples were able to stop speaking in tongues so that Peter could give his sermon to the assembled crowd. More explicitly, Paul says:

If any speak in a tongue, let there be *only two or at most three, and each in turn;* and let one interpret. But if there is no one to interpret, let each of them keep silence in church and speak to himself and to God. (1 Cor. 14:27–28)

Here Paul requires that those who speak in tongues take turns, and he limits the number to three, indicating clearly that those who spoke in tongues were aware of what was going on around them, and were able to control themselves so as to speak only when it was their turn, and when no one else was speaking. If there was no one to interpret, they were easily able to keep silence and not speak. All of these factors indicate a high degree of self-control and give no support to the idea that Paul thought of tongues as ecstatic speech of some kind.

e. Tongues Without Interpretation: If no one known to have the gift of interpretation is present in the assembly, the passage just quoted indicates that speaking in tongues should be in private. No speech in tongues without interpretation should be given in the church service.[47]

Paul speaks of praying in tongues and singing in tongues when he says, "I will *pray with the spirit* and I will pray with the mind also; I will *sing with the spirit* and I will sing with the mind also" (1 Cor. 14:15). This gives further confirmation to the definition given above in which we viewed tongues as something primarily directed toward God in prayer and praise. It also gives legitimacy to the practice of singing in tongues, whether publicly or privately. Yet the same rules apply for singing as for speaking: if there is no interpreter, it should only be done in private.[48]

In 1 Corinthians 14:20–25 Paul says that if believers speak in tongues without interpretation in church, they will be acting and thinking like "children" (1 Cor. 14:20). He first quotes a prophecy of judgment from Isaiah 28:11–12: "In the law it is written, 'By

---

[47]It is troubling that, in some churches today where speaking in tongues is allowed, those who do *not* give a message publicly (perhaps because it is not the appropriate time in the service or perhaps because they do not know if someone will interpret) will still sometimes speak in tongues not "silently" but so that four or five people nearby can hear their speech in tongues. This is simply disobedience to Paul's directive, and is not acting in love toward others in the church. Paul says to "keep *silence* in church" if one is not giving a public message in tongues. (Many who have spoken in tongues today say that it can easily be done in an inaudible whisper, so that no one else will hear, and Paul's directions will be obeyed.)

[48]Many churches today, however, practice what is sometimes called "singing in the Spirit," in which many or all the congregation will simultaneously sing in tongues, individually improvising their melodies around a certain dominant musical chord. While many people will testify that there is beauty and spiritual power in such occurrences, once again we must object that it is directly contrary to Paul's instructions in 1 Cor. 14:27–28, where those who speak in tongues are to take turns, and there are to be at most three in a worship service, and interpretation is to follow. Though this practice may sound beautiful to those who are familiar with it, and though God may at times graciously use it as a means of winning an unbeliever, Paul explicitly says that the expected result generally will be that unbelievers will say "that you are mad" (1 Cor. 14:23). An alternative to this practice, and one that would both be consistent with Scripture and follow the path of love toward outsiders, would be for everyone to sing in this way, not in tongues, but in an understandable language (whether English or whatever language is commonly understood in the area where the church assembles).

men of strange tongues and by the lips of foreigners will I speak to this people, and even then they will not listen to me, says the Lord' " (1 Cor. 14:21).

In the context of Isaiah 28, God is warning the rebellious people of Israel that the next words they heard from him would be words of foreigners that they could not under-stand—the Assyrian army would come on them as agents of God's judgment. Now Paul is about to take this as a general principle—when God speaks to people in language they cannot understand, it is quite evidently a sign of God's judgment.

Paul rightly applies that to the situation of speaking in tongues without interpretation in the church service. He calls it a sign (that is, a sign of judgment) on unbelievers:

> Thus, *tongues are a sign* not for believers but *for unbelievers, while prophecy is* not for unbelievers but *for believers.* If, therefore, the whole church assembles and all speak in tongues, and outsiders or unbelievers enter, will they not say that you are mad? (1 Cor. 14:22–23)

Here Paul uses the word "sign" to mean *"sign of God's attitude"* (whether positive or negative). Tongues that are not understood by outsiders are certainly a *negative* sign—a sign of judgment. Therefore Paul cautions the Corinthians not to give such a sign to outsiders who come in. He tells them if an outsider comes in and hears only unintel-ligible speech, he will certainly not be saved but will conclude that the Corinthians are mad, and the uninterpreted tongues will in his case function as a sign of God's judgment.

By contrast, Paul says that prophecy is a sign of God's attitude as well, but here a *posi-tive* sign of God's blessing. This is why he can say that prophecy is a sign "for believers" (v. 22). And this is why he concludes his section by saying, "If all prophesy, and an unbe-liever or outsider enters, he is convicted by all, he is called to account by all, the secrets of his heart are disclosed; and so, falling on his face, he will worship God and declare that God is really among you" (vv. 24–25). When this happens, believers will certainly realize that God is active among them to bring blessing, and prophecy will regularly function as a sign *for believers* of God's positive attitude for them.[49]

Nevertheless, however much Paul warns against using tongues without interpretation *in church,* he certainly views it positively and encourages it in *private.* He says, "He who speaks in a tongue *edifies himself,* but he who prophesies edifies the church" (1 Cor. 14:4). What is his conclusion? It is not (as some would argue) that Christians should decide not to use the gift or decide that it has no value when used privately. Rather he says, "What am I to do? I will pray with the spirit and I will pray with the mind also" (v. 15). And he says, "I thank God that I speak in tongues more than you all" (v. 18), and "Now *I want you all to speak in tongues,* but even more to prophesy" (v. 5), and "Earnestly desire to prophesy, and do not forbid speaking in tongues" (v. 39). If our previous understand-ing of tongues as prayer or praise to God is correct, then we would certainly expect that edification would follow, even though the speaker's mind does not understand what is

---

[49]For further discussion of this passage, see Wayne Grudem, "1 Corinthians 14:20–25: Prophecy and Tongues as Signs of God's Attitude," *WTJ* 41:2 (Spring 1979), pp. 381–96.

being said, but his or her own human spirit is communicating directly with God. Just as prayer and worship in general edify us as we engage in them, so this kind of prayer and worship edifies us too, according to Paul.

f. Tongues With Interpretation: Edification for the Church: Paul says, "He who prophesies is greater than he who speaks in tongues, *unless someone interprets,* so that the church may be edified" (1 Cor. 14:5). Once a message in tongues is interpreted, all can understand. In that case, Paul says that the message in tongues is *as valuable* to the church as prophecy. He does not say they have the same functions (for other passages indicate that prophecy is communication from God toward humans, while tongues is generally communication from humans to God). But Paul clearly says they have equal value in edifying the church. We may define the gift of interpretation as *reporting to the church the general meaning of something spoken in tongues.*

g. Not All Speak in Tongues: Just as not all Christians are apostles, and not all are prophets or teachers, and not all possess gifts of healing, so not all speak with tongues. Paul clearly implies this when he asks a series of questions, all of which expect the answer "no," and includes the question "Do all speak with tongues?" (1 Cor. 12:30). The implied answer is no.[50] Some have argued that Paul here only means that not all speak with tongues *publicly,* but that perhaps he would have admitted that all can speak in tongues privately. But this distinction seems foreign to the context and unconvincing. He does not specify that not all speak with tongues *publicly* or *in church,* but simply says that not all speak with tongues. His next question is, "Do all interpret?" (v. 30). His previous two questions were, "Do all work miracles? Do all possess gifts of healing?" (vv. 29–30). Would we wish to make the same arguments about these gifts—that not all interpret tongues *publicly,* but that all Christians are able to do it *privately?* Or that not all work miracles publicly, but that all are able to work miracles privately? Such a distinction seems unwarranted by the context in every case.

In actuality, the desire to say that every Christian can speak in tongues (even though Paul says that not all speak in tongues) is probably motivated in most cases by a prior doctrinal understanding that views baptism in the Holy Spirit as an experience subsequent to conversion, and sees speaking in tongues as an initial "sign" of receiving this baptism in the Holy Spirit.[51] But there are serious questions that remain about this doctrinal position. It seems better to take 1 Corinthians 12:30 to mean just what it says: not all speak in tongues. The gift of tongues—just like every other gift—is not given by the Holy Spirit to every Christian who seeks it. He "apportions to each one individually as he wills" (1 Cor. 12:11).

However, there is nothing in Scripture that says that only a few will receive the gift of speaking in tongues, and, since it is a gift Paul views as edifying and useful in prayer and worship (on a personal level even if not in church), it would not be surprising if the

---

[50]The Greek particle *mē,* which precedes this question, expects the answer "no" from the reader. The NASB captures this sense: "All do not speak with tongues, do they?"

[51]This is still the official doctrinal position of the Assemblies of God, for example.

Holy Spirit gave a very widespread distribution of this gift and many Christians in fact received it.[52]

h. What About the Danger of Demonic Counterfeit? At times Christians have been afraid to speak in tongues, wondering if speaking something they do not understand might involve them in speaking blasphemy against God or speaking something that is prompted by a demon rather than by the Holy Spirit.

First, it must be said that this is not Paul's concern, even in the city of Corinth where many had come from pagan temple worship, and where Paul had clearly said that "what pagans sacrifice they offer to demons and not to God" (1 Cor. 10:20). Nonetheless, Paul says, "I want you all to speak in tongues" (1 Cor. 14:5). He gives no warning that they should beware of demonic counterfeit or even think that this would be a possibility when they use this gift.

The theological reason underlying Paul's encouragement at that point is the fact that the Holy Spirit is working powerfully within the lives of believers. Paul says, "I want you to understand that no one speaking by the Spirit of God ever says 'Jesus be cursed!' and no one can say 'Jesus is Lord' except by the Holy Spirit" (1 Cor. 12:3). Here Paul reassures the Corinthians that if they are speaking by the power of the Holy Spirit working within them, they will not say, "Jesus be cursed!"[53] Coming as it does at the beginning of a discussion of spiritual gifts, 1 Corinthians 12:3 is intended to function as reassurance to the Corinthians who may have suspected some Christians who came from backgrounds of demon worship in the temples at Corinth. Might this demonic influence still affect their use of a spiritual gift? Paul lays down the ground rule that those who genuinely profess faith that "Jesus is Lord" are doing so by the Holy Spirit working within, and that no one speaking by the power of the Holy Spirit will ever speak blasphemy or curses against Jesus.[54] This fear, then, is not one that Paul seemed troubled by. He simply encouraged believers to pray in tongues and said that if they did so they would be edifying themselves.[55]

---

[52]Mark 16:17 is sometimes used to claim that all Christians can speak in tongues: "And these signs will accompany those who believe: in my name they will cast out demons; they will speak in new tongues." But in response to this verse it must be noted (1) that the verse probably was not originally part of Mark's gospel, since many early and very reliable manuscripts do not include Mark 16:9–20, and its doubtful status means that it is a precarious basis upon which to build doctrine (2) that even if it is not part of Scripture, it does of course bear witness to a very early tradition in the history of the church, but even in this case, it does not affirm that all believers will speak with tongues: the immediately following phrase says, "They will pick up serpents" (v. 18), something that no responsible interpreter would say should be true of every Christian; and (3) that no connection is made between speaking in tongues and baptism in the Holy Spirit in this passage.

[53]It might be objected at this point that speaking in tongues is not speech empowered by the Holy Spirit, but is speech that comes from the speaker's own human spirit. But Paul clearly

views all these spiritual gifts as generally *empowered* by the Holy Spirit, even the ones in which human personality comes fully into play. This would be true of teachers and helpers and administrators, as well as those who speak with tongues. In each of these cases the active agent in performing the activity is the Christian who has the particular gift and uses it, but all these are nonetheless empowered by the Holy Spirit in their functioning, and that would also be true of the gift of tongues as well.

[54]Also relevant at this point is John's reassurance to his readers, in the context of demonic spirits that had gone out into the world: "He who is in you is greater than he who is in the world" (1 John 4:4).

[55]Some popular books have given anecdotal accounts of Christians who say they spoke in tongues for a time and then found that there was a demon within them who was empowering this speech, and the demon was cast out. (See, for example, C. Fred Dickason, *Demon Possession and the Christian* [Westchester, Ill.: Crossway, 1987], pp. 126–27; 188–91; 193–97.) But this is just another example of a case where experience

i. Is Romans 8:26–27 Related to Speaking in Tongues? Paul writes in Romans 8:26–27:

> Likewise the Spirit helps us in our weakness; for we do not know how to pray as we ought, but the Spirit himself intercedes for us with sighs too deep for words. And he who searches the hearts of men knows what is the mind of the Spirit, because the Spirit intercedes for the saints according to the will of God.

Paul does not mention speaking in tongues explicitly here, and the statement is a general one concerning the life of all Christians, so it does not seem correct to say that Paul here is referring to speaking in tongues. He is referring to a more general experience that occurs in the prayer life of every Christian.

But what exactly is he talking about? Some have thought that he is referring to an intercessory activity completely imperceptible to us, in which the Holy Spirit intercedes for us by making sighs and groans to the Father. On this view, such intercessory work of the Spirit goes on continually, but we have no idea that it is happening (except for the fact that Scripture tells us this). In this way it would be similar to the intercessory work of Christ mentioned in Romans 8:34 and Hebrews 7:25.

But this does not appear to be a satisfactory explanation of the passage, for several reasons: (1) It would not seem probable that Paul would say that the intercessory work of the Holy Spirit, who is the infinite, omnipotent, omniscient God, would be carried out in "wordless *groans*" (literal translation of *stenagmois alalētois* in Rom. 8:26), especially

---

is to be subject to Scripture and tested by Scripture, and the teaching of Scripture should not be subject to experience. We must be careful that we not let such reports of experiences cause us to adopt a different position than Scripture itself on this issue. Specifically, if 1 Cor. 12–14 views tongues as a good gift from the Holy Spirit that is valuable for edification and for the good of the church, and if Paul can say, "I want you all to speak in tongues" (1 Cor. 14:5), then interpretations of contemporary experiences that, in effect, say, "I want you all to be afraid of tongues," go contrary to the emphasis of the New Testament. (Note Dickason's quotation of Kurt Koch: "Seeking this gift for ourselves can be a very dangerous experience" [p. 127].) This is just not the perspective Paul has in the New Testament.

I realize that Dickason has a cessationist view with respect to speaking in tongues today (see p. 189: "I told her I doubted that there were any genuine tongues from God today in the New Testament sense"). Therefore, from his perspective, he is not making Scripture subject to experience, but sees these experiences as confirming his understanding of Scripture. (I have discussed the cessationist position in chapter 10, section B.)

There is the possibility of demonic counterfeit of every gift *in the lives of unbelievers* (see Matt. 7:22). Therefore the fact that there is some kind of "speaking in tongues" in pagan religions should not surprise us or cause us to think that

all speaking in tongues is false. But *in the lives of believers,* especially when there is positive fruit in their lives and from their gifts, 1 Cor. 12:3, 1 John 4:4, Luke 11:11–13, and Matt. 7:16–20 tell us that these are not counterfeit gifts but real gifts from God. We must remember that Satan and demons do not do good; they do evil; and they do not bring blessing; they bring destruction.

(Neil T. Anderson, in *The Bondage Breaker* [Eugene, Oreg.: Harvest House, 1990], pp. 159–60, relates a story of a man who was apparently a Christian and who had a counterfeit gift of tongues. But Anderson notes that the gift was conferred on the man "by false teachers" [p. 159] and that this "gift" brought obviously destructive consequences in the man's life. These factors, and not just the words of a demon as the only evidence, gave clear indication of the counterfeit nature of that supposed "gift." Unlike Dickason, Anderson affirms that he is not opposed to speaking in tongues; see p. 160.)

An alternative explanation for the stories given by Dickason is to say that the demons who *said* they were "tongues spirits," and that they came in when some charismatics laid hands on the Christian in question, were lying. Satan "is a liar and the father of lies" (John 8:44), and he would love to have Christians afraid of as many of the Holy Spirit's gifts as possible.

when we realize that "groans" refers to the intense sighs of fatigue that are appropriate to weary, burdened creatures in a fallen world.[56] (2) Within the larger context the groanings in view seem to be those due to the burden of living in this present evil age, particularly the groans associated with our suffering in this age (see vv. 17, 18, 23). (3) The verb "helps" in Romans 8:26 ("The Spirit *helps* us in our weakness") does not refer to something the Holy Spirit does *apart from us and on our behalf,* but rather something the Holy Spirit does *in cooperation with us.* The verb Paul uses here (*sunantilambanomai*) is also used in Luke 10:40, where Martha wants Jesus to tell Mary "to *help* me"—certainly she does not want Mary to do the food preparation *instead* of her, but rather to come and take part *with* her in doing it.[57] Therefore Paul is not talking about something the Holy Spirit does completely apart from our participation, but something the Holy Spirit does in cooperation with our activity.

These reasons combine to indicate that Paul is not talking about a work of the Holy Spirit done apart from us and unknown by us, but about the inarticulate sighs and groans which we ourselves utter in prayer, which the Holy Spirit then makes into effective intercession before the throne of God. We could paraphrase, "The Holy Spirit assists our prayers when he intercedes (for us) by taking our wordless groans and making them into effective prayer."[58]

What is the relationship between this and speaking in tongues? There is some similarity because it is effective prayer which *we pray* even though we do not understand fully what we are praying. But there are some differences in that the sighs or groans that we utter in prayer very often relate to situations or hardships that we are very conscious of in our minds as we pray, so we know what we are praying about. But Paul says that we do not know how to pray for these situations as we ought to pray. Therefore the Holy Spirit helps us and intercedes in these situations "according to the will of God" (Rom. 8:27). There is no explicit mention of our spirit praying (though that may indeed be true as well), nor is there mention of our mind being unfruitful or lacking understanding (though that may at times be at least partially true). Nor do these sighs or groans come forth in anything that could be called "other tongues" or "other languages." So there are several differences, even though Romans 8:26–27 talks about intercession that we make in sounds that are not fully understood by us, and therefore it is a phenomenon that has some similarities to speaking in tongues.

---

[56]The word "groan" (*stenagmos*) is elsewhere used in the New Testament only at Acts 7:34, of the groanings of Israel under oppression in Egypt. But the related verb *stenazō* is used several times, always of finite creatures groaning under the burden of this fallen creation. In the immediately previous context *stenazō* refers to our groaning because our redemption is incomplete (Rom. 8:23; a related compound word is used in v. 22 of the creation itself). The verb is also used of finite creatures groaning under the burden of this creation in Mark 7:34 (Jesus as a man); 2 Cor. 5:2, 4 (believers who have a corruptible, earthly body); Heb. 13:17 (church leaders who may be tempted to groan under the burden of church leadership); and James 5:9 (a warning for Christians not to grumble or groan against one another). Though the verb was once used of Jesus who groaned while under the limitations of this human existence, it does not seem an appropriate term to use of the activity of the Holy Spirit, who would not experience a similar weakness because he never took on human nature.

[57]Though the word is not elsewhere used in the New Testament, its sense is also transparent from the *sun* ("with") prefix that Paul attaches to a very common word for "help."

[58]An alternative view is found in the helpful discussion by Douglas Moo, *Romans 1–8,* Wycliffe Exegetical Commentary (Chicago: Moody, 1991), pp. 559–63, who (hesitantly) understands the groans to be not ours but the Holy Spirit's.

F. Word of Wisdom and Word of Knowledge

Paul writes, "For to one is given the *word of wisdom* through the Spirit, and to another the *word of knowledge* according to the same Spirit" (1 Cor. 12:8 NASB). At the beginning of this discussion it must be understood that these two gifts are mentioned nowhere else in Scripture,[59] and no other early Christian literature outside the Bible has been found to use these phrases of any spiritual gift either. This means that the *only* information we have about these gifts is contained in this verse: we have the words used to describe these two gifts, and we have the context in which the phrases occur. No interpreter anywhere has any more information than this to work with. This warns us that our conclusions will probably be somewhat tentative in any case.

The major alternatives for understanding these gifts are two: (1) These gifts are commonly thought to be the ability to receive a special revelation from the Holy Spirit and on that basis to speak words that give wisdom in a situation or give specific knowledge of a situation in the life of someone present in a congregation. In this interpretation these gifts would be more "miraculous," in that they would call forth wonder and amazement from the people present since they would not be based on information ordinarily available to the person using the gift.

(2) The other interpretation of these gifts would see them as more "non-miraculous" or ordinary: the "word of wisdom" simply means the ability to speak a wise word in various situations, and "word of knowledge" is the ability to speak with knowledge about a situation. In both cases the knowledge and wisdom would not be based on a special revelation spontaneously given by the Holy Spirit, but would be based on wisdom acquired in the ordinary course of life, the knowledge and wisdom that would be characteristic of Bible teachers or elders and other mature Christians in a church, for example. These would be empowered by the Holy Spirit and thereby made effective when they were spoken. Examples of "words of wisdom" in this sense would be found in Acts 6:1–6 (the appointment of the first "deacons" or assistants to the apostles); Acts 6:10 (Stephen's wisdom in proclaiming the gospel); Acts 15:19–29 (the decision of the Jerusalem council); and even in King Solomon's statement, "Divide the living child in two, and give half to the one, and half to the other" (1 Kings 3:25; see also 1 Cor. 6:5–6).

In favor of the first interpretation, it might be argued that all the other seven gifts listed in 1 Corinthians 12:8–10 are in the "miraculous" category, and therefore these two gifts should be understood that way as well.

However, there are some weighty considerations against this view: (1) The words Paul uses for "word" (*logos*), "wisdom" (*sophia*), and "knowledge" (*gnōsis*) are not specialized or technical terms, but are extremely common words in the Greek New Testament. They are simply the ordinary words frequently used for "word" and "wisdom" and "knowledge." Moreover, they are not ordinarily used to denote miraculous events (as are the words *revelation* and *prophecy,* for example), but are simply the words used for human knowledge and wisdom. So from the meanings of the words themselves, no indication of a miraculous gift seems to be given.

---

[59]At least no other place in Scripture calls something a "word of wisdom" or "word of knowledge" or uses those phrases in any other way.

(2) In the context of 1 Corinthians 12:8, Paul's purpose in the argument seems to weigh against thinking of them as miraculous. Paul's larger purpose in verses 8–10 is to demonstrate that *no matter what kind of gift a person has,* he or she can be assured that that gift has been given by the Holy Spirit. He precedes the section by saying, "To *each* is given the manifestation of the Spirit for the common good," and follows this immediate section by saying, "All these are inspired by one and the same Spirit, who apportions to *each one* individually as he wills" (vv. 7, 11). But if Paul's purpose in this section is to show that *every Christian's gift* is given by the Holy Spirit, then that purpose would not be well served by giving only examples of miraculous gifts. If he did that, those with nonmiraculous gifts would feel left out of the argument and would not be persuaded that their gifts are included in Paul's discussion. Even more importantly, those with miraculous gifts might look at this list and conclude that *only* those with miraculous gifts really had the Holy Spirit at work within them to empower those gifts. This would lead to a dangerous kind of elitism in the congregation. Therefore it seems necessary that Paul would include some *nonmiraculous* gifts in his list in 1 Corinthians 12:8–10.

But which are the nonmiraculous gifts in this list?

Word of wisdom
Word of knowledge
Faith
Gifts of healings
Miracles
Prophecy
Distinguishing between spirits
Tongues
Interpretation of tongues

All the other gifts seem to fall in the more "miraculous" category (with the possible exceptions of speaking in tongues and perhaps faith). But that would make it almost necessary that word of wisdom and word of knowledge be nonmiraculous to guarantee that there are *some* nonmiraculous gifts in the list. This would demonstrate Paul's pastoral wisdom in selecting examples of different kinds of gifts being exercised in the actual congregation. So there must be some nonmiraculous gifts on the list—and if there are some, then these are very good candidates.[60]

(3) Probably the most decisive consideration is the fact that the New Testament already has a term to describe the action of receiving a special revelation from the Holy Spirit and reporting it in the congregation—this is what Paul calls "prophecy." Since he discusses prophecy at some length, describing it and regulating it, we can know fairly clearly what prophecy was. But to say that these other gifts functioned in exactly the same way (perhaps differing only in content) does not seem justified by anything in the text other than a preconceived notion of what these gifts should be.[61]

---

[60]Even if faith and tongues are considered non-miraculous, then we have a list that is a mixture of miraculous and non-miraculous gifts, and then there is no reason why word of wisdom and word of knowledge could not be considered non-miraculous as well, especially on the basis of the fact that the words used to describe them do not ordinarily denote miraculous events.

[61]In fact, everything that modern Pentecostal and charismatic Christians call "words of knowledge" and "words of wisdom" would fit exactly into the definition of prophecy

Therefore it would seem preferable to understand these in a "nonmiraculous" way, simply as the ability to speak with wisdom or with knowledge in various situations. What many people today call "word of wisdom" and "word of knowledge" in charismatic circles, it would seem better simply to refer to as "prophecy."[62]

G. Distinguishing Between Spirits and Spiritual Warfare

The gift of distinguishing between spirits is another gift that is mentioned only once in the New Testament (in the list at 1 Cor. 12:10), but the nature of this gift connects it with a number of other passages that describe the spiritual warfare that occurs between Christians and demonic spirits. We may define the gift of distinguishing between spirits as follows: *Distinguishing between spirits is a special ability to recognize the influence of the Holy Spirit or of demonic spirits in a person.*

In the perspective of the history of redemption, this gift also gives a foretaste of the age to come in that it is a foretaste of the ability to recognize Satan and his influence, which ability will be made perfect for us in heaven, when everything that is covered or hidden will be revealed and brought to the light (Matt. 10:26; cf. Rev. 20:11–15). This ability is probably also stronger than that possessed by most or all believers in the old covenant, where mentions of demonic activity are infrequent, and where demonic attacks against God's people most often were embodied in military attacks by unbelieving nations against the people of Israel, or in overt temptations to go and serve pagan deities. Demonic activity was therefore perceived primarily through observation of outward physical events and circumstances in which Satan's purpose was carried out, and which could be clearly seen.

This New Testament gift of distinguishing between spirits involves the ability to distinguish the presence of evil spirits from the presence of the work of the Holy Spirit in a person's life. Paul knows that the Corinthians previously were "led astray to dumb idols" (1 Cor. 12:2), and John similarly realizes that there is a need for Christians to "test the spirits to see whether they are of God; for many false prophets have gone out into the world" (1 John 4:1).

Beyond this, it is also possible that the gift would involve distinguishing between various *types* of evil spirits, such as a spirit of infirmity (Luke 13:11), a spirit of divination (Acts 16:16), a dumb and deaf spirit (Mark 9:25, 29), and a spirit of error (1 John 4:6). From a lexical and grammatical standpoint there is nothing that would prevent us from understanding the gift of "distinguishing between spirits" to include this kind of ability as well.[63]

---

as given by Paul, and should in fact be put under the general umbrella of prophecy. This would have the distinct advantage of making the use of this gift subject to Paul's rules for understanding and regulating prophecy in the church.

Will any harm come from continuing the fairly common practice of thinking of words of wisdom and words of knowledge as miraculous gifts that depend on a special revelation from God? One immediate danger might be that, whereas what is actually happening would be called "prophecy" by Paul, in some cases it is now being called something different, and that tends to distance it from the regulations for prophecy that Paul

gives in the New Testament. Whether that would lead to misuse of the gift at some point in the future is impossible to predict. But it does seem to be rather anomalous to have a miraculous gift that is quite widely used and that is only mentioned but never discussed or regulated at all in the New Testament.

[62]For further discussion of these gifts, see Wayne Grudem, "What is the Real Meaning of a 'Word of Wisdom' and a 'Word of Knowledge'?" in *Ministries Today* (Jan.–Feb. 1993), pp. 60–65.

[63]For a very extensive linguistic and grammatical analysis of this phrase, see Wayne Grudem, "A Response to Gerhard

Of course, to some degree the presence of demonic activity is outwardly evident, sometimes from the blurting out of blatantly false doctrinal statements (see 1 Cor. 12:2–3; 1 John 4:1–6), and sometimes from violent and bizarre physical actions, especially in the face of Christian preaching (see Mark 1:24; 9:20; Matt. 8:29; etc.). Satan's influence is characteristically destructive, and the person influenced by a demon will have a destructive influence on the church and others around him or her, and also a self-destructive influence that harms the life of the troubled individual himself or herself.

But in addition to these outward indications of demonic influence, there is probably also a more subjective perception that occurs at the spiritual and emotional level, whereby the presence of demonic activity is distinguished. When this is more highly developed, and is able to function for the benefit of the church as a whole, then Paul would no doubt call it a gift of distinguishing between spirits.[64]

QUESTIONS FOR PERSONAL APPLICATION

1. Have you ever experienced a gift of prophecy as defined in this chapter? What have you called it? Has this gift (or something like it) functioned in your church? If so, what have been the benefits—and dangers? If not, do you think this gift might be of help to your church? (Why or why not?)

2. Does the gift of teaching function effectively in your church? Who uses this gift in addition to the pastor or elders? Do you think your church adequately appreciates sound Bible teaching? In what areas (if any) do you think your church needs to grow in its knowledge and love of the teachings of Scripture?

3. Of the other gifts discussed in this chapter, have you ever used any of them yourself? Are there any which you think your church needs but does not have at this time? What do you think would be best for you to do in response to this need?

SPECIAL TERMS

(This list applies to chapters 10 and 11.)

apostle
cessationist
distinguishing between spirits
miracles
miraculous gifts
nonmiraculous gifts
office
prophecy

gifts of the Holy Spirit
healing
interpretation of tongues
speaking in tongues
teaching
word of wisdom
word of knowledge

Dautzenberg on 1 Cor. 12:10," in *Biblische Zeitschrift*, N.F., 22:2 (1978), pp. 253–70.

[64]Of course, no gift is perfect in any Christian in this age (1 Cor. 13:9–10), and we should not expect that this gift would be perfect, or that those who have it would never make mistakes. See chapter 10, section A.4, on the fact that spiritual gifts vary in strength.

BIBLIOGRAPHY

Baker, J. P. "Gifts of the Spirit." In *NDT*, pp. 269–71.

Bennett, Dennis and Rita. *The Holy Spirit and You*. Plainfield, N.J.: Logos, 1971. (Charismatic.)

Blue, Ken. *Authority to Heal*. Downers Grove, Ill.: InterVarsity Press, 1987.

Bridge, Donald. *Signs and Wonders Today*. Leicester: Inter-Varsity Press, 1985. (Charismatic.)

_____, and David Phypers. *Spiritual Gifts and the Church*. Downers Grove, Ill.: InterVarsity Press, 1973. (Charismatic.)

Budgen, Victor. *The Charismatics and the Word of God*. Phillipsburg, N.J.: Presbyterian and Reformed, 1985. (Cessationist.)

Carson, D. A. *Showing the Spirit: A Theological Exposition of 1 Corinthians 12–14*. Grand Rapids: Baker, 1987.

Chantry, Walter J. *Signs of the Apostles*. 2d ed. Edinburgh and Carlisle, Pa.: Banner of Truth, 1976. (Cessationist.)

Clements, Roy. *Word and Spirit: The Bible and the Gift of Prophecy Today*. Leicester: UCCF Booklets, 1986.

Deere, Jack. *Surprised by the Power of the Spirit: A Former Dallas Seminary Professor Discovers That God Still Speaks and Heals Today*. Grand Rapids: Zondervan, 1993. (This is the most balanced and persuasive argument I have ever read against the cessationist position.)

Edgar, Thomas. "The Cessation of the Sign Gifts." In *BibSac* 145:180 (Oct.–Dec. 1988), pp. 371–86. (Cessationist.)

Ellis, E. E. "Prophecy, Theology of." In *NDT*, pp. 537–38.

Farnell, F. David. "The Current Debate About New Testament Prophecy." In *BibSac* 149:595 (July–Sept. 1992), pp. 277–303.

_____. "Does the New Testament Teach Two Prophetic Gifts?" In *BibSac* 150 (Jan.–March, 1993), pp. 62–88.

_____. "Fallible New Testament Prophecy/Prophets? A Critique of Wayne Grudem's Hypothesis." In *The Master's Seminary Journal* 2:2 (Fall 1991), pp. 157–80.

_____. "The Gift of Prophecy in the Old and New Testaments." In *BibSac* 149:596 (Oct.–Dec., 1992), pp. 387–410.

_____. "When Will the Gift of Prophecy Cease?" In *BibSac* 150 (April–June, 1993), pp. 171–202.

Gaffin, Richard B. *Perspectives on Pentecost: Studies in New Testament Teaching on the Gifts of the Holy Spirit*. Phillipsburg, N.J.: Presbyterian and Reformed, 1979. (Cessationist.)

Gee, Donald. *Concerning Spiritual Gifts*. Springfield, Mo.: Gospel Publishing House, 1972 (revised edition). (Traditional Pentecostal.)

_____. *Spiritual Gifts in the Work of Ministry Today*. Springfield, Mo.: Gospel Publishing House, 1963. (Traditional Pentecostal.)

Gentry, Kenneth L., Jr. *The Charismatic Gift of Prophecy: A Reformed Response to Wayne Grudem*. 2d ed. Memphis, Tenn.: Footstool Publications, 1989. (Cessationist.)

Green, Michael. *I Believe in the Holy Spirit.* London: Hodder and Stoughton, and Grand Rapids: Eerdmans, 1975.

Greig, Gary, and Kevin Springer, eds. *The Kingdom and the Power: Are Healing and the Spiritual Gifts Used by Jesus and the Early Church Meant for the Church Today?* Ventura, Calif.: Regal Books, 1993.

Gromacki, Robert G. *The Modern Tongues Movement.* Rev. ed. Phillipsburg, N.J.: Presbyterian and Reformed, 1972. (Cessationist.)

Grudem, Wayne. "Does God Still Give Revelation Today?" In *Charisma*, Sept., 1992, pp. 38–42.

_____. *The Gift of Prophecy in 1 Corinthians.* Lanham, Md.: University Press of America, 1982.

_____. *The Gift of Prophecy in the New Testament and Today.* Westchester, Ill.: Crossway, 1988.

_____. *Power and Truth: A Response to the Critiques of Vineyard Teaching and Practice by D. A. Carson, James Montgomery Boice, and John H. Armstrong in Power Religion.* Anaheim, Calif.: Association of Vineyard Churches, 1993.

_____. "What Is the Real Meaning of a 'Word of Wisdom' and a 'Word of Knowledge'?" In *Ministries Today* (Jan.–Feb. 1993), pp. 60–65.

_____. "What Should Be the Relationship Between Prophet and Pastor?" In *Equipping the Saints* (Fall 1990), pp. 7–9, 21–22.

Hayford, Jack W. *The Beauty of Spiritual Language.* Irvine, Tex.: Waco, 1993.

Horton, Michael Scott, ed. *Power Religion: The Selling Out of the Evangelical Church?* Chicago: Moody Press, 1992.

Houston, Graham. *Prophecy: A Gift For Today?* Leicester and Downers Grove, Ill.: InterVarsity Press, 1989.

Hummel, Charles E. *Fire in the Fireplace: Charismatic Renewal in the Nineties.* Downers Grove, Ill.: InterVarsity Press, 1993.

MacArthur, John F., Jr. *Charismatic Chaos.* Grand Rapids: Zondervan, 1992. (Cessationist.)

_____. *The Charismatics: A Doctrinal Perspective.* Grand Rapids: Zondervan, 1978. (Cessationist.)

Mallone, George. *Those Controversial Gifts.* Downers Grove, Ill.: InterVarsity Press, 1983.

Moo, Douglas. "Divine Healing in the Health and Wealth Gospel." In *TrinJ*, Vol. 9 N.S., No. 2 (Fall 1988), pp. 191–209.

Nathan, Richard. *A Response to Charismatic Chaos.* Anaheim, Calif.: Association of Vineyard Churches, 1993. (An extensive response to John MacArthur's 1992 book.)

Osborne, Grant. "Tongues, Speaking in." In *EDT*, pp. 1100–1103.

Poythress, Vern. "Linguistic and Sociological Analyses of Modern Tongues-Speaking: Their Contributions and Limitations." In *WTJ* 42 (1979): 367–98.

Pytches, David. *Spiritual Gifts in the Local Church.* Originally published as *Come, Holy Spirit.* Minneapolis: Bethany, 1985. (Charismatic.)

Reymond, Robert L. *What About Continuing Revelations and Miracles in the Presbyterian Church Today?* Phillipsburg, N.J.: Presbyterian and Reformed, 1977. (Cessationist.)

Robertson, O. Palmer. *The Final Word.* Edinburgh and Carlisle, Pa.: Banner of Truth, 1993. (Cessationist.)

Ruthven, Jon. *On the Cessation of the Charismata: The Protestant Polemic on Post-Biblical Miracles.* Sheffield: Sheffield University Academic Press, 1993. (Charismatic; a revision and expansion of the author's Ph.D. dissertation, in which he responds to the arguments of cessationists from Warfield to the present.)

Saucy, Robert. "Prophecy Today? An Initial Response." In *Sundoulos* (Talbot Seminary; Spring 1990), pp. 1–5. (Cessationist.)

Schatzmann, Siegfried. *A Pauline Theology of Charismata.* Peabody, Mass.: Hendrickson, 1987.

Stephanou, Eusebius A. "The Charismata in the Early Church Fathers," *The Greek Orthodox Theological Review* 21:2 (Summer 1976), pp. 125–46.

Storms, C. Samuel. *Healing and Holiness: A Biblical Response to the Faith-Healing Phenomenon.* Phillipsburg, N.J.: Presbyterian and Reformed, 1990.

Thomas, Robert L. "Prophecy Rediscovered? A Review of *The Gift of Prophecy in the New Testament and Today.*" In *BibSac* 149:593 (Jan.–Mar. 1992), pp. 83–96. (Cessationist.)

Thompson, J. G. S. S. and Walter A. Elwell. "Spiritual Gifts." In *EDT*, pp. 1042–46.

Turner, M. M. B. "Spiritual Gifts Then and Now." In *Vox Evangelica* 15 (1985), pp. 7–64.

Warfield, Benjamin B. *Counterfeit Miracles.* London: Banner of Truth, 1972 (first published in 1918).

White, John. *When the Spirit Comes with Power.* Downers Grove, Ill.: Inter-Varsity Press, 1988.

White, R. Fowler. "Gaffin and Grudem on Ephesians 2:20: In Defense of Gaffin's Cessationist Exegesis." In *WTJ* 54 (Fall 1993), pp. 303–20. (Cessationist.)

_____. "Richard Gaffin and Wayne Grudem on 1 Corinthians 13:10: A Comparison of Cessationist and Noncessationist Argumentation." In *JETS* 35:2 (June 1992), pp. 173–82. (Cessationist.)

Wilkenson, J. "Healing." In *NDT*, pp. 287–88.

Wimber, John. With Kevin Springer. *Power Evangelism.* San Francisco: Harper and Row, 1986.

_____. *Power Healing.* San Francisco: Harper and Row, 1987.

SCRIPTURE MEMORY PASSAGE

1 Corinthians 12:7–11: *To each is given the manifestation of the Spirit for the common good. To one is given through the Spirit the utterance of wisdom, and to another the utterance of knowledge according to the same Spirit, to another faith by the same Spirit, to another gifts of healing by the one Spirit, to another the working of miracles, to another prophecy, to another the ability to distinguish between spirits, to another various kinds of tongues, to another the interpretation of tongues. All these are inspired by one and the same Spirit, who apportions to each one individually as he wills.*

HYMN

"Come, O Come, Thou Quickening Spirit"

(A possible alternative tune is the tune for "Guide Me, O Thou Great Jehovah.")

Come, O come, thou quick'ning Spirit, God from all eternity!
May thy power never fail us; dwell within us constantly.
Then shall truth and life and light banish all the gloom of night.

Grant our hearts in fullest measure wisdom, counsel, purity,
That we ever may be seeking only that which pleaseth thee.
Let thy knowledge spread and grow, working error's overthrow.

Show us, Lord, the path of blessing; when we trespass on our way,
Cast, O Lord, our sins behind thee and be with us day by day.
Should we stray, O Lord, recall; work repentance when we fall.

Holy Spirit, strong and mighty, thou who makest all things new,
Make thy work within us perfect and the evil foe subdue.
Grant us weapons for the strife and with vict'ry crown our life.

AUTHOR: HEINRICH HELD, 1664

We want to hear from you. Please send your comments about this book to us in care of zreview@zondervan.com. Thank you.

ZONDERVAN.com/
AUTHORTRACKER
follow your favorite authors